Handbook of Differential Treatments for Addictions

Editors:

LUCIANO L'ABATE

JACK E. FARRAR

DANIEL A. SERRITELLA

ALLYN AND BACON
Boston   London   Toronto   Sydney   Tokyo   Singapore

Library of Congress Cataloging-in-Publication Data

Handbook of differential treatments for addictions / Luciano L'Abate,
    Jack E. Farrar, and Daniel A. Serritella, editors.
       p.   cm.
    Includes bibliographical references and indexes.
    ISBN 0-205-13237-5
    1. Compulsive behavior—treatment.   2. Substance abuse—Treatment.
3. Psychiatry—Differential therapeutics.   I. L'Abate, Luciano,
1928-   . II. Farrar, Jack E.   III. Serritella, Daniel A.
    [DNLM: 1. Compulsive Behavior—therapy.   2. Substance Dependence—
    therapy.   WM 176 H236]
    RC533.H34 1991
    616.86′06—dc20
    DNLM/DLC
    for Library of Congress

                    91-26124
                       CIP

Printed in the United States of America

10 9 8 7 6 5 4 3 2   95 94 93 92

CONTENTS

iii

PREFACE

THE MAIN PURPOSE of this handbook is to stress differential psychotherapeutic, paratherapeutic, and pretherapeutic treatments for addictions. How are addictions to be treated? Are all addictions to be treated by the same approach? Are there commonalities in all addictions that dictate uniform treatment for all of them? In editing this handbook, we have attempted to stress differences among addictions rather than similarities, because this emphasis leads us to a more specific and more explicit formulation of various modes and modalities of treatment needed than would be possible otherwise. We stress the need to individualize treatment even within each addiction. This individualization of treatment is the responsibility of the many professionals specializing in working with addictions. We want to minimize theoretical and etiological considerations, because they have been expounded at length by many of the sources cited in the book. In most of these sources we found no specific and explicit guidelines for treatment of each addiction. This is also true for addictions that are not commonly considered in most professional books on addictions, such as excesses in work, exercise, love, spending, and religion.

The fallacy of uniformity in treatment approaches derives from common semantic errors that we accept uncritically in our everyday speech. If someone shows an addiction, that person automatically becomes an addict. Not only do we generalize across many different addictions, but by using the term "addict," we are committing another semantic error. We call a person who is blind according to the exhibited disability. By the same token, we call a person with an addiction "an addict." We are generalizing from the defect or disability to the person. Why not use a person's strengths instead? Why just limit ourselves to the negative side of a person? We are trapped in our semantic binds. Unfortunately, even in this handbook we cannot make an exception. We will try to use the term "addiction" as much as possible, rather than "addict." By the term "addict" we mean first and foremost *a person:* a complex, difficult, and even exasperating multiplicity of complicated needs, wants, desires, and habits. That person "has" an addiction, a handicap that eventually becomes a disability. We want to treat him or her like a person, differentiating as much as possible between one type of addiction and another, as well as within each addiction.

Addictions provide a great (if not the greatest) challenge to the psychotherapeutic community. We want to give to as many professionals as possible specific, explicit conceptual and practical tools to accomplish their therapeutic work more effectively. In addition to improving the specificity and explicitness of the differential psychotherapeutic approaches that already exist in tertiary prevention, we also want to make available tools for primary and secondary prevention, as illustrated by a continuum of interventions (to be elaborated in Chapter 3), ranging from primary to secondary and tertiary.

How can we cope with such a widespread phenomenon as addiction? Are we exaggerating the impact of addictions? Are addictions indigenous to this country, or are they present in other countries? Could we conceive of addictions as the price we pay for the relative affluence and abundance of goods the United States enjoys in comparison to other, less affluent countries? Are there countries just as affluent as we are that do not exhibit, as far as we know, such widespread, almost endemic, addictions? Are addictions the result of affluence and the availability of addictive substances in our society? Given the same availability and ease of access to these substances, why are there individuals who seem impervious to addictions? Are there self-indulgent personality patterns that interact with availability? If so, what are those patterns? Many of these questions will be answered, directly or indirectly, in the various chapters of this handbook. If some are not answered, it is because no answer could be found.

Acknowledgments

This book would have had a hard time coming into print, were it not for the dedicated help of the reference staff in the Pullen Library of Georgia State University, who helped us search, locate, and cross-reference a great deal of literature about the treatment of addictions. Among the many people on that staff, we want to recognize especially the help of Pauline Monaka, Ann Page Mosby, Christopher Raines, Mary Ann Raney, and Stanley M. Verhoeven. Without their help and the latest reference search technology, we would have found it at least ten times as difficult and time-consuming to locate what we needed. We are sorry if we have inadvertently left out the names of other kind, considerate, and helpful library personnel, who were always available to us in our moments of need, panic, and turmoil! We are also very grateful for a research grant from the Office of the Vice-President for Academic Affairs of Georgia State University, which enabled us to conduct this search.

Special thanks are due to Marilyn Roberts, M.S., for her help with Chapter 14 (Excessive Exercise). We also wish to express our appreciation to the following reviewers, whose insightful comments helped make this a better book: Mary Lenney of East Norwalk, CT; Dr. Robert Meyer of

Louisville, KY; Professor Soren Svanum of Indianapolis, IN; and Dr. Carolyn Virtunski of Cleveland, OH.

Luciano L'Abate
Jack E. Farrar
Daniel A. Serritella

CONTRIBUTORS

Louis P. Anderson, Ph.D., is Associate Professor in the Psychology Department at Georgia State University. His major interest is research in the outcomes of psychotherapy.

Linda P. Buchanan, M.Ed., is a psychotherapist specializing in eating disorders at the Atlanta Counseling Center. She is also enrolled in the doctoral program in Counseling Psychology at Georgia State University.

William L. Buchanan, Ph.D., is Consultant to the Laurelwood-Northeast Georgia Medical Center, Gainesville, Georgia. He is also in private practice in Gainesville, Georgia, specializing in eating addictions.

Judith Cooney, Ed.D., is University Professor in the Division of Psychology and Counseling at Governors State University in University Park, Illinois. Among her many publications is a book (in press) on sexual abuse.

Jack E. Farrar, Ph.D., is a licensed psychologist in private practice in Jonesboro, Georgia, specializing in individual, marriage, and family therapy.

Mary G. Harrison, M.S., is a doctoral candidate in the Counseling and Psychological Services program at Georgia State University. She is affiliated with the Brookwood Center for Psychotherapy; her major interests are marriage and the family.

Doris W. Hewitt, Ph.D., is senior therapist in the Cross Keys Counseling Center, Forest Park, Georgia, where she specializes in individual, marital, and family therapy and hypnosis. She is also Clinical Assistant Professor in the Psychology Department at Georgia State University.

Luciano L'Abate, Ph.D., is Professor Emeritus in the Department of Psychology at Georgia State University. He works part-time in private practice of marriage and family therapy and is consultant to the Cross Keys Counseling Center in Forest Park, Georgia.

Judith A. Lewis, Ph.D., is Professor in the Division of Health and Human Services at Governors State University. She is a licensed psychologist and author of several books, including *Community Counseling, Substance Abuse Counseling: An Individualized Approach, Counseling Programs for Employees in the Workplace,* and *Management of Human Service Programs.* She is also co-editor of *Counseling the Adolescent* and *Introduction to the Counseling Profession.*

Lynn F. Ranew, L.C.S.W., is Director at the Odyssey Family Counseling Center in Hapeville, Georgia, specializing in training and consultation.

Gregory T. Samples, A.C.S.W., is a psychotherapist in the Cross Keys Counseling Center in Forest Park, Georgia. He is an Approved Supervisor of the American Association for Marriage and Family Therapy.

Daniel A. Serritella, Ph.D., has been affiliated with the Odyssey Family Counseling Center in Hapeville, Georgia in various capacities and has been interested in addictions all of his professional career.

Robert W. Wildman II, Ph.D., is a licensed clinical psychologist in private practice in Reno, Nevada. He lectures and consults on problems of gambling and has published extensively on clinical issues in professional journals.

___ INTRODUCTION ___

LUCIANO L'ABATE, Ph.D.

THE PURPOSE OF THIS introduction is to argue for the need to treat addictions differentially. The many references on the topic of treatments for addictions fail to indicate the importance of differential treatment, since addictions are assumed to result from a common narcissistic personality core, supposedly present in many if not most addicted individuals (Chessick, 1985; Jaffe, Petersen & Hodgson, 1980; Milkman & Shaffer, 1985; Nirenberg & Maisto, 1987; Orford, 1985; Peele, 1988). In fact, in their preface to a recent text on this topic, Donovan and Marlatt (1988) commented: ". . . . there appear to be a number of processes that are common across a wide range of behaviors, such as drinking, smoking, eating, drug use, and gambling. Although the objects of addiction may vary both within and across individuals, the process of addiction appears comparable" (p. vii). In spite of this comparability, these authors propose a "biopsychosocial" model that includes "multiple causality, involvement of multiple systems, and multiple levels of analyses" (p. vii). Why not multiple avenues of treatment? This is the approach advocated here. This handbook, in spite of possible similarities in the process of addiction acquisition (that is, the "addictive personality"), is based on an assumption of diversity in treatments rather than on one of commonality. There may be some commonalities in the causes and processes of acquiring an addiction (Marlatt, 1988). However, we would maintain that not all addictions are the same, nor do they have similar causes, pathways, and outcomes. Hence, we want to treat them differently.

Psychotherapeutic guidelines will be given in general in Chapter 3, and also in the other chapters. These guidelines derive from the view that each form or type of addiction, in its content and its object of usage, is unique in its own way and therefore needs to be treated in ways different from other addictions.

First, what is an addiction? Marlatt, Baer, Donovan, and Kivlahan (1988) defined addictive behavior as "a repetitive habit pattern that increases the risk of disease and/or associated personal and social prob-

1

lems" (p. 224). We prefer to define addictive behavior as a persistent and intense involvement with and stress upon a single behavior pattern, with a minimization or even exclusion of other behaviors, both personal and interpersonal. In a way, addictions are monomanias; that is, they become all-encompassing preoccupations with one object (i.e., the addiction) that controls the individual's behavior. This control is extended to the point that the addiction becomes a compulsion, an obsession, influencing negatively the individual's behavior in many situations. Rather than the individual controlling it, the addiction controls him or her to the point of self- and other-defeating extremes.

Moreover, most addictions are forms of self-indulgence in the short haul that become extremely destructive in the long haul. This self-indulgence, which Marlatt et al. (1988) characterize as "immediate gratification" (p. 224), often takes place at the expense of other responsibilities and at the expense of other people, usually loved ones and family members who suffer the destructive consequences of that indulgence. Ultimately, single-minded emphasis on one behavior, to the exclusion of more helpful behavior toward oneself and toward loved ones, implies a certain degree of incompleteness or immaturity in the nature of self-definition. The individual is no longer in control of his or her life, and the addiction has achieved the position of controlling and determining most of that individual's behavior.

In fact, there is a trend toward defining most addictive behaviors as cases of extreme dependency on a particular substance, object, or person in a way that is self- and other-defeating. Thus, it may be helpful to conceptualize addictions along a continuum of dependence, rather than on an absolute basis, which the term addiction would imply. This continuum would consist of at least three steps, going from *usage,* which may consist of mild, occasional, short-lived, and still controllable experiences, to *abuse,* which may consist of more frequent, somewhat longer-lasting, and seemingly controllable experiences, to *addiction* proper, consisting of out-of-control dependency in which the individual can no longer control the addiction, and resorts to deception, theft, and even murder and other self-defeating behaviors, with a parallel deterioration in personal and interpersonal adjustment and relationships. Once this extreme is reached, the old truism about addictions ("Once an addict, always an addict") may possess a modicum of validity, in the sense that the individual has not learned or can no longer experience, withstand, or tolerate unpleasant, painful, and dysphoric tensions within the self. Could it be that if the individual has not learned to face and withstand these internal tensions, no further learning can ever take place?

Addictive behaviors are self-reinforcing because they produce a lessening or even cessation of internal pains or hurts that the individual has not been socialized and trained to endure; a reduction and relaxation of internal tensions that have been produced by internal stress, like anxiety or depression, or by interaction with external stressors, like home or work responsibilities and pressures; an increase in perceived status by giving the individual an ephemeral sense of self-importance, a boost to a sagging or already low self-esteem; or a euphoric rush that gives the individual an intense sensation of pleasure not achieved otherwise. A combination of all four possibilities may be closer to explaining why addictions are so self-reinforcing, without discounting the role of secondary reinforcers, such as the excitement of doing something forbidden or "evil;" the sense of belonging to a small, special, elite group who share the same experiences; or the perception of being seen as "macho," doing something dangerous and daring that increases the sense of self-importance, appearing to have achieved the status of an "independent" adult or an individual in charge of his or her life in the eyes of selected peers (Milkman & Shaffer, 1985; Orford, 1985). Addictions are one way of making oneself feel important, even though such a feeling of importance may be ephemeral, inappropriate, superficial, short-lived, and extremely costly in the long run.

From this viewpoint, many of us may be considered addicts if and when we stress unilaterally certain behaviors that diminish other, more helpful behaviors within ourselves, and discount the importance of loved ones around us. When all of the individuals involved in any of the types of addictive behavior considered in this volume are added up, we could conclude that, unhappily, approximately 50% of the population in the United States may well suffer from at least one addiction. Some addictions, such as exercise or diet, may be seen as helpful, but an excessive dose of anything may become harmful, as in the case of excessive exercise or a rigid diet.

One could argue that this pessimistic estimate is unduly harsh, unwarranted, and excessively alarmist. Let us consider the following statistics concerning alcohol usage. In 1986 more than 4 million adolescents from 14 to 17 years of age were arrested or involved in accidents because of alcohol; about 10,000 young people between 16 and 24 years of age are killed each year in alcohol-related accidents, including drowning, suicide, violent injuries, homicides, and fire; nearly 100,000 children between 10 and 11 years of age reported getting drunk at least once a week in 1985; children of alcoholics are at four times greater risk of becoming alcoholics than children of non-alcoholics; of the more than 28 million children of alcoholics in the United States today, more than 6 million are under the age of 18 (Burk & Sher, 1988). We grant that alcohol is the greatest drug problem and will yield the largest numbers statistically. However, alcohol and other addictions, all summed together, may not fall far from our original estimate.

The best predictor of future usage in adulthood is frequency of usage in high school (Bachman & Johnston, 1987). Extrapolating from the figures given above to other addictions in adulthood, *even if a more conservative estimate were given,* such as 25 percent of the population being *at risk* of needing help for addictive behaviors, this estimate would still yield more than 60 million people. An even more conservative estimate of 10 percent for populations *in need* would yield about 25 million, still a very high number. However, keep in mind three different levels of vulnerability: *risk,* for 50 percent of the population, *need,* for 25 percent of the population, and *crisis,* for 10 percent of the population.

In conclusion, in spite of their assumed commonalities, addictions need to be treated differentially, not only on grounds of multiple causality and levels of analysis, but also on grounds of individual differences. Addicts are not all alike just because they receive the same label. Each is different from all others, in spite of having or showing the same addiction. Two individuals labeled as "alcoholics" may have completely different socioeconomic, family, educational, personality, intellectual, and occupational characteristics. Consequently, we need to treat all addicts as important human beings, different in their ways from all other addicts. We are aware of how expensive individualized treatment of addictions is. We do not know of any shortcuts. However, suggestions will be given on how treatment costs and effectiveness can be improved.

References

Bachman, J. G., & Johnson, L. D. (1987). *Patterns of change and stability in drug usage among American young people.* Ann Arbor: Institute for Social Research, University of Michigan.

Burk, J. P., & Sher, K. J. (1988). The "forgotten children" revisited: Neglected areas of COA research. *Clinical Psychology Review, 8,* 285–302.

Chessick, R. D. (1985). *Psychology of the self and the treatment of narcissism.* New York: Jason Aronson.

Donovan, D. M., & Marlatt, G. A. (1988). Preface. In D. M. Donovan & G. A. Marlatt (Eds.), *Assessment of addictive behaviors* (pp. vii–x). New York: Guilford.

Jaffe, J., Petersen, R., & Hodgson, R. (1980). *Addictions: Issues and answers.* New York: Harper & Row.

Marlatt, G. A. (1988). Matching clients to treatment: Treatment models and stages of change. In D. M. Donovan & G. A. Marlatt (Eds.), *Assessment of addictive behaviors* (pp. 474–483). New York: Guilford.

Marlatt, G. A., Baer, J. S., Donovan, D. M., & Kivlahan, D. R. (1988). Addictive behaviors: Etiology and treatment. *Annual Review of Psychology, 39,* 223–252.

Milkman, H. B., & Shaffer, H. J. (1985). *The addictions: Multidisciplinary perspectives and treatments.* Lexington, MA: D. C. Heath.

Nirenberg, T. D., & Maisto, S. A. (Eds.). (1987). *Developments in the assessment and treatment of addictive behaviors.* Norwood, NJ: Ablex.

Orford, J. (1985). *Excessive appetites: A psychological view of addictions.* New York: Wiley.

Peele, S. (Ed.). (1988). *Visions of addictions: Major contemporary perspectives on addiction and alcoholism.* Lexington, MA: D. C. Heath.

_1

Major Therapeutic Issues

LUCIANO L'ABATE, Ph.D.

THE PURPOSE OF THIS chapter is to introduce major therapeutic issues that apply to individuals, couples, and families afflicted by addictions. Specific treatment issues concerned with each addiction will be considered in different chapters whose purpose is to review specific practices for each addiction. The rest of this chapter will be devoted to giving suggestions about the initial interview and about the evaluation of addictions and will make available references to simple rating scales for the assessment of dependencies and codependencies. In addition to evaluation, which is definitely a problem area in the treatment of addictions, six other problem areas will be considered.

Evaluation

Evaluation is neither welcome nor popular in the mental health field and in addiction treatment. After all, we all are supposed to evaluate as we interview an addict. What else do we need? We obtain complete background information from him or her and/or from the family. Furthermore, the type of addiction tells us all we want to know about that particular individual. Why should we evaluate further? Because, as we shall see throughout most chapters, the addiction in and of itself will not tell us a great deal about the addict as a person, unless we want to stereotype and consider addicts to be a homogeneous group that should be considered and treated uniformly. We are not willing to make this assumption. We assume, instead, that behind each addict is a wounded individual who needs and deserves the best service we can give. This service begins with a thorough interview about the historical, developmental, and situational factors that surround the etiology and maintenance of the addiction.

Interviewing is the most important part of the evaluation. It fulfills a variety of functions, such as obtaining relevant information about the patient, the addiction, and its etiology, as perceived by the patient and his or her family, and establishing rapport to the point that the patient feels comfortable being asked questions because the interviewer shows that he or she knows what he or she is doing by the questions asked. Rapport means that the interviewer can be trusted, is knowledgeable about the addiction, and gives hope about the possibility of help and improvement. Interviewing also begins the process of rehabilitation by helping the individual think in new and different ways that will be helpful in motivating him or her to continue treatment. The fact that the addict is present for the interview and cooperates in allowing himself or herself to be interviewed should be stressed as a definite asset. ("You care about yourself; otherwise you would not be here to answer my questions.")

Tomm (1988) suggested a helpful classification of questions to be asked in an interview, depending on four different types of intent on the interviewer's part: (a) *investigative,* to know more about the problem in terms of definitions and explanations; (b) *corrective,* to produce positive changes in the process of treatment through leading and confrontational questions; (c) *exploratory,* to see how contextually aware the individual (and his or her family) is about differences among family members and what behavioral effects they have on each other; and (d) *facilitative,* to deal with hypotheses about the future and with the interviewer's own perspective.

Within Tomm's framework (1988), one can then consider Shaffer and Neuhaus' approach (1985) of testing various hypotheses about addictive behavior by providing a complementary set of questions that are specifically directed toward assessment of the addiction. *Physiologically,* can the patient's problem be understood as a result of intoxication or withdrawal, or as a manifestation of genetic causes or predispositions, to the point that the addiction has altered neurological and/or psychological functioning? (Shaffer & Neuhaus, 1985, p. 93). *Psychodynamically,* can the addiction be understood as an attempt to reduce sad and dysphoric feelings through either compulsive or controlled usage that is antecedent to or a consequence of the addiction? (Shaffer & Neuhaus, 1985, pp. 94–95). *Sociologically,* is the addiction taking place within limited or varied environmental contexts, as an attempt to draw attention to familial problems or difficulties? (Shaffer & Neuhaus, 1985, p. 96). *Behaviorally,* can the addiction be understood as contingent on its primary and secondary reinforcing properties, bypassing the effects of rational and emotional resources? (Shaffer & Neuhaus, 1985, p. 97).

For therapists interested in treating addictions within the context of the family, we recommend the use of genograms (Gerson & McGoldrick, 1986) and global scales to assess family functioning (Kinston, 1988;

L'Abate & Bagarozzi, in press). Dunst, Trivette, and Deal (1988) have developed a battery of family-oriented tests worthy of consideration.

A different and novel type of evaluation suggested by Strayhorn (1988, pp. 28–29), although designed to evaluate children, may have potentially useful applications in the evaluation of addictions. Strayhorn suggested a skill-based evaluation according to nine groups of skills. Each group is defined by three or more objective items on a self-report or rating sheet. The nine groups can be divided into two major classes of skills. The first class relates to *presence* and to the ability to love, as in (a) closeness, trusting, and relationship building; (b) handling separation and independence; (c) dealing with frustration and unfavorable events; (d) celebrating good things and feeling pleasure; and (e) relaxing and playing. The second class of skills relates to the negotiation of *performance* and *production,* as in problem-solving and decision-making defined by (a) handling joint decisions and interpersonal conflict; (b) working for delayed gratification; (c) cognitive processing through words, symbols, and images, and (d) an adaptive sense of direction and purpose. The items that define the nine groups of skills could be used to evaluate how each addict rates in each of these skills. According to Strayhorn, this approach is more specific and clear than trying to define vague and undefinable personality and interpersonal dimensions from subjectively interpreted projective tests or from subjective impressions. However, we still need to rely on criteria external to the personal biases of the evaluator(s). The evaluator's subjective impressions need to be supported or contradicted by objective evidence.

Ryan, Ryan, Rosen, and Virsida (1986) suggested that in addition to common substance abuse tests or checklists, one last question should be asked: "Did you cheat on this test?" Furthermore, some pathognomomic indicators of alcohol or severe substance abuse are: feet wide apart when walking for better balance; convoluted logic; omnipotence, or "I know better than anybody else"; red herrings, focusing on completely irrelevant, secondary, or distracting issues; magic cures (vitamins, aerobics, spirituality, religion, etc.) or changes (job, partner, location, etc.); claimed inability to pay for treatment, although thousands of dollars have been spent on the addiction; the primary importance of job responsibilities, as if one were irreplaceable; ecstatic descriptions of the nirvana-like euphoria resulting from the addiction.

In assessing addictions, however, we insist that a battery of objective tests must be administered to fulfill the following functions: (a) discover the extent and type of dysfunctionality (physical, neurological, physiological, and psychological), especially in substance abuse, where organic and central nervous system injuries may have been produced by the addiction; (b) find the broader context of the addiction within the personality of the addict and of the family of the addict; (c) determine a treatment plan specific to that particular addiction and the personality of the individual addict and family; (d) establish an initial baseline to compare future treatment gains or losses; and (e) compare one form of treatment with other forms and identify the contribution that the therapist makes to the treatment outcome. Without evaluation as a standard operating procedure in the treatment of addicts, this field will not be able to progress as fast and efficiently as it needs to. Unfortunately, most therapists feel that an objective evaluation is cumbersome, costly, or irrelevant to the treatment process. Some therapists like to rationalize that evaluation may distract the therapist and the client from the main goals of treatment. Many of these fears and distortions, however, have no basis in evidence or in clinical practice. On the contrary, we would argue that the client would feel reassured when a thorough evaluation takes place.

Admittedly, we may need to streamline and make evaluative procedures more relevant to treatment planning. Most evaluative techniques in the past fulfilled merely a *descriptive* function; we need to create assessment instruments that are also *prescriptive*. That is, they can link evaluation to intervention, by specifying which particular area of deficit or dysfunction needs to be dealt with from the outset of therapy. This specificity of treatment is not possible as long as therapy is kept at a verbally interactive level. It will become possible, however, when we start relying on paratherapeutic workbooks that are based on the written rather than on the spoken medium and that allow patients to learn at a distance, without personal contact with a therapist. A variety of paratherapeutic instruments designed with this additional prescriptive function in mind, still in an experimental stage, have been developed by this writer and his coworkers (L'Abate, 1990, 1992).

Relevant to the process of evaluation are simple checklists that have been developed by, among others, Robert Dobes (1988). Table 1–1 was derived from the work of other authors (Black, 1984; Middleton, 1984; Woititz, 1983). Table 1–2 was developed by Dobes alone, and Table 1–3 was adapted and expanded from the work of Eve (1985). These and other checklists, as well as questionnaires that will be described later, can be classified into three different groups. One group deals with particular

Why Have a Checklist?

It is not unusual for individuals at times to question if they need counseling or outside help regarding their personal lives, their parenting role, or their workplace situations throughout life. Often these situations are unavoidable and are best dealt with by supportive help from personal resources or professionals. If you find that you have been unable to find or ask for support in dealing with personal crises, or if you know of someone who appears to be dissatisfied with the experience of life, this checklist will help to determine if counseling or therapy would be helpful.

TABLE 1–1 Primary Codependency Checklist

1. Do you make time to do things just for yourself each week?
2. Would you be embarrassed if people knew certain things about you?
3. Do you have difficulty with intimate relationships?
4. Do you judge yourself without mercy?
5. Do you take yourself very seriously?
6. Do you have unidentified loneliness and depression?
7. Do you feel that no one really knows you?
8. Do you have feelings of guilt and low self-esteem?
9. Do you find it easy to be critical of others, yet fear criticism and judgment?
10. Do you tend to be a perfectionist?
11. Do you fear losing control of feelings, behavior, or life in general?
12. Are you a workaholic or are you compulsive about eating, reading, spending, exercising, sex, helping, the need to be right, etc.?
13. Do you constantly seek approval or affirmation from others?
14. Are you super-responsible or super-irresponsible?
15. Do you have regrets about what you have done with your life?
16. Do you have a compelling need to achieve or have frequent fantasies of being in the spotlight, but feel unfulfilled after gaining attainable objectives?

If you have answered "yes" to three or more of these questions, your skill in achieving greater tranquility and balance in your life may need refinement or redirection through counseling.

methodologies to evaluate various addictions, as in the case of cigarette smoking (Coletti, Payne & Rizzo, 1987; Wurtele & Martin, 1987), obesity (Dubbert & Brubaker, 1987), alcohol and drug abuse (Foy, Cline & Laasi, 1987). A second group consists of checklists of a *specific* nature about various addictions, as in the case of substance abuse (Forman, 1982), or self-monitoring forms of bulimia (Fremouw, Wiener & Seime, 1987). Other checklists will be described in various chapters of this book, especially Chapter 18. A third group of checklists, of a more *generic* nature, are either global or directed toward tangential or secondary areas relevant to the addiction, such as adolescents (Stout, 1987); anger (Siegel, 1987); crises (Slaikeu, 1985); depression (Beckman, 1986; Linehan, 1985); health concerns (Spoth & Dush, 1988); mental status (Faiver, 1986; Spencer & Folstein, 1985); sexual history (Fabrick, 1985); social adjustment (Weissman, 1986); and stress (Lefebre & Sandford, 1986). A sentence completion manual, based on stems concerning a variety of areas, and closely resembling what could be conceived as a workbook, has been produced by Eimer (1988). There is no question, in this writer's opinion, that clinicians and therapists will need to rely on the written word and on prepackaged office forms (Meek & editors, 1985) for evaluation as well as treatment, if we want to use our energy and time in cost-effective ways and expand practice without cutting down on effectiveness.

More recently, Donovan and Marlatt (1988) have edited a text dedicated to the problem of evaluation and suggest what they call "the behav-

TABLE 1–2 Parenting Skills Codependency Checklist

1. Did your parents avoid open communication about family problems when you were growing up?
2. Do your children avoid discussing feelings and affection openly with you?
3. Do you openly compare your child's poor performance or behavior to that of other siblings or other children?
4. Do you say to your child, "Do as I say, not as I do"?
5. Do you make speeches to your child? For example, "When I was a child, we valued the privilege of going to school . . . ", etc.
6. Do you use phrases such as, "What's wrong with you?" or "Can't you do anything right?"
7. At times, do you expect your child to read your mind when you want something done?
8. Do you openly use different labels for your children, such as "the smart one," "the quiet one," "the bad one," etc?
9. Recall the last few instances when you corrected your child. Do you remember correcting your child, but do not remember having praised him at least the same number of times that day?
10. Do you believe that love and respect are the same thing?
11. Do you get angry when the child does not understand what you tell him the first or second time?
12. Have you noticed that your children do not ask you to play with them?
13. Are your children either great achievers or poor achievers?
14. Do you encourage your child by saying, "You can do better than that"?
15. When deciding on a family recreation, do the parents make the decision and later tell the children what the decision is?
16. Do you teach your children values by stating that there is a right way and a wrong way of doing things, and emphasize what will happen if they choose the wrong way?
17. Do you tell your children "You should be happy" at times when they seem indifferent?

If you have answered "yes" to three or more of the above questions, there is a reasonable probability that codependency may be parented to your children.

ioral assessment funnel," which is akin to what this author has called "successive sieves" or "hurdles" in evaluation and treatment (L'Abate, 1990). This model is elaborated by Marlatt (1988) in what he calls the "stages of change" model. Since an individual goes through a variety of changes as a result of treatment at various stages, Marlatt argues that evaluation should parallel such stages. Regardless of what model one wants to follow, it should be standard operating practice to evaluate *before* treatment, immediately *after* treatment, and after at least six months to a year as *follow-up* with continuous *check-ups* every year afterward for as long as necessary. Because of the frequency of proposed evaluations, follow-ups, and check-ups, by necessity they should be specific to the existence of addictive behaviors, relatively short but relevant to the overall functioning of the individual, and also, if possible, reliable.

TABLE 1–3   Workplace Codependency Checklist

1. Do you fear going to work?
2. Do you attempt to manipulate your supervisor to do something your way?
3. Do you avoid direct communication regarding problem areas, such as work environment, work relationships and work load?
4. Do you repress your feelings of hurt, anger, resentment, overwork, or being taken advantage of?
5. Do you ignore and/or avoid problems so as not to rock the boat?
6. Do you feel guilty for your employer's bad mood and behavior?
7. Do you take care of or protect your employer?
8. Do you dread evaluations?
9. Do you take responsibility for your assigned duties and those of co-workers or your employer?
10. Do you generally feel overworked and/or feel a sense of burnout?
11. Do you feel that your work is never good enough?
12. Do comments about aspects of your work needing improvement make you feel worthless as a person?
13. Do you avoid negative feelings related to work by drinking, eating, sleeping or isolating yourself at home?
14. Are your good feelings about yourself derived from your supervisor's praise?
15. Are your actions on the job determined by a fear of rejection?
16. Do you put your values aside to please your co-workers or supervisor?
17. Do you periodically feel guilty about your work?
18. Do you experience stress-related physical symptoms in relation to work, such as headaches, tight stomach, insomnia, backache, diarrhea, neck pains, etc.?

If you have answered "yes" to three or more of these questions, the issues of codependency may be affecting your workplace environment and career development. Counseling and/or employee assistance programs to improve job satisfaction, attendance, and productivity without burnout can be provided through The Dobes Center.

Problems in the Treatment of Addictions

Six of the most crucial problems in the psychological treatment of addictions and addictive dysfunctionalities are: motivation, denial, dual diagnosis, matching, control, and relapse. Some of these issues will be considered in greater detail in the discussion of codependency (Chapter 17).

Motivation for Treatment

A lethargic-apathetic style, which is characteristic of most addictions, would indicate that it would be very difficult for addicts to want to change. Their incomplete self-definition, manifested in either self-centeredness and egocentricity or in not caring for the self and considering others more important than oneself, would make change an external rather than an internal process. While selfless individuals may admit more readily to their "misdeeds," selfish individuals tend to avoid and deny personal responsibility, with a mixture of arrogance and denial of dependency on others, as in the "I know better" and "I will not be caught" positions (L'Abate, 1992). Hence, while selfless individuals may be good risks for psychotherapeutic interventions, selfish individuals are fairly poor risks, but not as poor as individuals who exhibit no-self characteristics such as apathy and abuse. Here is where paratherapeutic programmed materials and workbooks can be used initially to evaluate whether the patient is willing to work for change or not. With selfish individuals talk is cheap and commonly used to manipulate, deceive, and, ultimately, avoid coming to terms with and confronting one's self and the reality of a bleak situation. Since sad and unpleasant feelings are avoided and denied to begin with, any confrontation of a bleak reality will be avoided as well. Consequently, face-to-face confrontation and especially psychotherapy are seen as a threat to the balance of a tenuous sense of self; it is better to avoid confrontation than to approach it. Things will have to be considerably worse before this approach and confrontation can take place. In many instances approach and confrontation never take place.

In dealing with the poor motivation of addicts for treatment, Halleck (1988) argued that there is a continuum of excuse-making and excuse-giving that therapists need to be aware of, especially with addicts.

> *Once treatment begins, expectations of responsibility increase. One way of depicting this process . . . is that 'everyone is doing the best they can. But everyone can do better.' Perhaps this process is best illustrated by the manner in which we deal with addictive behaviors such as alcohol abuse and compulsive gambling. We often describe these behaviors as diseases and imply that they are beyond the patient's control. Yet, the essential ingredient in any treatment of addictive behavior is that the patient willfully stop indulging in it. . . . There is good reason to believe that treatment is more efficient when the physician [therapist] has a consistent model of excuse giving and excuse withholding. (pp. 348–349)*

One wonders whether Halleck ever heard of the positive reframing practice used by many therapists (Weeks & L'Abate, 1982) as a form of excuse-giving as well as a positive "explanation" for an otherwise bleak negativity in many dysfunctional people? Many addiction treatment approaches stress the importance of self-management and of major lifestyle changes (Marlatt, 1985a, 1985b, 1985c, 1985d, and 1985e; Shiffman, Read, Maltese, Rapkin & Jarvik, 1985). However, it will take more than explanations or "excuses" to help addicts move and work toward those changes.

In a review of motivation for treatment, Miller (1985) considered most of the personality factors that lower this motivation and the various therapeutic procedures that can be used to enhance it. None of these factors included the concept of self-importance, although self-esteem was considered. One would predict that selfish or self-centered, self-indulgent individuals would be resistant to any form of intervention designed to help them change, for the reasons previously given. Hence, one may need to wait until a critical stage is reached, when the addict faces imprisonment, divorce, or even death before he or she can ask for help. Once help is asked, one needs to question the motivation for change from the very beginning. The patient needs to demonstrate this motivation by actual behavioral changes, keeping agreements, following contracts, completing homework assignments, and demonstrating concretely the desire to change. Without concrete, specific, and measurable changes, even small ones, especially at the nonverbal level, it would be a waste of energy and time for any therapist to attempt to motivate addicts. Changes consist of new, positive, strong steps, different from any behavior used in the past. If people do not want to change, nobody is going to do it for them.

Meichenbaum and Turk (1987) suggested a list of ten guidelines to help in what they called "nonadherence," translated here as being an inadequate motivation for change. First, anticipate nonadherence, to the point of expecting, predicting, and planning for it, as noted earlier; then consider the prescribed self-care regimen from the patient's perspective; foster a collaborative relationship based on negotiation (we would also add "and on caring"); be patient-oriented; customize treatment; enlist family support; provide a system of continuity and accessibility; make use of other health care providers and personnel as well as community resources (as suggested by the continuum of preventive approaches presented earlier); repeat everything; and don't give up!

Denial

Addictions are derived in part from a defensive posture of denial, as the avoidance of sad or painful feelings or tensions. Indeed, one could say that poor motivation is the outcome of a strongly needed denial system that the addict's thinking finds necessary for survival. Whatever its sources, denial has an important function in the genesis and proliferation of addictions. No therapist can hope to deal successfully with addictions unless he or she is able to deal with this strong form of resistance to treatment.

Denial is common to almost all addictions. Forman (1988) listed four causes of denial: (a) memory loss, due to either physiological or psychological bases; (b) pride—"Denial of the addiction is a desperate attempt to hold on to the last shreds of an already devastated self-image" (p. 210); (c) love of the substance more than self or others; and (d) fear. For a satisfactory recovery or motivation for treatment, Forman maintained that three conditions are necessary: sufficient pain and fear of future pain, sufficient self-love, and sufficient knowledge about what actions to take. He suggested five sequential phases to deal with the denial: facing and confronting facts and mobilizing energies and resources; family education, involving having family members talk and express their feelings about the addiction; rehearsal and coaching about effective communication styles; intervening, with caring confrontation of the addiction within the context of positive regard ("I care about you . . . ") and concern about the destructive outcome of the addiction ("I am concerned about what _____ will do to you and to your loved ones"); and follow-up concerning the therapeutic outcome of the process.

Another way of dealing with denial is by using the analogy that no system, either mechanical or human, can heal itself without external intervention: "What would happen if you did not wash a small cut?" "How does your car (toaster, computer, etc.?) get fixed?" "Yet you expect to heal yourself without external help? Has it worked?" "You must be an exception to all living systems. No system heals itself, but you will?" If this analogy does not seem to make a dent in the addict's thinking, as often happens, perhaps one could use the program developed for each of the 15 MMPI-2 Content Scales (L'Abate, 1992). Among these scales is one entitled "Negative Treatment Indicators." This written program can be self-administered as a homework assignment; it poses many questions that would antagonize the addict if they were asked in a face-to-face situation. When administered impersonally through the written medium, these questions do not seem to arouse as many emotional reactions as a close and necessarily confrontational face-to-face relationship would. The use of this program has been found useful in the writer's own practice.

Dual Diagnosis

More often than not, addictions are accompanied by secondary diagnostic labels that may refer to the personality of the individual. For instance, an alcoholic may show secondary features of impulsive personality, or an embezzler may show a high level of depression. How are we going to deal with this issue? Because of the availability of programmed materials, to be discussed at greater length in Chapter 3, this should no longer be a problem. Verbal psychotherapy, for instance, could be oriented toward family problems that may have started or exacerbated the addiction, and programmed materials could be used to deal with the secondary diagnosis. In other words, these materials offer a wider range of options for both therapists and addicts than would otherwise be available. For instance, the addict could be seen in family therapy while working on a programmed workbook dealing with impulsivity; or the whole family, in addition to face-to-face sessions with a therapist, could be working on a depression workbook that would lead eventually toward learning how to negotiate and to love among family members (L'Abate, 1986, 1990, 1992).

Matching

What does the term "matching" mean? It refers to one of the major issues in psychotherapy: How can treatment fit a particular addiction? If the same form of treatment is administered indiscriminately with any kind of addiction, what will be the results? Can we and should we use just one type of therapy for all forms of addiction? If this is the case, what kind of therapy should we use—individual, group, marital, or family? Should the therapy be based on humanistic, behavioral, psychodynamic, or contextual principles? Which theory should be used to match an addiction with a specific type of treatment? Should we make an assumption of uniformity of treatment for all addictions, or should we try to specify which addiction should receive what form of treatment with which therapist and at what price?

Instead of a uniform approach, we lean toward a specificity approach, at least as far as treatment is concerned (McLellan, Woods, Luborsky, O'Brien & Druley, 1983). Each addiction should ideally receive the specific form of treatment most appropriate for dealing with it. How is such specificity to be achieved if psychotherapy and its process cannot be specified? As long as treatment is based on the oral medium, it remains vague, variable, general, and, more important, unverifiable. It varies from one therapist to another. It varies with the same therapist, and it varies from one clinical setting to another. There are nonspecific factors, like positive regard, warmth, acceptance, and empathy, *relationship skills* that some therapists, especially those of a humanistic bent, maintain are responsible for positive therapeutic outcome. Relationship skills may be responsible, at best, for approximately 50 percent of positive therapeutic outcomes. What about the other 50 percent of the outcomes? This second half is due to *structuring skills,* those skills that go above and beyond relationship skills. These skills provide the addict with a definite structure to follow during the process of treatment, as will be discussed later in this chapter.

Structuring skills are just as important as relationship skills. The ratio of one set of skills over the other may vary from one therapist to another, as well as in the interaction between therapist and patient. Relationship skills represent the *style* of the therapist, and structuring skills represent the *method* or approach the therapist uses to reach therapeutic objectives and goals. Both relationship and structuring skills are the responsibility of most professionals, acquired during many years of training under supervision. We will not be able to devote a great deal of attention to the former, but we hope to specify and structure different approaches for each addiction. In turn, eventually we plan to render such approaches even more specific and more explicit through the application of specially programmed, paratherapeutic workbooks for each addiction, based on the written rather than on the spoken word (L'Abate, 1990, 1992).

A good example of specificity in treatment is illustrated by the work of Cancrini, Cingolani, Compagnoni, Constantini, and Mazzoni (1988), who identified and classified juvenile heroin addicts and argued that heroin usage is not specific to a homogeneous population. In fact, they found four different patterns of usage: (a) traumatic, after a crucial event in the individual's life; (b) presence of an actual neurosis; (c) presence of transitional states, like affective disorders of a manic-depressive nature; and (d) presence of sociopathic conditions. On the basis of this classification, for instance, type a addicts would profit by individual therapy; type b addicts would profit more from structural family therapy; counterparadoxical techniques seem more likely to be effective with type c addicts, and type d addicts would benefit by network and community interventions. This important study initially consisted of only 131 subjects, but it is hoped that it will be extended to include a larger number of subjects, using more objective and specific measures of personality make-up and functioning, with a greater specificity of treatment modalities, as well as prolonged follow-up after treatment termination.

One could argue that as long as treatment methods continue to be based on the spoken rather than on the written word, it will remain difficult and expensive to evaluate and prescribe the process and outcome of such methods. Furthermore, as long as the spoken rather than the written word is used in such treatment methods, it will be difficult and expensive to match type of treatment with type of addiction or of psychological affliction. At best one can match clients with therapists. As Anderson and Carter (1982) argued, part of this matching should consider at least three variables: (1) gender of client and therapist; (2) social class or socioeconomic status of both; and (3) ethnic origin of both. Although the personalities of client and therapist cannot be ignored, matching could take place on the basis of Marlatt's stages of treatment model or the successive sieves or hurdles model proposed in Chapter 3. According to a process view of treatment, matching should take place according to specific deficits on the client's side and specific competencies on the therapist's side. Above and beyond this matching, a higher degree of specificity in matching will be achieved when a greater proportion of evaluation and treatment is based on the written rather than just the spoken word.

Control

Ultimately, many addictions are failures in self-control; hence, it is important for therapists to have some notions of the nature of control. What does it mean to control? What does control consist of? How can we teach people who have few or inadequate controls to learn to control themselves? How can we teach these controls if we do not have any idea, scientifically and professionally, about what control is? How can a therapist control a client without appearing to control?

Reinforcement theorists and behavioral practitioners stress the importance of using rewards or contingent consequences *after* the behavior has taken place. A different view of control, a contextual one, instead stresses its use *before* the beginning of the undesirable behavior rather than at the end (L'Abate, 1986). To achieve control one needs to stress *regularity and regulation* of behavior. However, therapists should learn to control without appearing to control, lest clients become threatened by what they may see as loss of control on their part. Consequently, therapists need to take control so that they can give it away from the very beginning. Some control and regularity is initiated by making regular weekly or bi-weekly appointments. In addition, one can insist from the very outset of treatment that clients make regular appointments with themselves to complete systematic homework assignments given to them (L'Abate, 1986). The main question to be asked about undesirable behavior ("*it*"), addictive or otherwise, is the same: "Do you want *it* to control you or do you want to learn to control *it*?" Emotional problems, like anxiety or depression, can be easily prescribed on a regular basis ("Stay with your depression for one hour every other day and write about it while you are depressed"), but addictions cannot and must not be encouraged. Hence, control principles that work with emotional issues may not work with addictive behaviors. Instead, the therapist could prescribe "pretend" behaviors or thinking about the addiction without prescribing the actual addictive behaviors. The addict can be asked to pretend being "hooked" on the addictive behavior, as if he or she were hooked or he or she could think about the addition without participating in it: "Write how you feel when you want (a drink, a fix, etc.)." In other words, writing becomes another way of interfering with feelings and thoughts that may lead toward the addiction.

Another way is to prescribe specific times (7 P.M. on Mondays, Wednesdays, and Fridays) to work on programmed weekly lessons derived from the Alcoholics Anonymous twelve steps. The major medium of control, instead of speech, has to be writing; that is, clients need to learn to communicate either through writing or, if they do not know how to write, to talk into a tape recorder at specified, prearranged times, frequencies, and durations (one hour, three times a week, at 7 P.M., for instance). Since some of the major characteristics of addicts are either depression or impulsivity, they have to work on weekly lessons from workbooks dealing with these topics (L'Abate, 1986, 1992). Once regularity and regulation are introduced in whatever they do, addicts start to become more controlled and controlling of their behavior. Compliance or non-compliance with homework assignments then becomes a good indication of motivation for change.

Relapse

Relapse in the treatment of addictions is to be expected, as recidivism is in the treatment of criminals (Maltz, 1984). In fact, relapse should be predicted and planned for as part of the whole treatment plan. Any treatment plan for addictions that lacks plans and preparations for relapse prevention should be considered incomplete and ultimately unacceptable. While a stage of recovery may have seemingly been reached, the professional needs to be aware that the strong probability of relapse lurks in *every* addiction. No addicted individual can be considered free of the addiction, even years after termination of the condition. No addiction can be considered cured, since it is a life-long pattern that can come back at any time (Marlatt, 1985a).

This strong possibility requires continuous vigilance on the therapist's part, with the possibility of relapse continuously present in treatment. What signs and symptoms should one use to evaluate this possibility? Booth (1988) listed eleven criteria to be kept in mind in the treatment of addictions, especially in patients dealing with the high of having reached a recovery stage. The criteria are denial and avoidance of certain realities in the addict's life; anger and irritability over small or irrelevant situations; isolation from others; fear of natural, non-threatening conditions; lethargy and apathy; problems in relationships; inability to sleep; erratic personality changes; poor eating habits; physical deterioration and not taking good care of oneself in grooming, appearance, and exercise; and mood swings and volatility, ranging from manic grandiosity and selfishness to opposite extremes of selfless altruism and overconcern for others rather than the self. To this list we would add completion of assigned tasks, such as written homework assignments and/or programmed materials.

Marlatt (1985a, 1985b, 1985c, 1985d and 1985e) and others (Donovan & Chaney, 1985; McCrady, Dean, Dubreuil & Swanson, 1985; Shiffman, Read, Maltese, Rapkin & Jarvik, 1985; Sternberg, 1985), have detailed a variety of relapse-prevention strategies that need to be mastered by any professional dealing with addictions. No competent therapist can assume that self-reports of well-being and contentment on the addict's part can be taken at face value. In fact, one should consider such claims as harbingers of a forthcoming relapse.

Conclusion

The treatment of addictions requires a great variety of human and professional skills, mixed with large doses of patience, forgiveness, and persistence. All of the six issues presented in the preceding pages point toward the melancholy fact that the treatment of addictions is not easy and is hampered by a great many difficulties, leading to frustration, despair, and giving up by many therapists. On the other hand, if we were to consider the treatment of addictions as the new frontier of psychological treatments, we would see addictions as challenging chances to use all of the therapist's resources, including creativity, knowledge, and skills. Success with addictions represents the highest level we can achieve in treatment. Many of us fall short of this goal, but we pick ourselves up to try again and again, because giving up may mean death for some of our patients.

References

Anderson, L., & Carter, J. H. (1982). Psychotherapy: Patient-therapist matching reconsidered. *Journal of the National Medical Association, 74,* 461–464.

Beckman, E. E. (1986). The coping strategies scales for depression. In P. A. Keller and L. G. Ritt (Eds.), *Innovations in clinical practice: A source book* (pp. 287–297). Sarasota, FL: Professional Resource Exchange.

Black, C. (1984). *Children of alcoholics.* Speech given at the Meadows Recovery Center, Gambrills, MD.

Booth, L. (1988). The spiritual key to relapse. *Professional Counselor, 3,* 8.

Cancrini, L., Cingolani, S., Compagnoni, F., Constantini, D., & Mazzoni, S. (1988). Juvenile drug addiction: A typology of heroin addicts and their families. *Family Process, 27,* 261–271.

Colletti, G., Payne, T. J., & Rizzo, A. A. (1987). Treatment of cigarette smoking. In T. D. Nirenberg & S. A. Maisto (Eds.), *Developments in the assessment and treatment of addictive behaviors* (pp. 243–276). Norwood, NJ: Ablex.

Dobes, R. W. (1988). Personal communication. The Dobes Center, 1322 Concord Rd., Smyrna, GA 30080.

Donovan, D. M., & Chaney, E. F. (1985). Alcoholic relapse prevention and intervention: Models and methods. In G. A. Marlatt & J. R. Gordon (Eds.), *Relapse prevention: Maintenance strategies in the treatment of addictive behaviors* (pp. 351–416). New York: Guilford.

Donovan, D. M., & Marlatt, G. A. (1988). Preface. In D. M. Donovan & G. A. Marlatt (Eds.), *Assessment of addictive behaviors* (pp. vii–x). New York: Guilford.

Dubbert, P. M., & Brubaker, R. G. (1987). Assessment of obese patients. In T. D. Nirenberg & S. A. Maisto (Eds.), *Developments in the assessment and treatment of addictive behaviors* (pp. 153–170). Norwood, NJ: Ablex.

Dunst, C., Trivette, C., & Deal, A. (1988). *Enabling and empowering families.* Cambridge, MA: Brookline Books.

Eimer, B. D. (1988). Sentence completions about relationships, experiences, and discomfort (SCARED): Introduction and clinical manual. In P. A. Keller & S. R. Heyman (Eds.), *Innovations in clinical practice: A source book* (pp. 337–349). Sarasota, FL: Professional Resource Exchange.

Eve, S. I. (1985). Takin' care of business and family. *Focus on the Family, 8,* 24–25.

Fabrick, S. D. (1985). The sexual history inventory (SHI). In P. A. Keller and L. G. Ritt (Eds.), *Innovations in clinical practice: A source book* (pp. 331–344). Sarasota, FL: Professional Resource Exchange.

Faiver, C. M. (1986). The mental status examination—revised. In P. A. Keller and L. G. Ritt (Eds.), *Innovations in clinical practice: A source book* (pp. 279–285). Sarasota, FL: Professional Resource Exchange.

Forman, B. D. (1982). A substance abuse screening check list. In P. A. Keller & L. G. Ritt (Eds.), *Innovations in clinical practice: A source book* (pp. 289–292). Sarasota, FL: Professional Resource Exchange.

Forman, R. F. (1988). A technique for overcoming substance abuse denial. In P. A. Keller & S. R. Heyman (Eds.), *Innovations in clinical practice: A source book* (pp. 209–216). Sarasota, FL: Professional Resource Exchange.

Foy, D. W, Cline, K. A., & Laasi, N. (1987). Assessment of alcohol and drug abuse. In T. D. Nirenberg & S. A. Maisto (Eds.), *Developments in the assessment and treatment of addictive behaviors* (pp. 89–114). Norwood, NJ: Ablex.

Fremouw, W. J., Wiener, A. L., & Seime, R. J. (1987). Self-monitoring forms for bulimia. In P. A. Keller & S. R. Heyman (Eds.), *Innovations in clinical practice: A source book* (pp. 325–332). Sarasota, FL: Professional Resource Exchange.

Gerson, R., & McGoldrick, M. (1986). Constructing and interpreting genograms: The example of Sigmund Freud's family. In P. A. Keller and L. G. Ritt (Eds.), *Innovations in clinical practice: A source book* (pp. 203–220). Sarasota, FL: Professional Resource Exchange.

Halleck, S. M. (1988). Which patients are responsible for their illnesses? *American Journal of Psychotherapy, 42,* 338–353.

Kinston, W. (1988). The family health scales for global assessment of family functioning. In P. A. Keller & S. R. Heyman (Eds.), *Innovations in clinical practice* (pp. 299–330). Sarasota, FL: Professional Resource Exchange.

L'Abate, L. (1986). *Systematic family therapy.* New York: Brunner/Mazel.

L'Abate, L. (1990). *Building family competence: Primary and secondary prevention strategies.* Newbury Park, CA: Sage.

L'Abate, L. (1992). *Programmed writing: A self-administered approach for interventions with individuals, couples, and families.* Pacific Grove, CA: Brooks/Cole.

L'Abate, L., & Bagarozzi, D. A. (in press). *Sourcebook of marriage and family evaluation.* New York: Brunner/Mazel.

Lefebre, R. C., & Sandford, S. L. (1986). The strain questionnaire. In P. A. Keller and L. G. Ritt (Eds.), *Innovations in clinical practice: A source book* (pp. 309–314). Sarasota, FL: Professional Resource Exchange.

Linehan, M. M. (1985). The reasons for living inventory. In P. A. Keller and L. G. Ritt (Eds.), *Innovations in clinical practice: A source book* (pp. 321–330). Sarasota, FL: Professional Resource Exchange.

Maltz, M. D. (1984). *Recidivism.* Orlando, FL: Academic Press.

Marlatt, G. A. (1985a). Relapse prevention: Theoretical rationale and overview of the model. In G. A. Marlatt & J. R. Gordon (Eds.), *Relapse prevention: Maintenance strategies in the treatment of addictive behaviors* (pp. 3–70). New York: Guilford.

Marlatt, G. A. (1985b). Situational determinants of relapse and skill-training interventions. In G. A. Marlatt & J. R. Gordon (Eds.), *Relapse prevention: Maintenance strategies in the treatment of addictive behaviors* (pp. 71–127). New York: Guilford.

Marlatt, G. A. (1985c). Cognitive factors in the relapse process. In G. A. Marlatt &

J. R. Gordon (Eds.), *Relapse prevention: Maintenance strategies in the treatment of addictive behaviors* (pp. 128–200). New York: Guilford.

Marlatt, G. A. (1985d). Cognitive assessment and intervention procedures for relapse prevention. In G. A. Marlatt & J. R. Gordon (Eds.), *Relapse prevention: Maintenance strategies in the treatment of addictive behaviors* (pp. 201–279). New York: Guilford.

Marlatt, G. A. (1985e). Lifestyle modification. In G. A. Marlatt & J. R. Gordon (Eds.), *Relapse prevention: Maintenance strategies in the treatment of addictive behaviors* (pp. 280–348). New York: Guilford.

Marlatt, G. A. (1988). Matching clients to treatment: Treatment models and stages of change. In D. M. Donovan & G. A. Marlatt (Eds.), *Assessment of addictive behaviors* (pp. 474–483). New York: Guilford.

McCrady, B. S., Dean, L., Dubreuil, E., & Swanson, S. (1985). The problem drinkers' project: A programmatic application of social-learning-based treatment. In G. A. Marlatt & J. R. Gordon (Eds.), *Relapse prevention: Maintenance strategies in the treatment of addictive behaviors* (pp. 417–471). New York: Guilford.

McLellan, A. T., Woods, G. E., Luborsky, L., O'Brien, C. P., & Druley, K. A. (1983). Increased effectiveness of substance abuse treatment: A prospective study of patient-treatment "matching." *Journal of Nervous and Mental Disorders, 17,* 597–605.

Meek, C. L., & editors. (1985). A collection of office forms. In P. A. Keller and L. G. Ritt (Eds.), *Innovations in clinical practice: A source book* (pp. 345–360). Sarasota, FL: Professional Resource Exchange.

Meichenbaum, D., & Turk, D. C. (1987). *Facilitating treatment adherence: A practitioner's guidebook.* New York: Plenum.

Middleton, J. (1984). *Children of alcoholics.* Paper read at the AHEC Annual Meeting, Boise, ID.

Miller, W. R. (1985). Motivation for treatment: A review with special emphasis on alcoholism. *Psychological Bulletin, 98,* 84–107.

Ryan, W. G., Ryan, N. J., Rosen, A., & Virsida, A. R. (1986). Practical issues for the clinician treating substance abuse. In P. A. Keller and L. G. Ritt (Eds.), *Innovations in clinical practice: A source book* (pp. 71–82). Sarasota, FL: Professional Resource Exchange.

Shaffer, H. J., & Neuhaus, C., Jr. (1985). Testing hypotheses: An approach for the assessment of addictive behaviors. In H. B. Milkman & H. J. Shaffer (Eds.), *The addictions: Multidisciplinary perspectives and treatments* (pp. 87–103). Lexington, MA: Lexington Books.

Shiffman, S., Read, L., Maltese, J., Rapkin, D., & Jarvik, M. E. (1985). Preventing relapse in ex-smokers: A self-management approach. In G. A. Marlatt & J. R. Gordon (Eds.), *Relapse prevention: Maintenance strategies in the treatment of addictive behaviors* (pp. 472–520). New York: Guilford.

Siegel, J. M. (1987). The multidimensional anger inventory. In P. A. Keller & S. R. Heyman (Eds.), *Innovations in clinical practice: A source book* (pp. 279–287). Sarasota, FL: Professional Resource Exchange.

Slaikeu, K. A. (1985). An assessment checklist for crisis therapy. In P. A. Keller and L. G. Ritt (Eds.), *Innovations in clinical practice: A source book* (pp. 267–284). Sarasota, FL: Professional Resource Exchange.

Spencer, M. P., & Folstein, M. F. (1985). The mini-mental state examination. In P. A. Keller and L. G. Ritt (Eds.), *Innovations in clinical practice: A source book* (pp. 305–310). Sarasota, FL: Professional Resource Exchange.

Spoth, R. L. & Dush, D. M. (1988). The adult health concerns questionnaire: A psychiatric symptom checklist. In P. A. Keller and S. R. Heyman (Eds.), *In-*

novations in clinical practice: A source book (pp. 289–297). Sarasota, FL: Professional Resource Exchange.

Sternberg, B. (1985). Relapse in weight control: Definitions, processes, and prevention strategies. In G. A. Marlatt & J. R. Gordon (Eds.), *Relapse prevention: Maintenance strategies in the treatment of addictive behaviors* (pp. 521–545). New York: Guilford.

Stout, C. E. (1987). Integrated forensic evaluation form for adolescents. In P. A. Keller & S. R. Heyman (Eds.), *Innovations in clinical practice: A source book* (pp. 289–293). Sarasota, FL: Professional Resource Exchange.

Strayhorn, J. M. (1988). *The competent child: An approach to psychotherapy and preventive mental health.* New York: Guilford.

Tomm, K. (1988). Interventive interviewing: Part III. Intending to ask lineal, circular, strategic, or reflective questions? *Family Process, 27,* 1–15.

Weeks, G. R, & L'Abate, L. (1982). *Paradoxical psychotherapy: Theory and practice with individuals, couples, and families.* New York: Brunner/Mazel.

Weissman, M. M. (1986). The social adjustment self-report inventory. In P. A. Keller & L. G. Ritt (Eds.), *Innovations in clinical practice: A source book* (pp. 299–308). Sarasota, FL: Professional Resource Exchange.

Woititz, J. G. (1983). *Adult children of alcoholics.* Hollywood, FL: Health Communication.

Wurtele, S. K., & Martin, J. E. (1987). Assessment of smoking. In T. D. Nirenberg & S. A. Maisto (Eds.), *Developments in the assessment and treatment of addictive behaviors* (pp. 115–152). Norwood, NJ: Ablex.

2

Differential Treatment Effects

LOUIS P. ANDERSON, Ph.D.

AS NOTED IN the previous chapter, at least one-fourth of the population of the United States engages in some form of addictive behavior. This figure translates into approximately 60 million people. Furthermore, national surveys point to the alarming rise in substance abuse among children and adolescents (Kumpfer, 1987). This trend in the early use and abuse of alcohol and drugs by children and adolescents is remarkable when we consider that 92 percent of all high school seniors report that they use alcohol, 69 percent smoke cigarettes, and 61 percent report the use of illicit drugs (Rhodes & Jason, 1988).

A decade ago, apart from alcohol and substance abuse, there was little interest in conceptualizing and/or identifying addictive behaviors in individuals. The current realization that addictive behavior is now widespread has prompted behavioral scientists, practitioners, therapists, and researchers to examine their theoretical models, research practices, and clinical applications.

As with any area that is rapidly expanding, there are often polemics regarding the severity of the concern and the effectiveness of existing treatment strategies. These polemics tend to be confusing and not useful to practitioners who have to prescribe treatment strategies for clients in need of immediate attention. Consequently, the purpose of this chapter is to provide parameters by which the reader can best understand the factors and techniques associated with therapeutic outcome.

Toward this end, there will be a reporting of the most salient issues in the area of addictive behavior. Examples will be drawn primarily from the alcohol abuse, substance abuse, and smoking cessation literatures, for two reasons. First, research in these areas has dominated the addiction literature (Donovan & Marlatt, 1988). It is unfortunate but true that our knowledge has derived primarily from research in these areas. Secondly, several researchers have argued convincingly that the course and relapse rates for treatment are similar for all addictions (Brownell, Marlatt, Lichtenstein & Wilson, 1986; Stall & Biernacki, 1986).

This chapter is divided into three major sections. In the first section demographic, personal, and environmental factors that affect treatment outcome are discussed. The second section reviews studies that examined therapeutic approaches to treatment. In the final section, methodological issues that most in the field consider to be important are presented. Given the incidence of addictive disorders in this country, research findings often will have direct implications for clinical application and preventive strategies. Thus, valid research in the area of addictive behavior is crucial.

Demographic, Personal, and Environmental Factors

The relationship between demographic factors and outcome has aroused very little attention and concern. Although our research into these factors is limited, several major trends are presented. Logically, if demographics contribute to outcome, then therapists can take certain precautionary steps in their approach to treatment.

Sex

The notion that there may be gender differences in outcome is confounded by how the addictive behavior is manifested. Most heavy drinkers and substance abusers are men (Miller & Joyce, 1979). Women experience more addiction to food and are more prone to abuse substances other than alcohol (Malhotra, Kapur & Murthy, 1978). Moreover, there tends to be a tremendous overlap between different forms of addictions in women (Miller, Yahne & Rhodes, 1990).

In one of the few studies that examined gender differences, Miller and Joyce (1979) discovered that when compared to women, men abstained at a higher rate, but women were more successful in attaining moderation. Significantly, the study also revealed that there were differences in the chronic and habitual patterns of abuse. Females reported less use and were not prone to be chronic abusers. The self-reports documented by Miller and Joyce (1979) were consistent with those reported in a survey of 871 subjects conducted by Brammer and Fritz (1981). Moreover, the survey revealed that females tended to attribute the origins of their addiction to prescribed medication. With regard to treatment outcome, evidence suggests that perhaps men are more vulnerable to relapse because they tend to be more susceptible to social pressures or negative emotional states (Annis & Kelly, 1984).

Race

The incidence of substance abuse and alcoholism in racial and ethnic minority populations is well documented. Substance abuse and drug addiction are disproportionately higher among Blacks, Hispanics, and American Indians (Ryan & Trimble, 1982; Nathan, 1983; LaFromboise, 1988). Such addictive behavioral patterns are related to the health risk of ethnic and racial minorities. Some have argued that these addictive behavioral patterns are maladaptive strategies that racial and ethnic minorities use to cope with racism, poverty, and other stressors (Allen & Stokes, 1982; Harper, 1988). American Indians are among the most adversely affected by substance abuse. Approximately 52 percent of urban Indian adolescents and an estimated 80 percent of reservation Indians engage in moderate to heavy alcohol or substance abuse (LaFramboise, 1988).

Mainly because of methodological problems in instances where both race and socioeconomic status are confounded, we do not know the specific effects race has on the outcome of treatment. One study did indicate that among Black Americans, outcome is highly dependent on gender. While the likelihood of a Black man's abstinence is not highly related to the course of treatment, the probability of a black woman abstaining is significantly enhanced if she enters treatment (Brunswick & Messeri, 1986). As is the case with most psychological disorders, the dropout rate in treatment for racial and ethnic minorities remains quite high (Nathan, 1983).

Consequently, either the treatment strategies are viewed by ethnic minorities as not being helpful or relevant, or the motivation needed for successful treatment is absent for many in this population. Regardless of the reason, research and increasing sensitivity to treatment of racial and ethnic minorities have to be priorities in light of the high incidence of several addictive behaviors in this population. Then too, research should be undertaken to determine cultural norms among ethnic minorities that influence their help-seeking behavior, tolerance of pathological behaviors, and knowledge of and access to treatment facilities (Snowden & Cheung, 1990).

Income/Socioeconomic Status

Results in this area have been equivocal. Willems, Letemendia, and Arroyave (1973a) found that low social class was related to poor outcome. Similar results have been reported by Moos and Bliss (1978) and Vogtsberger (1984). Miller and Joyce (1979) reported conflicting results.

In their study, socioeconomic status was inversely related to successful outcome for both men and women. Several methodological problems that characteristically plague the area may explain the conflicting results. The studies reviewed differed in sample size (62–429) subjects), number of days in treatment (20–82 days), and post-assessment follow-up period (5–12 months).

Age

A consistent trend in the literature indicates that older individuals (above 30) do better in treatment programs (Shiffman, 1987). Younger participants, particularly adolescents, are found to be non-compliant with treatment recommendations (Baskin & Missouri, 1983). The recidivism rates for younger clients are high, in part because of vulnerability to social pressures, interpersonal conflict, and negative emotional states (Annis & Kelly, 1984; Willis & Vaughan, 1989). On the other hand, older individuals have been discovered to be more motivated (Bradfer, 1974). Moreover, when relapse after treatment does occur, younger participants reported that they benefited least from treatment (Kolb, Gunderson & Bucky, 1977).

Two broad approaches (systems theory and cognitive-behavioral techniques) in combination have been successful in increasing adherence to treatment for adolescents and young adults. These approaches have focused on community-based programs that incorporate drug education, behavioral skills training, and prevention strategies aimed at young children (Rhodes & Jason, 1988). In part, the success of these strategies is due to the emphasis placed on the identification of factors that place the individual at risk for substance abuse. Once these factors are identified, the adolescent is then taught effective social coping strategies (Rhodes & Jason, 1988).

Marital Status

Converging lines of evidence strongly suggest that marital status is of central importance in understanding successful outcome to treatment. Studies have found that individuals who were married remained abstinent for a longer period of time than single individuals (Auger, Bragg, Corns & Milner, 1973). Specifically research participants described social support, care, and understanding from spouses, as well as the interpersonal sensitivity of other members of the family, as being instrumental in their recovery (Moberg, Krause & Klein 1982; Reynolds, O'Leary & Walker 1982). For some specific addictive behaviors (smoking, alcohol abuse) the cessation of that behavior by the spouse is a primary factor in recovery (Ward, 1981).

Family cohesiveness and the wife's self-report of support seem to be the primary factors in the abstinence of men with low self-esteem and/or men from lower class backgrounds (Orford, Oppenheimer & Edwards, 1976). Craig (1985) reported that in a study of 150 addicts, the third most frequent reason for early termination of treatment was family problems. Kaufman (1972) found that when addicts began to improve their social interactions, the length of time of abstinence increased. Family and/or couples therapy has become a standard in most substance abuse programs. Interestingly enough, comparing behavioral approaches with group therapy shows that married alcoholics in an established occupation did better than unmarried subjects with no occupational skills. The later were most successful with behavior therapy (Gallen, 1976).

Personality and Psychopathology

The clinical importance of personality factors has been examined in a number of studies. Based on the empirical literature in this area, by and large it appears that a specific, generalizable addictive personality type does not exist. For the most part this is because we do not have adequate theories or conceptual and methodological breakthroughs that would allow us to make such cause-and-effect statements. Nonetheless, it is safe to say that even identification of a specific, generalizable addictive personality type cannot predict with precision outcome in treatment.

In this area of research, measurement and conceptual problems exist. For example, research participants exhibiting similar clinical pictures often have received different diagnoses (Schuckit & Gunderson 1979). Then too, researchers with a behavioral orientation often are reluctant to apply diagnostic labels, thus limiting our ability to draw conclusions. Although some researchers (Schuckit & Gunderson, 1979; Sullivan, Guglielmo & Lilly, 1986) have concluded that diagnostic breakdowns and personality subtypes have limited prognostic significance, others have justified the use of assessing personality factors on clinical grounds (Felde, 1973). In Chapter 17 of this book, L'Abate provides a system for understanding the nature of the interpersonal dimension of addictions. The advantage of his system in comparison to others is its multidimensional, developmental focus. Although it should be evaluated empirically, the interpersonal model by L'Abate provides one of the few testable frameworks in which to evaluate the personality dimensions of addictions.

Using data on male alcoholics, O'Leary, Rohsenow, and Donovan (1976) discovered that those clients who dropped out of treatment were significantly lower in total and personal control when compared to successful clients. Interestingly, these subjects also reported a greater change in internal direction on the locus of control scale. Consequently, the results imply that as subjects begin to believe that they could exert influence over their condition, they may be at risk for dropping out of treatment.

A similar finding was present in a study by Scheller and Klein (1982). These investigations used the Levenson Locus of Control Scale to measure the therapeutic progress of 78 male alcoholics. Results revealed an increase in internal direction on the locus of control scale during treatment. Furthermore, a positive relationship was found between hopelessness and external locus of control for treatment failures. With regard to affective symptoms, Kanas, Cleveland, Pokorny, and Miller (1976) and Washton, Stone, and Hendrickson (1988) found that less favorable outcomes were associated when symptoms of depression and anxiety were present in clients with addictive behaviors. Interestingly enough, it was determined that treatment focused primarily on resolving underlying personality factors failed. Thus, Kanas et al. (1976) argued that symptom reduction (reducing the addictive behavior) should be given primary consideration in treatment approaches. The classification model of helping and coping, as outlined by Brickman, Rabinowitz, Karuza, Coates, Cohn, and Kidder (1982), is arguably the most popular framework for conceptualizing both the treatment and empirical work in the addiction area. Within this four-category framework, attributions for development and solution for the addiction are emphasized. Personality and forms of psychopathology are de-emphasized. Attributions and the symptom of the addiction are dealt with as a primary (concerns) disorder and not simply as a symptom of underlying psychopathology. With regard to severe psychopathology, Orford et al. (1976) found an inverse relationship between treatment, success, and psychopathology.

Motivation, Expectancy, and Self-Perception

Bromet, Moos, Bliss, and Wuthman (1977) investigated the post-treatment functioning of 429 alcoholic patients. Relative to those who showed no improvement, patients who were actively involved in their treatment experienced better outcome. The expectancy of therapist and patient was examined in a single study; Vannicelli and Becker (1981) examined expectancy along several dimensions, including role functioning, drinking behavior, and utilization of after-care services. Drinking behavior and use of after-care services were correlated with patient perception at 12-month follow-up. Therapists' expectations were unrelated to any of the criterion measures used. The researchers concluded that patients predict with regard to their own motivations and that therapists predictions were in accordance with the characteristics of the patients (Vannicelli & Becker, 1981).

Research on self-perceptions has led to results that are not easy to interpret. Results on self-perception of drinking behavior have suggested that major changes occur in the way an alcoholic perceives himself or herself. In a study by Heather, Edwards, and Hore (1975), significant changes were documented in subject's self-perception. However, patients who dropped out of treatment showed the greatest gain in self-respect and esteem. Similar findings were presented in an earlier section on locus of control. Possibly once a patient experiences a gain in confidence and gets what he or she wants out of treatment, that individual may be at risk to terminate treatment.

Several investigators have looked at the role the therapist plays in influencing a patient's response to treatment. In a study focused on reasons for patient dropout, Craig (1985) discovered that the incidence of dropout increased as absences by the patient's primary therapist increased. In another investigation, patients were asked to describe the most helpful aspect of a treatment program. Successful participants cited stability, consistency of staff, and realistic goal setting (Birmingham, 1986). Furthermore, therapists who were described as flexible and creative, and who strived to improve their patient's self-esteem worked best with individuals with addictive behaviors (Montalvo, 1985; Sullivan, Guglielmo & Lilly, 1986). Values of the therapist also play a major role in outcome. In at least one study, successful outcome was related to the values held by the therapist (Talbott & Gillen, 1978). Although the values of therapists, as measured by the Rokeach Value Scale, were related to outcome, no evidence indicated that convergence of values between therapist and patient did occur.

Length of Treatment

Studies of time spent in treatment have yielded important findings. Washton, Gold, and Pottash (1986) showed that with drug abusers, length of treatment is highly predictive of successful outcome. The influence of length of treatment on outcome is less clear with alcoholics. The Willems et al. study (1973b) found no differences in treatment between short-term (20 days) and long-term (82 days) treatment. Smart and Gray (1978) studied 520 alcoholics, 20 to 59 years old. They found that when compared to a control group, five times as many subjects in the long-term treatment group and three times as many subjects in the short-term treatment group remained abstinent one year after treatment. Unfortunately, the researchers had to qualify their conclusions, because when the total number of improved subjects was compared to the total not improved, no differences existed across treatment groups. Consequently, although a higher proportion of the subjects in the long-term group remained abstinent, no significant differences existed between the group on other measures of improvement such as social stability, physical health, and motivation for treatment.

Coercion

Coercion and confrontation are hotly debated therapeutic strategies. In looking at the components of successful treatment, Schramm and De-Fillippi (1975) determined that successful identification and referral of patients for treatment were far more predictive of success than any component of the treatment program. These results implied that spouses, parents, employers, and anyone in a position of power should not be hesitant about confronting and/or coercing the patient into treatment. Consistent with this view is Willems' research, which suggests that the threat of civil commitment reduced drug use, and increased employment and family responsibility in substance abusers (Anglin & Douglas, 1984).

Relapse

Inconsistency in treatment and follow-up care have been found to contribute to relapse. In Chvapil, Hymes, and Delmastro's study (1978), 70 percent of the patients relapsed after they were asked to seek treatment at another facility. The reverse (70 percent remained abstinent) was true for those who continued treatment at their original site. Results of Vanicelli's study (1978) suggested that motivation and involvement in after-care arrangements during the first three months following treatment were determining factors in favorable outcome. Litman, Eiser, and Rawson (1977) have taken an interactional position and have presented data to support the view that relapse is an interaction between: a) the degree of addictive behavior, b) environmental threat, c) coping strategies available for the individual, and d) perceived effectiveness of these coping strategies. Their principal components analysis revealed that threatening perceptions that lead to relapse could be categorized as lessened cognitive vigilance, social anxiety, unpleasant affect, or euphoric feelings.

Marlatt and Gordon (1980) have developed a social learning model of the relapse process. Their model has been well received by practitioners and researchers in the field. The model suggests that relapse follows the principles of cognitive dissonance. A major factor in relapse concerns how the individual is able to resolve the conflict between his or her new self-view of being an abstainer and the internal attribution that a slip means a lack of willpower. Thus, Marlatt and Gordon (1980) have suggested programming relapses and identifying high-risk situations and aversive conditioning. The Hunt and General (1973) review of research on relapse rates in smoking, heroin addiction, and alcoholism provides evidence that a negatively accelerated extinction curve is present in all three populations. Significantly, their data revealed that the process of relapse begins immediately after treatment ends. These results suggest a need to see treatment as a continuous process that includes attention being paid to aftercare and follow-up.

Treatment Strategies

In the previous sections, we examined how outcome is influenced by characteristics of substance abusers and their therapist. In this section, I will examine studies that deal with specific therapeutic interventions. Researchers have long been fascinated with comparing approaches to treatment and determining which intervention worked best. However, possibly because of the severity of addictive disorders, there is a paucity of comparative research studies done. Generally researchers from different schools evaluate their own approaches.

Behavioral/Cognitive-Behavioral Approaches versus Traditional Psychotherapies

Behavioral and/or cognitive-behavioral strategies have played a crucial role in treating individuals with addictive behaviors. Litman and Topham's review of the outcome literature for alcoholism (1983) found that behavioral techniques are at least as effective as traditional verbal treatment. Patients in behavioral programs stay in treatment longer (Litman & Topham 1983; Forrest, 1984). Moreover, the ease in using such standard behavioral techniques as contingency contracting makes this approach both economical and efficient for use by paraprofessionals and community ombudsmen. Perhaps such behavioral techniques as stress inoculation, social skills training and self-control procedures should be standard approaches in smoking, weight control and substance abuse programs (Grabowski & O'Brien, 1981).

An assumption in treating individuals with addictions is that they often cope with stressful situations inappropriately by engaging in addictive behaviors. Therefore, interventions are designed to help these individuals broaden their skills in coping with a variety of stressful situations. In a classic intervention study, Chaney, O'Leary, and Marlatt (1978) implemented a skill-training program that taught individuals appropriate problem-solving behaviors to use in self-identified target situations that triggered frustration, anger, and a negative emotional state, and interpersonal temptation. In comparison to a discussion group and a control group, the skill-training group showed significant improvement.

Moreover, these changes continued at a one-year post-treatment follow-up.

As indicated by studies reviewed earlier in this chapter success of treatment was influenced by such demographic factors as a person's gender (Miller & Joyce, 1979), socioeconomic status (Willems, Letemendia & Arroyave, 1973a), age (Shiffman, 1988), and marital status (Auger et al., 1973). Unmarried alcoholics with no occupational skills and lower IQ were found to do better with behavioral approaches, whereas married research participants with occupational skills did better with verbal forms of therapy. The only study that investigated the combination of behavioral and psychoanalytic techniques revealed that this combination is a remarkably effective treatment strategy (Grenier, 1985).

Family Intervention

Some form of family intervention is now the standard for both inpatient and outpatient treatment of addictive disorders. Successful outcome to treatment is related to family stability and support (Smart, 1978; Thomas, 1989). Family intervention is particularly effective when: a) individual psychotherapy is ineffective; b) the addiction affects the marriage; c) in cases of severe psychopathology; and d) when depression is present (Beavers, 1982). An underlying assumption of family intervention is that after a period of time a person's addictive-related behavior evokes negative emotion and behavior on the part of family members, thus leading to family dysfunction. Therefore, intervention strategies are introduced that allow family members to come to grips with their own interactional patterns. Structural and strategic approaches are used, as well as assertiveness training, rehearsal, contracting, and education about the addictive behavior. One study has shown that one-person therapy was as effective as co-joint therapy in improving family functioning with drug abusers (Szapocznik, 1986).

Inpatient Treatment

A basic intervention for life-threatening, severe addictive disorders is inpatient treatment. Reviews of inpatient programs have indicated that success rates are unrelated to length of treatment (Annis, 1986). However, personality factors such as motivation and willingness to participate in hospitalization are predictive of drinking and occupational and psychological functioning (Bromet, Moos, Bliss & Wuthmann, 1977). Social support and employee involvement also had a positive influence (Moberg, Krause & Klein, 1982). Family interventions that focus on self-awareness and interpersonal relationship were superior to detoxification alone in patient programs for substance abusers. (Cusack, 1985). In fact, a review by

Dole (1980) implied that without psychosocial intervention, relapse rates for substance abusers reach as high as 90 percent.

Annis (1986) has argued that partial hospitalization is more economical (one-third the cost) and a superior modality to inpatient hospitalization. The advantage of partial hospitalization is that it allows the patient more freedom and the opportunity to maintain some ties with his or her social environment.

Methodological Concerns

An important consideration in therapy outcome studies with addictive behaviors concerns appropriate pre-treatment assessment, diagnosis, and adequate measurement of treatment effects. Reliable, valid, and quantifiable measures are imperative (Nirenberg, Ershner-Hershfield, Sobell & Sobell, 1981).

As pointed out earlier, responsiveness to treatment can be influenced by a wide range of variables such as degree of pathology, marital status, age, and motivation. These factors and other pre-treatment differences must be considered. Therefore, an adequate screening process should allow the investigator to define the population under study. If this screening cannot or is not done, any possibility of change may be obscured by factors present that have little to do with the intervention. Furthermore, even if change occurs, it may be due to factors secondary to the intervention (Critelli & Neumann, 1984).

Research participants or patients may be differentiated by diagnosis (e.g., smokers, gamblers, substance abusers, or alcoholics) and randomly assigned to treatment or control groups, or their assignment to groups may be based on a criterion measure such as condition, frequency of target behavior, or a combination of both (e.g., gender plus diagnosis). (See Campbell & Stanley, 1963 and Kazdin & Wilson, 1978 for discussion.)

Regardless of how the population is selected, detailed and clearly defined criteria for inclusion in the study are warranted. A standardized instrument or diagnostic framework such as the DSM III-R should be employed. Alternatives such as using trained judges or experts in the area to rate target behaviors are frequently used and highly recommended. A reliability coefficient of 80 percent or greater is the minimum acceptable criteria for interrater reliability (Mitchell, 1979).

Outcome Measures

In order to answer the question, "Does treatment work?" the investigator has to assess outcome. Treatment-outcome results are influenced primarily by factors such as the selection and measurement of outcome measures. Emrick and Hansen (1983), in their review of the literature, recommended the use of multiple outcome criteria including length of treatment, recidivism, physical health indices, and social and emotional functioning, as well as an evaluation of the addictive behavior.

On the basis of an exhaustive review of over 211 studies in 50 journals, Milner, Freeman, Surber, and Goldstein (1985) also recommended the use of multiple outcome measures. Moreover, they concluded that objective measures should be augmented by the research participant's self-reports. This conclusion was based on studies indicating that subjective measures were more likely to yield significant findings of treatment success than either objective or behavioral measures.

However, another line of research suggests caution. Aiken (1986) discovered that research participants tended to distort their early self-presentation. Consequently, post-treatment change levels often are elevated artificially because of unrealistic pre-treatment levels. Single change scores in general and single scores on subjective measures in particular may be less than optimal indices of response to treatment.

Critical evaluation of treatment procedures via criteria measures should include an indicator of social functioning or adjustment. An over-reliance on the cessation of the addictive behavior as the sole criterion of success may be overly rigid, if not impractical. Maisto and Caddy (1981), in noting the importance of a multivariate approach, pointed out the value of assessing biological, psychological, and social factors. As L'Abate indicated in Chapter 1, the individual does not live in a social vacuum. Conversely the addict's health, emotional well-being, and interpersonal relationships are affected by the addiction.

With regard to follow-up assessment, three-month, six-month, and one-year follow-up periods are preferred and are now standard for articles accepted for publication in American Psychological Association journals. The longer the follow-up assessment, the less likelihood that the results would be due to placebo effects (Kazdin, 1978). Miller (1986) emphasizes the use of informants to ensure accurate follow-up information. Steps should be taken to ensure that contact is maintained with the research participants.

Design Dilemmas

In general, an investigator selects a design to account for expected change. For the most part, experimental designs can be grouped into either between-subjects or within-subjects types. Dilemmas generally arise in the area of addiction research when the investigator is not able to assign participants to groups randomly or is unable to locate a suitable control group. Since randomization is fundamental to scientific research, studies that do not take this into consideration are viewed unfavorably.

When randomization is not feasible, researchers have settled on various quasi-experimental designs, as well as covariance analysis to adjust statistically for group differences and to control for unsystematic error that may influence outcome. Within-subjects designs have become increasingly popular among addiction researchers. In within-subjects designs, the efficacy of a treatment is assessed by examining the change over time made by the research participant or a number of research participants across situations. Since the focus of within-subjects designs is on change within the individual and not change between groups, randomization is generally not necessary. However, a major weakness of within-subjects designs concerns the generalizability of their findings (Kazdin, 1982).

With regard to treatment studies, an assumption is that differences by group on outcome measures (e.g., dependent variables) are due to the treatment intervention. Although it is important to test for group differences in order to determine treatment effectiveness, an ethical dilemma occurs when treatment is withheld from participants in a control group. A number of investigations have offered solutions to this ethical dilemma. A useful alternative to the withholding of treatment is to administer different treatments to different groups of research participants. In this way each research participant receives treatment and an evaluation can be performed at the end of treatment to determine whether the different treatments produced different results (Chassan, 1979).

A second strategy involves administering various components of an established treatment program to groups of research participants, and then assessing the relative influence of each treatment component. A third strategy that has merit involves the use of a waiting-list control group. Research participants in the waiting-list control condition serve as a control group for those in the experimental group who receive the intervention. Waiting-list controls are then given the intervention treatment after the experimental group concludes treatment. Disadvantages of this strategy involve threats to the internal validity of the study. Factors such as history, maturation, and experimental mortality have to be controlled (Campbell & Stanley, 1963).

Conclusion

This chapter has summarized two broad areas of differential treatment effects. The areas discussed include demographics, personal and environmental factors, and therapeutic approaches to treatment. For the most part, the influence of demographic factors (e.g., gender, race, age, and marital status) remains unclear. For example, although response to treatment has been found to be influenced by gender, the differences found seem to be more dependent on moderating factors such as the type of addiction and the pattern of substance abuse.

With regard to race, racial and ethnic minorities make up a high percentage of substance abusers. Even with this being the case, research still has not offered clear guidelines regarding treatment effectiveness with this population. This raises the question of whether researchers have been asking the right questions. Given the high dropout rates in treatment, more time should be spent in determining why ethnic minorities do not complete treatment. In addition, research that attempts to address the high rates of addiction in this population should also confront questions concerning the history of chronic abuse within families of ethnic minorities, along with systemic issues such as poverty, unemployment, and severe health problems.

Several studies have suggested that younger individuals, particularly adolescents, are not motivated for treatment. Since adolescents are at greater risk of developing addictions but are not committed to treatment, greater attention should be placed on primary prevention strategies. Such strategies should involve families, schools, and all major institutions of society. The intent of primary prevention strategies should include altering the values, customs, and attitudes that encourage addictive behavior patterns among our youth.

As with age, research on marital status is far more definitive than is the case with gender or race. Marital status and support by spouse were found to be strong predictors of successful outcome to treatment. Conversely the lack of support of a spouse and/or family members can lead to unsuccessful treatment (Craig, 1985). Family involvement is therefore highly recommended in the development of treatment strategies for individuals manifesting addictions. The multi-dimensional framework presented in Chapter 1 points out directions for future research.

With regard to the therapeutic process, research has suggested that overemphasis on an assumed underlying cause of the addiction is unproductive and may actually increase the risk of early termination of treatment (Kanas et al., 1976). In addition, the values of therapists have been examined and determined to be an important ingredient affecting client change. Although the therapist's values are important, at this time it is not clear whether a convergence of the values of therapist and client is necessary for significant change to occur (Talbott & Gillen, 1978).

Therapist influence has also been studied in relationship to the incidence of relapse. Generally studies have found that continued follow-up and involvement in an after-care arrangement with the same treatment staff during the first three months after treatment ends reduce the rate of relapse.

Factors such as motivation (as measured by self-involvement), gain in self-respect, self-esteem, and internal locus of control seem to be strong predictors of outcome to treatment. These results provide some evidence to support future research on attributional styles. The work by Marlatt (1988) and others on matching attributional styles with treatment strategies appears promising. Surprisingly, it appears that clients are most at risk for dropping out of treatment if a significant change occurs in their self-respect or internal locus of control (Heather et al., 1975). Possibly as clients begin to feel a greater sense of control over their life, they also begin to feel as though they have mastered their addiction and thus see little need to continue treatment. These results provide evidence to support the need for conceptual and empirical work investigating the attributional styles of the addict.

Behavioral and cognitive-behavioral strategies have increased in popularity over the past decade. Such strategies are now standard in treating most addicts. Clients in behavioral programs stay in treatment longer, and these strategies have been found to be at least as effective as other interventions (Litman & Topham, 1983; Forrest, 1984). In the future we look forward to more sophisticated treatment strategies using behavioral approaches. For example, future clinical research is needed to determine the efficacy of extending behavioral approaches to the family and the larger social environment of the addict.

The most striking feature of the literature concerning differential treatment effects is the lack of methodologically sound applied and basic research. The lack of research rigor has greatly impeded both our understanding of the nature of addiction and how best to treat individuals manifesting addictive behaviors. Future research, involving greater attention paid to the pretreatment assessment and diagnosis of research participants, the use of multiple outcome criteria, and the use of more sophisticated designs and statistical procedures, may permit a better understanding of the differential treatment effects in the area of addiction.

References

Aiken, L. S. (1986). Retrospective self-reports by clients differ from original reports: Implications for the evaluation of drug treatment programs. *International Journal of the Addictions, 21,* 767–788.

Allen, W. R., & Stokes, S. (1982). Black family lifestyle and the mental health of Black Americans. In F. U. Munoz & R. Endo (Eds.), *Perspective on minority group mental health* (pp. 43–52). Washington, DC: United Press of America.

Anglin, M., & Douglas, W. H. (1984), Outcome of narcotic addict treatment in California. *National Inst. on Drug Abuse Research Monographs, 51,* 106–128.

Annis, H. M. (1986). Is inpatient rehabilitation of the alcoholic cost-effective? National Association on Drug Abuse Problems Conference on Controversies in Alcoholism and Substance Abuse: The scientific approach. *Advances in Alcohol and Substance Abuse, 5,* 175–190.

Annis, H. M., & Kelly, P. (1984, August). *Analysis of the Inventory of Drinking Situations.* Paper presented at the convention of the American Psychological Association, Toronto.

Auger, R., Bragg, R., Corns, D., & Milner, M. (1973). Preliminary assessment and prognostic indicators in a newly developed alcohol treatment program.

Newsletter for Research in Mental Health and Behavioral Sciences, 15, 21–24.

Baskin, D., & Missouri, C. (1983). How effective are alcohol halfway houses? A case in point. *Journal of Alcohol and Drug Education, 29,* 62–71.

Beavers, W. R. (1982). Implications and contradictions for couples therapy. *Psychiatric Clinics of North America, 5,* 469–478.

Birmingham, M. S. (1986). An outpatient program for adolescent substance abusers. *Journal of Adolescence, 9,* 123–133.

Bradfer, J. (1974). Comparative study of therapeutic and of clinical and psychosocial data from a medico-social guidance center for alcoholics. *Acta Psychiatrica Belgica, 74,* 617–629.

Brammer, H., & Fritz, W. (1981). Epidemiological study of some aspects of alcoholism: A pilot study. *International Journal of Rehabilitation Research, 4,* 554–558.

Brickman, P., Rabinowitz, V., Karuza, J., Coates, D., Cohen, E., & Kidder, L. (1982). Models of helping and coping. *American Psychologist, 37,* 368–384.

Bromet, E., Moos, R., Bliss, F., & Wuthman, C. (1977). Post-treatment functioning of alcoholic patients: its relation to program participation. *Journal of Consulting and Clinical Psychology, 45,* 829–842.

Brownell, K. D., Marlatt, G., Lichtenstein, E., & Wilson, G. T. (1986). Understanding and preventing relapse. *American Psychologist, 41,* 765–782.

Brunswick, A. F., & Messeri, P. A. (1986). Pathways to heroin abstinence: A longitudinal study of urban black youth. *Advances in Alcohol and Substance Abuse, 5,* 111–135.

Campbell, D. T., & Stanley, J. C. (1963). *Experimental and quasi-experimental designs for research.* Chicago: Rand McNally.

Chaney, E. F., O'Leary, M. R., & Marlatt, G. A. (1978). Skill training with alcoholics. *Journal of Consulting and Clinical Psychology, 46,* 1092–1104.

Chassan, J. B. (1979). *Research design in clinical psychology and psychiatry* (2nd ed.). New York: Wiley.

Chvapil, M., Hymes, H., & Delmastro, D. (1978). Oupatient aftercare as a factor in treatment outcome. *Journal of Studies on Alcohol, 39,* 540–544.

Craig, R. J. (1985). Reducing the treatment dropout rate in drug abuse programs. *Journal of Substance Abuse Programs, 2,* 209–219.

Critelli, J. W., & Neumann, K. F. (1984). The placebo: Conceptual analysis of a construct in transition. *American Psychologist, 39,* 32–39.

Cusack, S. (1985). Veritas Villa. *Journal of Substance Abuse Treatment, 2,* 193–194.

Dole, V. P. (1980). Addictive behavior. *Scientific American, 243,* 138–154.

Donovan, D. M., & Marlatt, G. A. (1988). *Assessment of addictive behaviors.* New York: Guilford.

Emrick, C. D., & Hansen, J. (1983). Assertions regarding the effectiveness of treatment for alcoholism: Fact or fantasy? *American Psychologist, 38,* 1078–1088.

Felde, R. (1973). Alcoholics before and after treatment: A study of self-concept changes. *Newsletter for Research in Mental Health and Behavioral Sciences, 15,* 32–34.

Forrest, G. G. (1984). Psychotherapy of alcoholics and substance abusers: Outcome assessment revisited. *Family and Community Mental Health, 7,* 40–50.

Gallen, M. (1976). Prediction of improvement in two contrasting alcoholism treatment programs. *Newsletter for Research in Mental Health and Behavioral Sciences, 18,* 31–32.

Grabowski, J., & O'Brien, C. P. (1981). Conditioning factors in opiate use. *Advances in Substance Abuse, 2,* 69–121.

Grenier, C. (1985). Treatment effectiveness in an adolescent chemical treatment program: A quasi-experimental design. *International Journal of the Addictions, 20,* 381–391.

Harper, F. D. (1988). Alcohol and black youth: An overview. *Journal of Drug Issues, 18,* (1), 7–14.

Heather, N., Edwards, S., & Hore, B. D. (1975). Changes in construing and outcome of group therapy for alcoholism. *Journal of Studies on Alcohol, 36,* 1238–1253.

Hunt, W. A., & Bespalec, D. A. (1974). Relapse rates after treatment for heroin addiction. *Journal of Community Psychology, 2,* 85–87.

Hunt, W. A., & General, W. R. (1973). Relapse rates after treatment for alcoholism. *Journal of Community Psychology, 1,* 66–68.

Kanas, T. E., Cleveland, S. E., Pokorny, A. D., & Miller, B. A. (1976). Two contrasting alcoholism treatment programs: A comparison of outcomes. *International Journal of the Addictions, 11,* 1045–1062.

Kaufman, E. (1972). Methadone and/or ex-addict therapy: Are they a "cure" for heroin addiction? *Contemporary Drug Problems, 1,* 207–223.

Kazdin, A. E. (1978). Methodological and interpretive problems of single-case experimental designs. *Journal of Consulting and Clinical Psychology, 46,* 629–642.

Kazdin, A. E. (1980). *Research design in clinical psychology.* New York: Harper & Row.

Kazdin, A. E. (1982). *Single-case research designs.* New York: Oxford University Press.

Kazdin, A. E., & Wilson, G. T. (1978). *Evaluation of behavior therapy: Issues, evidence and research strategies.* Cambridge, MA: Ballinger.

Kolb, D., Gunderson, E. K., & Bucky, S. F. (1977). Outcomes for recidivists in Navy alcohol rehabilitation programs. *Military Medicine, 142,* 435–437.

Kumpfer, K. L. (1987). Special populations: Etiology and prevention of vulnerability to chemical dependency in children of substance abusers. In B. S. Brown & A. R. Mills (Eds.), *Youth at risk for substance abuse* (pp. 87–119). Rockville, MD: National Institute on Drug Abuse, Department of Health Education and Welfare.

LaFromboise, T. D. (1988). American Indian mental health policy. *American Psychologist, 43*(5), 388–397.

Litman, G. K., Eiser, J. R., & Rawson, N. S. (1977). Toward a topology of relapse: A preliminary report. *Drug and Alcohol Dependence, 2,* 157–162.

Litman, G. K., Eiser, J. R., & Taylor, C. (1979). Dependence, relapse and extinction: A theoretical critique and a behavioral examination. *Journal of Clinical Psychology, 35,* 192–200.

Litman, G. K., & Topham, A. (1983). Outcome studies in alcoholism. *Recent Developments in Alcoholism, 1,* 167–194.

Maisto, S. A., & Caddy, G. R. (1981). Self-control and addictive behavior: Present status and prospects. *International Journal of the Addictions, 16,* 109–133.

Maisto, S. A. & Conners, G. J. (1988). Assessment of treatment outcome. In D. S. Donovan & G. A. Marlatt (Eds.), *Assessment of addictive behaviors* (pp. 421–453). New York: Guilford.

Malhotra, A., Kapur, R. L., & Murthy, V. N. (1978). Drug dependence: A preliminary survey of hospital registrations. *Indian Journal of Clinical Psychology, 5,* 131–137.

Marlatt, G. A. (1988). Matching clients to treatment. In D. M. Donovan & G. A. Marlatt (Eds.). *Assessment of addictive behaviors* (pp. 474–484). New York, Guilford.

Marlatt, G. A., & Gordon, J. R. (1980). Determinants of relapse: Implications for the maintenance of behavior change. In P. O. Davidson & S. M. Davidson (Eds.), *Behavior medicine; Changing health lifestyles* (pp. 410–452). New York: Brunner/Mazel.

Miller, S. (1986). How to tell if alcoholism treatment has worked: Assessing outcome studies. *Hospital and Community Psychiatry, 38,* 555–556.

Miller, W. R., & Joyce, M. A. (1979). Prediction of abstinence, controlled drinking, and heavy drinking outcomes following behavioral self-control training. *Journal of Consulting and Clinical Psychology, 7,* 773–775.

Miller, W. R., Yahne, C. E., & Rhodes, J. M. (1990). *Adjustment: The psychology of change.* Englewood Cliffs, NJ: Prentice-Hall.

Milner, D. M., Freeman, H. E., Surber, M., & Goldstein, M. S. (1985). Success in mental health treatment interventions: A review of 211 random assignment studies. *Journal of Social Science Research, 8,* 1–21.

Mitchell, S. K. (1979). Interobserver agreement, reliability and generalizability of results collected in observational studies. *Psychology Bulletin, 86,* 376–390.

Moberg, D. P., Krause, W. K., & Klein, P. E. (1982). Post-treatment drinking behavior among in-patients from an industrial alcoholism program. *International Journal of the Addictions, 17,* 549–567.

Montalvo, B. (1985). On blunder avoidance. *Family Therapy Networker, 9,* 51–53.

Moos, R. F., & Bliss, F. (1978). Difficulty of follow-up and outcome alcoholism treatment. *Journal of Studies on Alcohol, 39,* 473–490.

Nathan, P. (1983). Failures in prevention. *American Psychologist, 38,* 459–467.

Nirenberg, T. D., Ersner-Hershfield, S., Sobell, L. C., & Sobell, M. (1981). Behavioral treatment of alcohol problems. In C. K. Prolop & L. A. Bradley (Eds.), *Medical Psychology* (pp. 267–291). New York: Academic Press.

O'Leary, M. R., Rohsenow, D. J., & Donovan, D. M. (1976). Locus of control and patient attrition from an alcoholism treatment program. *Journal of Consulting and Clinical Psychology, 44,* 686–687.

Orford, J. (1976). The cohesiveness of alcoholism, complicated marriages and its influence on treatment outcome. *British Journal of Psychiatry, 128,* 318–339.

Orford, J., Oppenheimer, E., & Edwards, G. (1976). Abstinence or control: The outcome for excessive drinkers two years after consultation. *Behavior Research and Therapy, 14,* 409–418.

Reynolds, F. D., O'Leary, M. R., & Walker, R. D. (1982). Family environment as a predictor of alcoholism treatment outcome. *International Journal of the Addictions, 17,* 505–512.

Rhodes, J. E., & Jason, L. A. (1988). *Preventing substance abuse among children and adolescents.* New York: Pergamon.

Ryan, R. A., & Trimble, J. E. (1982). Toward an understanding of the mental health and substance abuse issues of rural and migrant ethnic minorities. In F. U. Munoz & R. Endo (Eds.), *Perspectives on minority group mental health* (pp. 23–48). Washington, DC: United Press of America.

Scheller, R., & Klein, M. (1982). Personality psychological determinants of therapeutic success with alcoholism. *Zeitschrift fur Differentielle und Diagnostische Psychologie, 3,* 47–54.

Shiffman, S. (1987). Maintenance and relapse: Coping with temptation. In T. P. Nirenberg (Ed.), *Advances in the treatment of addictive behaviors* (pp. 353–385). Norwood, NJ: Ablex.

Schramm, C., & DeFillippi, R. J. (1975). Characteristics of successful alcoholism treatment programs for American workers. *British Journal of Addiction, 70,*(3), 271–275.

Schuckit, M. A., & Gunderson, E. E. (1979). The clinical characteristics of personality disorder subtypes in naval service. *Journal of Clinical Psychiatry, 40,* 175–179.

Smart, R. G. (1978). Do some types of alcoholics do better in some types of treatment than others? *Drug and Alcohol Dependence, 3,* 65–75.

Smart, R. G., & Gray, G. (1978). Minimal, moderate and long-term treatment of alcoholism. *British Journal of Addiction, 73,* 35–38.

Snowden, L. R. & Cheung, F. K. (1990). Use of inpatient mental health services by members of ethnic minority groups. *American Psychologist, 45,* (3), 347–355.

Stall, R., & Biernacki, P. (1986). Spontaneous remission from the problematic use of substances: An inductive model derived from a comparative analysis of the alcohol, opiate, tobacco and obesity literatures. *International Journal of Addictions, 21,* 1–23.

Sullivan, A. P., Guglielmo, R., & Lilly, L. (1986). Evaluating prevention and intervention procedures. *Journal of Drug Education, 16,* 91–98.

Szapocznik, J. (1986). Conjoint versus one-person family therapy: Further evidence for the effectiveness of conducting family therapy through one person with drug-abusing adolescents. *Journal of Consulting and Clinical Psychology, 54,* 395–397.

Talbott, J. A., & Gillen, C. (1978). Differences between nonprofessional recovering alcoholic counselors treating Bowery alcoholics: A study of therapist values. *Psychiatric Quarterly, 50,* 333–342.

Thomas, J. C. (1989). An overview of marital and family therapy with substance abuse populations. *Alcoholism Treatment Quarterly, 6* (2), 91–102.

Vanicelli, M. (1978). Impact of aftercare in the treatment of alcoholics: A cross-lagged panel analysis. *Journal of Studies on Alcohol, 39,* 1875–1886.

Vanicelli, M., & Becker, B. (1981). Prediction outcome in treatment of alcoholism: A study of staff and patients. *Journal of Studies on Alcohol, 42,* 938–950.

Vogtsberger, K. N. (1984). Treatment outcomes of substance-abusing physicians. *American Journal of Drug and Alcohol Abuse, 10,* 23–37.

Ward, D. A. (1981). The influence of family relationships on social and psychological functioning: A follow-up study. *Journal of Marriage and the Family, 43,* 807–815.

Washton, A. M., Gold, M. S., & Pottash, A. C. (1986). Treatment outcomes in cocaine abusers. Proceedings of the 47th Annual Scientific Meeting of the Committee on Problems of Drug Dependence: Problems of drug dependence (1985, Baltimore, MD). *National Institute on Drug Abuse Research Monograph Series, 67,* 381–384.

Washton, A. M., Stone, N. S., & Hendrickson, E. C. (1988). Cocaine Abuse. In D. M. Donovan & G. A. Marlatt (Eds.), *Assessment of addictive behaviors* (pp. 364–388).

Willems, P. J., Letemendia, F. J., & Arroyave, F. (1973a). A categorization for the assessment of prognosis and outcome in the treatment of alcoholism. *British Journal of Psychiatry. 122,* 649–654.

Willems, P. J., Letemendia, F. J., & Arroyave, F. (1973b). A two-year follow-up study comparing short with long stay inpatient treatment of alcoholics. *British Journal of Psychiatry, 122,* 637–648.

Willis, T. A., & Vaughan, R. (1989). Social support and substance use in early adolescence. *Journal of Behavioral Medicine, 12* (4), 321–329.

3

Guidelines for Treatment

LUCIANO L'ABATE, Ph.D.

IN SPITE OF our initial and consistent emphasis on differential treatment for addictions, we cannot escape the inherent commonalities present in most modalities of treatment for addictions or for any other human problem. Furthermore, the confusing, maddening morass of psychotherapeutic treatments (Saltzman & Norcross, 1990; Zeig & Munion, 1990), begs the question about what commonalities there are among all of these treatments. Even if we find such commonalities, what will they mean for successful therapeutic outcome? Are these commonalities responsible for positive outcome or are there specific approaches in each addictive condition that are more responsible for that outcome? Further, what is the contribution of the style of the therapist rather than any particular method of treatment that he or she may follow? Can we make sense of this confusing cacophony of treatment approaches, each claiming, often without a shred of evidence, to be successful? These are some of the many questions that may remain unanswered here as well as in the field of addiction treatment.

Consequently, the twofold purpose of this chapter is to introduce a continuum of preventive approaches for the treatment of addictions and enumerate various modalities and preferences of treatment approaches that have been already reviewed in the previous chapter from a research viewpoint. Here this enumeration is given for the sole purpose of citing references that have specifically used a modality of treatment with an addictive population and that could become additional forms of preferred treatment in the future in combination with other forms of treatment.

Among institutionalized methods of treatment available to us, four models of helping were proposed by Brickman, Rabinowitz, Karuza, Coates, Cohn, and Kidder (1982): moral, medical, enlightenment, and compensatory. We tend to favor the compensatory one (Marlatt, Baer, Donovan & Kivlahan, 1988). Ultimately, as both the moral and compensatory models of treatment stress, responsibility for change and improvement remains in the hands of the individual. However, the compensatory model makes the individual responsible for the initiation and the termination of the addiction, without being responsible for what has happened in the past. From and for this compensatory model, there are at least three types of preventive interventions, in addition to education.

A Continuum of Preventive Approaches

Given the widespread incidence of addictions in our society, what are the most cost-effective ways of helping the individuals affected and their families? Will individual, group, or family psychotherapy, and environmental manipulation, such as halfway houses, hospitals, or prisons, be able to deal with the sheer number of addicts that already outstrips any existing therapeutic facility or model of treatment? We are dealing with millions of people who are either already addicted or at serious risk for future addiction. For instance, we have an estimated 28 million children of alcoholics, plus millions of illegitimate and unwanted children, children from single-parent families, and abused and neglected children. How are we going to take care of them all?

Traditional crisis-oriented psychotherapeutic approaches, as helpful as they may be, are and will be insufficient to deal effectively with the masses of individuals and families who are at risk, in need, or in crisis from addictions. In addition to a traditional crisis-oriented model used in the psychotherapies, we need to adopt a public health model that attempts to deal with problems before they take place, for whoever needs and wants help, regardless of cost. Instead of working with mutually exclusive practices, with treatment approaches separate from preventive approaches, ideally we would like to see both types of approach working together synergistically for the welfare and well-being of all addicted individuals and their families. How can this goal be achieved? We need a conceptual framework as well as new, practical tools that will fit together into an integrated and systematic whole.

To fulfill some of the foregoing needs, we have found it useful to distinguish a continuum of psychological interventions based on three different types of prevention: primary, secondary, and tertiary, as summarized in Table 3-1. This continuum covers at least three different degrees and extents of functionality, going left to right from the very functional to the very dysfunctional. We can distinguish among three degrees of functionality/dysfunctionality. Primary prevention deals with functioning individuals and their families who may be *at risk* for a variety of possible negative outcomes, including addiction. For instance, a child from an alcoholic family is already at risk for a repetition of alcoholism or other addictive behaviors in the future. This child may not be in need of treat-

TABLE 3–1   Criteria to Differentiate and Discriminate Among Preventive Approaches for Addictions

Criteria	Levels of Prevention		
	Primary	Secondary	Tertiary
	Pro-active Pre-therapeutic	Para-active Para-therapeutic	Reactive Therapeutic
1. Risk	Low to minimal	High: In need but not critical	Very high: Critical
2. Reversibility	High (100% to 66%)	Medium (66% to 33%)	Low to very low (33% to 0%)
3. Probability of breakdown	Low but potential	Medium but probable	High & real (actual)
4. Population	Nonclinical: Labeled but not diagnosable	Pre-clinical & diagnosable	Clinical: Critical & diagnosed
5. Ability to learn	High	Medium	Low
6. Goals	Increase competence & resistance to breakdown	Decrease stress & chance of crisis	Restore to minimum functioning
7. Type of involvement	Voluntary: Many choices	Obligatory: Decrease in choices	Mandatory: No other choices available
8. Recommendations	"Could benefit by it" "It would be nice"	"You need it before it's too late" "Recommended strongly"	"It is necessary" "Nothing else will do," "Other choices would be more expensive" (i.e., hospitalization, incarceration)
9. Costs	Low	Medium	High
10. Effectiveness	High (?)	Questionable	Low (?)
11. Personnel	Lay volunteers and Pre-para-professionals	Middle-level professionals	Professionals
12. Types of interventions Examples:	General strengthening Enrichment	More specific: Workbooks	Specific & specialized: Therapy
13. Degree of structure	High	Medium	Low
14. Degree of specificity	General/Low	Individualized/ Medium	Specific/High

From L'Abate (1990).

ment now, but chances are high that he or she will be, if no preventive intervention is applied in childhood, adolescence, or early adulthood. Secondary prevention deals with individuals (and their families) who not only are at risk but may also be *in need* of help, even though they may have not broken down to a critical level. For instance, out of 28 million children of alcoholics, at least 3 or 4 out of 10 are and will be in need of some type of intervention; that does not necessarily mean therapy. Tertiary prevention deals with individuals who have broken down and are *in crisis*. Conservatively, at least one out of ten children of alcoholics will be in crisis at least once during their lifetime.

Therefore, people *at risk* might benefit by primary prevention approaches, people *in need* could profit by secondary prevention approaches, and people *in crisis* should receive tertiary prevention, in the form of crisis-oriented psychotherapies. Consequently, from Table 3–1, it is possible to discriminate among three types of prevention according to fourteen different criteria, covering most possible dimensions of prevention. In the first place, the three levels of prevention are defined according to the nature of the activity required (pro-, para-, and re-active) and to the type of intervention involved (pre-, para-, and therapeutic). These distinctions will become clearer as they are elaborated. It should be noted, however, that the prefix "pre" means before, and the prefix "para" means taking place concurrently. Consequently, any pretherapeutic activity takes place or consists of approaches with functioning and functional populations who are able to learn and profit by whatever appropriate instructions they are given. Paratherapeutic approaches, like programmed materials and workbooks, can be administered before, during, in addition to, instead of, or even after therapeutic interventions.

Primary prevention consists of educational and psychoeducational skill training programs, such as assertiveness training, that will increase the level of competence of that individual and, one hopes, decrease the chance of his or her reaching a level of dysfunctionality when in need or in crisis (L'Abate & Milan, 1985). L'Abate and his associates have developed a whole library of pretherapeutic, structured enrichment programs for couples and families that could be administered by volunteers and paraprofessional personnel (L'Abate & Weinstein, 1987; L'Abate & Young, 1987).

Secondary prevention approaches up to now have been left undefined, conceptually and practically. As shown in Table 3–1, the fourteen criteria used to differentiate conceptually among the three levels of prevention allow us to define secondary prevention with greater clarity than has been the case heretofore. Practically, this level of prevention can be operationally defined by specially written, programmed workbooks, administered by middle-level professionals working alongside and under supervision of upper-level therapists. With corrective feedback from therapists, these workbooks could fulfill paratherapeutic functions. Without any feedback, when administered to functional populations, the same programmed materials and workbooks could serve a pre- or post-therapeutic function (L'Abate, 1990, 1991).

The first five criteria of Table 3–1 attempt to describe the characteristics of the population; the remainder of the criteria, from six to fourteen, pertain to the characteristics of treatment approaches and the professionals offering them. In the first place, individuals in crisis need to receive help through the whole gamut of tertiary prevention approaches, including traditional psychotherapeutic approaches as well as medical, physical, and rehabilitative approaches that are already institutionally available and in place in most communities. They have been reviewed in Chapter 2 in terms of outcome, and will be reviewed again briefly at the end of this chapter in terms of presenting the whole gamut of approaches available to full-fledged professionals and semi-professionals.

The first three dimensions in Table 3–1 (risk, reversibility, and probability of breakdown) refer to the intensity and severity of the addiction, from non-existent but potential, to actual. An adult child of alcoholic parents is at greater risk for addiction or emotional breakdown than a child whose parents are free of addictions and of emotional and interpersonal problems. An adult child of alcoholics from a single-parent household with many other children is going to be at such high risk that he or she will need any possible intervention available, even if no addiction is yet present. When one adds a low socioeconomic level to the above characteristics, the chances of acquiring an addiction of some type are high.

One needs to consider that now and especially in the future, help for many populations at risk and in need will not be available from full-fledged professionals (M.D.s or Ph.D.s). Therapeutic and preventive approaches will be administered by middle-level professionals (M.A. or equivalent) and by paraprofessionals and volunteers (B.A. or equivalent). The reason for this trend lies in the fact that the cost of professional help is becoming prohibitive for many addictions. There are too many addicted individuals to take care of and there never will be a sufficient number of full-fledged professionals to take care of them. (L'Abate, in preparation; L'Abate, 1990).

We need to equate degrees of functionality/dysfunctionality with the ability to learn and to retain relevant information. The greater the degree of dysfunction from the addiction, the greater will be the impairment in the ability to learn and to retain (Schaeffer & Parsons, 1987). Consequently, the healthier the individual, the greater will be the ability to learn, retain, and even apply what has been learned. Learning, however, would need to be along experientially active and interactive lines, not just book learning. This dimension suggests that primary prevention approaches could use, among many other programs, an enrichment model that attempts to make things better than they are already (L'Abate & Weinstein, 1987; L'Abate & Young, 1987).

One unique feature of this handbook, derived from the stated need for specificity and explicitness in treatment (Chapter 1), is the planned creation and construction of written paratherapeutic materials and workbooks that, one hopes, will be isomorphic with the therapeutic guidelines given in each chapter for each separate addiction. We believe that these workbooks can and will expand greatly the cost-effectiveness and usage of traditional therapeutic interventions in the hands of top-level and middle-level professionals. They are mass-producible, cost-effective tools of secondary prevention that have been, thus far, unavailable on a large scale. They can facilitate research efforts that are traditionally very expensive in the mental health field.

Modalities of Treatment

Modalities of treatment can be classified in a variety of ways. The phenomenal and widespread proliferation of treatment approaches makes it impossible to review all of them. This section limits itself to suggesting the most common, known, and used avenues of treatment available currently. None of them, in and of themselves, guarantees a positive outcome. The best one can hope for is to keep the patient in treatment with a variety of approaches that will allow a successful completion of treatment, if there can be one. If the patient is still free of the addiction three to five years after cessation of the addicted condition, treatment has been successful.

We have chosen to classify therapeutic approaches according to three major headings that refer to preferences in composition, medium to be used, and therapeutic emphasis. In dealing with addictions, no one can assume that a single type of composition, medium, or therapeutic emphasis will suffice. Each addiction will need the concerted and concentrated efforts of a variety of treatment modalities, with one or more compositions of patients, one or more media, and more than one therapeutic emphasis. No single treatment approach can be sufficient in dealing with addictions. In fact, we suggest that tertiary prevention approaches by themselves will not be sufficient, but will need to rely on the synergistic combination of primary and secondary approaches to deal with the immensity of the problem.

Preferred Composition

Composition refers to the presence in the therapist's office of one or more patients. Again, composition does not mean fixed format. One person could be seen alone with one therapist, and also participate in group therapy sessions, with two therapists being aware of the duality of parallel treatments. In addition, the same patient might attend a support group in the specific addiction that made him or her seek help. Variations and permutations of treatment compositions differ from setting to setting and from therapist to therapist. In some cases, at one extreme, therapists will allow freedom to go from one composition to another. At the extreme, psychologists may not be allowed by professional rules to put the patient in jeopardy by allowing participation in different treatment modalities. Mixing modalities might result in increases of conflict and confusion in an already confused individual.

What is best for the patient? Will participation in different treatment modalities unduly increase conflict and confusion? Here is where a *successive sieves or hurdles* approach (L'Abate, 1990, 1992), may be useful. This approach sees treatment as going from the simplest and cheapest form to the more complex and expensive forms of treatment. For instance, one may start with individual therapy, but as one learns more about the patient's condition, one may recommend hospitalization. Going from one sieve of treatment to another is also accomplished by gradually increasing the patient's involvement in ordered and planned sequences of participation in different treatment compositions and modalities (Haugaard & Reppucci, 1988). From an initial stage of crisis intervention with the primary goal of symptom reduction and of rapport and trust building, one can then proceed to a stage of secondary prevention, using workbooks to educate and to enlighten. A third stage of enrichment, using group and/or family approaches, would lead toward termination. Between the first and second stage, relapse prevention should be the major focus of treatment, while between the second and third stages, maintenance and added learning, including lifestyle changes, should be stressed.

The crucial issue here lies in identifying who is responsible for making these choices. Should the patient be allowed to participate in as many treatment compositions as he or she wants or needs, or should the therapist be the final judge and arbiter of what is best for the patient? This is a gray area where professional experience, maturity, and availability of treatment resources come together in the professional decision-making process of individualized treatment planning. Decisions should be made on the basis of careful evaluation of the individual's level of functioning; type of addiction; availability of resources from the patient (insurance, funds, family members interested in becoming involved in the treatment, etc.); and availability of external resources relating to ease of access to additional treatment modalities different from the preferred treatment composition, such as support groups and training programs.

For instance, interventions can be divided into at least three different phases: (a) *crisis*, probably requiring individual therapy or tertiary prevention approaches at the beginning of treatment, proceeding then to (b) *rehabilitation*, using secondary prevention approaches with paratherapeutic workbooks, in addition to either therapy, or (c) *tertiary prevention*, such as psychoeducational skills training and enrichment with groups and families (L'Abate, 1986, 1992; L'Abate & Milan, 1985). In other words, the more "normal" the patient becomes, the more training and experiences he or she will be able to absorb and to retain, moving from tertiary to secondary, and finally primary prevention. This successive sieves approach includes the fact that relapse, as mentioned earlier, is to be considered as par for the course in the treatment of addictions (Marlatt & Gordon, 1985; Shiffman, 1987). Consequently, the rationale for suggesting a standard operating procedure of successive sieves combines sequentially tertiary with secondary and with primary prevention approaches. This approach also takes into consideration the recovery phase, the prevention of relapse, and the maintenance phase in the treatment of addictions.

Individual Psychotherapy   This remains the major and most widely used form of treatment in dealing with all sorts of psychopathology and addictions (Garfield & Bergin, 1986). Often this is still the sole form of non-medical treatment available in dealing with addictions. In fact, many therapists, especially psychoanalytically oriented ones, seem convinced that individual therapy is the *only real and ultimate* form of therapy and that all the other modalities of treatment are secondary and ancillary to it (Brown, 1985; Frosch, 1985; Kertzner, 1987; Nace, 1987). Certainly, initial individual contact and rapport with one specific therapist during the peak of the crisis is necessary for the individual addict to feel safe and secure. Ultimately, this individual relationship can be used to allow the patient to branch out, so to speak, and experience a certain degree of freedom in learning more from other addicts in group therapy, as well as from family members.

The first major difficulty in dealing with individuals without anyone else in the therapy office who knows them lies in *reality testing*. What is the therapist to believe and how can the patient's perceptions and accounts be validated? A great deal of time could be spent dealing with fabricated or distorted past or present events that may or may not have relevance to the addiction. A second difficulty with individual psychotherapy is cost and cost-effectiveness. Professional time is by necessity costly. Furthermore, there are insufficient numbers of trained professional therapists to deal realistically with the myriad of addictions facing us. How are we to use professional time and expertise best without shortchanging our clients? Again, a successive sieves approach can be used in dealing with a team approach that makes the professional primarily and ultimately responsible for the quality of treatment and for the welfare of the patient. More and more professionals will be obliged to delegate therapeutic responsibilities, at the initial stage of crisis intervention, to middle-level professionals. Paratherapeutic practices such as programmed workbooks in the secondary stage of treatment, and pre-therapeutic assignments, like enrichment in the primary stage of treatment, as with more structured tasks and assignments, can be delegated to less trained but more specialized personnel.

Groups of Individuals   Group psychotherapy is indicated in a variety of addictions because it has advantages over individual psychotherapy by being more cost effective per unit of professional time; any therapeutic modality involving more than one patient per unit of professional time is going to be less expensive. The issue here, of course, is whether it will be equally effective. Group psychotherapy is also more oriented toward testing the perception of reality for each individual in the group; one could argue that individual therapy is unduly artificial, because it does not allow the therapist to see the patient in action, so to speak, in front of and in relationship to other similarly troubled human beings. Additionally, group psychotherapy provides a natural support group that allows for close and intimate ties with other individuals, an experience not possible in individual therapy with the exception of the relationship with the therapist. Group approaches have been applied to Alcoholics Anonymous, cocaine abuse (Spitz, 1987), and sexual abuse (Haugaard & Reppucci, 1988), among others.

Marital Therapy   The spouse's involvement in the process of change is strongly recommended in the treatment of alcoholism (Lawson, Peterson & Lawson, 1983; Maisto & Carey, 1987) and obesity (Brownell, 1987), and in most other addictions.

Groups of Couples   This type of composition does not seem popular in the treatment of addictions, to the extent that no relevant references could be found in the current literature.

Family Therapy   Many claims have been made about the cost-effectiveness of family therapy over more traditional forms such as individual and group therapy (Hansen & L'Abate, 1982). Family therapy has been found useful in the treatment of alcohol abuse (Brown, 1985; Lawson, Peterson & Lawson, 1983; Steinglass, Bennett, Wolin & Reiss, 1987; Todd, 1988); cocaine abuse (Rosencrans, Spitz & Gross, 1987; Spitz & Spitz, 1987); and sexual abuse (Haugaard & Reppucci, 1988). Just as the non-addicted spouse is affected by the addiction, so are the children. Special attention to the children of alcoholics has been suggested by Brown (1985), Lawson, Peterson and Lawson (1983), Metzger (1988), and Steinglass et al. (1988).

Groups of Families   No relevant references could be found in the literature on treatment of addictions, although claims have been made in the past about the usefulness of this approach with families of schizophrenic patients (Hansen & L'Abate, 1982).

Preferred Medium

Preferred media of treatment can be classified according to the ERAAwC model, and may become a useful integration of various therapeutic emphases (L'Abate, 1986). For instance, Emotionality (E) on the experiencing, subjective, input side of receiving information would align itself with the Existential-Humanistic school, which includes a variety of offshoots, like the non-directive, phenomenological, and communication approaches, among many others. This school stresses the importance of internal states, such as anxiety, fear, guilt, and shame (Fossum & Mason, 1986), or stress (Sher, 1987). Rationality (R) would include the psychodynamic and/or rational approaches, like psychoanalysis (Frosch, 1985; Nace, 1987), the rational-emotive school of Albert Ellis, and the reality school of Glasser, as well as expectancy theory (Goldman, Brown & Christiansen, 1987) and the self-handicapping model of addictions (Berglas, 1987).

Activity (A) would include all the various behavioral approaches (Marlatt & Gordon, 1985; Shaffer & Schneider, 1985) that use classical conditioning and deconditioning, instrumental reinforcement, and social-learning interactional methods (Abrams & Niaura, 1987; McCrady, Dean, Dubreuil & Swanson, 1985; Zinberg & Shaffer, 1985). Awareness (Aw) would include all of the various body-oriented, Gestalt-type approaches (Zarcone, 1984) that border on the existential-humanistic, but which stress that awareness of internal cues is more important than awareness of the external Context (C). The importance of context is stressed instead by the interactional school (Savada, 1987) and the family therapy movement (Fossum & Mason, 1986; Hansen & L'Abate, 1982; L'Abate, Ganahl, & Hansen, 1986; Steinglass et al., 1987).

This model is supported by the work of Karasu (1986), who specified the relationship between specific techniques of different schools of psychotherapy in a way very similar to the ERAAwC model (L'Abate, 1986). Karasu differentiated among Affective Experiencing (E), Cognitive Mastery (R), and Behavioral Regulation (A), in a way that is consistent with the ERAAwC model. For instance, Affective Experiencing consists of the following techniques: encounter, flooding, meditation, shared dialogue, body manipulation, group regression, massage, free association, isolation, role playing, and intravenous drugs. These techniques are respectively represented by the following schools: existential analysis, implosion therapy, Arica, gestalt therapy, rolfing, Erhard seminars, psychoanalysis, primal scream, psychodrama, and narcotherapy. Cognitive Mastery consists of techniques such as interpretation, clarification, attacking irrational ideas, providing information, thought stopping, search for meaning, correcting false beliefs, analysis of transference, paradoxical intention, analysis of body armor, and confronting decisions. The respective schools representing these techniques are: psychoanalysis, supportive therapy, rational therapy, sex therapy, behavior therapy, logotherapy, cognitive therapy, character analysis, and direct decision therapy. Behavioral Regulation consists of the following methods: conditioning, teaching and coaching, direct feedback, giving rewards, direct modeling, suggestion, punishment, and relaxation. These techniques are matched by the following schools: behavior therapy, assertiveness training, biofeedback, token economies, modeling therapy, hypnotherapy, aversiveness training, and systematic desensitization. Karasu did not include marital or family therapies, which would encompass the contextual (C) dimension not considered by his otherwise apt classification. The same ERAAwC model was applied by L'Abate, Ulrici, and Wagner (1982) to a classification of psychoeducational skill training programs.

To elaborate on the same model, another way to classify therapies is on the basis of the medium of exchange: oral, nonverbal, or written.

Oral   The spoken word has been, is, and will remain the main medium of exchange and dialogue between and among individuals, reflecting the universality of this medium. Unfortunately, its usefulness becomes limited when it is used as the only medium. As we shall see, there is more to human behavior than language. Yet, even within the oral medium, there are different emphases that determine different outcomes. One of the major theoretical and therapeutic battlegrounds lies in the differential emphasis on the affective versus cognitive approaches.

Affective-emotive   L'Abate (1986) classified the humanistic school with its many offshoots (existentialism, experientialism, phenomenology, etc.) as stressing the subjective side of experiencing. Consequently, depending on the theoretical position of the therapist, this aspect may or may not be stressed in the client's language and thinking. If feelings and emotions are deemed important to adjustment, the therapist will tend to reinforce them directly and indirectly, influencing the patient in that direction. If one puts emotions and feelings primary for human existence, then rationality may take second place, unless one were to consider both processes as equally important but with different functions (L'Abate, 1986). Unilateral stress on feelings and emotions at the expense of rationality might lead one to learn to be intimate, but still unable to negotiate.

Rational-cognitive   By the same token, if the therapist's biases are toward the rational-cognitive realm, as in the psychodynamic, rational-emotive, and reality schools, he or she will tend to stress logical and rational processing, making, directly and indirectly, rationality primary over emotionality. The outcome of this emphasis may lead toward learning how to think better, but without being able to use feelings and emotions as resources to get close to significant others.

Behavioral-activity Oriented   Using the same criterion, behavioral approaches at the expense of either affective or cognitive resources may lead toward improvement in the ability to negotiate, but would make it difficult to become intimate with loved ones. Hence, an eclectically comprehensive and integrative approach that stresses the importance of all three different media (oral, nonverbal, and written) would differentiate them by the specificity of situations and of settings, as suggested by a continuum of interventions presented earlier in this chapter.

Nonverbal-experiential   This aspect of adjustment has been stressed especially by the humanistic school and its closely allied human potentials movement. This school and many of its derivatives (phenomenology, existentialism, expressionism, etc.) have reminded us of the importance of being in touch with our bodies and with our bodily processes, sensations, feelings, and emotions. This emphasis needs to be included in treatment plans as being synergistic with the strictly rational and intellectual emphases of the rationally-oriented psychodynamic school, that, by not paying attention to feelings and emotions, may eventually lead some patients to undue intellectualization and defensiveness. Perhaps in reaction to the psychodynamic emphasis, the last two or three decades have seen the increase of treatment approaches that stress the importance and relevance of: (a) *movement*, like dancing and aerobics; (b) *body-work*, like massage, rolfing, and muscle relaxation; (c) *exercise*, like sports, running, calisthenics, and walking; (d) *breath-work*; and (e) *"energy"* work, like polarity therapy, Shiatsu, and therapeutic touch. Unfortunately, we were not able to find relevant references on this particular area as applied to addictions, suggesting that many of these experiences need to be considered as part of a comprehensive treatment plan.

A fourth nonverbal medium that, like those listed above, needs to be explored in regard to addictions is *art therapy*, which Lawson, Peterson, and Lawson (1983) have applied to the treatment of alcoholism.

Writing   The importance of the written word as a therapeutic medium has not been stressed as much as it deserves to be. Indeed, it could be argued that as long as treatment methods continue to be based strictly on the spoken modality, it will be difficult and expensive to evaluate their outcomes. The spoken word cannot be controlled, programmed, predicted, or prescribed as the written word can. The possibility of using writing as therapy or as part of therapy, as a paratherapeutic modality is still completely untapped. Through the written word we will be able to control and improve what we do and how we intervene in people's lives.

Writing can be classified according to four different types, going from the least to the most structured: (a) *open*, as in diaries and journals; (b) *focused*, as in the assignment of writing about a specific topic, i.e., depression or anxiety; (c) *guided*, where a variety of questions are asked; and (d) *programmed*, as in the case of specifically written workbooks for depression, negotiation, and intimacy in couples and families (L'Abate, 1986); individual workbooks for the treatment of impulsivity, anxiety, and marital relationships; or written homework assignments to deal with fighting, sibling rivalry, or temper tantrums in families (L'Abate, 1992). Whether writing is therapeutic depends a great deal on the corrective feedback given by the therapist after each assignment.

Hypnosis   Bocci (1983a) reported on 9 of 17 drug (marijuana and heroin) addicts who responded well to hypnosis during the process of detoxification. However, family therapy was also used in conjunction with hypnosis; possibly "magical" views about hypnosis were used at the beginning of therapy to obtain a "positive transference." In some cases, on the basis of post-hypnotic suggestion, states of terror during drug use were reported. Bocci (1983b) also combined hypnosis with calcium treatment and acupuncture, claiming that satisfactory therapeutic outcome was mainly due to the forced confinement in the hospital that kept patients away from the availability of drugs. Since no control group was used, it is impossible to determine which treatment modality produced which outcome.

Vandamme (1986) presented a case study of a 20-year-old female heroin addict, treated with hypnosis, who was free of addiction 18 months after termination of treatment. Mann, Johnson, and Levine (1986) also suggested the use of hypnosis in the treatment of tobacco dependence. However, as in the case of many reports in this section, no results were reported. By the same token, Cohen (1984) treated five long-term smokers with a combination of meditation and hypnosis plus behavioral techniques. His results were unsatisfactory because many other social and family stressors had not been allowed for in the treatment. The author concluded that "even when an individualized approach and a combination of techniques are used, long-term success in smoking cessation cannot be achieved if the patients are under severe stress and have little or no social support" (p. 39). This conclusion justifies the need for treatment approaches that consider the family context of the patient. Moses (1987) proposed a radical view of smoking as a skill and a role rather than a habit or an addiction. He used a combination of discussion and hypnosis that, according to him, led to abstinence from smoking. Objective results to support this view were not included, thus raising questions about the validity of his opinion.

Psychodrama   Descombey (1982) suggested the use of psychodrama in addition to individual psychoanalytic therapy and group techniques. In fact, most advocates of psychodrama recommend its use in combination with other expressive modalities of treatment integrating music and art, leading to greater self-awareness that would follow from free and uninhibited self-expression (Adelman & Castricone, 1986). Tolesand, Kabat, and Kemp (1983) also recommended a treatment "package" that included psychodrama with Gestalt exercises, behavioral contracting, and contingency-management. In applying this package to 39 people participating in a 20-hour, 9-session smoking cessation program with 15 controls, these investigators used a carboximeter to measure physiologically concomitant self-reports from the experimental subjects. Complete stoppage of smoking was reported by 47 percent of these subjects; 38 percent decreased the number of cigarettes smoked; 13 percent did not change at all; and 2 percent had increased their habit. None of the control group stopped smoking, 27 percent had decreased, 60 percent had made no changes, and 13 percent had increased intake. At a three-month follow-up, however, only 36 percent of the experimental subjects had remained abstinent, indicating how important a relapse prevention component is in any form of treatment for addictions.

Role-playing   Kolko, Sirota, Monti, and Paolino (1985) used 50 role-playing scenarios to find which of them would be rated as representing difficulties in coping with addicts. These investigators found five "high stress" scenarios: coming home to find no dinner prepared by your mate; dealing with a friend unwilling to pay a debt owed to you; approaching a friend found with your wallet; confronting a friend who lied about you to the boss; and expressing a different opinion from a friend's. One hopes these scenarios can be applied in practice to help addicts learn how to cope with stressful situations.

Meditation   Nespor (1985) suggested the combination of yoga with traditional psychotherapy and hypnosis. It stands to reason that, if addictions result from impulsivity and immediacy, learning to meditate, to delay, and to postpone gratification may be useful adjuncts to verbal therapy. This conclusion is supported by suggestive results of various studies where combinations of progressive muscular relaxation and meditation were used in treatment of addictions. Nespor concluded that the evidence was equivocal because of many conceptual and methodological inadequacies in these studies. Rather than decreased anxiety, which had been used as a hypothetical result to justify the use of relaxation and meditation, increased perceived control might be a more plausible and likely explanation for positive outcome. Calajoe (1986) also claimed that yoga combined with meditation "can be effective in helping patients regain their vital center" (p. 46). No evidence was presented to support this conclusion, as in the case of similar claims made by many well-meaning therapists.

Games   Jordan (1985) described a group therapy game in which the addict's lifestyle is acted out, to yield a more realistic view of the drug subculture and its inherently self-destructive qualities. The game can be adapted to various addictions. Players follow instructions of special cards that designate three different areas of relevance to the addict's experience: on the streets, in jail, and in therapy. Players must move through these three areas to learn to "negotiate" toward successful completion of treatment.

Therapeutic Emphasis

In a way, overlap exists between a treatment medium used and one's preferred method of treatment. This overlap, however, extends only to the oral category, since most therapeutic emphases rely on the spoken word. It would be repetitive to review here all of the various available therapeutic emphases. Any classification presented here is to illustrate the wide scope of therapeutic emphases and to show how many options both therapists and patients have. Unfortunately, each of these emphases takes a lifetime of study. Consequently, we cannot expect therapists to be knowledgeable and experienced in all of them. Mastery of one therapeutic emphasis is all one can aspire to during one's professional career. However, most therapists admit to relying on eclectic combinations of more than one approach, recognizing that human behavior, especially addiction, is too variable and too wide-ranging to be encompassed by a single therapeutic emphasis. Thus, most therapists combine a variety of therapeutic emphases to the best of their knowledge and experience.

Each school of therapy stresses one aspect of behavior from the viewpoint of information processing within extremes of an experiencing-expressing continuum summarized in the ERAAwC model. While the humanistic school stresses receptive experiencing on the input side, the psychodynamic school stresses the rational processing of information (throughput) within the middle of this continuum, and the behavioral school stresses the expressive output side. Awareness would represent the change-oriented corrective feedback loop that gives this model the circularity so important to system theorists, going from A back to E, R, A, and C, and the family context (C) gives meaning and significance to the development and maintenance of addictive behaviors. All five of these aspects are important and all need to be stressed in treatment for a successful outcome.

Combination of Treatments   No therapist treating addictions can be so narrow-minded as to believe that a single treatment modality will make a significant change in and by itself. Supposed cases of successful treatment using a single modality do not reach the light of publication or do not hold up under controlled scrutiny. Furthermore, only a prolonged period of abstinence can define "success" in the treatment of addictions. As one can see from the reports reviewed above, most professionals working with addictions advocate the use of multiple modalities of treatment, either consecutively, in tandem, or in parallel. Successful combinations recognized repeatedly are the cognitive-behavioral treatment of problem drinking (Emrick, Hansen & Maytag, 1985), and the multimodal approach of A. A. Lazarus (Frye, 1985).

In addition to combinations of various treatment modalities, in the future we will see more frequent combinations of preventive approaches with various treatment approaches, as suggested by the work of Lawson, Peterson, and Lawson (1983) in the treatment of alcohol, and by Haugaard and Reppucci (1988) with sexual abuse of children. Of course, Alcoholics Anonymous and similar support groups used in conjunction with various types of psychotherapy are among the most common combinations (Brown, 1985), second only to the combination of medication and any type of psychotherapy. In the future we will also see greater therapeutic and preventive effort with special populations (Lawson & Lawson, 1989).

Conclusion

A continuum of preventive interventions with a lattice of pre-, para-, and full-fledged professionals will allow us to satisfy the need for systematic models of interventions, integrating various types of prevention with systematic evaluation and follow-up. A successive sieves approach, going from the least to the most expensive approach, is also suggested to combine various treatment and preventive modalities. No single type or modality of treatment is or will be sufficient to stem the tide of addictions in this country. We will need not only the efforts of professionals, semi-, para-, and pre-professionals, but also the contribution of volunteers and former addicts to help us deal with one of the most dangerous epidemics our country has ever known.

References

Abrams, D. B., & Niaura, R. S. (1987). Social learning theory. In H. T. Blane and K. E. Leonard (Eds.), *Psychological theories of drinking and alcoholism* (pp. 131–178). New York: Guilford.

Adelman, E., & Castricone, L. (1986). An expressive arts model for substance abuse group training and treatment. *Arts in Psychotherapy, 13*, 53–59.

Berglas, S. (1987). Self-handicapping model. In H. T. Blane and K. E. Leonard (Eds.), *Psychological theories of drinking and alcoholism* (pp. 305–345). New York: Guilford.

Bocci, U. (1983a). Esperienze ipnoterapeutiche in tossico-dependenti. *Rivista Internazionale di Psicologia e Ipnosi, 24*, 31–37.

Bocci, U. (1983b). In tema di tossicodependenti: Contributo clinico. *Rivista Internazionale di Psicologia e Ipnosi, 24*, 231–243.

Brickman, P., Rabinowitz, V. C., Karuza, J., Coates, D., Cohen, E., & Kidder, L. (1982). Models of helping and coping. *American Psychologist, 37*, 368–384.

Brown, S. (1985). *Treating the alcoholic: a developmental model of recovery*. New York: Wiley-Interscience.

Brownell, K. D. (1987). Obesity: Understanding and treating a serious, prevalent, and refractory disorder. In T. D. Nirenberg & S. A. Maisto (Eds.), *Developments in the assessment and treatment of addictive behaviors* (pp. 213–241). Norwood, NJ: Ablex.

Calajoe, A. (1986). Yoga as a treatment component in treating chemical dependency. *Alcoholism Treatment Quarterly, 3,* 33–46.

Cohen, B. B. (1984). A combined approach using meditation-hypnosis and behavioral techniques in the treatment of smoking behavior: Case studies of five stressed patients. *International Journal of Psychosomatics, 31,* 33–39.

Descombey, J. P. (1982). La dependance alcoolique: Problèmes de théorie freudienne et de technique psychotherapique. *Information-Psychiatrique, 58,* 505–515.

Dunst, C., Trivette, C., & Deal, A. (1988). *Enabling and empowering families: principles and guidelines for practice*. Cambridge, MA: Brookline Books.

Eimer, B. D. (1982) A substance abuse screening check list. In P. A. Keller and L. G. Ritt (Eds.), *Innovations in clinical practice: A source book* (pp. 289–292). Sarasota, FL: Professional Resources Exchange.

Emrick, C. D., Hansen, J., & Maytag, J. C. (1985). Cognitive-behavioral treatment of problem-drinking. In H. B. Milkman & H. J. Shaffer (Eds.), *The addictions: Multidisciplinary perspectives and treatments* (pp. 161–173). Lexington, MA: Lexington Books.

Fossum, M. A., & Mason, M. J. (1986). *Facing shame: Families in recovery,* New York: W. W. Norton.

Frosch, W. A. (1985). An analytic overview of addictions. In H. B. Milkman & H. J. Shaffer (Eds.), *The addictions: Multidisciplinary perspectives and treatments* (pp. 29–37). Lexington, MA: Lexington Books.

Frye, R. V. (1985). A multimodal approach to the treatment of addiction. In H. B. Milkman & H. J. Shaffer (Eds.), *The addictions: Multidisciplinary perspectives and treatments* (pp. 75–182). Lexington, MA: Lexington Books.

Garfield, S. L., & Bergin, A. E. (Eds.). (1986). *Handbook of psychotherapy and behavior change*. New York: Wiley.

Goldman, M. S., Brown, S. A., & Christiansen, B. A. (1987). Expectancy theory: Thinking about drinking. In H. T. Blane and K. E. Leonard (Eds.), *Psychological theories of drinking and alcoholism* (pp. 181–226). New York: Guilford.

Hansen, J. C., & L'Abate, L. (1982). *Approaches to family therapy*. New York: Macmillan.

Haugaard, J. J., & Reppucci, N. D. (1988). *The sexual abuse of children: A comprehensive guide to current knowledge and intervention strategies*. San Francisco: Jossey-Bass.

Jordan, J. B. (1985). "Drugs on the street": A group therapy game for drug abusers. *Small Group Behavior, 16,* 105–109.

Karasu, T. B. (1986). The specificity versus nonspecificity dilemma: Toward identifying therapeutic change agents. *American Journal of Psychiatry, 143,* 687–695.

Kertzner, R. M. (1987). Individual psychotherapy of cocaine abuse. In H. I. Spitz & J. S. Rosencrans (Eds.), *Cocaine abuse: New directions in treatment and research* (pp. 138–155). New York: Brunner/Mazel.

Klajner, F., Hartman, L. M., & Sobel, M. B. (1984). Treatment of substance abuse by relaxation training. *Addictive Behaviors, 9,* 41–55.

Kolko, D. J., Sirota, A. D., Monti, P. M., & Paolino, R. M. (1985). Peer identification and empirical validation of problematic interpersonal situations of male drug addicts. *Journal of Psychopathology and Behavioral Assessment, 7,* 135–144.

L'Abate, L. (1986). *Systematic family therapy.* New York: Brunner/Mazel.

L'Abate, L. (1990). *Building family competence: Primary and secondary prevention strategies.* Newbury Park, CA: Sage.

L'Abate, L. (1992). *Programmed writing: A self-administered approach for interventions with individuals, couples, and families.* Pacific Grove, CA: Brooks/Cole.

L'Abate, L. (in preparation). *The laboratory method in clinical psychology.*

L'Abate, L., Ganahl, G., & Hansen, J. C. (1986) *Methods of family therapy.* Englewood Cliffs, NJ: Prentice-Hall.

L'Abate, L., & Milan, M. (Eds.). (1985). *Handbook of social skills training and research.* New York: Wiley.

L'Abate, L., Ulrici, D., & Wagner, V. (1982). The ERA model: A heuristic framework for classification of skill training programs for couples and families. *Family Relations, 30,* 307–315.

L'Abate, L., & Weinstein, S. (1987). *Structured enrichment programs for couples and families.* New York: Brunner/Mazel.

L'Abate, L., & Young, L. (1987). *Casebook of structured enrichment programs for couples and families.* New York: Brunner/Mazel.

Lawson, G. W., & Lawson, A. W. (Eds.). (1989). *Alcoholism and substance abuse in special populations.* Rockville, MD: Aspen.

Lawson, G., Peterson, J. S., & Lawson, A. (1983). *Alcoholism and the family: a guide to treatment and prevention.* Rockville, MD: Aspen.

Maisto, S. A., & Carey, K. B. (1987). Treatment of alcohol abuse. In T. D. Nirenberg & S. A. Maisto (Eds.), *Developments in the assessment and treatment of addictive behaviors* (pp. 173–211). Norwood, NJ: Ablex.

Mann, L. S., Johnson, R. W., & Levine, D. J. (1986). Tobacco dependence: Psychology, biology, and treatment strategies. *Psychosomatics, 27,* 713–718.

Marlatt, G. A., & J. R. Gordon (Eds.). (1985). *Relapse prevention.* New York: Guilford.

Marlatt, G. A., Baer, J. S., Donovan, D. M., & Kivlahan, D. R. (1988). Addictive behaviors: Etiology and treatment. *Annual Review of Psychology, 39,* 223–252.

McCrady, B. S., Dean, L., Dubreuil, E., & Swanson, S. (1985). The problem drinkers' project: A programmatic application of social-learning-based treatment. In G. A. Marlatt & J. R. Gordon (Eds.), *Relapse prevention* (pp. 417–471). New York: Guilford.

Metzger, L. (1988). *From denial to recovery: Counseling problem drinkers, alcoholics, and their families.* San Francisco: Jossey-Bass.

Moses, F. (1987). Treating smoking behavior by discussion and hypnosis: Destroying the myths of habit, addiction, and will power. *Psychology: A Quarterly Journal of Human Behavior, 24,* 1–9.

Nace, E. P. (1987). *The treatment of alcoholism.* New York: Brunner/Mazel.

Nespor, K. (1985). The combination of psychiatric treatment and yoga. *International Journal of Psychosomatics, 32,* 24–27.

Rosencrans, J. S., Spitz, H. I., & Gross, B. (1987). Contemporary issues in the treatment of cocaine abuse. In H. I. Spitz & J. S. Rosencrans (Eds.), *Cocaine abuse: New directions in treatment and research* (pp. 299–323). New York: Brunner/Mazel.

Saltzman, N., & Norcross, J. C. (1990). *Therapy wars: Contention and convergence in differing clinical approaches.* San Francisco: Jossey-Bass.

Savada, S. W. (1987). Interactional theory. In H. T. Blane and K. E. Leonard (Eds.), *Psychological theories of drinking and alcoholism* (pp. 90–130). New York: Guilford.

Schaeffer, K. W., & Parsons, O. A. (1987). Learning impairment in alcoholics: Using an ecologically relevant test. *Journal of Nervous and Mental Disease, 175,* 213–218.

Shaffer, H. J., & Schneider, R. J. (1985). Trends in behavioral psychology and the addictions. In H. B. Milkman & H. J. Shaffer (Eds.), *The addictions: Multidisciplinary perspectives and treatments* (pp. 39–55). Lexington, MA: Lexington Books.

Sher, K. J. (1987). Stress response dampening. In H. T. Blane and K. E. Leonard (Eds.), *Psychological theories of drinking and alcoholism* (pp. 227–271). New York: Guilford.

Shiffman, S. (1987). Maintenance and relapse: Coping with temptation. In T. D. Nirenberg & S. A. Maisto (Eds.), *Developments in the assessment and treatment of addictive behaviors* (pp. 353–385). Norwood, NJ: Ablex.

Skodol, A. E. (1987). Diagnostic issues in cocaine abuse. In H. I. Spitz & J. S. Rosencrans (Eds.), *Cocaine abuse: New directions in treatment and research* (pp. 119–137). New York: Brunner/Mazel.

Spitz, H. I. (1987). Cocaine abuse: Therapeutic group approaches. In H. I. Spitz & J. S. Rosencrans (Eds.), *Cocaine abuse: New directions in treatment and research* (pp. 156–201). New York: Brunner/Mazel.

Spitz, H. I., & Spitz, S. T. (1987). Family therapy of cocaine abuse. In H. I. Spitz & J. S. Rosencrans (Eds.), *Cocaine abuse: New directions in treatment and research* (pp. 202–232). New York: Brunner/Mazel.

Steinglass, P., Bennett, L. A., Wolin, S. J., & Reiss, D. (1987). *The alcoholic family.* New York: Basic Books.

Todd, T. C. (1988). Treating families with a chemically dependent member. In E. W. Nunnally, C. S. Chilman, & F. M. Cox (Eds.), *Mental illness, delinquency, addictions, and neglect* (pp. 88–107). Newbury Park, CA: Sage.

Tolesand, R. W., Kabat, D., & Kemp, K. (1983). Evaluation of a smoking-cessation group treatment program. *Social Work Research and Abstracts, 19,* 12–19.

Vandamme, T. H. (1986). Hypnosis as an adjunct to the treatment of a drug addict. *Australian Journal of Clinical and Experimental Hypnosis, 14,* 41–48.

Weissman, M. M. (1986). The social adjustment self-report questionnaire. In P. A. Keller and L. G. Ritt (Eds.), *Innovations in clinical practice: A source book* (pp. 299–307). Sarasota, FL: Professional Resource Exchange.

Zarcone, V. (1984). Gestalt techniques in a therapeutic community for the treatment of addicts. *Journal of Psychoactive Drugs, 16,* 43–46.

Zeig, J. K., & Munion, W. M. (Eds.). (1990). *What is psychotherapy? Contemporary perspectives.* San Francisco: Jossey-Bass.

Zinberg, N. E., & Shaffer, H. J. (1985). The social psychology of intoxicant use: The interaction of personality and social setting. In H. B. Milkman & H. J. Shaffer (Eds.), *The addictions: Multidisciplinary perspectives and treatments* (pp. 57–74). Lexington, MA: Lexington Books.

4

Treating the Alcohol-Affected Family

JUDITH A. LEWIS, Ph.D.

ALCOHOL PROBLEMS ARE both "systems-maintaining and systems-maintained" (Kaufman, 1985, p. 37). Alcohol abuse by one family member can become so central to a family's functioning that it actually becomes the primary organizing factor in the system's structure, with the family learning to maintain its homeostasis around the individual's drinking behavior. In fact, alcohol may even become a stabilizing factor, producing "patterned, predictable and rigid sets of interactions which reduce uncertainties" (Steinglass, 1979, p. 163). A number of families studied by Steinglass (1978) used the alcohol-dependent individual's intoxicated state as a way both of dealing with conflict and of restabilizing their interactions. For many of the married couples who were studied, alcohol played a problem-solving role. When problems arose, whether psychological problems, family conflicts, or conflicts between the family and the environment, intoxication provided temporary stabilization of the marital system.

Steinglass's findings need not be interpreted to mean that unstable family dynamics "cause" the development of alcohol dependence, nor do they imply that the homeostasis found in alcohol-affected family systems is healthy. These findings do imply, however, that families develop consistent, predictable methods for adapting to alcohol problems, just as they build patterns for dealing with other pressures. At the same time, "alcohol or drug abuse may also be one method—if a spectacularly ineffective one—for coping with the stresses of a family system" (Lewis, Dana & Blevins, 1988, p. 171). Kaufman (1985) points out that drinking behavior "interrupts normal family tasks, causes conflict, shifts roles, and demands adjustive and adaptive responses from family members who do not know how to appropriately respond" (p. 30). However, the reverse effect occurs simultaneously. Family conflicts, rules, styles, and interactive mechanisms can support and maintain alcohol problems, with alcohol abuse serving as a way of coping with family problems or acting as a symptom of some dysfunction in the family system. Thus, alcohol problems are "systems-maintaining" in that the drinking behavior of one family member and the responses of others can allow the family to keep its equilibrium and avoid change. They are "systems-maintained" in that family members may consistently play roles that allow—even encourage—alcohol abuse to continue.

Traditionally, many treatment providers have viewed alcoholism as though it were simply a personal characteristic or an individual dysfunction developed in isolation from the social environment. Recognition of the importance of the family system in alcoholism brings with it drastic alterations in perceptions and processes. A treatment provider with a family-systems orientation views the individual with alcohol problems as the identified symptom bearer in the family, not necessarily as the sole focus of attention. Thus, a therapist needs to know what function the individual's drinking behaviors may play in the family unit and which family behaviors enable the alcohol abuse to continue. As Steinglass (1979, p. 165) states, "If alcohol consumption is part of an ongoing interactional pattern within the family system, then the traditional therapeutic intervention aimed toward abstinence is totally inadequate to the task."

Acceptance of the importance of family interactions in the creation and maintenance of alcohol problems has major treatment implications. Family therapy must proceed on the basis of a perspective that sees the entire family as the patient. This approach is in opposition to an intervention that involves the family members solely for the purpose of improving treatment with the identified patient: the alcoholic. If Steinglass's perspective is accepted, the therapist works primarily with interactions, rather than with intrapsychic phenomena, and treatment goals tend to focus on improvements in the functioning of the entire family. Changes in drinking behaviors are important, but are not the only outcomes being sought.

If the family system as a whole is viewed as the client, any treatment that is considered must be based, not just on a diagnosis of the drinking problem, but on a thorough consideration of the family situation. Moreover, the family situation must be assessed in terms of the nature of the system at the time the intervention is to begin. Different stages in the development and resolution of alcohol problems present widely varying challenges and goals.

Stages in Recovery

Bepko and Krestan (1985) suggest that generalizations can be made about the needs of alcohol-affected family systems at various stages of the recovery process. Their model involves three stages in treatment, each of which has accompanying goals. According to their conceptualization, the first stage, *attainment of sobriety,* involves unbalancing the system. The goal of the second stage, *adjustment to sobriety,* is stabilizing the system. *Long-term maintenance of sobriety* requires that the system be rebalanced.

Thus Bepko and Krestan see systems interventions as being very different, depending on whether the treatment is being provided while alcoholic drinking is present, at the point of change in the alcoholic's drinking behavior, or after initial abstinence has become established.

Schlesinger and Horberg (1988) also suggest that families have divergent attitudes and needs at different stages in the development and resolution of addiction problems. Their model takes families on a journey through three "regions": exasperation, effort, and empowerment. While the family is in the region of exasperation, it is characterized by chaos, shame, and helplessness. Individual family members and the family as a whole feel that their needs are not understood, see major differences between their standards and their own behaviors, and feel overwhelmed and panicky. In the region of effort, the family's focus is on the escape from chaos. Family members see few rewards but struggle on in the vague hope that life will improve. Satisfaction comes from choosing bland, socially acceptable lifestyle alternatives. Entering the region of empowerment brings a sense of meaning and purpose in life. Family members now feel able to dream, to make real commitments, and to believe in their own competence. Both positive and negative feelings can be experienced fully. Schlesinger and Horberg, like Bepko and Krestan, see recovery as a process, rather than an event, and recognize that the family's needs may differ at various points in time.

It may well be that families move through the process of change in predictable stages that parallel the stages that have been identified for individual clients. An example of a comprehensive, stage-based model of change is provided by Prochaska and DiClemente (1988), who see individual change as moving from pre-contemplation to contemplation to action, and finally to maintenance. They suggest that therapeutic interventions are likely to be effective only if they are matched to the client's stage of change. Thus, clients who are beginning to contemplate the need for change may be open to consciousness-raising and educational interventions. Those who are at the action stage need opportunities to practice autonomy, training in effective behavior change, and support in their efforts. Clients who have succeeded in making initial changes need help with the maintenance stage, when they assess the conditions under which relapse may occur, consider the alternatives they have for coping, and develop "the sense that one is becoming more of the kind of person one wants to be" (Prochaska and DiClemente, 1988, p. 10).

Families, too, may move from contemplation through action to maintenance, and systems interventions are likely to be most effective if they are appropriate to family members' level of readiness. Family change may be more complex than individual change because all family members do not necessarily reach the point of readiness concurrently. Yet any one participant who chooses to remove himself or herself from the ongoing pattern of interaction can transform the system. As long as other family members fail to play their customary roles, major changes can take place whether or not the alcohol-abusing family member stops drinking. Perhaps the most accurate way of describing the process of change in the family is to reconcile the models described above and to begin thinking in terms of the following general stages:

> Stage 1: Interrupting Ongoing Patterns
> Stage 2: Facing the Reality of Change
> Stage 3: Deepening and Maintaining Change

Interrupting Ongoing Patterns

The ideal situation is one in which the family as a unit moves together to take the first steps toward recovery. In fact, however, family members frequently find that they need to begin the change process without the participation of the alcohol-abusing member. Those family members who are ready to make a commitment to change need to be encouraged to move ahead. Schlesinger and Horberg (1988) encourage family members to take steps toward improving family life, even if the substance abusing individual refuses to participate. They suggest that other family members can grow and change even if the drinker tries to undermine their efforts. Before he or she is ready to change, other family members can begin to extricate themselves from chaos.

The key to this approach is that the family members must set their goals not just in terms of the alcohol-dependent person's behavior but in terms of their own health and growth. In the first stage of treatment, the therapist's approach must involve helping family members to interrupt patterns that have been characteristic of the family system in the past. As Bepko and Krestan (1985, p. 96) point out, what the therapist is doing is helping the family to gain a structure that is more functional and that eliminates the need for alcohol as an "interactional fulcrum."

Part of the therapist's role at this point involves helping the family to decide whether it might be possible and appropriate to press the alcohol-dependent member into accepting treatment. Kaufman and Pattison (1981) differentiate between actions that lead directly to achieving a "dry system" and actions that help the family disengage from the ongoing "wet system." They suggest that the therapist may initiate family actions to confront and change drinking behaviors, thus attempting to achieve a dry system. As either a separate or a complementary action, the family may move in the direction of another option: disengaging from alcoholismic behaviors, clarifying family definitions of responsibility, and changing behaviors that might in the past have served to perpetuate the wet system.

Family action to achieve immediate sobriety often takes the form of an intervention that forces the alcoholic to examine his or her drinking behaviors and encourages immediate treatment. Although active intervention is not always workable, it does represent an option to be considered by family members interested in interrupting current patterns. The idea underlying family intervention is that if family members protect the alcohol-dependent individual from the negative effects of his or her drinking, they may unwittingly encourage the behavior to continue. Allowing the drinker to deal with the consequences of his or her alcohol abuse may make a difference. An intervention into this situation involves allowing a crisis to occur and then offering help when the need for it is recognized. Miller and Gorski (1982), writing in support of the intervention mechanism, point out that the goal of the intervention is to "intensify the pain of drinking above the pain of not drinking and produce within the alcoholic the awareness that drinking is the source of pain" (p. 45). First, family members try to stop protecting the individual from the consequences of his or her drinking. Second, they confront the individual with concrete evidence of his or her alcohol-related behavior in the hope that the reality of the alcohol problem will become apparent. Thus, the family members engage in a two-pronged effort: using natural consequences to affect drinking behavior, and gathering together people who are significant to the alcohol abuser and who can force the issue by confronting the individual as a group. As part of the intervention process, family members, friends, and associates gather together to present their perception of the problem. All of the participants share their concerns, describing specific behaviors that have been troubling to them and attempting to show the individual how his or her drinking has affected them. The goal of the process is the alcohol-abusing individual's recognition of the problem and acceptance of the need for treatment.

It must be recognized that the intervention process is far from a panacea. Although this approach has become very popular among some treatment providers and families, it does have a major shortcoming in that it tends to oversimplify problem attribution. If families see alcohol treatment as a happy ending, they may fail to recognize the urgent need to make systemic changes in the family situation. At the same time, a situation in which the treatment option is not accepted by the alcohol-affected family member may still bring positive growth for the family as a whole if other members can achieve a degree of detachment.

A process of disengagement can help the family draw clearer boundaries among subsystems, interrupt rigid patterns of interaction, and recognize the impossibility of accepting responsibility for the behavior of others. For many families, a referral to Al-Anon or another self-help organization provides much-needed support as sober family members attempt to withdraw from the performance of roles that have enabled the alcohol abuser to avoid the negative social consequences of problem drinking.

One way to look at the appropriate direction for therapy is to consider Ackerman's (1983) conceptualization of the family's potential for moving from a "reactive" mode to an "active" one. When the family is in a reactive state, family dynamics are dominated by reactions to the drinking behavior. Ironically, family members' attempts to be very cautious and avoid difficulties may actually exacerbate the problem; their adaptations to an unhealthy situation allow it to continue. The reactive state is characterized by the attempts of family members to deny the existence of the alcohol problem. Parents try to protect children by covering up problems and by avoiding discussion of unpleasant realities. The family as a whole becomes isolated from others and emotions are buried.

Ackerman's idea is that a family can exchange a reactive state for an active state even though the individual affected may still be drinking. The difference lies in the reactions of the other family members. They begin to consider their own needs, to take an interest in themselves, to "decenter" from the alcohol. Most important, they may end their self-imposed isolation and seek support and help from others.

If the family system as a whole has developed mechanisms to clarify individual responsibilities and withdraw from enabling patterns, family members are likely to be able to make the difficult adaptations involved when the individual does eventually stop drinking.

Facing the Reality of Change

When an alcohol-abusing family member does achieve sobriety, the family may unexpectedly be thrown into crisis. Pittman (1987, p. 4), in his discussion of family crisis situations, says that "a crisis results when a stress comes to bear upon a system and requires change outside the system's usual repertoire." Clearly, the new-found sobriety of a family member who has had a history of dependence on alcohol does require that family members learn to behave in ways that are outside their customary repertoires. Families that have developed transactional patterns based on alcoholism find it difficult to adapt to the sudden need for change. Sometimes they have difficulty finding a new homeostatic state. Often they face disappointment when they realize that every aspect of their lives does not immediately improve.

Usher, Jay, and Glass (1982) point out that an individual's act of giving up alcohol is stressful for his or her entire family. Daily living without the buffer of alcohol may be unfamiliar and therefore frightening. The fact that abstinence does not automatically solve problems in family relationships may be surprising; family members find that old conflicts and emotional dysfunctions remain, but that they can no longer attribute all of these issues solely to alcohol. The frustration and anger that come to the surface may inhibit the alcoholic's attempts at a sober lifestyle.

Usher et al. (1982) warn that the alcohol abuser's family may choose any one of several responses to the crisis of abstinence. In many instances, families reintroduce alcohol into the system; old patterns are reestablished and the familiar "alcoholismic homeostasis" returns. Some families separate shortly after sobriety is attained, exchanging accusations, blaming one another for newly uncovered problems, or insisting that the alcoholic, although sober, has not made real behavioral changes. Another frequent response involves making minimal changes in family structures while family members seek support from outside sources such as Alcoholics Anonymous. The fourth option, seen as the optimal solution, is a more basic change, with the family learning to interact more effectively, to achieve closeness, and to find ways to meet one another's emotional needs.

Moving a family in the direction of such lasting changes requires first that the system be helped to weather the immediate crisis. What Bepko and Krestan (1985) suggest as appropriate short-term goals at this point involve keeping the system as calm as possible, focusing on stepping down the conflict, addressing individual issues that may be important to family members, encouraging family members to focus on themselves and their own needs, and anticipating extreme reactions to the crisis on the part of the sober family member who has been most involved in and affected by the alcohol problem. Fears that the family might have concerning relapse need to be addressed while new coping skills are developed and minor structural changes are made.

As family members face the reality of change they must also face the limitations of change. For example, the alcohol-dependent individual may expect upon achieving abstinence to be entrusted immediately with responsibilities that had been relinquished years before. He or she needs help in recognizing that trust needs to be rebuilt slowly, that other family members may have reasonable concerns about relapse, and that customary roles and behaviors are not amenable to sudden change. Other family members, after years of attributing all of their problems to alcohol, may be surprised, disappointed, and angry when they realize that long-standing problems do not melt away. They need help and support as they learn to address problems, issues, and conflicts more directly. Both the former alcohol abuser and the other family members need to identify some basic needs and goals that they, as individuals, want to meet. They need training in how to negotiate so that all members feel that some of their own needs are being met and that they are, at the same time, successfully helping the others. The anger that has built up over the years needs to be addressed and understood. Once these basic steps toward stability have been taken, the family as a whole can learn to reframe issues in systems terms and start to build a more solid foundation for future growth.

Deepening and Maintaining Change

It is in the realm of long-term recovery that the major theories of family therapy can be most helpful. The broad theoretical perspectives in which family therapists have been trained can be adapted very successfully to the needs of recovering families (Lewis, Dana & Blevins, 1988). Among the models that have been used most widely are structural family therapy (Minuchin, 1974, 1979), communication models (Haley, 1976; Madanes, 1981), experiential/humanistic therapy (Satir, 1967, 1972), and behavioral family therapy (Liberman, 1981).

Structural Family Therapy

Structural family therapy, with its strongly systems-oriented approach, has had a major impact on family practice. To Minuchin (1974, 1979), a family system can be understood only if its basic structure is recognized. The "enduring interactional patterns that serve to arrange or organize a family's component subunits into somewhat constant relationships" (Umbarger, 1983, p. 13) regulate the family's transactions and allow the system to remain consistent.

Study of the family's structure includes attention to its sub-systems. An enmeshed family system is characterized by an absence of clear boundaries differentiating one subsystem from another. In contrast, disengaged family systems have rigid boundaries between subsystems and great personal distance among family members. A pathologically enmeshed family has overly rigid boundaries separating the family system from its environment, while the disengaged family complements rigid internal boundaries with a lack of clear boundaries separating it from the outside world.

Family systems may be enmeshed or disengaged to varying degrees. A structure is dysfunctional to the degree that its rigidity interferes with the system's ability to adapt in response to changing circumstances. What Minuchin (1979) calls a "pathogenic family" is a family that has become trapped in patterns that fail to help members in their attempts at coping and adaptation. Such a family rigidly maintains stereotyped interactions, unable to see any possible alternatives. Although one family member may have been defined as the "identified patient," the family system as a whole is dysfunctional and will remain so until the process of over-focusing on one member has been reversed.

Minuchin's description of the pathogenic family is highly descriptive of the alcoholismic structure. In alcohol-affected families, focus on the individual alcohol abuser tends to be almost total, with other family members developing roles and patterns of interaction that are based on the presence of abusive drinking practices. The family structure tends to be rigid, with this problem exacerbated by the secrecy that protects the drinker from interference by outsiders. The popular literature has, in recent years, discussed extensively the role of the "codependent," who is seen as having a major role in the alcohol-dependent person's continued drinking. In fact, what is seen as codependency could be more accurately described as enmeshment. Wegscheider's (1981) description of the alcoholic family presents a picture of a system characterized by enmeshment and rigidity. Wegscheider points out that members of families affected by alcohol tend to feel that they are so completely trapped in these disordered systems that they have no options available to them. Although it would be healthier if family members were to speak out, voice their concerns, face their problems, and try to save themselves, most choose instead to try to adapt to the existing family system and hide their real feelings.

Structural family therapy approaches this problem through the therapist's leadership. Once the short-term crisis of sobriety has been weathered, the therapist can gradually confront the family's view of the problem, moving attention from the individual symptom-bearer to the family system, manipulating subsystem boundaries, presenting alternate concepts of reality, and encouraging the family's attempts to grow. Ultimately, the aim of the therapy is to change the structure of the family system, making it more functional in its own environmental context.

The Communications Model

The communications model also exemplifies a systems framework. Much of the pioneering work in applying systems theory to the study of family relationships was begun in the 1950s by a group organized in Palo Alto, California, under the leadership of Gregory Bateson. Bateson did much to move family therapy away from over-concentration on the individual and toward a focus on information processing in the systems context. "He called instead for an epistemological shift—to new units of analysis, to a focus on the ongoing process, and to the use of a new descriptive language that emphasizes relationships, feedback information, and circularity" (Goldenberg & Goldenberg, 1985, p. 6).

Bateson's interdisciplinary team, which included Jay Haley, John Weakland, and Donald Jackson, focused attention on communications models for understanding families and other human systems. It is now well understood by family therapists that communications have both content and command aspects, and that the command aspects, or metacommunications, define relationships.

The communications approach of today is exemplified by strategic therapy (Haley, 1976; Madanes, 1981), which focuses on active methods for changing repetitive communication patterns among family members. Haley (1976, p. 9) says, "If therapy is to end properly, it must begin properly—by negotiating a solvable problem and discovering the social situation that makes the problem necessary." If problems or symptoms serve a purpose in the social context, they can be resolved only through a strategy that focuses on interpersonal relationships.

The application of this conceptualization to alcohol-affected family systems is clear. Instead of looking at alcoholism as a self-contained problem, the strategic therapist searches for the purpose that the alcohol problem plays in the system. This conceptualization pinpoints the shortcomings of the disease concept for working with families. While the disease concept insists that alcoholism is always the "primary" problem, and therefore the first cause of other issues, the strategic model helps families to recognize that such causal relationships are oversimplified and inadequate.

To Haley, Madanes, and other communications theorists, the best way to eradicate a problem or symptom is to make it unnecessary for the stability of the family system. Once a problem has been redefined in terms that make it solvable, the strategic therapist develops a strategy unique to the needs of the specific family system. The therapist redefines the symptom, whether it is alcoholism or another problem, in terms of the purpose it serves for the family. This method forces change in the perceptions of family members and thus allows for long-term systems changes of real depth.

Experiential/Humanistic Therapy

The work of Virginia Satir (1967, 1972) has been closely associated with that of the communications theorists, but Goldenberg and Goldenberg (1985) place it in its own category of experiential/humanistic approaches because of the strongly humanistic and feeling-oriented underpinnings of the approach. Although Satir recognized the presence of family rules that maintain each family's system, she saw as most important those rules relating to self-esteem. Her therapeutic focus involved working to build self-esteem in both parents and children and to change family communications in such a way that the self-worth of each member would be enhanced. Thus, systems thinking and humanistic influences come together in this therapeutic approach.

Family therapy based on Satir's model focuses on the communication patterns that typify the functioning of the specific family. Satir differentiates between dysfunctional communication styles and congruent communications that express messages clearly and genuinely. One of the goals of family therapy practiced by Satir and other humanists is to make congruent communication the norm for the family as a whole.

The family members' self-esteem and the rules that govern family interactions are closely connected to the communication patterns. In functional families, the self-esteem of individual members is enhanced and the system as a whole is free to develop reasonably flexible rules that encourage open communication. In dysfunctional families, unwritten rules limit authentic communications and the members' self-esteem is not maintained. The alcoholic family, with its shame, guilt, and secrecy, is at high risk for developing dysfunctional interpersonal mechanisms. Even after drinking behaviors have been addressed and changed, family members are people in pain. Therapy, over the long term, attempts to help the family heal itself by moving away from destructive patterns and toward congruent, flexible, and open transactions.

Behavioral Family Therapy

Liberman (1981) points out that problem behaviors are learned in a social context and that these behaviors will be maintained as long as the social system is organized in a way that reinforces them. Behaviorally based family therapy uses learning theory to bring about changes in the contingencies that affect each family member's behaviors. The therapist tries to help family members identify what they see as desirable behaviors and reinforce these behaviors, withholding reinforcement of the negative behaviors that might previously have been encouraged. Liberman, like other family therapists with behavioral or social learning perspectives, focuses attention on specific, measurable behaviors and on the environmental contingencies that tend to develop and maintain these behaviors. When behavioral therapists work with families, they set concrete goals to increase positive behaviors and attempt to alter the patterns of reinforcement offered in the family milieu. At the same time, the therapist provides skills training for family members, focusing on such issues as communication methods, stress management, and behavioral self-control training.

These methods can be especially important for the long-term recovery of the alcohol-abusing client. As Finney, Moos, and Mewborn (1980) point out, "therapeutic efforts must go beyond the patient to deal with the contexts in which the patient functions after treatment" (p. 28). Once an individual has achieved sobriety, his or her risk for relapse has to be addressed within the context of the family and other social settings. If the behaviors of other family members reinforce sobriety, the risk of relapse is reduced. If the behavioral repertoire of family members remains unchanged, customary drinking behaviors are reinforced as strongly as they were in the past and long-term sobriety is endangered. The recovery of the alcoholic and his or her family depends on the development of new coping skills, new interactive behaviors, and new methods of dealing with internal and external stressors. Addressing drinking behaviors is only the first step in the long process of recovery.

In the final analysis, all of these approaches to family therapy seek verifiable changes both in the behaviors of family members and in family relationships. Although the alternate perspectives vary in their emphases, they all recognize the importance of the family as a social system that influences and is influenced by individual behaviors. As Finney, Moos, and Mewborn (1980, p. 27) have found, "The more cohesive and supportive the family . . . the better the prognosis for an individual who has been treated for alcoholism." Family systems certainly affect the outcome of treatment for individuals, but just as important is the notion that the family system itself can be seen as the most appropriate target for change.

In a stage-based process, the initial change in the family system involves an interruption in the customary patterns of interaction that have grown up around one member's alcoholism. The second stage brings an initial, adaptive reorganization to respond to change. Only in the third stage does the family system develop the basic, structural changes that can stand the test of time. At each stage, however, the family as a whole—not just the identified, alcohol-abusing client—is seen as the appropriate target of intervention.

Effects on Children

A systems-based focus on alcohol-affected families brings with it a recognition of the special problems faced by children. The problems inherent in the alcohol-affected family system have important developmental implications for children whose preadolescent and adolescent years are spent coping with an unusual set of stressors. Of course, there are vast differences among alcohol-affected families and numerous alternatives for children in terms of the coping mechanisms they employ. However, some common patterns do emerge.

If a family is affected by parental alcohol abuse, there is likely to be at least some impairment in the ability of parents to provide consistency in child-rearing practices. The behaviors of the drinking parent may show extreme variations that are difficult for children to understand. The other parent may also be impaired because of his or her focus on the alcohol problem. In some alcohol-affected families, neither parent is truly available to the child on a consistent basis (Lewis, Dana & Blevins, 1988).

What is being described here, of course, is a situation in which the structure and boundaries of the family system are dysfunctional. Within the family unit, boundaries between subsystems may be weak. Often, the unity of the parental subsystem is broken. At the same time, children frequently take on what are normally thought to be parental responsibilities. The boundaries between the family and its environment may also be problematic; as the family tries to maintain secrecy about the alcohol problem, isolation from others becomes extreme. Children who are unable to count on consistent support from their parents may also be prevented from reaching out to other adults for fear of breaking the family's rule of silence. The delicate homeostasis of the alcoholic family is maintained, but at high cost to all of its members, including the children.

Many children respond to this situation by working to provide for themselves the order and consistency that is missing from parental behaviors. These children adjust in such a way that the system's structure becomes regularized at the cost of a real childhood. As Black (1981) points out, children need consistency and structure. As alcohol problems become more severe, both parents become more and more preoccupied, leaving the children without consistent parenting. In these situations, children may find ways to provide for themselves the structure and order that they have been missing. Black suggests that children may restructure family systems by playing some combination of three family coping roles: the responsible one, the adjuster, and the placater.

The responsible one takes over parental roles on a routine basis, thereby providing consistency and structure for himself or herself and his or her siblings. This role may bring the child a degree of comfort and stability and may also provide a semblance of order for younger children. This phenomenon is not an unmixed blessing. These overly responsible children learn to rely on no one but themselves, thus helping to maintain the family's alcohol-based homeostasis.

The adjuster, in contrast, copes with a disorganized family system by detaching, going along with events, and thinking about family crises as little as possible. The placater copes by focusing on the needs of others and trying to salve the family's wounds. He or she tries to lower the family's tension level and to "fix the sadness, fears, angers and problems of brothers, sisters, and certainly, of Mom and Dad" (Black, 1981, p. 24).

Wegscheider (1981) also identifies a typology of basic roles that children may adopt in alcohol-affected families, as follows:

1. The family hero
2. The scapegoat
3. The lost child
4. The family mascot

The family hero, like Black's "responsible one," takes over functions that would normally be performed by the parents, assumes responsibility for solving family problems, and tries to provide stability for himself or herself and also for younger children. This coping method may be carried over into other childhood situations, including school, and into adulthood, so the family hero may be outstanding in many arenas. The scapegoat is the troublemaker in the family and receives attention for his or her misbehavior; he or she may at times be an identified patient who brings the family into therapy. The lost child remains in the background, gives the impression of needing very little attention, and, in fact, tends to receive almost no notice. The mascot, like Black's placater, tries to fix things. He or she tries to lessen anxiety and distract the family from tension-filled problems by clowning and seeking attention.

Although the roles described by Black and Wegscheider differ slightly, they share an emphasis on the notion that these roles are used both by individual children as coping mechanisms and by family systems as a set of transactions that help to maintain homeostasis. It is, of course, an oversimplification to identify and label a limited number of roles played by children of alcoholics and to assume that these roles differ in any basic way from those played by children in other families. Still, it is clear that the alcohol-affected family is at risk of being dysfunctional and that children might need to develop extraordinary mechanisms for coping.

Black (1986) says that children of alcoholics may have fewer physical, social, emotional, and mental resources available to help them cope, and at the same time they are faced with an unusual degree of stress. Their physical resources may be sapped because they are tired due to a lack of sleep at night, because they have internalized stress, because they have been abused, or because they are victims of fetal alcohol syndrome. Their social resources may be limited because of the rigid boundaries between the family system and its social environment. They may hesitate to bring other children into the home because of their shame at what might be encountered. They may cut off ties with outsiders—whether adults or children—because of their reluctance to share information about their families. In either instance, their social resources are lessened. Emotional resources may also be affected; the fear, pain, and embarrassment that come with unstable living arrangements, financial difficulties, broken promises, accidents, and public intoxication leave their mark. Even what Black calls mental resources may be affected because of difficulties in maintaining regular school attendance along with a lack of parental help and support for scholarship. The combined effects of increased stress with lack of personal resources and support may make children of alcoholics sufficiently vulnerable to warrant extra attention to their special developmental needs.

Children in the Alcohol-Affected Home Environment

Addressing the needs of children still living in the alcoholic environment often requires that hidden family dynamics be brought to the surface. Hastings and Typpo (1984) describe such family situations in their workbook for children by saying that living with a family where alcohol is a problem is like living with an "elephant in the living room." The elephant is seen by everyone in the family; in fact, people have to be careful to avoid it, yet the presence of the elephant is ignored. Each child learns that it is against the rules to talk about it, but each child may worry about its presence and wish it could be discussed.

Therapeutic interventions with children require strong levels of empathy and support as their customary secrecy is shed. Children need help in developing coping skills that can serve them more effectively both in the current situation and in the future; they need to deal with their current uncertainties and at the same time gain the strengths that can prevent the development of chronic emotional problems.

One of the most useful approaches to take with children may be to move them from a reactive to an active state (Ackerman, 1983), encouraging them to recognize and try to meet their own needs. If they are isolated in their home environments, they need help in reaching out to others. If they are afraid of their feelings, they need to recognize and express their previously forbidden emotions. If they feel alone in their situation, they need to know that others share their problems. They need to know that they are not to blame for family difficulties and that their attempts to meet their own needs are appropriate. This level of awareness can be reached most successfully in group settings. Brown and Sunshine (1982) have found that a group intervention can be successful in bringing the "family secret" out into the open, thus providing immediate relief for a child who would otherwise be burdened by shame and isolation. They point out that children from alcohol-affected families may also have deficits in social development and peer interaction and that this factor provides an even stronger rationale for group as the treatment of choice.

Group counseling can use a structured, educational approach, combining a cognitive dimension with a focus on affect and skill acquisition. The Hastings and Typpo (1984) design, for instance, includes materials dealing with the following topics:

1. *Drinking and drug problems* (cognitive materials designed to build knowledge concerning alcohol and other drugs)
2. *Feelings* (exercises to elicit awareness of negative and positive emotions and to encourage sharing)
3. *Families* (discussions of family rules and relationships)
4. *Coping with problems* (exercises dealing with coping methods to be used for dealing with general or alcohol-related family problems)
5. *Changes* (material encouraging children to make changes in the areas over which they have most control, especially in taking care of themselves)
6. *Choices* (decision-making exercises)

Such structured approaches can help children develop the skills and resources they need for coping with family stress. Ideally, they can also help to prevent problems that might otherwise follow these children into adulthood.

Adult Sons and Daughters of Alcohol Abusers

The coping mechanisms that work for children in alcohol-affected homes may not serve them well in adulthood. In therapeutic interventions with adults, it is not always possible to work with the family of origin. However, therapists should examine current behaviors in the context of the systems functions they were developed to meet.

Many children growing up in alcohol-affected families learn to respond by exerting control and burying their feelings. In adulthood, they may pay a price for this kind of adjustment. Seixas and Youcha (1985, pp. 47–48) ask adult children of alcoholics whether they identify with the following list of prevalent feelings and attitudes:

Lack of trust?
Feel isolated and lonely?
Deny or suppress deep feelings?
Feel guilty?
Feel unnecessarily embarrassed and ashamed?
Wish for closeness, yet fear it?
Have a low opinion of yourself?
Feel sad?
Need to control yourself?
Need to control others?
Split the world into all good or all bad?
Have an exaggerated sense of responsibility?

Want desperately to please?
Have trouble standing up for your own needs?
Overreact to personal criticism?

It would be absurd to believe that only adult children of alcoholics exhibit these kinds of attitudes and behaviors. However, their burgeoning self-help movement does seem to indicate that a significant number of "ACOAs" identify with these problems, feeling that they have unusual difficulty in trusting others, relinquishing control, identifying and expressing emotions, or changing rigid behaviors. Malone (1987) discusses a number of personality characteristics that she sees herself as sharing with other adult children of alcoholics. Among the phenomena she identifies are high achievement combined with "a knack for sabotaging success" and difficulty in enjoying it; an overdeveloped fear of losing control that can lead to perfectionism and rigidity; a long-term sense of guilt and sadness; a high tolerance for very unusual behavior; a strong sense of being different from others; an inappropriate sense of loyalty; and a lack of self-esteem. Coping mechanisms that worked in the context of the alcoholic family system are clearly less appropriate for a mature life style.

Black (1986) suggests that therapy with adult children of alcoholics should have two components. First, clients should be encouraged to face their fears of loss of control and express their guilt, sadness, and anger. Subsequently, this catharsis should give way to an attempt to learn new behavioral skills. If clients' needs are addressed through a group process, emphasis should be placed on the development of such adult competencies as assertion, relaxation, stress management, and interpersonal communication. Although the group can also serve the purpose of providing an understanding of the systems issues in alcoholism, it is probably less useful to focus on children of alcoholics as a risk group than to emphasize the individual's potential for successful adaptation and self-control. In actuality, the therapeutic process for children of alcoholics may parallel that for the alcoholic family: interrupting ongoing behavioral patterns; facing the reality of change; and, finally, taking steps to deepen and maintain those changes that lead toward health.

Case Study: The Marshall Family

The Marshall family once exemplified the problems inherent in the alcoholic family system. When the Marshalls were first seen in treatment, Don Marshall was forty-two and had been drinking heavily since adolescence. The last few years had brought an increase in Don's drinking and an intensification of his and his family's problems. Don was finding it more and more difficult to maintain even a semblance of normality in his life; his "few beers on the way home from work" now stretched into late-night drinking bouts that often made it necessary for him to miss his mornings at work. His job as an insurance adjuster in a large company seemed stable, but his career development had been stalled over the last few years.

Don's wife, Peggy, was busy with her job as a nurse's aide, but she found time to help Don with his work. Frequently, he brought paperwork home instead of taking care of it at the office. Peggy had learned enough about the insurance business over the years that she was able to complete the work; no one at the company seemed to notice the difference. Peggy also took care of the family's finances and took responsibility for any supervision needed by their two children, Janie and Jim.

Janie, age 16, had always helped with the housework after school. Now that she had her driver's license, she was also able to do some of the grocery shopping and to chauffeur her 14-year-old brother, Jim, to swimming practice and other after-school activities. Sometimes, when her mother worked the evening shift, Janie had to pick her father up at the bar where he did most of his drinking after work. Jim maintained a strong interest in athletics and avoided staying home as much as he could.

Over the last few years, Peggy had become increasingly concerned and frustrated about Don's drinking. It seemed to be getting continually worse, and he was less and less able to do his work or communicate with the children. She continued to call his office to make excuses for him when his hangovers were too severe for him to go to work, but she thought she detected some suspicion on the part of his boss. She began to fear that his job might not be as secure as it had seemed.

Interrupting Ongoing Patterns

Peggy was able to make the first break in the family's established patterns when she began attending meetings of Al-Anon, a support group to which she had been referred. Here, she was encouraged to try to find ways to meet her own needs, rather than to continue focusing solely on the problem of Don's drinking. She also learned that she could change the current pattern of family interactions only if she could force herself to stop protecting Don from the effects of his alcohol abuse.

Peggy made two immediate changes. First, she made the decision to return to school in a program that would allow her to become a registered nurse through two intensive years of study. Involvement in this program made her feel that she might be able to support herself and the children by herself if it became necessary. Peggy also made the decision to stop protecting Don at work. She was now involved in her own career and made it clear to Don that she would no longer have time to do his work as well. It took a great deal of courage for her to explain this to Don and to let him know that she would no longer be calling his boss to explain his absences.

This change in the family's pattern did finally bring about a change in Don's drinking behavior, not because of a family confrontation but because of an ultimatum from his supervisor. When Peggy removed herself as a buffer between Don and the possibility of job-related disaster, she helped to create a crisis at work. The impact of this crisis was ultimately positive: Don was told that he would have to change his job performance immediately or face dismissal. The company was willing to give Don time off for alcoholism treatment that would be covered by his health insurance. Don took advantage of this opportunity and achieved abstinence through an inpatient program at a local hospital. He immediately became actively involved in Alcoholics Anonymous, attending meetings almost daily as soon as he was released from treatment.

Facing the Reality of Change

All of the members of the Marshall family were surprised by the difficulties they faced in adjusting to a change that they had believed would be an entirely positive event. More than anything else, the source of the crisis could be attributed to the differences among them in their expectations.

Don expected that the family would go back to the way it had been years ago, before his drinking had gotten out of hand. At that time, he had been the chief decision maker in the family, taking responsibility for all financial matters and acting as the primary disciplinarian for the children. He now expected that he would immediately resume his former authority, taking back the checkbook that Peggy had been maintaining and, even more important, making decisions for and about the children. He was especially concerned about Janie, who seemed to be resisting his authority and who was adamant about continuing to see her boyfriend, even though Don felt that this relationship was too intense for such a young girl. Don was also concerned about Peggy, who he believed was putting too much time and energy into her nursing program. Most of all, Don was hurt because he thought that the family was not as supportive of his sobriety as he believed they should be. They failed to see the importance of Alcoholics Anonymous in his life, and they failed to trust and compliment him on his sobriety.

What Don could not see was that family life had changed drastically in the last few years. Although Peggy honestly wanted Don's sobriety, she had very mixed feelings concerning power and responsibility in the family. She had no intention of giving up her own career goals, nor did she see any reason to withdraw from the decision-making authority concerning family finances. If anything, she felt that the family should be more supportive of her efforts, providing extra help so that she would have time to study and freedom to attend classes without worry.

Janie and Jim were also caught up in this crisis. If anything, Peggy's interruption of the family's ongoing patterns had left the children more than ever to their own resources. Her attendance at nursing school left more and more household responsibilities to Jane and allowed Jim almost complete freedom of movement. The children had been accustomed to taking care of themselves and saw no reason to return authority to their father. Jane liked being in charge at home and did not see why she should cede authority to the man she had had to drag home from the bar so many times. Jim had been deeply hurt by his father's failure to provide consistent parenting. He wanted to spend time with his father, but he was afraid of being disappointed and was very distrustful. He was also hurt because his father spent time at many A.A. meetings but said that he did not have time to watch Jim's swimming meets or soccer games.

The therapist working with the Marshalls helped them to weather this crisis by teaching them to identify realistic expectations and to negotiate so that each family member could have some of his or her goals met. The family understood that they could identify short-range solutions to their problems and that, once Don's sobriety had become more established, they could consider the possibility of deeper and more long-lasting changes. The goal of therapy at this point involved lowering the level of conflict and helping the family to adjust to the major changes taking place in their lives. Focus was placed on individual needs so that family members could begin to relearn the process of helping and supporting one another.

As a result of this therapeutic intervention, the family negotiated some short-term changes that succeeded in making them all more comfortable. For instance, Peggy, Janie, and Jim agreed to attend an Alcoholics Anonymous breakfast with Don every Sunday morning, thus giving the family some time to be together while concurrently showing their support for his sobriety and becoming involved with other recovering families. Janie agreed to limit her dating to the weekends, with her parents allowing her to see her boyfriend as long as curfew was maintained and no drinking or drug use occurred. She continued to do the grocery shopping and had access to the car when her mother did not need it for going to class. She was in charge of planning the family's meals, but the other family members were expected to help with the cooking and clean-up. Don, Janie, and Peggy took turns driving Jim to swimming practice, with Don and Peggy agreeing that one of them would watch Jim's swimming matches or soccer games at least once a week. The family agreed to give Peggy quiet time for studying; Don agreed to take care of family needs on the two nights a week that she had evening classes. Thus, each of the family members had an opportunity both to meet some of his or her own needs and to be supportive of the others.

Deepening and Maintaining Change

The Marshall's efforts at rebuilding their family life and negotiating supportive compromises enabled them to weather the storm of change, but long-term stability would require more drastic measures. The family members needed to learn how to view the family unit as an ongoing system. They needed to develop deeper changes in their interactive patterns so the alcoholism that had once been central to the family's functioning would no longer have a potential role to play.

The interventions used by a family therapist working with the Marshalls would differ in accordance with his or her theoretical framework, but the differences would be subtle. A structural family therapist might have focused on the family sub-systems, recognizing for instance that stronger differentiations would need to be made between the parental subsystem and the sibling subsystem before the family structure could become truly functional. A strategic therapist, like the structural therapist, might have focused on the question of why this family system needed Don's alcoholism. The therapist would have helped the family to recognize that the focus on Don as the identified patient served primarily to disguise more basic dysfunctionality in the system. As long as Peggy and Janie continued to take full responsibility for the family's well-being, Don and Jim would both tend to take on less and less responsibility. Moreover, Jim might be at risk for the development of problem behaviors. An experiential/humanistic therapist would also attend to the systemic dysfunctions of the family, but his or her most basic question would ask how these family members could learn to be supportive and encouraging to one another. Every member of this family had been bearing his or her pain in loneliness and isolation; a deep healing process would have to take place in the context of a highly supportive therapeutic process. The behavioral family therapist would help the family develop mechanisms for reinforcing positive behaviors. Thus, Don's performance of responsible behaviors, as well as his sobriety, would be recognized and reinforced by other family members. At the same time, Peggy's attempts to build a satisfying career, Janie's growth into independent maturity, and Jim's closer involvement with the family might be seen and reinforced as positive behaviors. Each of these approaches to family therapy might differ in its primary emphases. All would have in common a focus on helping the family develop consistent interactive patterns to enhance the development of each of its members and eradicate the need for alcohol as a unifying force. Success in this endeavor would improve the family's current well-being and also help the children to avoid carrying dysfunctional coping mechanisms into adulthood.

Conclusion

The family system of the alcoholic is not able to differentiate itself. Each family member reacts to the unusual, disruptive, and frustrating behavior in ways that somehow reinforce the addiction itself. Even if these members are able to behave at their best and not to react, the addicted member often has an investment in eliciting and provoking their reactions, perhaps as a form of reassurance or affirmation. However, no one wins in this system. The alcoholic member will use the behavior of other family members to justify his or her behavior and to decrease responsibility for it. Treatment without an analysis of these frustrating and defeating transactions can be only partial, because all family members, including the alcoholic, ultimately need to confront issues of closeness and intimacy that have been masked by the symptom.

References

Ackerman, R. J. (1983). *Children of alcoholics: A guidebook for educators.* Holmes Beach, FL: Learning Publications.

Bepko, C., & Krestan, J. A. (1985). *The responsibility trap: A blueprint for treating the alcoholic family.* New York: Free Press.

Black, C. (1981). *It will never happen to me.* Denver: M.A.C.

Black, C. (1986, March). *Children of alcoholics.* Paper presented at the Conference on Children of Alcoholics, Gestalt Institute for Training, Chicago.

Brown, K. A., & Sunshine, J. (1982). Group treatment of children from alcoholic families. *Social Work with Groups, 5* (1), 65–72.

Finney, J. W., Moos, R. H., & Mewborn, C. R. (1980). Posttreatment experiences and treatment outcome of alcoholic patients six months and two years after hospitalization. *Journal of Consulting and Clinical Psychology, 48*(1), 17–29.

Goldenberg, I., & Goldenberg, H. (1985). *Family therapy: An overview* (2nd ed.). Pacific Grove, CA: Brooks/Cole.

Haley, J. (1976). *Problem-solving therapy.* New York: Harper & Row.

Hastings, J. M., & Typpo, M. H. (1984). *An elephant in the living room.* Minneapolis: CompCare Publications.

Johnson, V. (1973). *I'll quit tomorrow.* New York: Harper & Row.

Kaufman, E. (1985). *Substance abuse and family therapy.* Orlando, FL: Grune & Stratton.

Kaufman, E., & Pattison, E. M. (1981). Differential methods of family therapy in the treatment of alcoholism. *Journal of Studies on Alcohol, 42,* 951–971.

Lewis, J. A., Dana, R. Q., & Blevins, G. A. (1988). *Substance abuse counseling: An individualized approach.* Pacific Grove, CA: Brooks/Cole.

Liberman, R. (1981). Behavioral approaches to family and couple therapy. In G. D. Erickson & T. P. Hogan (Eds.), *Family therapy: An introduction to theory and technique* (2nd ed.) (pp. 152–164). Pacific Grove, CA: Brooks/Cole.

Madanes, C. (1981). *Strategic family therapy.* San Francisco: Jossey-Bass.

Malone, M. (1987, February). *Dependent on disorder.* Unpublished manuscript, pp. 50–55, 76–78.

Miller, M., & Gorski, T. T. (1982). *Family recovery: Growing beyond addiction.* Independence, MO: Independence Press.

Minuchin, S. (1974). *Families and family therapy.* Cambridge, MA: Harvard University Press.

Minuchin, S. (1979). Constructing a therapeutic reality. In E. Kaufman & P. Kaufmann (Eds.), *Family therapy of drug and alcohol abuse* (pp. 5–18). New York: Gardner.

Pittman, F. S. (1987). *Turning points: Treating families in transition and crisis.* New York: W. W. Norton.

Prochaska, J. O., & DiClemente, C. C. (1988). Toward a comprehensive model of change. In W. R. Miller & N. Heather (Eds.), *Treating addictive behaviors: Processes of change* (pp. 3–28). New York: Plenum.

Satir, V. M. (1967). *Conjoint family therapy* (2nd ed.). Palo Alto, CA: Science and Behavior Books.

Satir, V. M. (1972). *Peoplemaking.* Palo Alto, CA: Science and Behavior Books.

Schlesinger, S. E., & Horberg, L. K. (1988). *Taking charge: How families can climb out of the chaos of addiction.* New York: Simon & Schuster.

Seixas, J. S., & Youcha, G. (1985). *Children of alcoholism: A survivor's manual.* New York: Harper & Row.

Steinglass, P. (1978). The conceptualization of marriage from a systems theory perspective. In T. J. Paolino & B. S. McCrady (Eds.), *Marriage and marital therapy: Psychoanalytic, behavioral, and systems theory perspectives* (pp. 298–365). New York: Brunner/Mazel.

Steinglass, P. (1979). Family therapy with alcoholics: A review. In E. Kaufman & P. Kaufmann (Eds.), *Family therapy of drug and alcohol abuse* (pp. 147–186). New York: Gardner.

Umbarger, C. C. (1983). *Structural family therapy.* New York: Grune & Stratton.

Usher, M. L., Jay, J., & Glass, D. R. (1982). Family therapy as a treatment modality for alcoholism. *Journal of Studies on Alcohol, 43,* 927–938.

Wegscheider, S. (1981). *Another chance: Hope and health for the alcoholic family.* Palo Alto, CA: Science and Behavior Books.

5

Substance Abuse and Addiction

LYNN F. RANEW,
M.S.W.

DANIEL A. SERRITELLA,
Ph.D.

WHAT DEFINES HIGH RISK factors for drug addiction? Is it genetics, environment, learning, intrapsychic issues, interpersonal issues, or early life experiences? Is addiction multi-generational and if so, is it a result of genetics or of learned behavior? These are unanswered questions that make the field of drug addiction complex and challenging for the practitioner. The pathogenesis of drug addiction is unknown. It may, as some postulate, involve neurochemical changes (Miller, Dackis & Gold, 1987).

Further, genetics may be involved in the transmission of substance abuse. Goodwin (1979) estimated that first-degree relatives of alcoholics have at least a fivefold increase in their risk for alcoholism compared to the general population. Adoption studies have provided additional insight into the nature versus nurture question of alcoholism. The rate of alcoholism was four times as great among adopted children whose biological father was alcoholic (Wender & Klein, 1981). Incidences of alcoholism were significantly less among adoptees who had environmental influence of alcoholism but had no biological parental link to the disease.

Substance abuse can be viewed as a means to change a psychophysiological state from one of less comfort to one of more comfort. Influences from the environment, social stimulus situation, and internal body chemistry all interact with early learning, perception, and heredity. Two individuals who carry similar genetic predispositions may play out their life stories in very different ways. One may choose a lifestyle that triggers the genetic risk factor; the other may choose a lifestyle that places the individual at limited risk of triggering the genetic link. Recognizing and identifying those individuals at greater risk for substance abuse is the next frontier of prevention work.

There are multiple causal theories in the area of substance abuse and addiction (Lettieri, Sayers & Pearson, 1980). The theoretical and research base is continually expanding. A comprehensive addiction theory would draw from multiple disciplines, including biochemistry, genetics, behavioral learning theory, social learning, psychoanalytic doctrine, social control, and cultural, environmental, and economic approaches. An integrated theory of the etiology of drug addiction is needed.

Personality Dynamics of the Substance Abuser

Personality dynamics of substance abusers have been of increasing interest. Cox (1979) offers two common and generally accepted postulates that correlate drive states with addiction.

1. Substance abusers are oral, dependent individuals who seek to gratify their cravings for dependency through alcohol or drugs.
2. Substance abusers are individuals with an intensified drive for personal power, who seek to gratify this drive through substance abuse.

Most researchers have simplistically looked at substance abusers as if they were of a single personality type (Craig, 1979). It appears likely that individuals with a variety of personality organizations may compulsively use drugs (Penk, 1981). The individual's background, ethnicity, and interpersonal history appear to interact with his or her drug of choice. Consequently, addicted individuals do not exhibit one personality type. Nonetheless, many substance abusers do exhibit common factors such as impulsivity, failure to inhibit behavior that has previously led to negative consequences, and valuing immediate euphoria. In one study, demographic and personality dynamics of 533 addicted individuals were observed, and the researchers concluded that substance abuse was associated with a variety of antisocial indices including number of arrests, legal problems, and antisocial personality disorders (Kosten & Rounsaville, 1986).

Inman, Bascue, and Skoloda (1985) found that 56 percent of substance abusers admitted for treatment were identified as having borderline personality disorders. Additionally, substance abusers are frequently characterized as being extremely impulsive in ways that are self-damaging. Many suffer from affective instability marked by shifts in moods from depression, irritability, or anxiety. Khantzian and Treece (1985) found that 93 percent of all substance abusers had diagnosable personality disorders, with over two-thirds exhibiting a lifetime history of affective disorder. A review of the literature on substance abuse and personality disorders found that 80 percent of all studies show a positive association between the two (Lewis, Cloninger & Pais, 1983; Grande, 1984).

Affective illness within the substance abusing population is also an area of interest. An increasing prevalence of affected illness is appearing in opiate, central nervous system stimulant, and depressant drug abusers. Findings support that a minority of opiate users suffer from an underlying depression pre-dating their drug problems. Stimulant and depressant abusers may often be self-medicating underlying depression or dysphoric mood (Mirin & Weiss, 1986). Dackis and Gold (1986), however, suggest that the depression and other emotional states associated with drug addiction may be the result, and not the cause, of abuse.

Addictive Family Systems

Research has shown a unique pattern of characteristics in families with substance abuse and addiction. When looking at the causes of addiction, we should not overlook family dynamics that greatly affect initial drug use, course of addiction, and recovery. Addicts' fathers have been found to be detached, passive, and inadequate as role models. Several studies have shown that addicts and their families were aware of the self-destructive nature of the addiction (Stanton, 1979a). Since many interpersonal skills are learned within the family context, families of substance abusers appear to have a deficiency of role models and opportunities to acquire interpersonal skills.

Enmeshed Families

Families can be viewed as enmeshed, disengaged, or healthy. Generally, substance abuse families show strong enmeshment (Madanes, Dukes & Harbin, 1980). These are families that do not let go of their offspring, that cling to their children and tolerate all kinds of abuse from them, including substance abuse. Often we see intense enmeshment between parents and opposite-sex children. The family message seems to be, "We will suffer almost anything, but please don't leave us" (Stanton, Todd, Heard, Kirschener, Kleiman, Mowatt, Riley, Scott & Van Deusen, 1978).

The enmeshed family system embraces the addicted individual well beyond the adolescent years, a fact that should dispel the popular image of the abuser isolated and alone or absorbed into an addicted peer culture. Stanton and Todd (1982) reported that 64 percent of heroin addicts were in daily telephone contact with one parent. Of multiple-drug abusers, 51 percent were in daily telephone contact with a parent; in the population at large, only 9 percent of adults contact a parent by phone on a daily basis.

Other studies found that two-thirds of male drug abusers under the age of 35 live with the people who raised them. Of drug abusers under age 35, 80 percent are in at least weekly contact with home (Stanton & Todd, 1982).

Multi-Generational Addiction

The addicted individual usually does not stand alone within a family. In a family history, multi-generational issues of substance abuse quickly surface. The substance may change from generation to generation, but the thread of addiction seems to remain present. Family therapists pay particular attention to a three-generational frame of reference. A family history, gathered in the form of a genogram, will often show a symbolic display of relationships and key events in a family's life. Genograms depict marriages, divorces, births, deaths, and major influences on the family. The pattern of addiction is often graphically displayed as a family relates its history.

Often one sees other patterns of addictions appearing in the family history. Patterns of addiction may include gambling, eating disorders, or even behaviors as simple as compulsive television-watching.

Children of Addiction

Children growing up in homes where there is substance abuse are at risk to become addicted. Families with parental addictions risk higher incidence of emotional, physical, social, and psychological deprivation. There appears to be a set of common factors in homes where there is parental addiction. These families frequently limit their contacts with other members of the community, thereby reinforcing social withdrawal and isolation. Families that are withdrawn are less welcoming to their children's friends. Children are more reluctant to invite peers home, since they are never sure what condition their addicted parent may be in when they get there. Addicted families are closed rather than open systems.

Children growing up in substance-abusing families often suffer from emotional neglect. Parents under the influence of drugs are less able to be emotionally available to their children's needs. Likewise, such parents are less sensitive to the changing moods and emotions of other family members. There may be varying degrees of emotional numbing. In some families angry feelings are vented, but intimate emotions of caring go unexpressed. In other families the angry feelings are anesthetized; anger becomes repressed and unexpressed. Healthy ways of defusing anger are not learned or exercised as drugs often become the means to cope with stress.

A primary task of any parent is to set age-appropriate limits. In substance-abusing homes these limits frequently never are established. The child, experiencing little external limit on his or her behavior, has little opportunity to internalize a set of controls on his or her behavior or impulses. Children growing up in homes where there is substance abuse habitually experience confusion and disruption. Communication is apt to be incongruent and unclear and is accompanied by inconsistent discipline. Substance-abusing families exhibit a higher incidence of parental quarreling and family violence. Additionally, these families experience elevated rates of divorce and separation. Also, boundaries recurrently become violated, resulting in higher frequencies of child abuse and sexual abuse.

Childhood responses to parental drug abusers are similar to the experiences of children whose parents are alcoholic. Similar family dynamics for the child are present. Roles have been identified by which children attempt to resolve the conflicts and confusions in their addictive home. These roles have been identified by Wegscheider (1981) as hero, mascot, scapegoat, and lost child.

Substance Abuse Treatment

The treatment of drug addiction is complex and multi-faceted. Detoxification, methadone maintenance programs, methadone-to-abstinence programs, individual outpatient drug-free counseling, day programs, inpatient programs, court-mandated treatment, and group and family therapy are some of the many treatment modalities currently employed.

The ultimate goal in most drug treatment counseling is total abstinence for long periods of time and no addictive substitutions. This ideal goal can be achieved by setting small but achievable short-term goals. By definition, an effective treatment of addiction takes time, as fundamental changes in the individual's lifestyle must occur. The treatment of addiction is a long-term process. Grandiose expectations at the outset of treatment set up both client and therapist for failure.

Motivation for Change

The individual's motivation for change must be present before substance abuse treatment can be effective. Parents, spouses, employers, and others identifying the problem and seeking treatment for the abuser are insufficient. Family involvement assists in the long-term treatment, but the individual substance user must reach a point where he or she acknowledges that drugs are a problem, and must be in enough psychological and emotional pain to have a desire to stop using drugs.

Factors have been identified that increase the prognosis for favorable treatment outcome. These traits include being well socialized, absence of personality disturbances, and strong ties to other persons (Blum, 1972). Treatment may work best on those who need it least.

Treatment is not effective if the person does not view the substance abuse as a problem. If the individual perceives the drug use as under control, pleasurable, or causing no negative social consequences, the individual is unlikely to seek treatment. A cultural milieu that supports and condones drug use reduces the effectiveness of any intervention. However, significant others who do not condone drug use may eventually have an influence in initiating treatment and in the course of treatment. Spouses, in-laws, and parents may be the helpful resources who assist in terminating drug use. Individuals who have been successful in ending their drug addiction often describe the importance of strong and caring people who influenced them to get off drugs (Blum, 1972). Attempts to achieve stable abstinence are enhanced by mobilizing a social network, used for social support in assuring compliance with the treatment regimen and to undercut denial (Galanter, 1986).

Treatment Modalities

In drug therapy the least restrictive environment that can provide positive outcome is the first treatment of choice. Individuals who can maintain a drug-free lifestyle through outpatient counseling (individual, family, or group) are best served in this environment. Day treatment during which an individual lives at home but maintains daily intensive work at a treatment center is the second level of intervention. Hospitalization, in which the individual enters a 30- or 60-day in-hospital treatment program with detoxification and intensive therapy represents a restrictive treatment environment. Long-term residential treatment is another treatment option in which the individual gradually earns more and more privileges to enter job and outside activities. The client resides in a residence that focuses on drug treatment and living skills for a drug-free life style.

Although the different treatment options may follow dissimilar patterns, detoxification is always an initial treatment issue. Many therapists contend that insight-oriented therapy is useless during a period when a person is frequently using drugs. Drugs often interfere with the individual's ability to gain insight into behavior and limit the application of new skills. Frequently, drug abusers report continued drug use as a means to avoid withdrawal rather than to achieve the euphoric high they sought at earlier stages in their drug dependency. Detoxification treatment has as its primary goal the relief of the withdrawal symptoms while the body adjusts to a drug-free state. Detoxification is seen as a precursor to long-term treatment. Medical supervision is advisable during the detoxification process. Medical interventions create an opportunity to orient the client to treatment resources following detoxification. Detoxification is a prerequisite to enrollment in drug-free programs.

Family Therapy

Enabling behavior is a difficult program in many drug-abusing families. Issues of codependency, where family members are caught up in and reactive to the substance user, create unhealthy patterns of behavior throughout the family. Enabling behavior by other family members allows the drug user not to feel the full consequences of behavior. Family members cover up, make excuses, and overload themselves in trying to cover for the irresponsible drug user. However, their behavior merely reinforces the substance abuse. It may be difficult and painful for the families, but family members must allow the drug abuser to suffer the consequences of behaviors related to substance abuse, in order to create motivation for change.

The literature on family treatment for drug abuse has been increasingly studied (Stanton, 1979b; Heath and Atkinson, 1988; Stanton, 1988). Most researchers agree that family members need to be involved early in the treatment process. Acknowledging family members' pain and frustration, their disappointment and hurt, their sense of being overburdened, and their feelings of helplessness can help establish a bond of trust and rapport with the family. Family members are hurting. Their pain is real, and their lives have been as affected and impaired by the substance abuse as that of the individual who is ingesting or injecting the drugs. Understanding the family's pain is the beginning.

Families need help in learning to set limits for the abuser. The substance abuser must experience the consequences of his or her behavior. Therapy must help the parents to cooperate in dealing with their offspring rather than undercutting each other, and also to understand the impact of their behavior, such as in bailing their 40-year-old son out of jail repeatedly. Many times the parents of the substance abuser are dealing with the separation issues of adolescents even with their middle-aged child (Stanton et al., 1982). Parents must learn to work together, to set limits on what behavior they will and will not tolerate, to spell out the consequences of negative behavior, and to set standards for the substance abuser's continued use of their home and resources.

Family therapy is the treatment of choice for adolescents. Helping the family and child to negotiate needs, set limits, and work toward the emerging independence of the teen is best accomplished in family therapy. When the teen shows responsible behavior, more freedom is earned. Irresponsible behavior reduces the teen's freedom. Parents frequently need help setting these guidelines. Only when a family system is so toxic that separation from a harmful and chronically abusive family system is in the best interest of the teen, should family therapy not be advised. In such cases, alternative living arrangements with supportive surrogate parents should be provided until the teen is old enough to be independent. Even when other living arrangements are found for the dependent adolescent, the ties that bind the child to the toxic family system will remain. Additional family work may still be in order. Short-term residential drug treatment programs for adolescents should incorporate a family therapy component.

The issue of triangulation is an element in the dynamics of family therapy with substance abusers. In triangulated relationships communication is not straightforward. Communications, expectations, and disappointments repeatedly move through a third party. In substance-abusing homes this third party frequently is the substance-abusing child, caught between the parental dyad. Family therapy creates an opportunity to see these communication patterns and redirect them. Again, we are speaking of major changes of entrenched patterns and behaviors. Working to have the couple speak directly to each other about their fears, their angers, and their needs may seem very frightening. Therapists must move carefully into the underlying pain that may be present in the marital relationship. Otherwise the family will feel too exposed too quickly and may terminate therapy early.

If an abuser is married, it is advisable to bring the spouse in during the course of treatment. The dynamics of the marital relationship will affect the course of recovery. If both partners are substance abusers, much of their relationship and behavior may be drug-related. It is difficult for one partner to change without seeing change in the other. Partners who are users may sabotage treatment by maintaining a high profile of drug-related behavior.

Marital partners of substance abusers are often caught up in over-responsible roles and enabling roles. Helping to acknowledge the burdens and giving permission not to take care of everyone else may be part of treatment. Often second-generation substance abuse becomes a focus for the therapy as a history of substance abuse in the family of origin of one or both spouses becomes evident.

If substance abusers have children in their custody, family therapy should include the children. Addressing the needs, confusion, and emotional stress of the children is a form of prevention. The children experience the trauma of growing up in an addictive home; speaking to their needs now may help prevent the pain and dysfunction experienced in childhood from becoming a lifelong pattern. Parenting skills, developmental stages of children, and the emotional and psychological needs of children are all addressed in family sessions.

Group Therapy

Group therapy is frequently seen as a therapy of choice for substance abuse; it is included in most day treatment and hospitalization programs. All members are in the group to deal with substance abuse problems. Substance abuse is frequently a peer-supported activity. When surrounded by like-minded individuals who support the drug experience, an abuser will find it difficult to make a break into new behavior. Through the group process, individuals can struggle along with others who have similar experiences. Issues of denial can be strongly confronted in the groups. Attempts to minimize drug use can also be challenged. Individuals have the opportunity to learn from, support, and confront each other. Individuals at different stages of the recovery experience can become role models. An individual who has been clean for three months can relate his experience to a person just coming out of detoxification. When individuals relapse, the group is there to confront the drug-taking behavior and support the continuing effort to stay drug-free. Drug abusers may have learned excellent deceiving skills. Other abusers see through the games and help individuals confront reality. The therapeutic community has developed as a treatment modality for addiction in the United States in the past 20 years (Rosenthal, 1989). The psychodynamic features of the therapeutic community appear to have an impact on character disorder by encouraging and supporting social learning and relearning.

Therapeutic Issues—Individual

Therapy with substance abusers focuses on the drug-taking behavior as a monitor in the recovery process but goes beyond just weekly check-ins. Therapy is a three-tier process. The first tier is educational. Through the therapeutic process, the individual may become educated about his or her addiction. Information dissemination about the life cycle of addiction and the recovery process is necessary. The second tier of therapy is skill building. Here the individual learns skills that have been deficient or replaces old, dysfunctional skills with new skills. Communication skills, assertiveness skills, time management skills, stress management skills, and parenting skills are just some features of the skill-building process. The third tier of therapy is insight-oriented. As discussed earlier, the pathogenesis of addiction often occurs in the early developmental stages of life. Thus, for treatment to be effective it must deal with past issues in the abuser's life. Kohut (1977) sees addiction as a disorder that is a reflection of a fundamental weakness in the individual's self. Several proponents of Kohut's idea have postulated a theory that drug addiction may be more of a deficit in psychic structure than a physical or biochemical abnormality (Krystal, 1982; Wurmser, 1978, 1987).

One research study looked at the self-concept and self-esteem issues of substance abusers. Douglas and Nutter (1986) found that therapy provided an avenue for change of the self-image toward a more balanced self-perception. An improved self-image held true particularly in the male population. The authors speculated that male substance abusers may experience more role conflict than addicted women.

Many psychosocial factors support the drug-using behavior. Family of origin, fear of failure, intimacy issues, grief issues, and suicidal and self-destructive behavior patterns all may be addressed in the individual therapy. Again, an individual needs to maintain some period of drug-free behavior to make use of insight-oriented therapy.

One theme that plays a role in drug therapy is locus of control. Individuals with substance abuse problems frequently exhibit an external locus of control. They blame their problems and behavior on everyone else and see themselves as victims of circumstance. "If the parole officer would just get off my back," or, "If the police had not stopped me for that sixth breathalyzer test," or, "If the boss had not arrived in the middle of that fight," or, "If my wife would stop being so demanding," the problems would disappear. Individuals with an external locus of control feel little ownership of their behavior. They blame others for the problems that have befallen them. In contrast, individuals with an internal locus of control feel a sense of control over their lives and their circumstances. They learn from the consequences of their behavior. They recognize that they are able to make choices and that the choices they make affect what happens to them. They feel a sense of control. When they make an error, they can accept and acknowledge their mistake, learn from it, and move on. Locus of control becomes an appropriate therapeutic issue.

Studies have shown that substance abusers take steps to dull their emotions, have a fear of feeling, and share common fears that lead them to protect themselves. Pacing factors may be needed for the focusing of emotions during the recovery process. Learning effective ways to express emotions may be a new experience. Tools that may be helpful in the emotive area are the naming of shades of feelings and learning a feeling vocabulary, and separating thoughts from emotions. Stress management skills and assertiveness training skills may also be helpful (Lacks & Leonard, 1986).

Guilt is a theme that is also addressed in the recovery process. As an individual recovers and takes responsibility for behaviors, the wrongs and hurts that were part of the drug addiction come to the fore. Feelings of guilt are one reason addicts give for continued drug use. When they are high, they do not have to feel guilty. Forgiveness themes, including forgiveness of self as well as of others, play a role in the resolution of guilt.

Individual approaches have developed some interesting formulations about the dynamics of drug abuse, but individual therapy has by and large demonstrated little efficacy in getting people free of their addiction. Individual approaches to therapy are strengthened when accompanied by other treatment modalities including family and group therapy.

Conclusion

The role of recovery is multi-faceted. The practitioner has many programs and options to consider in planning appropriate treatment. Outcome studies may help in assessing what form of treatment provides the most effective results with what population.

One study of gender differences found that the overall probability of abstinence did not differ between the two sexes. However, women entering treatment maintained a significantly higher abstinence level (Brunswick & Messeri, 1986). Kosten, Rounsaville, and Kleber (1986) studied 268 addicts to assess effectiveness of treatment. They concluded that longer treatment programs, time-wise, were associated with a greater percentage of long-term abstinence. The authors suggested that time in treatment increased abstinence by improving subjects' ability to cope with depression and life crisis.

Overall, the self-help, abstinence-oriented recovery model is the treatment of choice for motivated individuals in an early stage of drug abuse. The residential, therapeutic community treatment approach is appropriate for individuals with antisocial behavior (Klein & Miller, 1986).

Understanding and treating addiction would be simplified if the causes of addiction could be isolated. Study of effectiveness of treatment approaches has only preliminary research support. Isolating causes of addiction is extremely difficult and may prove to be impossible. Multiple causation should be accepted as a reality by the addiction-treatment community. A unified treatment approach is not embraced, nor should it be, with the present knowledge in the addiction-treatment field.

This paper acknowledges the growing body of knowledge about a biochemical role in the origin of addiction and has chosen to focus primarily on the intra- and interpersonal dynamics of addiction. Family interaction processes contribute to the maintenance of substance abuse. The intrapsychic phenomena that contribute to increased risk factors of substance abuse may also be influenced by early experiences in the family of origin.

An effective treatment model should encompass multiple theories and a diversity of programmatic and treatment strategies in order to develop individualized treatment plans. Treatment should be client-centered rather than program-centered. Researchers and therapists eager to add to the body of knowledge must work together as they seek new directions and understand that conclusions drawn at any given time may not endure. An openness to new information and a desire to provide effective treatment to individuals and families suffering from addiction are ongoing challenges.

References

Blum, R. H. (1972). *The dream sellers*. San Francisco: Jossey-Bass.

Brunswick, A. F., & Messeri, P. A. (1986). Pathways of heroin abstinence: A longitudinal study of urban Black youth. *Advances in Alcohol and Substance Abuse, 5,* 111–135.

Cox, W. M. (1979). The alcoholic personality: A review of the evidence. In B. Maher (Ed.), *Progress in Experimental Personality Research* (Vol. 9). New York: Academic Press.

Craig, R. J. (1979). Personality characteristics of heroin addicts: A review of the empirical literature with critique. Part I. *International Journal of Addictions, 14,* 513–532.

Dackis, C. A., & Gold, M. S. (1986). More on self-mediation and drug abuse. *American Journal of Psychiatry, 143,* 1309–1310.

Douglas, J., & Nutter, C. P. (1986). Treatment-related change in sex roles of addicted men and women. *Journal of Studies on Alcohol, 47,* 201–206.

Galanter, M. (1986). Social network therapy for cocaine dependence. *Advances in Alcohol and Substance Abuse, 6,* 159–175.

Goodwin, D. W. (1979). Alcoholism and heredity. *Archives of General Psychiatry, 36,* 57–61.

Grande, T. (1984). Associations among alcoholism, drug abuse, and antisocial personality: A review of literature. *Psychological Reports, 55,* 455–474.

Heath, A. W., & Atkinson, B. J. (1988). Systematic treatment of substance abuse: A graduate course. *Journal of Marital and Family Therapy, 14,* 411–418.

Inman, D. J., Bascue, L. O., & Skoloda, T. (1985). Identification of borderline personality disorders among substance abuse inpatients. *Journal of Substance Abuse Treatment, 2,* 229–232.

Khantzian, E. J., & Treece, C. (1985). DSM-III. Psychiatric diagnosis of narcotic addicts: Recent findings. *Archives of General Psychiatry, 42,* 1067–1071.

Klein, J. M., & Miller, S. I. (1986). Three approaches to the treatment of drug addiction. *Hospital and Community Psychiatry, 11,* 1083–1085.

Kohut, H. (1977). Preface in psychodynamics of drug dependence. *National Institute on Drug Abuse Research Monograph 12.* Washington DC: United States Department of Health Education and Welfare.

Kosten, T. R., Gawin, F. H., Rounsaville, B. J., & Kleber, H. D. (1986) Abuse of cocaine with opiates: Psychological aspects of treatment. *National Institute on Drug Abuse Research Monograph Series, 67,* 278–282.

Kosten, T. R., & Rounsaville, B. J. (1986). Psychopathology in opioid addicts. *Psychiatric Clinics of North America, 9*(3), 515–532.

Kosten, T. R., Rounsaville, B. J., & Kleber, H. D. (1986). A 2.5 year follow-up of depression, life crises, and treatment effects on abstinence among opioid addicts. *Archives of General Psychiatry, 43,* 733–738.

Krystal, H. (1982). Character disorders: Characterological specificity and the alcoholic. In M. E. Pattison and E. Kaufman (Eds.), *Encyclopedia of Alcoholism.* New York: Gardner.

Lacks, H. E., & Leonard, C. A. (1986). Fear of feeling: Addressing the emotional process during recovery. *Alcoholism Treatment Quarterly, 3,* 69–80.

Lettieri, D. J., Sayers, M., & Pearson, H. W. (1980). *Theories on drug abuse.* NIDA

Research Monograph #30. Washington, DC: US Government Printing Office.

Lewis, C. E., Cloninger, C. R., & Pais, J. (1983). Alcoholism, antisocial personality and drug use in a criminal population. *Alcohol & Alcoholism, 18,* 53–60.

Madanes, C., Dukes, J., & Harbin, H. (1980). Family ties of heroin addicts. *Archives of General Psychiatry, 37,* 889–894.

Miller, N. S., Dackis, C. A., & Gold, M. S. (1987). The relationship of addiction, tolerance and dependence to alcohol and drugs: A neurochemical approach. *Journal of Substance Abuse Treatment, 4,* 197–207.

Mirin, S. M., & Weiss, R. D. (1986). Affective illness in substance abusers. *Psychiatric Clinics of North America, 9,* 503–514.

Penk, W. E. (1981). Assessing the substance abuser with the MMPI. In J. Butcher, G. Dahlstrom, M. Gynther, & W. Schofield (Eds.), *Clinical Notes On the MMPI Number 7.* Minneapolis: University of Minnesota; National Computer Systems.

Rosenthal, M. S. (1989). The therapeutic community: Exploring the boundaries. *British Journal of Addiction, 84*(2), 141–150.

Stanton, M. D. (1979a). Drugs and the family: A review of the recent literature. *Marriage and Family Review, 2,* 1–10.

Stanton, M. D. (1979b). Family treatment approaches to drug abuse problems: A review. *Family Process, 18,* 251–280.

Stanton, M. D. (1988). Coursework and self-study in the family treatment of alcohol and drug abuse: Expanding Health and Atkinson's curriculum. *Journal of Marital and Family Therapy, 14,* 419–427.

Stanton, M. D., Todd, T. C., et al. (1982). *The family therapy of drug abuse and addiction.* New York: Guilford.

Stanton, M. D., Todd, T. C., Heard, D. B., Kirschener, S., Kleiman, J. I., Mowatt, D. T., Riley, P., Scott, S. M., & Van Deusen, J. M. (1978). Heroin addiction as a family phenomenon: A new conceptual model. *American Journal of Drug and Alcohol Abuse, 5,* 125–150.

Wegscheider, S. (1981). *Another chance: Hope and health for the alcoholic family.* Palo Alto, CA: Science and Behavior Books.

Wender, P. H., & Klein, D. F. (1981, February). The promise of biological psychiatry. *Psychology Today,* 25–41.

Wurmser, L. (1978). *The hidden dimension: Psychodynamics in compulsive drug use.* New York: Jason Aronson.

Wurmser, L. (1987). Flight from consciousness: Experiences with the psychoanalytic treatment of compulsive drug abusers. *Journal of Substance Abuse Treatment, 4,* 157–168.

6

Tobacco Addiction

DANIEL A. SERRITELLA, Ph. D.

THIS CHAPTER WILL FOCUS on the psychologically addictive effects of smoking and review the effectiveness of treatment programs available.

As late as 1962 the World Health Organization's Expert Committee on Drug Dependence stated definitively that nicotine was not physically addictive. Cigarettes' nonaddictive quality was echoed by the first Surgeon General's Report on Smoking and Health in 1964.

In 1980 the American Psychiatric Association finally classified tobacco use as an addiction under its substance use disorders (American Psychiatric Association, 1987). For decades the social acceptance of cigarette smoking prevented recognition of the fact that most regular smokers are addicted to nicotine. For millions of Americans (26 percent of all adults), smoking remains a powerful addictive force in their lives. Over 300,000 Americans die each year from cigarette-related smoking illnesses such as heart disease, cancer, and lung diseases (Schwartz, 1987).

The Surgeon General's 1988 Report clearly accepts tobacco as an addiction. The Surgeon General stated unequivocally that "cigarettes and other forms of tobacco are addicting in the same sense as are other drugs such as heroin and cocaine" (Koop, 1988, p. 4). The report states that of all the addictions, tobacco is by far the largest killer; alcohol accounts for 125,000 deaths annually; heroin, 4,000; cocaine, 2,000; and cigarettes, 300,000. Six hundred billion cigarettes continue to be consumed each year.

Nicotine is a fast-acting stimulant that triggers chemicals in the brain that stimulate pleasurable sensations that are inevitably reinforcing. Tobacco smoking is the most important cause of morbidity in the world.

More than 4,000 chemicals have been identified in cigarette smoking; little is known about most of these (Schwartz, 1987). The three major components of cigarette smoke are tar, carbon monoxide, and nicotine. Nicotine appears to most researchers to be the drug responsible for the pharmacologically addictive nature of smoking. Smokers subconsciously attempt to achieve a blood-nicotine level that falls between upper and lower regulatory boundaries, with the upper defined by dizziness, sweating, nausea and ill health, and the lower defined by characteristic withdrawal symptoms.

Both pharmacological and psychosocial factors in nicotine addiction have powerful but varying effects on and within the individual. For example, the pharmacological effects of nicotine take place at the upper and lower biological limits of the individual. When too little nicotine is consumed, withdrawal effects take place. When too much nicotine is consumed, toxic effects occur.

Psychological or psychosocial factors also occur within this range. This area has been termed the area of indifference, in which factors such as self-control, the presence of others smoking, and stressful situations govern smoking behavior. Psychological and pharmacological addictions were only moderately correlated and had different relationships with age, in a study by Bosse, Garvey, and Glynn (1980). Their work supports the notion of two levels of addiction, one psychological and the other pharmacological. Older smokers exhibited a higher score on psychological addiction but did not consume more tar or nicotine than younger smokers. On five out of six factors for measuring the strength of motives for smoking, significant longitudinal increases on three factors suggested that older smokers are more psychologically involved or get more out of smoking than younger smokers (Bosse, Garvey & Glynn, 1980).

Tobacco as an Addiction

The World Health Organization's Expert Committee (Expert Committee, 1950) initially defined addiction as a state of periodic and chronic intoxication that is detrimental to the individual and to society, produced by the repeated consumption of a drug. The term "addiction" became so widely used that it became a misnomer. In 1965 the World Health Organization replaced "addiction" with the currently used term "dependence," which was preferred because few individuals apparently succumb entirely to the pharmacologic properties of drugs. An addiction has come to be defined as a strong dependence, both physiologically and emotionally, on some substance. Intake of the drug gradually increases to a level where the taking of the drug becomes compulsive. Finally, the presence of this substance in the individual's body becomes necessary in order to maintain functioning. When the drug is curtailed or stopped, physiological distortion occurs in addition to other withdrawal symptoms.

For decades scientists and smokers suggested that smoking and nicotine were addictive. However, rigorous investigation did not begin until the 1970s (Edwards, 1986). Since that time there have been attempts to emphasize the commonalities of addictions. The National Institute of Drug Abuse (1979) found theoretical and functional similarities between smokers, drug abusers, alcoholics, and overeaters. To strengthen this view, relapse rates were studied across addictions. Identical patterns of relapse were found among heroin addicts, smokers, and alcoholics (Marlatt & Gordon, 1985; Niaura, Rohsenow, Binkoff, Monti, Pedraza & Abrams, 1988).

The process of smoking moves from a single incident to a continuous process within a short period. The typical pattern of nicotine use is not daily, like other drugs, but several times hourly. Dependence on cigarette smoking is easier to develop, since its administration is continuous, whereas other drugs are used on a more episodic basis. The effects of nicotine pass through the body quickly. Within 30 minutes after smoking a cigarette, the nicotine has made its rounds of the brain, liver, kidneys, and stomach. Tobacco is addictive by every important measure of addiction: psychoactive effects, habitual use leading to dependence and compulsive abuse, physiological and psychological distress upon discontinuance, and a tendency to recidivism (Ravenholt & Pollin, 1983). This conclusion was echoed by Henningfield (1984), whose research supported the notion that nicotine addiction shares commonalities, including self-regulation and intake, with other addictions. Henningfield contended that tobacco use shares many factors with previously studied forms of drug abuse. This linkage includes historical regulatory, acquisition, maintenance, social relapse, tolerance, dependence, and deprivation factors (Henningfield, 1984).

Tobacco withdrawal is the result of a decrease in tobacco use and is characterized by a craving for nicotine, irritability, anxiety, difficulty concentrating, restlessness, headaches, drowsiness, and gastrointestinal disturbances (American Psychiatric Association, 1987).

Most experts today agree that cigarette smoking is as addictive as drugs or alcohol. For many it is nearly impossible to quit.

Smoking Cessation

The Surgeon General's 1988 report (Koop, 1988) stated that 75 to 85 percent of the nation's 51 million smokers would like to quit but are unable to do so. Over one-third of all Americans who continue to smoke are searching for ways to quit (Gorman, 1988). Forty-three million Americans have quit, the majority on their own. Many ex-smokers experienced several failed attempts before they succeeded in quitting. The key for many appears to be the desire to quit, accompanied by the emergence of, or heightened awareness of, negative health consequences, plus support from family, friends, and co-workers.

Once an individual decides to quit smoking, an often-asked question is, "What is the best way to stop?" Unfortunately, the answers are many and confusing. As with many addictions, ingredients are present for unscrupulous and unethical practitioners to pander their theories and methods. As discussed briefly, there are many possible reasons for the pathogenesis of smoking. Logically then, there are many methods that may be helpful in the cessation of smoking. Many smokers use programs and forms of psychotherapy to attempt to stop smoking. Below is an attempt to outline several different programs, each with discussion of which type of person would benefit most from its efforts.

Nicotine Chewing Gum

Nicotine is viewed by many scholars as the key element in smoking addiction. Ferno, Lichtneçkert, and Lundgren (1973) developed Nicorette, a prescription gum that is a substitute for nicotine. Ferno's (1980) rationale for developing nicotine gum was to provide an alternate source of nicotine to persons wishing to stop smoking, so they would only have to combat their psychological dependence.

Nicorette is currently produced by Lakeside Pharmaceuticals, a division of Merril Dow. Each Nicorette dose contains 2 mg of nicotine that is absorbed through the buccal mucosa when chewed. Nicorette is bound to an ion exchange resin that ensures that the nicotine does not become released in significant quantity if swallowed to cause overdose. Nicotine has effects on the sympathetic ganglia and on the chemoreceptors of the aorta and carotid bodies. Its overall effect on the cardiovascular system includes an increased heart rate, peripheral vasoconstriction, and elevated blood pressure. Nicorette has been shown to produce similar effects on the cardiovascular system.

One of the major advantages of Nicorette is its ability to prevent withdrawal symptoms. Russell, Sutton, Feyerabend, Cole, and Saloojee (1977) looked at blood levels of subjects using Nicorette or cigarettes and concluded that Nicorette produced sufficient levels of nicotine to prevent withdrawal. It appears that nicotine replacement through the use of Nicorette can reduce the unpleasant effects of withdrawal such as irritability and anxiety. Another benefit is that the gum may actually suppress weight gain (Gross, Stitzer & Maldonado, 1989).

The manufacturer stipulates that Nicorette is only a safe adjunct to smoking cessation and thus should be used in conjunction with other treatment methods. The possibility exists for a transfer of addiction to Nicorette, so three months appears to be the optimal time of usage. A gradual withdrawal after this period facilitates a lower relapse rate.

Nicorette has been investigated widely both in the United States and abroad. The investigations concentrated on the use of Nicorette as the primary treatment versus Nicorette with a behavior modification/cessation program. For a high number of individuals who chew the gum and receive therapy, counseling, or some type of support, the success rate appears to be good. Some smokers who are heavily addicted may either use the gum for short periods of time without counseling or use the gum and continue to smoke. In either case the success rate of such an individual is extremely low. Findings appear to indicate that the common use of Nicorette by the family physician (i.e., the practice of giving the patient a three-month prescription for Nicorette without offering counseling or support) is ineffective, with success rates at 10 percent and under (Fee & Stewart, 1982). In contrast, Fagerstrom (1982) was able to demonstrate a near-50 percent success rate with the use of nicotine chewing gum and psychotherapy.

Nicorette appears to be an effective tool to help with the cessation of smoking for persons who are so motivated. Methodological concerns, such as who can most benefit from Nicorette, long-term effectiveness rates, and follow-up studies, are as yet unanswered. However, the ongoing interest in research on the effectiveness of Nicorette is encouraging. Preliminary data suggest that Nicorette is most effective with smokers who are less addicted to nicotine and probably more psychologically addicted (Hughes & Miller, 1984).

The use of Nicorette raises ethical and treatment issues that are beyond the scope of this chapter. However, one area that must be addressed is the need for physicians to be wary of prescribing Nicorette without first assessing the individual's level of addiction and motivation and offering the individual avenues of seeking therapy, counseling, or support. Nicorette is an effective smoking cessation method only when coupled with counseling. Only then does it appear to give a motivated individual an even chance to break his or her addictive cycle.

Behavior Modification Methods

Many have used the analogy of behavior therapy as being like a river with different tributaries, all equally important in feeding the larger body of knowledge. Behavior therapy is probably the single largest treatment modality used to treat nicotine addiction and perhaps one of its least understood. When talking about the use of behavior therapy, one needs to be very specific about the type. Contemporary behavior therapy has fallen into three major camps: aversive theory, learning theory, and self-management built on a mixture of the preceding two. The predominant approach used today for treating nicotine addiction is aversive.

Aversive techniques used to treat nicotine addiction have varied widely. Some techniques have included electric shock, and others use bad tastes, smoke, noise, or smells. Perhaps the most recognized technique is known as rapid smoking. This technique has a person chain-smoke rapidly while hot, stale, smoky air is blown into his or her face. Some impressive results utilizing this technique were presented by Lichtenstein, Harris, Birchler, Wahl, and Schmahl (1973).

A comprehensive review of rapid smoking studies was presented by Danaher (1977). He looked at twelve different studies and concluded that the rapid smoking technique provided effective results. However, the need for a caring relationship with a therapist was the key ingredient for success. Often rapid smoking techniques are coupled with other treatment techniques that confound the results of rapid smoking alone (Schwartz, 1987).

A related aversion method often used is satiation. In satiation the individual gradually increases the rate of his or her smoking. For example, if the person smokes one pack per day he or she may be asked to smoke two packs per day. Schwartz (1987), based on his comprehensive survey, reported that rates of quitting have averaged between 6 and 67 percent. The median quit rate after one year was 25 percent. According to Schwartz, after one year there have been quit rates above 50 percent. However, these rates combined rapid smoking with other techniques such as training in self-control or relaxation.

Another approach has been that of stimulus control, which involves the attempt to alter the stimulus situation in which the addiction occurs. Although there are a number of strategies of stimulus control, there are two major approaches. The first is to increase the interval at which the individual responds to the stimulus. One way this outcome can be achieved is to have the individual agree to smoke only every time a watch strikes the hour. Gradually the time between cigarettes is lengthened until the smoking is phased out. A second approach has been hierarchical reduction, in which participants monitor their own smoking behavior to determine the situations in which smoking is likely to occur. A hierarchy is developed for the individual, specifying where stopping smoking would be the hardest to give up down to where it would be the easiest. Smoking behavior is then eliminated in a progressive fashion from the easiest situations to the hardest.

Evaluation of the effectiveness of behavioral programs is difficult for several reasons. The first is the wide variety of methods used, and often more than one method is used at the same time. Thus, the findings on behavioral programs have usually been mixed. Differences between behavioral programs are equally difficult to discriminate. Glasgow, Morray, and Lichtenstein (1989) found no differences between two types of behavioral-cognitive smoking programs. Schwartz (1987) presented a detailed follow-up report on quit rates from 1974 to 1986. The quit rate for behavioral methods is between 8 and 39 percent. Some findings suggested that aversive techniques produce only short-term change because they do not provide alternative responses for the individual to use in long-term management.

The more effective behavioral programs are those in which multiple treatment approaches are used. Hall (1980), described a model that included both behavioral and cognitive skills in the treatment of nicotine addiction. Her behavioral methods were coupled with relaxation training, cognitive training on the costs and benefits of smoking, and relapse training through role play. Behavioral programs are intensive and long-term (the average is 10 to 14 sessions). It appears that the use of "pure" behavioral methods would be most beneficial to long-term smokers who are having trouble breaking the smoking habit. However, smoking, as discussed, is a complex phenomenon that requires long-term change. Thus, unless behavioral methods are coupled with methods that also address cognitive, emotional, and maintenance issues, they will probably fail.

Transdermal Nicotine Patch

In 1988 the Elan Corporation of Ireland unveiled its plans for licensing a major American multinational pharmaceutical corporation to begin producing a transdermal nicotine patch that had been under development. The Elan Corporation has been a pioneer in the development of transdermal technology. The transdermal nicotine patch is designed to be used once a day as a temporary aid to the smoker trying to quit. The Elan Corporation stressed that the patch should be used in conjunction with behavioral modification programs under the supervision of a physician.

The theory behind the patch is that through smoking a cigarette a smoker receives an initial burst of nicotine into his or her bloodstream, after which nicotine level rapidly declines. The urge to smoke increases as the nicotine level drops below a given level in the system. This level varies with each individual. To overcome this drop in nicotine, which triggers smoking, a transdermal nicotine patch is affixed to the skin like a bandage. Nicotine, in the patch, is then constantly absorbed through the skin directly into the bloodstream to maintain regular and constant nicotine levels in the blood. The need to smoke a cigarette is theoretically eliminated or at least reduced. The program recommends successive lowering of the strength of the nicotine patch over a series of weeks or months. The steady decrease gradually reduces the nicotine level in the blood system and thus reduces dependency.

Research on the transdermal nicotine patch continues to develop. Initial corporate studies have shown success rates approaching 50 percent after a six-week, medically supervised program. Additionally, those who were not able to stop smoking showed an overall decrease in cigarettes consumed. Hartman, Jarvik, Murray, and Wilkins (1989) found that moderate smokers (smoking one or two packs per day) substantially decreased their consumption when the patch was worn.

Since development of the transdermal nicotine patch is a commercial venture, research has been closely guarded and not published in major scientific journals. Usually articles are published prior to the release of a product to the market to boost interest and sales. Corporate officials estimate that the patch will receive FDA approval by 1992. It is important to remember that a behavioral program is recommended in conjunction with the patch. This method for smoking cessation is continuing to develop and merits watching.

Hypnosis

Hypnotism was made popular by Franz Mesmer, an Austrian physician, in the late 1700s. Mesmer claimed that magnetic fluids given off by the sun and stars affected peoples' well-being. His mode of treatment included waving of magic wands and giving hypnotic suggestions. In 1784 Mesmer was branded a fraud by a special committee of the Academy of Sciences in Paris, which included Benjamin Franklin, then the American ambassador to France (Buranelli, 1975). Hypnotism continued to flourish in both Europe and America despite the mounting evidence against Mesmer's theories. Hypnotism was studied seriously by Jean Martin Charcot in the late 1800s as an aid to treating nervous diseases. Charcot's students, Sigmund Freud and Alfred Binet, would later use hypnosis in their work. Therapeutic hypnosis is usually of two types, superficial and deep. Superficial hypnosis involves an individual not being asleep, but rather lying still and listening with eyes closed. The individual may feel fatigued and feel a heaviness of limbs but might open his or her eyes if desired. A deep trance is when the individual is unable to remember after awakening what was said during the trance. The effectiveness of hypnosis is as controversial today as it was in the 1700s. However, it has become a popular mode of treatment for everything from weight loss to anxiety reduction to smoking cessation.

Moses (1964) pioneered the technique of using hypnosis as a smoking cessation method. Later Speigel (1970) popularized the method by combining psychotherapy and hypnosis in an attempt to decrease smoking. Speigel felt that hypnosis in and of itself was not enough to help someone quit smoking, but rather that quitting depended on the individual's motivation. Generally, there are five approaches for using hypnosis in smoking cessation: (1) giving the smoker a direct suggestion to change his/her behavior; (2) using hypnosis to alter the individual's perceptions of smoking; (3) using hypnosis as an adjunct to traditional psychotherapy; (4) using hypnosis for aversive imagery as an element in smoking cessation; and (5) teaching the client self-hypnosis to reinforce continuing hypnosis therapy (Simon & Salzberg, 1982).

Hypnosis as a method for smoking cessation is confusing to attempt to delineate, as there are no standardized procedures for a treatment program. Each program reviewed was unique and relied heavily on behavioral methods of imagery, desensitization, aversive techniques, reinforcement, and suggestion. Hypnosis covers such a wide spectrum of techniques and assumptions that it has lost its descriptive value as a therapy (Wadden & Anderton, 1982). In fact, investigators using hypnosis so frequently failed to specify their techniques that the research is often suspect. Results obtained under the guise of hypnosis are usually research in name only.

Schwartz (1987) analyzed over 50 studies that utilized hypnosis as the primary treatment method. Only one third of the studies reviewed used a one-year follow-up. Most of the studies included other techniques such as behavioral methods or counseling, which clouds assessment of the effectiveness of hypnosis alone. Schwartz concluded, as did Wadden and Anderton, that although hypnosis may be effective with addictive behavior, therapeutic success can usually be credited to nonhypnotic factors. Hypnotism appears to have some limited clinical value in the cessation of smoking only when coupled with other forms of treatment.

Educational Methods

For several years educational approaches have been used in a variety of health fields as an accepted treatment approach, and the smoking field is no different. Smoking cessation programs are offered by a variety of organizations in the United States including the American Cancer Society, American Lung Association, Seventh Day Adventist Church, schools, colleges, hospitals, private businesses, social service agencies, and federal, state and local governments. Each program is unique, but many of these programs utilize behavioral concepts and are intended to impart information and leave it up to the individual to decide if he or she wants to change. Teaching methods include lectures, films, pamphlets, instructions on how to quit, and the answering of questions and self-tests. Sessions are usually didactic and can last from a one-hour presentation to a three-month commitment.

In 1960 the Seventh Day Adventist Church began offering its five-day plan. To date over 14 million smokers have entered the program worldwide. The program consists of five consecutive daily two-hour sessions with several follow-up sessions. The plan includes instructions on diet modification, exercise, vitamins, prayer, and development of a buddy system. Presenters give lectures that relate to the medical, spiritual, and psychological aspects of life. The program was revised in 1985 and renamed the Breathe-Free Plan to Stop Smoking (General Conference of Seventh Day Adventists 1985). The revised program places more emphasis on motivation and self-concept.

Many other educational programs are available to the public through profit and nonprofit sources. The American Cancer Society offers a standardized program nationwide called Fresh Start. The program consists of four one-hour sessions that provide educational materials and give practical information on understanding why people smoke, withdrawal symptoms and ways to counteract them, handling obstacles such as weight gain, and new ways of dealing with stress.

Educational media campaigns have been initiated by the U.S. Government during the last two decades to combat smoking. Media campaigns are primarily of two types. The first seeks mainly to impart information on the health hazards of smoking and where to go to seek further information or help. These public service announcements are intended to help the public develop negative attitudes about smoking and motivate some to seek help in quitting. The second generation of media announcements consists of what many term "psychological inoculation". Youngsters are warned in advance that they may encounter pressure to try smoking. The announcements warn youngsters of the dangers and assure them that there are many healthy activities that can take the place of smoking. "Psychological inoculation" involves teaching not only the dangers of smoking but also alternative ways to feeling important and independent.

Educational programs to stop smoking appear to be proliferating in our society. Evaluation of the effectiveness of specific educational programs is available and the results look promising. Overall effectiveness rates for media educational programs appear to be favorable. Many programs are offered in the workplace and have had good success (Cummings, Hellmann & Emont, 1988). Media attention to smoking perhaps has as its greatest asset the ability to motivate people to think about quitting smoking rather than actually helping them to quit. Educational programs appear to be more effective when a number are linked together. For example, a media program can generate interest in quitting smoking, but citizens must also be given information about where they can participate in intensive instructional and motivational programs such as the Breathe-Free Plan to Stop Smoking or the Fresh Start program. The bottom line is that smokers must receive more help than just the sharing of information to cope with their addiction. Educational programs appear to work best with smokers who are motivated to quit but need the help and support of a peer group.

Relapse

Perhaps no subject is of greater importance, when talking about the treatment of an addiction, than relapse. A lapse, where the individual slips or makes a mistake, is a fairly common occurrence in the treatment of addictions. A lapse can lead to a relapse, defined as the recurrence of symptoms of a disease after an initial period of improvement. Relapse rates for the various addictions have been estimated as high as 90 percent, which points to the need for our attention to the problem.

The reader is referred to the works of Marlatt and Gordon (1980, 1985). Their model indicates that an individual's cognitive-affective reaction to a lapse is the key to whether the lapse will escalate into a full-blown relapse. Their model, which they term the abstinence violation effect (AVE), focuses on the individual's causal attribution of responsibility for the slip and his or her affective reaction to the attribution (Curry, Marlatt & Gordon, 1987). The intensity of the AVE appears to increase as the cause of the lapse is attributed by the individual to internal, stable, and global factors that are largely perceived as uncontrollable, such as a lack of willpower. The emotional reactions of guilt and self-blame associated with these attributions may hamper recovery from a slip (Curry, Marlatt & Gordon, 1987). The intensity of the AVE is decreased if the cause for the slip is attributed to external, unstable, and controllable causes, such as a failure to use effective coping skills.

Success in avoiding relapse appears to lie in the reasons the individual ascribes to his lapse. The individual must take responsibility for his or her own behavior. Thus, it would not be appropriate to try and blame relapse on external events. However, Curry, Marlatt, and Gordon warn against blaming relapse on uncontrollable characterological deficits such as poor willpower. Rather, an appropriate goal might be to help individuals to attribute personal responsibility to controllable behavioral factors such as a lack of coping skills that can be learned and practiced.

Other researchers feel that relapse occurs primarily in social occasions. Lichtenstein and Mermelstein (1984) stated that their findings indicate that over 80 percent of relapses occur with other people present, and that over 60 percent of the other individuals present were smoking. Social situations apparently raise many feelings in individuals, ranging from feeling good to feeling anxiety, which often precipitates a slip. Smoking, eating, and drinking occur in a high percentage of social situations. A slip, in most cases, leads to total relapse (Marlatt & Gordon, 1980). The situations in which smokers tend to relapse have been described by several authors. Smokers tend to relapse: (1) in social situations where the drinking of alcohol is also present; (2) at home, usually after a meal; (3) at work when unexpected or anxiety-producing situations occur; or (4) at home when the individual is alone and feeling depressed, and unexpected or anxiety-producing situations occur (Shiffman, Read & Jarvik, 1985; Shiffman, 1986).

It appears that the more coping strategies an individual can add to his armory, the more likely that he or she will be able to handle stressful situations without relapsing. Individuals who relapsed employed fewer coping skills and strategies than those who were able to abstain from smoking (Ashenberg, 1983). Likewise, individuals who learned a number of coping strategies were successful in combatting lapses (Stevens & Hollis, 1989).

Brown and Lichtenstein (1980) devised a relapse-prevention program that is based on five components. The first is to help the individual recognize high-risk situations. Second is the teaching and rehearsal of coping strategies. Third is avoidance of the abstinence violation effect (AVE) (Marlatt & Gordon, 1980, 1985). Fourth is balancing of the individual's lifestyle; this could include diet and exercise. The final component is a system for self-rewards. As Curry, Marlatt, and Gordon (1987) have discussed, clinicians should develop a model that addresses cognitive restructuring and role playing for coping with initial relapses. Self-efficacy is a valuable and useful construct to explore for successful changes in addictive behaviors including smoking (DiClemente, 1986). Self-efficacy is a common cognitive mechanism that mediates behavior change. If properly assessed, self-efficacy expectations can assist in the prediction of relapse and in designing programs for relapse prevention.

Another major fear that has been linked to the prospect of relapse is weight gain (Hall, McGee, Tunstall & Duffy, 1989). Two new discoveries have been made as to why smokers have a tendency to gain weight after they give up smoking (Nesmith, 1988). One study has shown that smokers have elevated levels of a mood-controlling brain chemical called serotonin, which induces relaxation and a feeling of well-being. High serotonin levels can be caused by either nicotine or the consumption of carbohydrates. Researchers now suggest that smokers, after depriving themselves of nicotine, return to carbohydrates as a form of self-medication against anxiety and they gain weight as a result. Another study suggested that former smokers' heightened desires for sweets may be related to the nicotine's depression of the level of insulin, the substance that allows the body to utilize sugar. When the effects of nicotine wear off, the body's insulin levels rebound, creating a craving for sweets (Nesmith, 1988). In effect, food consumption may be considered as self-administration of a psychopharmacologic agent to regulate the effect of nicotine withdrawal (Nesmith, 1988).

Clearly the area of relapse and long-term maintenance is a frontier for continued exploration. The major causes of relapse appear to be anxiety, stress, frustration, depression, low self-esteem, and fear of weight gain. Breaking the smoking habit is only the first step in a lifetime struggle for many smokers.

Conclusions

Cigarette smoking has been clearly established as addictive. Cigarette smokers know the true meaning of the word "hooked" (Gorman, 1988).

The effects of nicotine reach the brain within seven seconds, twice as fast as intravenous heroin. Within minutes, nicotine levels in the blood spiral. Only recently have all of the physiological effects become apparent. Nicotine in the brain triggers arousal and creates increased alertness, heart rates, and blood pressure. Concurrently, nicotine is known to relax muscles and trigger the release of endorphins, natural opiates produced by the body to reduce stress. Nicotine is also known to reduce circulation to the extremities and to suppress appetite for carbohydrates.

The long-term effects of cigarette smoking are devastating. The constant, and consequently reinforcing, use of cigarettes quickly leads from habit to addiction. Smoking is a powerful addiction because it is self-administered, with 300 to 500 puffs or short bursts of nicotine per day. Many individuals use cigarettes to control their moods and performance.

Science is only now looking at the two contradictory moods, alertness and relaxation, that cigarettes produce. Cigarette smoking is a very seductive addiction, in that its effects on the body are not readily apparent. Only after 15 to 20 years do the consequences of cigarettes to the heart, lungs, and respiratory system begin to emerge. The number of Caucasian men who smoke has been steadily declining during the past two decades, and their incidence of lung cancer has also been steadily declining. Recent surveys reveal that for all women and black males, consumption of cigarettes is only now slowing, according to the National Cancer Institute. For all women, mortality from lung cancer is expected to top that from breast cancer this year. Concurrently, black men have a much higher annual rate of lung cancer than their white male counterparts. An appreciable decrease in lung cancer rates among black males and all women is still 15 to 20 years away.

Today many Americans are seeking help to end their smoking addiction by a variety of clinics or programs. Most of the cessation methods and programs described above had about the same success rate. The key to success lies in the amount of face-to-face encouragement smokers get while quitting (Gorman, 1988) and in their motivation to quit (Marlatt, Curry & Gordon, 1988).

Nicotine addiction can be cured through several factors. The first is the individual's resolve to break the addictive cycle by quitting. Second is the learning, practicing, and internalizing of a repertoire of coping skills. Third is the short-term and long-term support of family, friends, and co-workers. Fourth is learning techniques and methods to deal with lapses and relapses, and last is the commitment to long-term change.

References

American Psychiatric Association. (1987). *Diagnostic and statistical manual of mental disorders* (3rd ed., revised). Washington, DC: Author.

Bosse, R., Garvey, A., & Glynn, R. (1980). Age and addiction to smoking. *Addictive Behaviors, 5,* 341–351.

Brown, R. A., & Lichtenstein, E. (1980). *Effects of a cognitive-behavioral relapse prevention program for smokers.* Paper presented at the 88th Annual Convention of the American Psychological Association, Montreal.

Buranelli, V. (1975). *The Wizard from Vienna: Franz Anton Mesmer.* New York: Coward.

Cummings, K., Hellmann, R., & Emont, S. (1988). Correlates of participation in a worksite stop-smoking contest. *Journal of Behavioral Medicine, 11*(3), 267–277.

Curry, S., Marlatt, A., & Gordon, J. R. (1987). Abstinence violation effect: Validation of an attributional construct with smoking cessation. *Journal of Consulting and Clinical Psychology, 55,* 145–149.

Danaher, B. G. (1977). Research on rapid smoking: Interim summary and recommendations. *Addictive Behavior, 2,* 151–166.

DiClemente, C. C. (1986). Self-efficacy and the addictive behaviors. *Journal of Social and Clinical Psychology, 4,* 302–315.

Edwards, D. D. (1986). Nicotine: A drug of choice? *Science News, 129,* 44–45.

Expert Committee on Drugs Liable to Produce Addiction. (1950) *Second report* (Tech. Rep. No. 21). Geneva, Switzerland: World Health Organization.

Fagerstrom, K.-O. (1982). A comparison of psychological and pharmacological treatment in smoking cessation. *Journal of Behavioral Medicine, 5,* 343–351.

Fee, W. M., & Stewart, M. J. (1982). A controlled trial of nicotine chewing gum in a smoking withdrawal clinic. *Practitioner, 226,* 148–152.

Ferno, O. (1980). Nicotine chewing gum as an aid in smoking cessation. *World Smoking and Health, 5,* 24.

Ferno, O., Lichtneckert, S., and Lundgren, C. (1973). A substitute for tobacco smoking. *Psychopharmacologia, 31,* 201–204.

General Conference of Seventh-Day Adventists. (1985). *Introducing the Breathe-Free Plan to Stop Smoking.* Unpublished paper. Washington, DC: Seventh-Day Adventists Health and Temperance Department.

Glasgow, R., Morray, K., & Lichtenstein, E. (1989). Controlled smoking versus abstinence as a treatment goal: The hopes and fears may be unfounded. *Behavior Therapy, 20*(1), 77–91.

Gorman, C. (1988). Why it's so hard to quit smoking. *Time, 131,* 56.

Gross, J., Stitzer, M., & Maldonado, J. (1989). Nicotine replacement: Effects on postcessation weight gain. *Journal of Consulting and Clinical Psychology, 57*(1), 87–92.

Hall, S. M. (1980). Self management and therapeutic maintenance: Theory and research. In P. Karoly and J. Steffan (Eds.), *Improving the long term effects of psychotherapy.* New York: Gardner Press, pp. 263–300.

Hall, S., McGee, R., Tunstall, C., & Duffy, J. (1989). Changes in food intake and activity after quitting smoking. *Journal of Consulting and Clinical Psychology, 57*(1), 81–86.

Hartman, N., Jarvik, M., Murray, N., & Wilkins, E. (1989). Reduction of cigarette smoking by use of a nicotine patch. *Archives of General Psychiatry, 46*(3), 289.

Henningfield, J. E. (1984). Pharmacologic basis and treatment of cigarette smoking. *Journal of Clinical Psychiatry, 45*(12), 24–34.

Hughes, J. R., & Miller, S. A. (1984). Nicotine gum to help stop smoking. *Journal of American Medical Association, 252,* 2855–2858.

Hyde, M. O. (1978). *Addictions: Gambling, smoking, cocaine use, and others.* New York: McGraw-Hill.

Koop, C. E. (1986). The quest for a smoke-free young America by the year 2000. *Journal of School Health, 56,* 8–9.

Koop, C. E. (1988). *The health consequences of smoking: Nicotine addiction.* Washington, DC: U.S. Government Printing Office.

Lichtenstein, E. & Mermelstein, R. J. (1984). Review of approaches to smoking treatment: Behavior modification strategies. In J. D. Matarazzo, S. M. Weiss, J. A. Herd, N. E. Miller, and S. W. Weiss (Eds.), *Behavioral health: A handbook for health enhancement and disease prevention.* New York: Wiley.

Lichtenstein, E., Harris, D. E., Birchler, G. R., Wahl, J. M., & Schmahl, D. P. (1973). Comparison of rapid smoking, warm, smoky air, and attention placebo in the modification of smoking behavior. *Journal of Consulting Clinical Psychology, 40,* 92–98.

Lieberman Research Incorporated. (1981). *A study of the impact of alternative American Cancer Society quit smoking clinics.* New York: American Cancer Society.

Marlatt, A., Curry, S., & Gordon, J. R. (1988). A longitudinal analysis of unaided smoking cessation. *Journal of Consulting and Clinical Psychology, 56*(5), 715–720.

Marlatt, A., & Gordon, J. R. (1980). Determinants of relapse: Implications for the maintenance of behavior change. In P. O. Davidson & S. M. Davidson (Eds.), *Behavioral medicine: Changing health lifestyles.* New York: Brunner/Mazel.

Marlatt, A., & Gordon, J. R. (Eds.). (1985). *Relapse prevention: Maintenance strategies in the treatment of addictive behaviors.* New York: Guilford.

Moses, F. M. (1964). Treating smoking habit by discussion and hypnosis. *Diseases of the Nervous System, 25,* 184–188.

National Institute of Drug Abuse. (1979). *Behavioral analysis and treatment of substance abuse* (Research Monograph No. 25). Washington, DC: U.S. Department of Health, Education and Welfare.

National Institute of Health. (1986). *The health consequences of using smokeless tobacco. A report of the advisory committee to the surgeon general, 1986* (NIH Publication Number 86-2874). Washington, DC: U.S. Department of Health and Human Services.

Nesmith, J. (1988, May 24). Studies examine why ex-smokers put on pounds. *Atlanta Journal.*

Niaura, R., Rohsenow, D., Binkoff, J., Monti, P., Pedraza, M., & Abrams, D. (1988). Relevance of cue reactivity to understanding alcohol and smoking relapse. *Journal of Abnormal Psychology, 97*(2) 133–152.

Ravenholt, R. T., & Pollin, W. (1983). Tobacco addiction and other drug abuse among American youth. In W. F. Forbes, R. C. Frecker, & D. Nostbakken (Eds.), *Proceedings of the Fifth World Conference on Smoking and Health* (Vol. 1). Winnepeg: Canadian Council on Smoking and Health.

Russell, M. A. H., Sutton, S. R., Feyerabend, C., Cole, P. V., & Saloojee, Y. (1977). Nicotine chewing gum as a substitute for smoking. *British Medical Journal, 1,* 1060–1063.

Schwartz, J. L. (1987, April). Review and evaluation of smoking cessation methods: The United States and Canada, 1978–1985. Washington DC: U.S. Department of Health and Human Services.

Shiffman, S. (1986). A cluster analytic classification of relapse episodes. *Addictive Behavior, 11,* 295–317.

Shiffman, S., Read, L., & Jarvik, M. E. (1985). Smoking relapse situations: A preliminary typology. *International Journal of Addiction, 20,* 311–318.

Simon, M. J., & Salzberg, H. C. (1982). Hypnosis and related behavioral approaches in the treatment of addictive behaviors. In M. Hersen, R. M. Eisler, & P. M. Miller (Eds.), *Progress in behavior modification,* (Vol. 13). New York: Academic Press.

Speigel, H. (1970). A single treatment method to stop smoking using ancillary self-hypnosis. *International Journal of Clinical Experimental Hypnosis, 18,* 235–250.

Stevens, V., & Hollis, J. (1989). Preventing smoking relapses, using an individually tailored skills-training technique. *Journal of Consulting and Clinical Psychology, 57*(3), 420–424.

Wadden, T. A., & Anderton, C. H. (1982). The clinical use of hypnosis. *Psychological Bulletin, 9,* 215–243.

_7_

Domestic Violence as Addiction

DANIEL A. SERRITELLA, Ph.D.

THIS CHAPTER IS in many respects a companion to Chapter 9 (Interpersonal and Love Relationships). The most common yet least recognized form of addiction may be interpersonal dependence. Dependence on a violent or destructive relationship has gradually become accepted as an addiction.

In an abusive relationship the need to remain overdependent on a specific person, despite danger or harm, appears to be the addictive ingredient. D.H. Lawrence used the term "egoisme a deux" for two people bonded together not because of love but because of over-entanglement and mutual self-deprivation (Peele & Brodsky, 1975). With such interdependence a couple can move to a closed and isolated position, breaking with family and friends.

Partners in abusive marriages are often people who grew up in abusive homes. As a group, such people suffered early disturbances in parent-child relationships. Instead of having unconditional love and support, these children were often abused, exploited, and neglected. Frequently an "infinite loop" of disappointment and despair was created (Wood, 1987). Those who grew up in abusive homes and children of alcoholics share similar characteristics: (1) great difficulty in separating and individuating from their family; (2) trouble maintaining adequate and stable levels of self-esteem; (3) Trouble making steadfast commitments to work or love; (4) inability to resist alcoholic lifestyle; and (5) likelihood of becoming deeply and painfully involved with partners, causes, and compulsions that endanger their physical, psychological, and spiritual well-being (Wood, 1987).

Many feel that the essence of this addiction is that the individual has never learned who he or she is and if he or she is loved. Thus, he or she continually and habitually seeks love, reassurance, and closeness through another individual.

Personality Dynamics of Men Who Batter

Although there is no single personality profile of the abuser, some general behaviors are common among men who batter their partners; these include: (1) holding traditional views of sex roles and parenting; (2) demonstrating extreme jealousy and possessiveness; (3) denying or minimizing the seriousness of the violence; and (4) refusal of responsibility for the abuse, often blaming it on chemicals, stress, or even the victim.

Joseph (1983) looked at 34 couples to study the personality and interactive styles of abusive and non-abusive couples and found that abusive men tended to be less dominant and less assertive than non-abusive men. Doherty (1983) used the Taylor Manifest Anxiety Scale, the Tennessee Self-Concept Scale, and the Rotter Incomplete Sentence Blank to examine the levels of self-esteem, anxiety, and dependency in men who batter their female partners. His findings indicate that men who batter have lower self-esteem than men who do not. He also found that anxiety, as well as dependency, were higher. Caesar (1985) concluded that male batterers tended to have substance abuse problems and were married to women who also had substance abuse problems. Additionally, batterers were more likely to have witnessed marital violence in their family of origin.

Hamberger and Hastings (1985) examined personality profiles of men who were participating in court-mandated programs. Three major personality factors (schizoid/borderline, narcissistic/antisocial, and passive/dependent) were established. Likewise, Stewart and deBlois (1981) found pathology, such as personality disorders and incidence of alcoholism, more prevalent among batterers than non-batterers.

Batterers as a group seem to lack insight and have low frustration levels and poor control of anger, characteristics that result in violent outbursts. Often they exhibit codependency problems and high levels of self-criticism and guilt feelings. However, many therapists argue that violence in a relationship should not be considered a mental illness. Rather, it should be viewed as a reflection of learned behavioral choices.

Personality Dynamics of Women in Battering Situations

There is increasing research interest in women who are battered. Why a battered woman continues to stay in an abusive situation is generally ascribed to legal problems, sex-role socialization, economic dependency, or unsupportive institutions (Archer, 1989).

Aguirre (1985) surveyed 1,024 residents of shelters for abused women. Her findings confirmed that the wife's economic dependence on her husband almost always ensured that she would return to the relationship. Many women continue to live in abusive marriages and assume the blame for their own victimization. Often these women experience overwhelming guilt, perceiving themselves as failures in their primary roles of mother, wife, and mate. Many battered women develop intense feelings of inferiority, feeling that they do not merit more positive attention. Only when violence spills over to the children will most women mobilize into action.

Battered women stay in abusive relationships due to a complex set of factors that includes a fear for their lives or the lives of their children, financial and emotional dependence, religious beliefs, family pressure, and isolation from support systems (Schrader, 1990). Some stay in the relationship because of low self-esteem and learned helplessness. Increasingly, a great majority of women do not stay in a battering situation but seek the help of shelters and prosecute their assailants.

Middle-class women are often underrepresented in statistics that focus on battered women. These women as a group have the resources and support systems to leave abusive partners but often choose not to. Why then do these women choose to stay in battering situations?

Theories of Why Women Stay in Abusive Relationships

Why a woman chooses to stay in a battering situation is a complex issue and often the result of long-term circumstances including intergenerational concerns (Walker, 1984). Primarily, women stay in the relationship because they are afraid for their own lives and the lives of their children. Many theories have been postulated as to why a woman would stay in a battering situation, including post-traumatic stress.

Masochism

Masochism may be thought of as a self-defeating personality disorder that can be defined as a pervasive pattern of self-defeating behavior. The origin of masochistic behavior has its roots in the child's search for intense emotional contact (Naylor, 1986) and/or repeated abusive behavior from the family of origin.

Many therapists see the term "masochistic" as imprecise and stigmatizing, as it blames women for societal failure and excludes the social realities of the battering (Bograd, 1984; Franklin, 1987). Psychoanalytic theory, however, looks at masochism as a concept thought to underlie women's conflicts about their own autonomous achievements (Kanefield, 1985; Warren, 1985).

There may indeed be factors in the course of female development that predispose some women to masochism. These factors include early identification with a mother who has a negative or depreciatory attitude toward her femininity and/or greater parental and societal controlling attitudes, excessive frustration, and interference with self-assertive and autonomous behavior of females (Bernstein, 1983).

Most battered women do not stay in a battering relationship because they are masochistic or enjoy frequent beatings, nor do most battered women choose to be battered because of personality defects. Personality symptoms often develop because of the violence (Schrader, 1990).

Clinicians often mistake a battered woman's survival strategy for a psychotic episode or long-term personality disorder (Rosewater and Walker, 1985). Rosewater (1985) contended that a battered woman's MMPI profile closely resembled schizophrenic and/or borderline profiles. However, this is misleading. Many women who have been battered suffer from post-traumatic stress syndrome, which can present a number of symptoms, including depression, paranoia, and dissociation. Dissociation occurs as a response to the trauma of battering. Many of the most seriously battered women often block all or part of their experiences in an attempt to anesthetize their feelings.

Walker (1984) found that battered women were candidates for major depression. Evidence suggests that many battered women minimize their depression in verbal interviews. Battered women, feeling a lack of rapport with other people, often withdraw from meaningful relationships.

Learned Helplessness

Another theory of why women choose to stay in battering situations is that of learned helplessness (Campbell, 1989). Learned helplessness develops when an individual does not believe that control of an outcome is possible. Women who are in battering situations are vulnerable because they are unable to predict when they will succeed and when they will fail in keeping themselves safe from abuse. A battered woman becomes unable to trust her own judgment. Her repertoire of responses continually narrows until she feels that she has little control over her situation; she feels that new responses, including seeking help, will not rescue her. After repeated traumas over a period of time, the woman becomes immune, numb, depressed, and convinced that she cannot do anything to help herself (Schrader, 1990). The battered woman's world continually shrinks as she terminates friendships and relationships and relies on the distorted perceptions of the batterer; this often makes her impervious to the seriousness of the violence. The woman's family and marital systems become closed, shutting her off from contact with the outside world and reality (Walker, 1977, 1979, 1984).

Learning Theory

Over 50 percent of all battered women come from families of origin in which they experienced or witnessed interpersonal violence (Giles-Sims, 1983; Walker, 1984; Straus, Gelles & Steinmetz, 1980). The evidence for modeling (Baker & Ball, 1969; Bandura, Ross & Ross, 1963; Tannenbaum & Zillman, 1975) is sufficient to conclude that the impact of growing up in a home where violence occurs is likely to cause the violence to be repeated in future generations. Even witnessing the mildest form of abuse is traumatic for a child and he or she develops a deep sense of betrayal of trust (Colrain & Steele, 1990).

Several researchers have looked at the issues of intergenerational violence (Owen & Straus, 1975; Kalmuss, 1984; Carroll, 1980; Post, Willet, Franks & House, 1984) and concluded that the roles of the aggressor and/or victim can be modeled and transmitted intergenerationally. Other childhood factors that can contribute to a woman's inability to leave a battering situation include rigid sex-role socialization in the family of origin, sexual abuse as a child, and the occurrence of uncontrollable events in the child's life, such as the sudden death of a parent.

Treatment Issues

The battering relationship is a symbiotic and addictive relationship, with a power imbalance based on violence (Schrader, 1990). For the treatment of any addicted individual the foremost treatment issues are dealing with denial, fears, and resistance. For those in a battering relationship, this may be complicated (Hamilton, 1989).

The paramount treatment issue is to convey the clear message that there is no justification for violence except in rare cases of self-defense or defense of others. Treatment must begin with a period of freedom from battering. In a violent marriage or relationship such freedom is not often possible. After the violence, the husband is often calm and humble. This behavior often re-entangles the woman, seducing her into thinking her situation will change. Despite the calm, a period of separation is crucial for effective treatment. Temporary freedom from battering often brings about improvement in conditions previously blamed by the addict as his or her reason for staying in an abusive relationship. It is impossible for one to confront repression or denial if the violence continues.

Freedom from battering alone, however, does not cure the addiction.

Addiction is not in the violence itself but rather in one's orientation to it. Often the more vicious and destructive a relationship becomes, the more intensely the partners become connected to each other; they lose their identity and their own sense of self-worth. Many individuals in abusive relationships give up on their ability to make it on their own. Thus, a period of freedom from battering is the beginning of a process to allow the individual to confront motivations and learn methods of coping on a day-to-day basis.

The healing process involves the lessening of the individual's denial while increasing self-disclosure. The individual must begin to let go of the blaming and focus on responsibility for actions.

Often a woman's initial request for treatment is for couples therapy. Couples therapy is usually requested because of the woman's traditional hope of holding her marriage together at all costs. Realistically, she may be asking for couples therapy in response to her fears. She probably is unable to assess the dangers to her in a rational manner. Under no circumstances is couples therapy appropriate as long as the woman lives in fear of her partner.

Treatment for the battered woman often follows the model of treatment for the victim of a rape. The major difference, however, is that the woman often needs to leave the home and seek the services of a shelter (Schrader, 1990). Treatment begins, as it does for the male, with the woman addressing the treatment issues of dealing with her denial, fears, severity of the violence, and resistance.

The next step towards recovery is to acquire a peer support group. Many cities across the United States have support groups for battered women, usually administered in conjunction with a shelter. A group can help the woman deal with her feelings, both positive and negative, on a day-to-day basis. The healing process becomes complete when feelings and behaviors become tied together and the woman learns that she is not responsible for the violence. Behaviors once thought uncontrollable and unpredictable now become understandable and manageable.

Because battering is a learned behavior, it can be unlearned. The primary treatment for the male batterer must be centered around helping him stop his violent behavior as well as eliminating sexual and psychological abuse. Often the most effective intervention is to make the batterer's behavior known to the police. From 1978 to 1982 the National Crime Survey showed that once a woman was victimized by domestic violence, her risk of being victimized again was high. Approximately 41 percent of the women who did not call the police were victimized again within 6 months. Of the women who did call the police, 15 percent were reassaulted (Langan & Innes, 1986). Police may represent the threat of punishment and that may deter men from new acts of violence. The criminal justice system may also order the batterer into treatment. Treatment does not center on psychotherapy but rather on teaching how to choose and develop nonviolent behaviors, emotions, and attitudes. This has traditionally been accomplished by developing anger management skills in a group treatment setting (Sonkin, Martin & Walker, 1985).

Secondary treatment goals include helping the male to decrease feelings of isolation and develop an interpersonal support system; increase feelings of personal control and self-esteem; increase responsibility for personal behavior; and increase awareness of the dangerousness of violent behavior. Additional goals are an increased acceptance of consequences of violent behavior; development of communication skills and assertiveness skills; an increase in the ability to empathize with partners; development of control over alcohol and/or drugs; and support from others in their lives. Treatment groups should in no way give the impression that it is not the man's responsibility to control his violence.

Structure of the groups usually includes anger management material as well as an opportunity for the men to work on other issues, especially those related to their families of origin. Discussions are always fo-

TABLE 7.1   Position Paper on Batterers' Services and Programs
Georgia Network Against Domestic Violence (March 1987)

1. The primary goal of all interventions must be the safety of the victim.
2. Shelter services must be available in the community before a batterers' program/ services is instituted.
3. Batterers' services must be accountable to the battered women's community and must state agreement with the Georgia Network Against Domestic Violence (GNADV) mission statement.
4. A batterers' program must challenge a man's belief in his right to greater power and privilege. Behavioral change results from changed beliefs.
5. Batterers' services/programs must have a philosophical base which holds that battering is a crime and that the perpetrator must be held responsible for his violence. This includes his assuming financial responsibility for any treatment so as not to compete with the meager resources available to shelters and services for battered women.
6. Batterers' services/programs will not do couples counseling or mediation. When a batterer's group is offered within a community mental health agency/family counseling center, men participating in the group will not be seen in couples counseling.
7. The appropriate role of the program within the criminal justice system is as alternative sentencing, not as a diversion.
8. Batterers' services/programs must take an active role in community education about the root causes of battering and work actively to change those systems and cultural norms that historically have given tacit approval of battering.
9. Although batterers' programs must be accountable to the battered women's community, it is not the responsibility of the battered women's advocates to "educate" batterers' service providers. They must take responsibility for learning about battered womens' reality themselves through reading and purchase of in-services, training, monitoring, etc.

cused onto the men's relationship to anger and violence. Men who are separated often experience high levels of anger, frustration, and hurt. They are at risk for further violence. Feelings are often projected onto others they love, including parents and/or children. A primary goal for these groups is the safety of the women and children.

Batterers can change their behavior. Through support, confrontation, and new information, men can learn new ways of behaving that are nonviolent.

A batterers' support group should not be an unstructured setting where men complain about their wives but should be a supportive environment where men can find empathy and develop new skills. Equally important, the group should be a place where men can begin to work on recovery. The Georgia Network on violence has presented a position paper on services to batterers that is a useful guideline (Table 7.1). A peer group allows each individual in the group not only to share his thoughts, fears, and doubts but also to share in self-acceptance, constructive confrontation, and identification with others.

Conclusions

Domestic violence, it appears, can never be eradicated from our society, as it is woven into the very fabric. Despite the changes in public perception, many civic officials continue to overlook violence in the family due to legal, ideological, practical, and political considerations (Ferraro, 1989). It is clear that society will be slow to change. What can be changed, however, is individuals. Each partner in a relationship is empowered to change his or her own behavior and take action to end the violence and heal his or her spirit and self-esteem. Addictions are modified by changing habits and behaviors.

The classification of domestic violence as an addiction is complex and relatively new. Violence as an addiction has been discussed in terms of personality dynamics, socialization, and feelings of hopelessness. Addiction is both on the individual and couple level with the interlocking consciousness and being of two separate individuals. It is both similar to and different from other addictions. Each individual in the couple reacts to violence in a different manner, based on his or her unique personality. Treatment of this addiction is possible only if partners focus on their individual responsibility and power to change. The ultimate responsibility for the treatment of violence as an addiction, for both males and females, lies with the individual.

The field of domestic violence is fraught with danger for both the individuals involved in the violence and the professional. We have passed through a phase that has been divisive and blaming. In truth, however, we have all become more sensitized to the problem of violence. The challenge is now to move beyond blame and understanding, to find long-term solutions for the millions that are affected by domestic violence in America today.

References

Aquirre, B. E. (1985). Why do they return? Abused wives in shelters. *Social Work, 30*(4), 350–354.

Archer, N. H. (1989) Battered women and the legal system: Past, present and future. *Law and Psychology Review, 13,* 145–163.

Baker, R. & Ball, S. (1969). *Man, media and violence* (Vol. 9). Washington, DC: U.S. Government Printing Office.

Bandura, A., Ross, D., & Ross, S. (1963). Transmission of aggression through imitation of aggressive models. *Journal of Abnormal Social Psychology, 66,* 3–11.

Bernstein, I. (1983). Masochistic pathology and feminine development. *Journal of the American Psychoanalytic Association, 31,* 467–486.

Bograd, M. (1984) Family systems approaches to wife battering: A feminist critique. *American Journal of Orthopsychiatry, 54,* 558–568.

Caesar, P. L. (1985). *The wife beater: Personality and psychological characteristics.* Unpublished doctoral dissertation. California School of Professional Psychology, Los Angeles.

Campbell, J. C. (1989). A test of two explanatory models of women's responses to battering. *Nursing Research, 38*(1), 18–24.

Carroll, J. C. (1980). A cultural consistency theory of family violence in Mexican American and Jewish ethnic groups. In M. A. Straus & G. T. Hotaling (Eds.), *The social causes of husband-wife violence.* Minneapolis: University of Minnesota Press.

Colrain, J., & Steele, K. (1990). Taking the blame. *Insight, 11*(2), 6–9.

Doherty, J. F. (1983). *Self esteem, anxiety and dependency in men who batter women.* Unpublished doctoral dissertation. Boston: Boston University School of Education.

Ferraro, K. J. (1989). Policing woman battering. *Social Problems, 36*(1), 61–74.

Franklin, D. (1987). The politics of masochism. *Psychology Today, 21,* 52–57.

Giles-Sims, J. (1983). *Wife battering: A systems theory approach.* New York: Guilford.

Hamberger, L. K., & Hastings, J. E. 1985, (March) *Personality correlates of men who abuse their partners: Some preliminary data.* Paper presented at the meeting of the Society for Personality Assessment, Berkeley, CA.

Hamberger, L. K., & Hastings, J. E. (1986). Personality correlates of men who abuse their partners: A cross-validation study. *Journal of Family Violence, 1,* 323–341.

Hamilton, J. A. (1989). Emotional consequences of victimization and discrimination in "special populations" of women. *Psychiatric Clinics of North America, 12*(1), 35–51.

Joseph, S. G. (1983). *Abusive and non-abusive couples' performance on the consensus Rorschach.* Unpublished doctoral dissertation. Hofstra University, Hempstead, NY.

Kalmuss, D. (1984). The intergenerational transmission of marital aggression. *Journal of Marriage and the Family, 46,* 11–19.

Kanefield, L. (1985). Psychoanalytic constructions of female development and women's conflicts about achievement: II. *Journal of the American Academy of Psychoanalysis, 13,* 347–366.

Langan, P., & Innes, C. (1986). *Preventing domestic violence against women.* Washington, DC: U.S. Department of Justice, Bureau of Justice Statistics. (NCJ–102037)

Naylor, B. A. (1986). Sadomasochism in children and adolescents: A contemporary treatment approach. *Psychotherapy, 23,* 586–592.

Owen, D. M., & Straus, M. A. (1975). The social structure of violence in childhood and approval of violence as an adult. *Aggressive Behavior, 1,* 193–211.

Peele, S., & Brodsky, A. (1975). *Love and addiction.* New York: Taplinger.

Post, R. D., Willet, A. B., Franks, R. D., & House, R. M. (1984). Childhood exposure to violence among victims and perpetrators of spouse battering. *Victimology, 6,* 156–166.

Rosewater, L. B. (1985). Schizophrenic or battered? In L. B. Rosewater & L. E. Walker (Eds.), *Handbook of feminist therapy: Woman's issues in psychotherapy.* New York: Springer.

Rosewater, L. B., & Walker, L. E. (Eds.). (1985). *Handbook of feminist therapy: Woman's issues in psychotherapy.* New York: Springer.

Schrader, S. (1990). Ending the violence. *Insight, 11*(2), 10–15.

Sonkin, D. J., Martin, D., & Walker, L. E. (1985). *The male batterer: a treatment approach.* New York: Springer.

Stewart, M. A., & deBlois, C. C. (1981). Wife abuse among families attending a child psychiatry clinic. *Journal of the American Academy of Childhood Psychiatry, 20,* 845–862.

Straus, M. A., Gelles, R., & Steinmetz, S. K. (1980). *Behind closed doors: Violence in the American family.* Garden City, NY: Doubleday/Anchor.

Tannenbaum, P. H., & Zillman, R. (1975). Emotional arousal in the facilitation of aggression through communication. *Advances in Experimental Social Psychology, 8,* 149–192.

Walker, L. E. (1977). Battered women and learned helplessness. *Victimology, 2,* 525–534.

Walker, L. E. (1979). *The battered woman.* New York: Harper & Row.

Walker, L. E. (1984). *The battered women syndrome.* New York: Springer.

Warren, V. (1985). Explaining masochism. *Journal for the Theory of Social Behavior, 15*(2), 103–129.

Wood, B. L. (1987). *Children of alcoholism: The struggle for self and intimacy in adult life.* New York: New York University Press.

8

Sexual Abuses and Offenses

JUDITH COONEY, Ed.D.

THE FOCUS OF THIS chapter is the misuse of sexuality in which children are victimized. Because much of the sexual abuse and exploitation of children is never reported, there is no accurate accounting of victims or perpetrators. Recent figures indicate that one of four females and one of four or five males will be sexually abused before reaching age 18 (Waterman & Lusk, 1986).

The sexual abuser who abuses only within the family may have one or two victims. Pedophiles, who prey on all children, may have hundreds or even thousands of victims. In their study of child molesters, Abel, Beck, Mittleman, Cunningham-Rathner, Rouleau, and Murphy (1987) found that the average female-oriented pedophile had 20 victims and the average male-oriented pedophile, 150 victims. Goldstein (1984) cites the case of the 52-year-old man who had molested 5,000 boys prior to his apprehension. He also reports that a 62-year-old oil executive admitted molesting one boy a day for 30 years. The fact that each individual was undetected for many years attests to the wiles of these perpetrators as well as the reluctance of victims to come forward.

Typically, many consider sexual abuse to be a euphemism for intercourse. Actually, sexual activity involving an adult perpetrator and a minor encompasses a range of activities, some of which do not include physical contact. If the perpetrator has access to the victim over time, the sexual activity tends to escalate from less intimate activity to physical contact.

Sgroi, Blick, and Porter (1982, pp. 10–12) have identified 14 sexually abusive behaviors. They include:

1. *Nudity:* The adult appears nude in front of all or some family members or visitors.

2. *Disrobing:* The adult disrobes in front of the child.
3. *Genital exposure:* The adult exposes his or her genitals to the child.
4. *Observation of the child:* The adult surreptitiously or overtly watches the child undress, bathe, excrete, or urinate.
5. *Kissing:* The adult kisses the child in a lingering and intimate way.
6. *Fondling:* The adult fondles the child's breasts, abdomen, genital area, inner thighs, or buttocks. The child may be directed to fondle the adult similarly.
7. *Masturbation:* The adult masturbates while the child observes; the adult observes the child masturbating; the adult and child observe each other while masturbating themselves; or the adult and child engage in mutual masturbation.
8. *Fellatio:* This type of oral-genital contact requires the child to take a male perpetrator's penis into his or her mouth, or the adult to take the male child's penis into his or her mouth.
9. *Cunnilingus:* This type of oral-genital contact requires the child to place mouth and tongue on the vulva or in the vaginal area of an adult female, or the adult will place his or her mouth on the vulva or in the vaginal area of the female child.
10. *Digital penetration of the anus or rectal opening:* This involves penetration of the anus or rectal opening by a finger or inanimate objects.
11. *Penile penetration of the anus or rectal opening:* This involves penetration of the anus or rectal opening by a male perpetrator's penis. A child can often be rectally penetrated without injury due to the flexibility of the child's rectal opening.
12. *Digital penetration of the vagina:* This involves penetration of the vagina by a finger or inanimate object.
13. *Penile penetration of the vagina:* This involves penetration of the vagina by a male perpetrator's penis.
14. *"Dry intercourse":* This is a slang term in which the adult rubs his penis against the child's genital-rectal area or inner thighs or buttocks.

Another category of sexual abuse could be labeled "allowing a child to be sexually abused by others." Such activities as offering a child to others for prostitution or forcing a child to appear in pornographic photos or films would be included in this category. Recently an Ohio mother of six children, ages 3 to 11, was arrested after lining her children up and asking several men to pay $50 to spend an hour with the child of their choice.

Although exact figures are not known, there is sufficient documentation regarding the sexual abuse of children to provide information about the victims and the victimizers, the problem and its effects, and current treatment approaches. Two categories of sex offenders will be discussed in this chapter. The first is the pedophile; the second is the sexual abuser.

The Pedophile

Literally, the word "pedophile" means lover of children. Although technically the term "pederast" is applicable when the perpetrator targets boys between the ages of puberty and sixteen (Rossman, 1976), "pedophile" is commonly used as a generic label for anyone who molests minors. Pedophilia is considered a mental disorder.

The pedophile or child molester is not a twentieth century phenomenon. Children have been sexual targets of adults throughout history. Sexual abuse of boys, in particular, was a common practice in ancient Rome and Greece. Boy brothels flourished in most large cities (de Mause, 1974). Literature and art confirm the sexual use of slave boys by their masters and students by their teachers. Rossman (1976) reports that the Roman emperor Hadrian ordered statues of his favorite boy to be erected and worshipped throughout the empire.

Children have not fared better in modern times. The attitude that a child is less than a person continues today in the United States, Europe, Sri Lanka, and many Moslem countries, where child prostitution and pornography are officially condemned but unofficially tolerated (Kempe & Kempe, 1984).

Portrait of the Pedophile

The image of the pedophile has traditionally been one of the dirty old man. It has only been in the last decade that the realization that women also can be pedophiles has reached the general public. Two cases, both of which began to unfold in the fall of 1983, changed the public's concept of who molests children.

The small town of Jordan, Minnesota, seemed an unlikely location for criminal activity of any consequence. National attention focused on this suburban community throughout late 1983 and into the spring of 1984 as 24 of its citizens, male and female, were implicated in sexual abuse cases for victimizing their own children as well as the children of neighbors and friends. The faces of the accused were those of women and men in their 20s, 30s and 40s. They did not look menacing. They looked like what they were: middle-class, white, employed, solid citizens for the most part (Crewdson, 1988). Stories of sex games and parties, of child swapping and sex contests, of mothers and fathers and grandparents as sexual abusers fascinated and confused the public. There were no furry-faced monsters in this group.

At almost the same time the Jordan cases were unfolding, the McMartin Preschool in Manhattan Beach, California, was becoming familiar to viewers of the nightly news. Also familiar were the faces of Virginia

McMartin, her daughter, her grandson, her granddaughter, and three other female teachers who were indicted by the Los Angeles County grand jury in March, 1984 (Crewdson, 1988). The concept of pedophilia as a male-only crime was crumbling.

Female Pedophiles

Finkelhor and Williams (1988b, p. 40) report that in their study of 270 cases of day-care sexual molestation, 147 of the perpetrators were females. Of the boys who were victimized, 59 percent were abused by females; 50 percent of the female victims were molested by female perpetrators. The female perpetrators in this study ranged in age from 16 to 77, with a median age of 35; 63 percent were married and 68 percent had children of their own. Almost 50 percent owned or directed the day-care facility; the other half were child-care workers or teachers.

Interestingly, women in this study were much more likely than men to be involved in multiple-offender cases. That is, 73 percent of the female perpetrators molested children in the presence of other abusers, male or female. The investigators developed a typology of sexual abuse by women. They identify the following categories:

1. *Lone woman.* This was the least frequent scenario. A woman, acting alone, abused one child or several children over time.
2. *Multiple perpetrators: women as initiators.* The women in this category seemed to exercise control over the other perpetrators as well as the children. There are indications that the initiating women may also physically or sexually abuse the other perpetrators.
3. *Multiple perpetrators: women as followers.* These women tended to be socially isolated and dependent people who were influenced by women from the preceding category or by male initiators. (p. 45–49)

The concept of the female pedophile is new. Day-care cases have only recently come to the attention of professionals. There are few treatment programs specifically directed toward female offenders. Day-care cases are extremely difficult to prove. Therefore women accused of pedophilia are unlikely to be convicted. The literature related to treatment programs and pedophilic behavior continues to refer only to male pedophiles. Questions related to the numbers of cases and the characteristics of female pedophiles pose new research challenges.

Male Pedophiles

Much more is known about male pedophiles than about their female counterparts. Males have been studied in correctional settings and in treatment programs. Foremost among those who have studied incarcerated pedophiles is A. Nicholas Groth, director of the sex offender program at Somers State Prison in Connecticut. Groth, Hobson, and Gary (1982) have identified two types of pedophiles: fixated and regressed. For each they have identified eleven characteristics.

The fixated molester:

1. *Primary sexual orientation is to children.*
2. *Pedophilic interests begin at adolescence.*
3. *No precipitating stress/no subjective distress.*
4. *Persistent interest and compulsive behavior.*
5. *Premeditated, preplanned offenses.*
6. *Identification: Offender identifies closely with the victim and equalizes his behavior to the level of the child and/or may adopt a pseudo-parental role to the victim.*
7. *Male victims are primary targets.*
8. *Little or no sexual contact initiated with agemates; offender is usually single or in a marriage of convenience.*
9. *Usually no history of alcohol or drug abuse and offense is not alcohol-related.*
10. *Characterological immaturity; poor sociosexual peer relationships.*
11. *Offense represents a maladaptive resolution of life development (maturation) issues. (p. 134)*

This category is described in the DSM-III-R (American Psychiatric Association, 1987) as the exclusive type. This person is sexually addicted to children and devotes most of his time to his addiction.

The regressed molester:

1. *Primary sexual orientation is to agemates.*
2. *Pedophilic interests emerge in adulthood.*
3. *Precipitating stress usually evident.*
4. *Involvements may be more episodic and may wax and wane with stress.*
5. *Initial offense may be impulsive and not premeditated.*
6. *Substitution: Offender replaces conflictual adult relationship with involvement with a child; victim is a pseudoadult substitute, and in incest situations the offender abandons his parental role.*
7. *Female victims are primary targets.*
8. *Sexual contact with a child coexists with sexual contact with agemates; offender is usually married or in a common-law relationship.*

> 9. *Offense is often alcohol-related.*
> 10. *More traditional lifestyle than fixated molester but underdevel-oped peer relationships.*
> 11. *Offense represents a maladaptive attempt to cope with specific life stresses. (p. 134)*

In the DSM-III-R the regressed molester is described as the nonexclusive type.

Mayer (1985) has added a third category of molester which she refers to as the mysopedic pedophile. This is a person whose sadistic and vicious behavior may result in the mutilation and murder of his victims. It is believed that this group is much smaller in number than fixated or regressed pedophiles. John Gacy represents the extreme of this category.

Adolescent Pedophiles

The fixated abuser is likely to have a history of sexual deviancy that began in adolescence. Their behavior differed from the awkward exploration usually associated with the onset of puberty. O'Brien and Bera (1986) have developed a typology of adolescent sexual offenders that could be especially helpful in treatment planning.

The first type is the naive experimenter. He is described as young (11–14) and with little history of acting out. He takes advantage of an unplanned situation with a much younger child. Sexual feelings are new to him and he explores them in a single instance or a few instances. He requires short-term intervention of an educational nature.

Type two is the undersocialized child exploiter. He is socially isolated from agemates and spends his time with younger children. His self-esteem and self-identity are enhanced by his ability to trick and manipulate his young victims. This individual needs assistance in developing social skills with his peers. Family therapy as well as individual and group therapy are indicated.

The third type is the pseudo-socialized child exploiter. Unlike the second type, this boy is a high achiever with good social skills. He may have been a victim of early abuse or neglect himself. He rationalizes his behavior and demonstrates little remorse or guilt. Without intervention he is at high risk to become a life-long pedophile. A residential program may be necessary for this individual. Another candidate for a residential program is the sexually aggressive adolescent. This fourth type is inclined to use force or violence in attacking children, peers, or even adults. He comes from a disorganized and abusive family and has a history of antisocial behavior.

Type five is the sexual compulsive who comes from a family in which intimacy and emotions are not expressed. He engages in repetitive, sexually arousing behavior that does not include physical contact with his victims. Obscene phone calls, window peeping, exhibitionism, and fetish burglary are often accompanied by masturbation. The degree of addiction will determine whether or not he will require residential treatment.

The sixth type, the disturbed impulsive, will require placement in either an inpatient psychiatric unit or a residential sex offender treatment program. He is a threat to children, peers and adults. His behavior is sudden and unpredictable. Substance abuse may be a factor. The last type is the group-influenced offender who abuses someone he knows in the presence of his peers. He may be either the leader or a follower in the abusive activity. Group members should be separated in treatment. Each must own responsibility for the abuse.

Not all adolescent sex offenders go on to become adult offenders. Early identification combined with appropriate treatment decisions increases the prevention potential.

General Characteristics

Pedophiles can be male or female, adolescents or octogenarians or anywhere in between. Their preferences may be for one sex or either sex. Pedophilia crosses all ethnic and socioeconomic levels. There have been numerous attempts to identify other characteristics of pedophiles. Most of the studies have been based on self-reports of incarcerated males. One such study (Tingle, Barnard, Robbins, Newman & Hutchinson, 1986) focused on the childhood and adolescence of pedophiles and rapists. In this study the pedophiles claimed to have had very close relationships with their mothers and a lack of closeness with their fathers. Many had been molested by family members and a significant number had been physically abused. Most of the molesters indicated that they had no friends or few friends when growing up. This "loner" status is consistent with research showing pedophiles "to be markedly introvert and lacking in social skill and confidence" (Wilson & Cox, 1983, p. 328).

Despite variations in age, race, socioeconomic level, education, and personal experiences as victims, pedophiles utilize similar types of faulty logic. Five categories of erroneous thinking have been identified by Smith (1989):

Denial. The offender claims that nothing happened.

Minimization. The offender admits that something happened but feigns shock that anyone would believe that he could do whatever has been described. "Yes, I took off her slacks, but you know I didn't actually touch her."

Projection of blame. The offender blames the victim. One offender told the judge that the sexy negligee that his victim wore was too much for any man to resist. He was describing a 5-year-old!

Distortion. The victim is described as having an adult's sexuality. "I knew she wanted this to happen. It was just a matter of who made the first move."

Justification. The offender admits molesting the child but rationalizes that this was an appropriate behavior. "At least he learned something from me," or "It kept me from having an affair and breaking up our family." (p. 4)

Whether the offender actually believes these verbal machinations or is simply trying to avoid dealing with the reality of events and their consequences is a question for the therapist to pursue.

Mayer (1988) characterizes pedophiles as immature, socially isolated, inept, lonely, shy, and passive men. Like other sex offenders, they demonstrate low impulse control, irresponsible behavior, and objectification of others. Many also share a hobby; some are producers and most are consumers of child pornography.

Treatment Issues and Options

Few crimes evoke the reaction that child molestation does. If one were to survey the general public regarding the disposition of cases involving a pedophile, suggestions would include using tools of the Inquisition, castration, and the death penalty. "Treatment" might not even appear on the list. However, since civilized society rejects the eye-for-an-eye concept, the pedophile need not fear the rack or the stake.

Treatment of pedophiles is dependent upon identification. Rarely do pedophiles come forward seeking help. Their strong denial and rationalization systems stand in the way of problem-recognition. Therefore treatment usually becomes an issue when the pedophile is charged with a criminal offense. Depending upon the location, a judge may have up to four sentence options in felony cases of child molestation.

Incarceration

Most people would assume that convicted pedophiles are destined to serve time in a correctional facility. In fact, the pedophile need not concern himself with thoughts of going to jail in many jurisdictions. It has been estimated (Goldstein, 1984) that 95 percent of the child molesters arrested in California do not serve any time.

For the relatively small number of pedophiles who serve time, prison will confirm that "baby-rapers" occupy the bottom rung of the prison hierarchy. Because of this status, they present security problems within the institution that officials prefer to avoid. As model prisoners their time served will be brief compared to societal expectations. Nonviolent offenders are certain to be included among the prisoners who receive "early out" furloughs due to overcrowding. The U.S. Department of Justice reported that first-time child molesters serve an average of less than one year in jail across all fifty states (Smith, 1989). If he is untreated, the likelihood is that the pedophile will return to his addiction and continue to be a threat to children.

Incarceration and Treatment

Particularly for the violent offender, incarceration is a necessity. A treatment program specifically designed for sex offenders is the ideal. Many institutions offer very limited services for this population. Mayer (1988) reports that the first four corrections-based programs in the United States were established in California (1948), Wisconsin (1958), Massachusetts (1958), and Washington (1958). These programs have provided viable treatment models as well as significant data about this special population.

Residential Treatment Facility

In place of a correctional facility, a residential treatment center has become an option, especially for first-conviction offenders and adolescent offenders. Programs vary but usually include intensive individual and group work, with components to address unique needs such as educational remediation, substance abuse recovery, or job skill development.

Community-Based Treatment Program

The offender may be diverted to such a program or may "graduate" from a correctional or residential program to this less restricted alternative. In many instances offenders participate as a condition of probation or parole. One of the most successful programs of this type is Northwest Treatment Associates of Seattle, Washington. This program enlists the support and cooperation of the offender's extended family and friends in monitoring deviant behavior. Community-based programs represent 75 percent of all sex offender treatment programs in the United States (Laws, 1988).

Treatment Modalities

Most pedophiles are never identified, never incarcerated, and never treated. The offender who does receive treatment is usually an involuntary client under the direction of the criminal justice system. Treatment modalities include:

Physiological Approaches   The physiological approaches to treating pedophiles and other sex offenders include castration and chemotherapy. Castration is a surgical procedure in which the testes are removed in order to lower the testosterone level. "The idea of lowering testosterone in the case of the pedophile is to try to decrease the intensity of his sexual cravings, which are for children" (Berlin & Krout, 1986, p. 23). Although voluntary castration has been utilized in Europe as a treatment option, it is not an accepted approach in the United States. It has been proposed by a few judges as an alternative to incarceration, but appeals courts have blocked the exercising of the option.

Testosterone levels can also be reduced by chemotherapy or chemical castration. The drug most often used for this purpose is medroxy-progesterone acetate (MPA), which is marketed as Depo Provera. MPA is injected intramuscularly. It adheres to the muscle and is gradually released into the blood stream over the course of several days (Berlin & Krout, 1986). In order to be effective, injections must given every seven to ten days. The pedophile's sexual orientation does not change as a result of using MPA, but the intensity of the desire for children is decreased. Although the use of MPA may seem ideal for some offenders, there have been many problems associated with its use:

1. Side effects are numerous and include weight gain, headaches, lethargy, sweats, nightmares, dyspnea, hyperglycemia, hypogonadism, leg cramps, thrombotic disorders, depression, fluid retention, infertility, liver damage, and diabetes.

2. The underlying assumption justifying use of Depo Provera appears to be that hormones cause sexual assault and molestation. Currently there are insufficient data to justify this assumption.

3. Sexual assault is defined as a crime of violence. There is no certainty that the chemical reduction of the libido also reduces aggression.

4. Use of Depo Provera necessitates costly medical procedures involving comprehensive hormone studies and ongoing testosterone-level monitoring.

5. Reliance on chemically controlling behavior removes individual accountability from the sex offender and does not address the issue of causation.

6. Because of the side effects, Depo Provera must be used with ex-

treme caution with individuals with certain physical diseases such as epilepsy, migraines, asthma, and renal and cardiac dysfunction.

7. When patients stop taking Depo Provera, sexual fantasies and libido return. Hence, the drug must be used indefinitely and be carefully monitored. Psychotherapy often is combined with the use of Depo Provera, but implementation is not always feasible. Since Depo Provera lowers arousal, behavioral management techniques such as desensitization may prove ineffective while the drug is being used.

8. Depo Provera affects arousal but not direction. Pedophiles, who seek emotional intimacy with children and for whom sexual arousal often is of secondary importance, may not benefit from the use of the drug.

9. While Depo Provera diminishes arousal, it does not affect penile reactions. When using antiandrogens, it is necessary to have a coordinated treatment plan involving a multitude of supportive and educational interventions including provisions for substitute sexual outlets for offenders in therapy (Mayer, 1988, pp. 115–117).

New and more sophisticated drugs may replace Depo Provera in the future. In the meantime, drug treatment may be appropriate for a limited number of offenders for whom other treatments have proved ineffective (Lanyon, 1986).

Psychoanalytic Approaches Although psychoanalytic therapy was the sole treatment method for child molestation prior to the 1960s, little evidence suggests that this approach is effective in treating pedophilia (Berlin & Krout, 1986; Lanyon, 1986). In their comparative study of the effectiveness of group psychotherapy in addition to probation versus intensive probation supervision, Romero and Williams (1983) found the recidivism rate was higher for those who participated in the group. This 10-year follow-up study does not so much negate the effectiveness of group psychotherapy as it promotes interest in making probation supervision more intensive. Self-reports of pedophiles combined with arrest records of a population that specializes in not getting arrested cannot be relied upon for purposes of generalization.

The major concern about psychoanalytic treatment is that even if the offender comes to an understanding of his sexual preference, there is no indication that this insight will result in behavior change. The client may simply understand why he continues to molest.

Cognitive-Behavioral Approaches A review of behavioral techniques used through the early 1980s to reorient pedophiles (Kelly, 1982) resulted in the identification of more than 20 different procedures; 75 percent of these used aversion therapy techniques including electric shock and noxious auditory feedback. In most studies the adversive techniques constituted one segment of a multicomponent approach. At least partial success in de-

creasing pedophilic urges and behaviors was reported in all 32 studies reviewed. However, as Kelly hastens to point out, success in a research setting does not ensure success in the community.

The behavior therapy program at Seattle's Northwest Treatment
Associates is designed to help offenders decrease their deviant urges
(Salter, 1988). The clients are seen individually and in groups. Extensive
assignments are given to group members to work on outside of the group.
These assignments require perpetrators to study their own deviant history and the effects of deviancy on their victims and significant others.
Combined with individual assignments, homework occupies much of the
offender's time between sessions. The less free time the offender has, the
less opportunity he has to pursue deviant activities. Clients are required
to make boredom tapes designed to reduce deviant arousal by satiation.
The client masturbates while recording an appropriate adult-to-adult fantasy; then continues to masturbate for an additional 45 minutes while recording inappropriate fantasies. Covert sensitization is used to combine
the attempt to initiate abusive behavior with thoughts and feelings that
are so negative that they will reoccur when the thought of abusing reoc-
curs (Salter, 1988). Another imagery technique combines the abuse initiation with an interruption that results in the molestation not taking place
and the client feeling rewarded for not molesting. Social skills training,
assertiveness training, and sex education may also be provided for offenders as needed. Cognitive restructuring and thought stopping using ammo-
nia or rubber bands is also integrated into the treatment.

Other Options   Behavioral techniques in sex offender treatment programs seem to be the norm. However, most programs integrate other
techniques as well. Laws (1988) describes a community-based program
that uses rational-emotive therapy to challenge deviant thinking, behavior therapy to decrease deviant sexual arousal, and relapse prevention to
halt pre-offending behaviors. Naitove (1988) reports on the use of art therapy in the assessment and treatment of offenders. In groups and individually, the art therapist, using drawings or collages, can assist these offenders in expressing their feelings, developing self-awareness, enhancing
self-esteem, and exploring an alternative outlet for expressing anger and
loneliness. Dance, movement, and drama can be utilized to achieve similar
goals.

Treatment Goals and Obstacles

Langevin and Lang (1985) have identified treatment guidelines for those
who work with pedophiles. Professionals must accept the fact that they
cannot change the client's preference for children. There are no programs

that claim to cure pedophiles. The primary treatment goal is to help the client manage his urges.

The client will be reluctant to give up sexual behavior that he perceives as positive and rewarding. The counselor will attempt to help the client recognize a need to change his behavior. This requires a continuous attack on the pedophile's denial system. Most offenders have spent years keeping secrets and pretending to be anything but child molesters.

To assist the pedophile in deciding to change his behavior, Langevin and Lang (1985) suggest three therapeutic goals:

1. *Moving the offender to admit to this sexual preference and to the actual extent of his sexual involvement with children.*
2. *Helping him see the child as a victim rather than as a consenting partner.*
3. *Overcoming rationalizations about his own motives for sexual involvement with children. (p. 411)*

The pedophile is an especially difficult client. In most instances he is an involuntary client who is aware of the counselor's decision-making role in his life. He may attempt to manipulate the treatment provider by blaming his pedophilic behavior on addiction to alcohol or drugs. One hears this claim from men who have never taken a drink or an aspirin in their lives. Sobriety is then claimed as proof of being "cured." The other oft-encountered tactic is that the pedophile finds religion and states that he is no longer a threat. He has been saved! Invariably this conversion/salvation experience is short-lived.

There are no academic programs that prepare counselors to work specifically with this population. Those who work with offenders should have a minimum of a master's degree of counseling or social work. For specific training in the area of sexual deviance, counselors must rely on continuing-education conferences, workshops, and professional reading. Beyond the basic academic credentials, the counselor must have expertise in the following areas:

A. Sexual deviancy and offender issues

  1. Deviant arousal patterns
  2. Arousal support mechanisms
  3. Methods for altering arousal

B. Victimization issues

  1. Relevance to offender treatment
  2. Decisions regarding reunification
  3. Protection of the victim

C. Criminal justice issues

1. Knowledge of the system
2. Knowledge of local resources
3. Acquiring information from the system

D. Community Resources

1. Victim services
2. Community protection agencies
3. Other offender therapists
4. Testing resources
5. Substance abuse programs
6. Employment services
7. Housing services
8. Financial resources. (O'Connell, Leberg & Donaldson, 1990, pp. 39–47)

Individuals who choose to work with sex offenders must recognize that they have chosen an extremely stressful profession. Burnout prevention for staff members is a mandatory component in any treatment agency. O'Connell, Leberg, and Donaldson (1990) identify the following personal traits and abilities of effective counselors of sex offenders:

1. Ability to cope with stress.
2. Ability to discuss sexual matters openly (especially deviant sexuality).
3. Ability to be precise in gathering and verifying information.
4. Ability to maintain objectivity.
5. Ability to remain realistic about sex offenders and their potential for reoffense.
6. Freedom from a deviant/criminal history. (pp. 54–60)

The individual who possesses the essential knowledge, skills, and personal qualities to work with pedophiles can apply these abilities in a number of treatment settings and modes.

Summary

Pedophiles present a challenge to the creativity, patience, and skills of the practitioner. Assessment leading to appropriate placement is essential to the treatment process. Follow-up and monitoring are crucial to society's safety. There is no cure for pedophilia, but excellent programs can assist in the management of deviant urges and desires.

The Pedophile/Sexual Abuser Issue

Family members who molest other family members are termed sexual abusers, incest offenders, intrafamilial abusers, or some combination of these titles. Professionals do not agree on the relationship between sexual abusers and pedophiles. On one side are those who consider sexual abusers to be a special category of pedophile (Groth, Hobson & Gary, 1982; American Psychiatric Association, 1987). On the other side are those who consider pedophiles and sexual abusers as two distinct populations (Giarretto, 1982; Langevin, 1983; Cooney, 1987). Both sides agree that the pedophile is a threat to all children and that the sexual abuser is more selective in his choice of victims. The criminal code distinguishes between pedophiles and incest offenders. The largest number are child sexual abusers, not pedophiles (Giarretto, 1982). Experts generally concur that there are some differences between sexual abusers and pedophiles. They disagree on the question of how much similarity there is between the two groups (Finkelhor, 1984).

Further confusing the issue is the acknowledgment by both sides that it is possible to be both a sexual abuser and a pedophile. If he were also molesting children outside the family, he would be considered a pedophile when molesting neighborhood children. To minimize confusion, the term "sexual abuser" will be used to describe the person who molests children only within the family.

Portrait of the Sexual Abuser

The sexual abuser is often a respected member of the community. He never speeds, never has had a parking ticket, never misses church, and would never cheat on his wife. He will continue his sexual involvement with his daughter. The sexual activity will escalate. His daughter is not likely to tell anyone about her father's behavior. He is good to her in many ways. She is not close to her mother and is certain that her mother would never believe her. Telling anyone outside of her family would not be advisable. Everyone knows and respects her father. He could be the next mayor of their town. Who would believe that he is also a sexual abuser?

The sexual abuser may be male or female. In some instances both parents may be molesting the same child or children. Like the pedophile, sexual abusers vary in race, religion, age, and socioeconomic status. They are not a homogeneous group (Finkelhor & Williams, 1988a). However, it is generally agreed that sexual abusers do share some characteristics. In a recent study (Ballard, Blair, Devereaux, Valentine, Horton & Johnson, 1990), 373 incest perpetrators were profiled. The abusers were drawn from both institutional and community-based treatment programs. Of those in institutional settings, 63 were in prison and 41 were in mental health facilities. Within the community, 240 were in Parents United groups and 39 were being treated by private practitioners. A composite summary of the perpetrator indicates that he (97.9 percent) is white (84.6 percent), a high school graduate (12.1 years of education) in good health (44.3 percent) who never or seldom uses alcohol (79 percent) or drugs (94.9 percent). His mean age is 38.8, he is Protestant (47.1 percent) and he is married (56.2 percent). He was physically (52 percent) or sexually (53.5 percent) abused as a child.

State reporting statistics constitute another source of demographic data regarding sexual abusers. In fiscal year 1988, 5,295 sexual abusers were identified in Illinois (Illinois Department of Children and Family Services, 1989). The offenders were predominantly male (80.5 percent) in the 30 to 40 age group (28.3 percent). They were most likely to be white (58.5 percent), as were their victims (63 percent). Their victims were usually females (78.8 percent), of whom the abuser was the natural parent (32.7 percent) or step-parent (9.2 percent).

Demographic information is useful in destroying some of the myths related to sexual abuse. For instance, the "dirty old man" myth and the stepfather myth are not supported by reported data. However, demographics do not provide insight into the personality traits of sexual abusers. Groth (1982) has identified several characteristics that are common to incest offenders. These include:

1. The offender experiences himself as a victim of external forces and events, rather than as a person in charge of his life.
2. Psychologically, the abuser is a loner, emotionally separate and apart from others. He lacks any sense of attachment or relatedness to others.
3. He lacks self-esteem and self-confidence. He is depressed and fearful. He views the world as hostile and rejecting.
4. In order to feel more comfortable and secure, he avoids anxiety-producing adult relationships. He projects his own needs and desires on his child victim.

Implied in these characteristics is a narcissism that allows the abuser to put his needs and desires above the welfare of anyone else in the family. Closely aligned with the traits of the abuser are the traits of the family in which sexual abuse occurs.

Female Sexual Abusers

One of the last taboos related to child sexual abuse has been the acknowledgment that mothers sometimes molest their own children. Justice and Justice (1979) describe the sexually abusive mother as someone who "tries to use sex as the means to establish closeness and warmth with another human being. Often she either has no husband or he is extremely passive or absent from the home most of the time" (p. 102).

In her study of 29 mother offenders, McCarty (1986) devised a three-part typology. *Independent offenders* were mothers who were living without a husband or husband figure when they molested a son or daughter. These offenders had a troubled childhood (92 percent) during which they were sexually abused (78 percent), usually by a brother. They were of average intelligence (100 percent) and able to maintain steady employment (67 percent). They married as teenagers (83 percent) and that was their only marriage (75 percent). All are now living independently (67 percent). They may abuse drugs (46 percent) and may be seriously emotionally disturbed (50 percent). Their victims were most often their daughters (60 percent), whom they view as extensions of themselves (67 percent). The average age of the female victims was 6; the male victims, 10.

The *co-offenders* molested their children with male partners. Co-offenders also reported troubled childhoods (100 percent) during which they were molested (100 percent), not by a sibling but by an adult caretaker. They married in their teen years (100 percent) and were in their second (44 percent) or third (44 percent) marriages. Co-offenders had a history of sexual indiscretion (56 percent) and were neglectful parents (66 percent). Their victims were as often their sons (average age 9) as their daughters (average age 7).

The *accomplices*, who assisted male molesters, were of average intelligence (80 percent) and married as teenagers (60 percent). Their victims were most often daughters (75 percent) whose average age was 13. Both co-offenders and accomplices placed their need for a man over the needs of their children.

The study and treatment of female sexual abusers is in the nascent stage. When identified, female offenders are less frequently charged, convicted, or incarcerated than their male counterparts (Rencken, 1989). Thus, they are less available for treatment and follow-up.

The Incestuous Family

Although sexual abuse appears in a variety of types of families, these families share some characteristics. Hilman and Solek-Tefft (1988) summarize these commonalities:

> *Blurred boundaries.* Role definitions and distinctions between parents and children are extremely unclear. Sexual boundaries are equally unclear.
>
> *Role reversal.* The victim is placed in an adult role of parent and

spouse. The nonabusing spouse is often relegated to a needy-child role.

Isolation. The family members view outsiders with distrust. They turn inward for support and intimacy, rather than reaching out to non-family members.

Lack of privacy. There is little physical or psychological privacy in the family. Doors cannot be locked and family members have the right to invade each other's rooms and personal belongings.

Mishandling of power. Power is not shared in the family. The perpetrator is most likely to be the only family member with any power.

Low self-esteem. Individual family members as well as the family as a whole are lacking in self-confidence and a positive self-image.

Fear of breaking up. The fear of disintegration is much greater than the distress resulting from the sexual abuse.

Lack of assertiveness and independence. Family members are extremely dependent on one another and do not risk confrontations with one another.

Poor communication. Keeping the peace is a family goal that interferes with dealing with conflicts and disagreements. Discussions are kept at a surface level.

Rigidity. The family supports a strongly conventional moral code. Rigid rules apply to all family activities.

Lack of appropriate sympathy. Family members are extremely self-involved and lack the ability to sympathize or empathize with others in the family.

Denial. Family members, led by the perpetrator, deny that they have any problems or require any assistance from the outside world.

Secrecy. Sexual abuse is one of many secrets kept in this family. Members do not share anything meaningful with one another.

Sexually abusive families tend to exhibit one of the following patterns (Cooney, 1987).

The Absent Spouse   Due to death, divorce, illness, or abandonment, some children live with only one of their parents. The oldest child is often elevated to a parenting role and becomes a substitute adult companion for the remaining parent.

Dependent Husband/Domineering Wife   A second family pattern observed in child sexual abuse cases is that of the hostile, angry wife who is in charge of the family, and the passive, dependent husband who is in charge of nothing. Although they may be close in age, the domineering wife complains that her husband is an additional child requiring her care. The dependent husband leaves all decisions and choices to his wife. He seeks affection from her but is unsuccessful in obtaining it. He feels inadequate and angry with his wife but would never challenge her authority directly. He is inclined to turn to his daughter, a less threatening female.

Possessive Husband/Passive Wife   This is the reverse of the second pattern. In this family the husband controls everything. His family members are his possessions. They exist to meet his needs. Although he is often considered a model citizen outside his home, he is a tyrant within it. He can be violent toward his wife or his children, and no one who lives in his domain will risk his wrath.

The passive wife has very low self-esteem. She believes that she is nothing without her husband. She may have been physically or sexually abused as a child. She then married a man who confirmed her worthlessness. She is totally dependent financially and emotionally on her husband. Holding on to her marriage is more important than anything else to her.

Although the husband enjoyed his role of king in the early years of marriage, eventually he becomes angry and disgusted with his clinging wife. He considers his daughters to be more adult than their mother.

Dependent Husband/Dependent Wife   In some instances, two adults who have difficulty managing their own lives marry with the expectation that someone will finally take care of them. When the need for care cannot be met by either spouse, they look to their children to meet these needs. The children are expected to parent the adults in this family.

The Normless/Chaotic Family   In this family sexual boundaries may not exist. Sleeping arrangements and overnight guests may vary from night to night. Drug or alcohol abuse may be prevalent. Rules and accountability are for other people.

None of these families welcome intervention nor are they inclined to seek professional or legal intervention voluntarily. The victim sometimes indirectly reveals abuse by acting out sexually, running away, abusing drugs or alcohol, or attempting suicide. Several precipitating factors might motivate a sexually abused teen to risk direct disclosure (Cooney, 1988, p. 8).

1. The abuser is beginning to demand full sexual intercourse. When the victim reaches puberty, the abuser rationalizes that the child is now an adult.
2. The abuser becomes more possessive and restrictive toward the victim. The victim, now a teenager, does not want to live with rules and innuendos about dating. Other members of the family may attempt

to intervene when the parent is obviously unreasonable, and the resulting family arguments make it more difficult for everyone to ignore the inappropriate relationship.
3. The teen becomes more informed about sexuality. The relationship
that the abusing parent described as normal is no longer considered
normal by the adolescent.
4. The teen becomes aware that the abuser is a threat to other siblings.
Although disclosure is painful, it is the only recourse for the adolescent who wants to protect younger family members.

Many forms of sexual abuse occur within the family. We will consider some of the most common variations.

Father-Daughter Sexual Abuse

Until fairly recently, father-daughter sexual abuse was considered the
only type of sexual abuse. It remains the most frequently reported form.
The women's movement has been a powerful force in bringing this problem to public attention. Feminist theory perceives father-daughter sexual
abuse as the "most extreme manifestation of the power imbalance and a
within-the-family conditioning of women to their roles in society"
(Courtois, 1988, p. 119). Women are conditioned to be passive and dependent, and men are conditioned to dominate females. Judith Herman (1981)
states that "as long as fathers rule but do not nurture, as long as mothers
nurture but do not rule, the conditions favoring the development of father-daughter incest will prevail" (p. 206). The imbalance of power in the
family can only be corrected by a change in the structure of the family.
The father in father-daughter sexual abuse has not fallen in love with
his daughter. He uses sexual activity to meet his needs for power, control,
or comfort. If he is not reported, it is likely that he will molest other children in his family.

Father-Son Sexual Abuse

Same-sex sexual abuse does not imply homosexuality in the perpetrator
or the victim. It has been hypothesized (Kempe & Kempe, 1984) that fathers who molest their sons may be performing the same sexual activities
that were performed on them by their fathers at the same age. The negative effects of this family tradition are compounded by the male victim's
concerns about his own sexuality. His reluctance to report the abuse is
partially based on his concern that others will identify him as a homosexual (Cooney, 1987). He has also been socialized to handle problems himself, rather than requesting help from others.
Boys are molested by their fathers and by other male relatives. They

are also more likely than girls to be victimized by males outside the family (Finkelhor, 1984).

Mother-Son Sexual Abuse

Information about the prevalence of mother-son sexual abuse is limited and contradictory. Kempe and Kempe (1984) describe a scenario in which the father is absent and the boy is considered the man of the house. He replaces his father as a sexual partner for his mother.

The recognition that mothers are capable of molesting their sons has been impeded by professional denial. Allen (1990) points out that the same professionals who have no difficulty accepting father-daughter sexual abuse, characterized mother-son sexual abuse as an extremely rare aberration. It is also a threat to the beliefs and theories that followed Freud's original formulations. The incidence of sexual abuse by females is not known, nor has there been sufficient research to formulate theories or treatment protocols. What is known about this form of sexual abuse originates primarily from anecdotal reports by adult survivors. Their credibility is questioned by a society that confuses sex with sexual abuse.

Mother-Daughter Sexual Abuse

If possible, even less is known about mothers who molest their daughters than is known about mothers who molest their sons. It is considered the rarest and least discussed form of incest (Waterman & Lusk, 1986). Mrazek (1981) describes a scenario in which the mother sleeps with her daughter to avoid sexual contact with her husband. A more graphic picture of mother-daughter sexual abuse was painted in *Sybil* (Schreiber, 1974), a popular nonfiction book that was made into a movie. The author described the sadistic torture and sexual abuse perpetrated by a mother over many years. The book focused attention on the connection between extreme abuse and the development of multiple personalities.

Sibling Abuse

It is believed by many experts (Laredo, 1982; Kempe & Kempe, 1984; Pierce & Pierce, 1990) that the incidence of sibling abuse is extremely underestimated by professionals. Brother-sister incest is the most common type of sibling incest reported (Laredo, 1982). In some instances the brother actually has a parent role in the family. He may be a source of income and emotional support for his mother and have disciplinary responsibilities as well. The victim may feel that she is actually experiencing father-daughter exploitation in this case. Whether the sibling abuse involves sisters, brothers, or a combination of both, the issues of intimidation, threat, physical force, and consent must be explored. The clinician must be attuned to the differences between exploration and sex play versus sexual abuse among siblings. The continuing increase in the number of "blended" families expands the potential for sibling abuse.

Issues that must be addressed in the treatment of adolescent sibling abusers include: the offender's low self-esteem; the social isolation experienced by offenders; the need for sex education; and the need of offenders to recognize their pattern of behavior antecedent to incestuous activity (Pierce & Pierce, 1990).

Abuse by Other Relatives

Children are abused by grandparents, aunts, uncles, cousins, and other family members. Some abusers may be parental substitutes who have direct responsibility for their victims. As family members, they have access to the victims and the trust of parents. Others may be pedophiles who use children whenever they are available.

The effects of sexual abuse vary depending upon the duration of the abuse, the age of onset, and the closeness of the relationship of the victim to the abuser (Cooney, 1988).

Treatment Issues and Options

A major difference in the treatment of sexual abusers and pedophiles is that members of the sexual abuser's family are included in the treatment program. By definition, the victim is a member of the abuser's family. The spouse of the abuser is also encouraged to participate in treatment. The pedophile is likely to be treated in isolation from his or her family.

Groth (1982) provides treatment considerations for the practitioner who works with incest perpetrators. He suggests the following:

1. You are dealing with an unmotivated client. He is not self-referred. It will therefore be important to ensure his cooperation in a treatment program by having his participation mandated by an external authority such as a court.

2. His sexual offense is not only a symptom, it is also a crime and needs to be dealt with on both levels, requiring combined mental health, social service, and criminal justice intervention.

3. He fears the adverse social and legal consequences of disclosure and will therefore tend to deny the offense or minimize his responsibility for his actions. He must not be allowed to deny his offense, minimize the

seriousness of his behavior, or project responsibility for his actions elsewhere.

4. He has operated from a position of power in regard to his victim and has maintained his control by effecting secrecy about his offense. The conventional therapeutic contract typically involves confidentiality. For this type of client, confidentiality contributes to the dynamics of secrecy and reinforces the offender's position of power and control. It should be waived. Not only must any suspected or known incident of incestuous behavior be reported to the proper authorities but also, if the offender's spouse is not aware of the situation, he must inform her of it, describing what has occurred. In the case of sibling incest, the parents must be similarly informed.

5. Although incest is a sexual offense, it is not predominantly motivated by sexual needs. It is the sexual expression of nonsexual needs. An incest offender does not commit a sexual offense primarily to satisfy a sexual need, any more than an alcoholic drinks to quench a thirst. It will therefore be necessary to help the offender uncover the underlying nonsexual needs and issues prompting his offense, and to discover why sexuality has become the mode of expression for these unmet needs or unresolved issues.

6. Although other family members may play a contributing role in the evolution of the incestuous relationship, the offender's responsibility for the offense cannot be mitigated by viewing incest as solely the product of family dysfunction. The offender must be held accountable, and therefore family therapy should not be the only, and especially not the initial, plan of action. It must be preceded by individual treatment.

7. The offender generally feels himself to be overwhelmed by life-demands and to be the helpless victim of social forces and life events outside of his control. Thus, in addition to conventional, insight-oriented psychotherapy, he needs to be provided with types of treatment that will help him develop skills and techniques to cope more adequately with life-demands: biofeedback and relaxation exercises to diminish anxiety, assertiveness training, parent effectiveness training, and the like. (Groth, 1982, pp. 236–237)

Groth's concern that family therapy not be the primary treatment mode has been expressed by other treatment providers as well. Meiselman (1978) has summarized the objections of clinicians who work with sexual abusers. The incestuous parent is unlikely to cooperate in the family therapy process, which he or she experiences as a mortifying process; individual counseling for the offender seems to be more effective. Secondly, most incestuous families have sexual problems in the spousal relationship; the parents should not be expected to deal with these issues in the presence of their children. Finally, the underlying assumption in family therapy that all family members share responsibility for the family's difficulties is contrary to the reality of sexual abuse. The abusing adult is totally responsible for the molestation; the victim is guiltless. Family therapy has a role in the treatment of sexual abuse, but it is a secondary one that may follow the treatment of each family member individually, in dyads, and in groups (Giarretto, 1982).

The treatment options for pedophiles that were previously identified in this chapter are also options for sexual abusers. Incarceration or placement in a residential treatment facility are appropriate for the few violent sexual abusers. The majority of sexual abusers, if identified, will be required to participate in a community-based treatment program. Depending upon the jurisdiction, some will also serve jail time or participate in a work-release program that includes community-based treatment. The largest such program is the Child Sexual Abuse Treatment Program (CSATP) in Santa Clara County, California.

Central to the treatment program are the many groups available to family members. There are groups for mothers, groups for fathers, groups for children and/or adults, parenting groups, etc. Parents attend Parents United meetings; children attend Daughters and Sons United groups.

Play therapy, puppetry, and art therapy are used with young children. Great emphasis is placed on working with the nonabusing spouse and victim together. Giarretto has found that this relationship is the key to healing in the family (Cooney, 1988). The longer it takes to reconstruct the parent-child bond, the less likely it is that the victim can return to the home.

Other Treatment Options

Sexual abusers and their family members are treated in private practice as well as in a variety of community agencies and institutions. In a survey of treatment providers, group therapy was the treatment modality most often reported used by community-based programs and institutional treatment providers (Plyer, Woolley & Anderson, 1990). Individual therapy was the second choice. Cognitive and behavioral approaches were most commonly used with sexual abusers. The length of treatment varied from months to years.

Treatment Goals and Philosophy

Salter (1988) identified the goals of therapy for offenders. These are:

1. A primary goal is for offenders to learn to control their deviant arousal patterns.

2. A second goal is to place obstacles in the path of converting nonsexual problems into sexual behavior. These may include removing the father from the home, developing a better mother-child relationship, and improving the ability of the victim to be assertive and to report any attempts at remolestation. A key to minimizing the risk of reoccurrence is to strengthen the positive qualities of the mother-child relationship.

3. A third goal of therapy is for offenders and their families to learn to solve nonsexual problems in nonsexual ways. For example, the offenders need to deal with marital problems, depression, and other life problems directly, without the use of inappropriate sexual acting-out. (pp. 66–67)

The practitioner or team of practitioners who work with sexual abusers and their families must consider the welfare and safety of the children as the primary concern. Therefore the reunification of the family, if desired, must of necessity be a slow and deliberate process. Minimal requirements for considering family reunification include:

(a) The abuser acknowledges the behavior, takes responsibility for the abuse, and does not project blame on the victim.
(b) The nonabusing parent does not hold the victim responsible for the abuse.
(c) The nonabusing parent demonstrates the ability to protect the child from abuse.
(d) The victim demonstrates the ability to obtain professional help if approached by the abuser.
(e) The therapist and all family members express reasonable assurance that the victim is safe from future abuse.
(f) The family has been restructured with more appropriate role boundaries and an improved marital relationship.
(g) The therapist and family members are certain that sufficient progress has been made on short- and long-term treatment goals. (Walker, Bonner & Kaufman, 1988, p. 137)

Conclusions

Sexual abuse is a symptom of a family in crisis. All members of the family are affected by the abuse and the other problems with which abuse is associated. Interventions must extend beyond the perpetrator to family members and the family structure. Clinicians will encounter extremes of denial, anger, and secrecy in working with sexual abusers and their families. A multi-modal approach is required in order to circumvent the barriers to treatment. Reporting is the first step toward family reconstruction.

A difference of opinion remains on the disposition of cases involving pedophiles and sexual abusers. On one side are cries for mandatory incarceration and lengthy sentences. On the other are those who advocate for treatment rather than punitive measures. While adults contemplate the advantages of each choice, children continue to be sexually abused in their own homes and other "safe" places by family members and caretakers. There are more questions than answers in the area of sexual misuse of children. The skilled and informed clinician may change that ratio.

References

Abel, G., Beck, J., Mittleman, M., Cunningham-Rathner, J., Rouleau, J., & Murphy, W. (1987). Self-reported sex crimes of nonincarcerated paraphilacs. *Journal of Interpersonal Violence, 2,* 3–25.

Allen, C. M. (1990). Women as perpetrators of child sexual abuse: Recognition barriers. In A. L. Horton, B. L. Johnson, L. M. Roundy & D. Williams (Eds.), *The incest perpetrator: A family member no one wants to treat* (pp. 108–125). Newbury Park, CA: Sage Publications.

American Psychiatric Association. (1987). *Diagnostic and statistical manual of mental disorders.* (3rd ed., revised). Washington, DC: Author.

Ballard, D., Blair, G., Devereaux, S., Valentine, L., Horton, A., & Johnson, B. (1990). A comparative profile of the incest perpetrator: Background characteristics, abuse history, and use of social skills. In A. L. Horton, B. L. Johnson, L. M. Roundy & D. Williams (Eds.), *The incest perpetrator: A family member no one wants to treat* (pp. 43–64). Newbury Park, CA: Sage Publications.

Belanger, A., Connor, J., Copenhafer, D., D'Agostino, R., Gould, R., Guio, J., Guio, M., Locker, M., Montan, C., Rodgers, T., Similes, K., & Swartz, M. (1984). Scope of the problem: Investigation and prosecution. In A. Burgess (Ed.), *Child pornography and sex rings* (pp. 25–50). Lexington, MA: D. C. Heath.

Beranbaum, T., Burgess, A., Cucci, J., Davidson, H., McCaghy, T., & Summit, R. (1984). Child pornography in the 1970s. In A. Burgess (Ed.), *Child pornography and sex rings* (pp. 7–23). Lexington, MA: D. C. Heath.

Berlin, F., & Krout, E. (1986). Pedophilia: Diagnostic concepts, treatment, and ethical considerations. *American Journal of Forensic Psychiatry, 7*(1), 13–30.

Cooney, J. (1987). *Coping with sexual abuse.* New York: Rosen.

Cooney, J. (1988). Child abuse: A developmental perspective. *Counseling and Human Development, 20*(5), 1–10.

Courtois, C. (1988). *Healing the incest wound: Adult survivors in therapy.* New York: W. W. Norton.

Crewdson, J. (1988). *By silence betrayed: Sexual abuse of children in America.* New York: Harper & Row.

de Mause, L. (1974). The evolution of childhood. In L. de Mause (Ed.), *The history of childhood: The untold story of child abuse* (pp. 1–73). New York: Psychohistory Press.

Finkelhor, D. (1984). *Child sexual abuse: New theory and research.* New York: Free Press.

Finkelhor, D., & Williams, L. (1988a). The characteristics of incestuous fathers: A review of recent studies. In W. Marshall, D. Laws & H. Barbee (Eds.), *The handbook of sexual assault: Issues, theories and treatment of the offender.* New York: Plenum.

Finkelhor, D., & Williams, L. (1988b). *Nursery crimes: Sexual abuse in day care.* Newbury Park, CA: Sage.

Giarretto, H. (1981). A comprehensive child sexual abuse treatment program. In P. B. Mrazek & C. H. Kempe (Eds.), *Sexually abused children and their families* (pp. 179–197). New York: Pergamon.

Giarretto, H. (1982). *Integrated treatment of child sexual abuse.* Palo Alto, CA: Science and Behavior Books.

Giarretto, H., & Einfeld-Giarretto, A. (1990). Integrated treatment: The self-help factor. In A. L. Horton, B. L. Johnson, L. M. Roundy & D. Williams (Eds.), *The incest perpetrator: A family member no one wants to treat* (pp. 219–226). Newbury Park, CA: Sage Publications.

Goldstein, S. (1984, January). Investigating child sexual exploitation: Law enforcement's role. *FBI Law Enforcement Bulletin,* pp. 22–31.

Groth, A. N. (1982). The incest offender. In S. Sgroi (Ed.), *Handbook of clinical intervention in child sexual abuse* (pp. 215–239). Lexington, MA: D. C. Heath.

Groth, A. N., Hobson, W. F., & Gary, T. S. (1982). The child molester: Clinical observations. In J. R. Conte & D. A. Shore (Eds.), *Social work and child sexual abuse* (pp. 129–144). New York: Haworth.

Herman, J. (1981). *Father-daughter incest.* Cambridge, MA: Harvard University Press.

Hillman, D., & Solek-Tefft, J. (1988). *Spiders and flies: Help for parents and teachers of sexually abused children.* Lexington, MA: D. C. Heath.

Illinois Department of Children and Family Services. (1989). *Child abuse and neglect statistics: Annual report. Fiscal year 1988.* Springfield, IL: State of Illinois.

Justice, B., & Justice, R. (1979). *The broken taboo: Sex in the family.* New York: Human Sciences Press.

Kelly, R. (1982). Behavioral reorientation of pedophiliacs: Can it be done? *Clinical Psychology Review, 2*(3), 387–408.

Kempe, R., & Kempe, C. H. (1984). *The common secret: Sexual abuse of children and adolescents.* New York: W. H. Freeman.

Langevin, R. (1983). *Sexual strands: Understanding and treating sexual anomalies in men.* Hillsdale, NJ: Erlbaum Associates.

Langevin, R., & Lang, R. (1985). Psychological treatment of pedophiles. *Behavioral Sciences and the Law, 3*(4), 403–419.

Lanning, K. (1984). Collectors. In A. Burgess (Ed.), *Child pornography and sex rings* (pp. 83–92). Lexington, MA: D. C. Heath.

Lanyon, R. (1986). Theory and treatment in child molestation. *Journal of Consulting and Clinical Psychology, 54*(2), 176–182.

Laredo, C. (1982). Sibling incest. In S. Sgroi (Ed.), *Handbook of clinical intervention in child sexual abuse* (pp. 177–189). Lexington, MA: D. C. Heath.

Laws, R. (1988). Treating pedophiles in the community. *Preventing Sexual Abuse, 1*(3), 8–11.

Lew, M. (1988). *Victims no longer: Men recovering from incest and other sexual child abuse.* New York: Nevraumont.

Mayer, A. (1985). *Sexual abuse: Causes, consequences, and treatment of incestuous and pedophilic acts.* Holmes Beach, FL: Learning Publications.

Mayer, A. (1988). *Sex offenders: Approaches to understanding and management.* Holmes Beach, FL: Learning Publications.

McCarty, L. (1986). Mother-child incest: Characteristics of the offender. *Child Welfare, 65*(5), 447–458.

Meiselman, K. (1978). *Incest: A psychological study of causes and effects with treatment recommendations.* San Francisco: Jossey-Bass.

Mrazek, P. (1981). The nature of incest: A review of contributing factors. In P. Mrazek & C. H. Kempe (Eds.), *Sexually abused children and their families* (pp. 97–107). New York: Pergamon.

Naitove, C. (1988). Using the arts therapies in treatment of sexual offenders against children. In S. Sgroi (Ed.), *Vulnerable populations* (pp. 265–298). Lexington, MA: D. C. Heath.

O'Brien, M., & Bera, W. (1986). Adolescent sexual offenders: A descriptive typology. *Preventing Sexual Abuse, 1*(3), 1–4.

O'Brien, S. (1983). *Child pornography*. Dubuque, IA: Kendall/Hunt.

O'Connell, M., Leberg, E., & Donaldson, C. (1990). *Working with sex offenders*. Newbury Park, CA: Sage Publications.

Pierce, L., & Pierce, R. (1990). Adolescent/sibling incest perpetrators. In A. L. Horton, B. L. Johnson, L. M. Roundy & D. Williams (Eds.), *The incest perpetrator: A family member no one wants to treat* (pp. 99–107). Newbury Park, CA: Sage Publications.

Plyer, A., Woolley, C., & Anderson, T. (1990). Current treatment providers. In A. L. Horton, B. L. Johnson, L. M. Roundy & D. Williams (Eds.), *The incest perpetrator: A family member no one wants to treat* (pp. 198–218). Newbury Park, CA: Sage Publications.

Rencken, R. (1989). *Intervention strategies for sexual abuse*. Alexandria, VA: American Association for Counseling and Development.

Romero, J., & Williams, L. (1983). Group psychotherapy and intensive probation supervision with sex offenders. *Federal Probation, 47*(4), 36–42.

Rossman, P. (1976). *Sexual experience between men and boys*. New York: Association Press.

Salter, A. (1988). *Treating child sex offenders and victims*. Newbury Park, CA: Sage Publications.

Schreiber, F. (1974). *Sybil*. New York: Warner Books.

Sgroi, S., Blick, L., & Porter, F. (1982). A conceptual framework for child sexual abuse. In S. Sgroi (Ed.), *Handbook of clinical intervention in child sexual abuse* (pp. 9–37). Lexington, MA: D. C. Heath.

Smith, T. (1989). Masks and metaphors. *Preventing Sexual Abuse, 1*(4), 4–7.

Tingle, D., Barnard, G., Robbins, L., Newman, G., & Hutchinson, D. (1986). Childhood and adolescent characteristics of pedophiles and rapists. *International Journal of Law and Psychiatry, 9*, 103–116.

Walker, C., Bonner, B., & Kaufman, K. (1988). *The physically and sexually abused children: Evaluation and treatment*. New York: Pergamon.

Waterman, J., & Lusk, R., (1986). Scope of the problem. In K. MacFarlane, J. Waterman, S. Conerly, L. Damon, M. Durfee & S. Long (Eds.), *Sexual abuse of young children* (pp. 3–12). New York: Guilford.

Wilson, G., & Cox, D. (1983). Personality of paedophile club members. *Personality and Individual Differences, 4*(3), 323–329).

_9

Interpersonal and Love Relationships

JACK E. FARRAR, Ph.D.

THE GENERAL PUBLIC in recent years has been flooded with books about "women who love too much" and about women loving men who hate them. Also, there is much written about the spouses who remain in physically and psychologically dependent and destructive relationships (see Chapter 7). What are the reasons so many people stay in seemingly unhealthy relationships? It hardly seems possible that individuals would voluntarily choose to stay with something that in no way is rewarding and, from a behavioral point of view, is psychologically and physically unhealthy for them. At some level, however, these individuals are receiving powerful reinforcement for their loyalty. There must be some underlying function or purpose for the structure and maintenance of these relationships. McClelland, Atkinson, Clark and Lowell (1953) proposed through a "discrepancy hypothesis" the theory that people tend to conduct their lives in a manner that is not discrepant from past experiences; that is, it is much easier, safer, and less threatening to perform tasks that are similar to those to which they have been accustomed.

This country seems to be experiencing an epidemic of interpersonal turmoil. The divorce rate for first marriages is close to 50 percent—and even higher for second marriages. Many people seem to be merely existing in bad relationships, unable to free themselves from partners who provide little positive reinforcement. With many of these unhealthy and often emotionally damaging relationships, people choose to tough it out. Why is this? Why do people passively and helplessly remain in harmful and sometimes even fatal relationships? Many experts (Halpern, 1983; Peele, 1985) are claiming that individuals in couples similar to ones described are in fact addicted to one another and are helpless to leave each other. These individuals, it seems, are striving to get a "fix" from their mate in order to live their lives. The addiction is in the form of a special kind of love. Lionells (1986) refers to this kind of love as hysteria that has a deep dependency on approval-seeking as the integral form of the interpersonal interaction.

Simon (1982) compared two kinds of love, suggesting that love can either have a severe addictive quality or can be a source of self-realization. According to Simon, an addiction to a love relationship is one in which each person needs the other in order to survive (symbiosis). On the other hand, the self-realization aspect of love refers to the constructive, intimate relationship in which each partner adds to the richness of the other's experience. In summary, individuals caught in symbiotic relationships tend to feel incomplete without their partner, and those in constructive intimate relationships tend not only to feel complete without their partner, but also to feel that their partner has added to their own independence and sense of self.

Case Study Number 1

Roger and Ann were a childless couple in their mid-thirties, caught in a love relationship that was clearly addictive. The couple was referred for treatment due to severe marital problems and was seen over a 4-year period. They had been together for 14 years of marriage in what, from the outside, appeared to be an intense love-hate relationship. This couple acted out a pursuer-distancer dynamic perfectly. When Roger made attempts to pursue Ann, she wanted nothing to do with him. When Ann attempted to be close, Roger's temper would flare and frighten Ann back into a distant stance. Although the relationship was neither rewarding nor boring, it was dramatically suspenseful, highly intense, extremely chaotic much of the time, and highly predictable. Seldom, and for only brief periods of time, was the relationship calm. It was as if calmness in the relationship did not confirm an aliveness in each partner. Intense chaos and dramatic intensity were necessary for these people to feel viable, confirmed, and validated. The intense chaos seemed to mirror the behavior patterns historically experienced in each of these individuals' families of origin.

Neither set of parents had good relationships during Roger's and Ann's life at home. Both set of parents were described as being distant and uninvolved. Both Roger and Ann needed a great deal of love that had not been forthcoming in their childhoods, and they were tremendously frightened of letting their partner close enough that they would begin depending on that closeness. Rather, both set up a paradox in their relationship. A closeness was desired, and even expected of the other partner, but it was too frightening. Both were so hungry for the closeness that they became terrified of getting it, for fear that it would be taken from them;

both felt that they could not handle the devastation if this were to happen to them. The relationship progressed, with neither partner succeeding in being close to the other at the same time.

This couple used their therapy to look at the possibility of ending this unfulfilling relationship, although neither had seriously thought about ending it until this point. Both had learned from their parents that marriage was forever, no matter whether there was happiness. Once they both became clear that much of their emotional turmoil within the relationship was due to repetition of behaviors reinforced in their respective nuclear families, individual therapy was begun.

Initially, individual therapy was chosen over couples therapy due to the issues presented, which were intrapsychic and related much more to the dynamics of the family of origin and less directly to the partner in the relationship. The relationship was merely the sphere in which these dynamics were being acted out.

Deep Commitment Versus Addiction

One of the dilemmas for Roger and Ann was that they were on an endless treadmill that repeated the same painful struggle. They were stuck in the addictive patterns of their relationship. The following are several criteria that differentiate this pattern of addiction from relationships built on deep, growing commitments to another person.

1. Does each individual within the relationship value his or her own development first? Does each person have important interests outside the relationship, including significant personal relationships?

2. Is the relationship seen as a separate entity from each individual, or do individual and couple blend together without clear boundaries?

3. Is the relationship an open system that encourages the two members to venture out and explore and also encourages others to enter the system, or is the system closed to outsiders and outside influence?

4. Is the energy in the relationship system synergistic and alive rather than subtractive and flat? Does the relationship fulfill these individuals so that they are able to live a higher-quality, more productive, and more enriching life outside the relationship?

5. Is each person beyond being possessive or jealous of the other's growth and expansion of interests? (Fromm, 1956)

6. When a person takes steps to end the addictive relationship, does he or she suffer acute withdrawal symptoms, including physical distress, that can only be relieved by reestablishing contact? (Halpern, 1983)

7. When the relationship is really over (or a partner fantasizes that it has ended), does either partner feel the lostness, aloneness, and emptiness of a person exiled, with that feeling often followed or even accompanied by a feeling of liberation? (Halpern, 1983)

Addictive relationships are ones in which one or both partners are diminished when together. They either close others out and deprive themselves of nurturing from an outside support group and/or they put a lid on the development of their individual selves.

Systemic Issues in Relationship Addictions

In systems terminology, relationship addicts maintain a closed system. Other people do not enter the system, nor do members of the relationship leave the system. The important key in any kind of relationship addiction is that the system remains closed. This ingredient guarantees the ongoing nature of the addiction. A self-perpetuating homeostasis has been established; it not only feeds off itself in a symbiotic manner but also, through the use of internal intermittent reinforcement, acts to generate energy from within the system. External energy entering the system is discouraged and usually not accepted. Therefore, the internal system merely stagnates and continuously cycles through the same dynamics.

Addicted individuals lose sight of the other partner in the relationship at the time the addiction is cemented, and the symbiosis is locked into place at this point in the relationship. Both partners provide each other with blind security and a safety net of *sameness*. As a result of the sameness, and the often boring quality of the relationship, the couple's system forms repetitive patterns of behavior. This repetition tends to reduce the fear of change and hence of possible loss.

With so much sameness the couple has to have a means of capturing each other's attention. This capture can take many forms, such as developing a dynamic of distance (separating) and pursuing (coming closer) or an abuser-victim dynamic or one of many different routines to raise the emotional ante through increased chaos and nonrational behavior. This process tends to recharge the intensity of the addictive commitment cycle. It is as if each person in the couple activates the other to inject life (although negative and destructive much of the time) back into the relationship, thus ensuring the couple's intense negative involvement with one another.

Relationships can either be growth-oriented and fulfilling or consuming and addictive. Put another way, relationships may be addictive or synergistic. Each person brings to the relationship something of his or her own and adds it to the pool of partnership characteristics, thus making the relationship fuller than it could be with either of the members of the couple functioning independently. Greer (1971) suggested that relationship addiction involves a couple sacrificing their initial positive love for the mutual dependence of symbiosis, resulting in a relationship where there is barely a whole human being between the two.

Individuals who have not previously struggled with their own separateness from their family of origin have tremendous difficulty in perceiving themselves as capable of emotionally surviving as separate, independent individuals. They do what is most comfortable and at the same time least threatening: hook up with another human being who will provide the kind of external confirmation that they cannot provide for themselves. This type of dynamic is often observed in members of a couple who after divorce need immediately to attach to another person who looks different from their ex-spouse but who turns out to have similar dynamics; the separateness of being alone is too overwhelming. These individuals proceed through life carrying the emotional remnants of past marriages and the unfinished business from their families of origin.

Case Study Number 2

This vignette describes an adolescent who grew up in a family that formed a closed system. This young man was discouraged from going outside the family system for any of his need fulfillment.

Wayne was a 16-year old boy who had been in therapy for a long period of time. When the therapist started seeing Wayne, he had been removed from his home after a suicide attempt. Wayne said that his mother was very weak and could not take care of herself emotionally and that his father was an alcoholic. Wayne had not been allowed to go to other boy's homes to play but had to remain at home after school to take care of his younger brother physically and take care of his mother emotionally. He was clearly a "parentified child." By the age of 15, when he entered therapy, it became clear that he was intensely involved in an addicted relationship with a girlfriend. Needing to be loved, Wayne traded caretaking of Margaret, his girlfriend, for the constant attention and affection she gave in return. Due partially to growing up in a closed family system, Wayne would become very jealous and angry if Margaret talked to other boys. He became very territorial about her, even when she spent time with her girlfriends. Actually, he became angry if Margaret spent any time or energy outside their symbiotic relationship.

Up to this point the roles of individual and couple issues in the development of relationship addictions have been examined, but this only describes part of the problem. Family dynamics that feed into an individual's relationship addiction should also be studied.

Boundaries and Hierarchy Issues

A predominant issue in families that produce an addicted child is the lack of good, clear interpersonal boundaries. Little clear separateness is evident in these families, and often one parent is seen as helpless. As a result, one of the children takes over the parental responsibility that the helpless parent has given up. Also, since parents in these systems do not relate well together, it is not unusual for the parenting child to be involved in an "emotional marriage" with one of the parents. Individuals who become addicted to relationships begin this conditioning process within this kind of family structure at a very early age. The structure for the development of an addiction of this sort is clearly established in the first two or three years of life.

Within-family fears and heightened anxieties are often passed on to the children. Problems arise when the children are nonverbally expected to do something to alleviate the fear of their mother or father. The children, especially the one least emotionally separated from his or her parents, are usually tuned into family pain, anxiety, and fear. The child feels helpless and at the same time is called upon to "emotionally rescue" the frightened part of the family system.

Children caught in a dilemma like this often attempt a variety of behaviors to reduce perceived neediness in the parents. The rescuing kinds of behaviors required by the system are less important than the effect that this kind of (often) nonverbalized request has on the children. The child is encouraged to play a certain role that does not focus on the growth or development of emotional security. The child, in essence, is frozen in his or her individual development, with no adult model to provide a sense of control over the environment. Recoiling and nonexploratory behavior are reinforced when risk-taking behavior is not modelled, supported, or practiced in the family.

Family systems that produce relationship addictions are highly anxious and fearful and feel little control over the outside world. Many of these families tend to deny their basic feelings of insecurity, which are masked in different ways. For many of these families the denial of the insecure feelings will be presented as reaction formations. For instance, families feeling a lack of control in their external world will be very controlling within the family. This process sets up all sorts of double messages within the family. For example, when a child attempts to do something that suggests an attempt at mastery of some task in his or her world, the parents will often deprecate this behavior or ignore it altogether.

The role that most often is selected by these children, who later become addicted to relationships, is the role of rescuer. Later in life, this role is one of the functional elements that acts to cement the relationship addiction. The rescuer is seen by his or her partner as very helpful, giving, and caretaking—all of the attributes that were desired from the parents but that were not present. The rescuer often secretly fantasizes that he or she will also be given the same rescuing treatment. This fantasy played out by the adult couple may replicate what went on in these individuals' relationships with their parents. The rescuer replays the dynamics that occurred in his or her early childhood. Each time this struggle is reenacted, there is the opportunity to have emotional roles reversed, resulting in the rescuer being cared for and the original psychological damage being repaired. The unconscious hope is that the emotional relationship will be healed, to provide a way for the early developmental intrapsychic deficits played out in relationships to be corrected.

Destructive Impact of Addictive Relationships

Two emotionally needy individuals manage to find each other, and they quickly progress into a state of limerence (Tennov, 1979). *Limerence* is a state of acute longing for the object of one's passionate desire. The exuberance and buoyancy experienced when thinking of the other person completely obscure any negative aspects or deficits in the relationship. The partners in such a relationship are primarily motivated by their own need for security rather than by appreciation of the personal attributes and qualities that their partner brings to the relationship. What these individuals most want from their partners is reassurance of constancy (Peele & Brodsky, 1975). The basis of constancy and movement away from change lead to the couple's progression toward a closed system, one in which others do not participate and one that the partners do not leave.

Such partners do require each other to change in certain ways, but the adaptations expected or demanded are entirely toward each other and do not entail an improved ability to deal with other people or the world. The changes one partner expects of the other to satisfy his or her needs are almost always harmful to the other's general development as a person. In fact, a lessened ability to cope with anything or anyone else is welcomed as a stronger guarantee of allegiance to the relationship. This is why jealousy and possessiveness are so much a part of addictive love. An addict actually hopes that his or her lover will not meet new people and enjoy the world, since such an expansion suggests competing ties and interests that would make the partner less available or dependent.

Treatment of Relationship Addictions

How then do people addicted to relationships go about stopping this negative, painful cycle? When treating addiction to relationships and love, the following should be considered: intrapsychic issues, interpersonal issues, and issues related to the nuclear family and family of origin.

Several means are cited in research literature, by which a relationship addiction can be broken (Halpern, 1983; Peele & Brodsky, 1975; Forward, 1986; Norwood, 1985). Perhaps the most important ingredient in breaking any relationship addiction is the awareness that an addiction is present. Without at least one person in an addicted relationship admitting that an addiction is present, there is no way the addiction can be broken.

Many authors make recommendations about breaking addictions to relationships, breaking the dependent force that causes loss of selfhood in addiction, and encouraging development toward the personal fulfillment found in a more independent lifestyle. The first step in breaking an addiction to another person is a true self-confrontation. This often means coming to grips with one's aloneness and sense of personal emptiness. It also indicates a need to reach greater awareness of one's projective identification onto others and an honest attempt to acknowledge the unfinished business that underlies this projection (Peele & Brodsky, 1975).

Halpern (1983) treats relationship addicts through the use of the informational statements that provide insight into the relationship addiction. Halpern employs such statements as, "You can live without him/her (probably better)," "Limerence is not enough," "You can't always work it out, no matter how much you may want to," and "When you feel inadequate, incomplete, or worthless apart from him/her, childhood feelings are taking over" (pp. 240–241). Halpern's psychotherapy uses statements similar to these to encourage his patients to confront their addictive dynamics, to either change the relationship or move out of it.

The following statements (not included in Halpern's list) provide additional information to be used with individuals in addictive relationships. These formulations tend to help individuals to become more aware of ways in which they get stuck and cannot leave hurtful, addictive relationships.

1. Past behavior is the best predictor of present and future behavior. If the person you are living with has behaved the same way throughout the relationship, don't expect major changes in the future.

2. Major change in your partner will not come about without some sort of external change intervention (i.e., serous involvement in psychotherapy or a group experience similar to Alcoholics Anonymous).

3. If an intervention such as therapy is initiated, it is important that your spouse or partner take responsibility for his or her change. You cannot force your partner to change. No significant change will come about unless your partner sincerely desires to change. Attendance in therapy or any other major change intervention, under any circumstances other than willing participation, leads to superficial and usually short-lived change at best.

4. Although there will be anxiety, loneliness, and depression if you end your relationship, remember that all of these intense feelings were present many times during your relationship. One partner in an addicted relationship reported, "I have never been more lonely and depressed than I was at the low periods in that marriage."

A similar but alternative approach to treating those caught in a codependent relationship is discussed in Chapter 17.

Treatment Guidelines

Part of the treatment focus with addicted clients requires that these individuals be given the opportunity to do some reparative work that they have been unsuccessful in accomplishing through their addicted relationship. Since the treatment of a relationship addiction affects the entire couple and family system, it is important to inform the client that any change in him or her will result in reverberating effects on the system with the spouse and other members of the family.

Halpern (1983) employed writing and psychomotor sculpting techniques in his treatment of relationship addictions. Treatment was initially oriented toward the addicted person gaining greater awareness and understanding of his or her addicted relationship. Once the person became aware of the emotional and behavioral patterns in the relationship, he or she was guided and gently pushed toward reduced dependence on the partner and toward a choice of greater independence. Treatment included behavioral techniques such as monitoring specific behaviors and experiential psychotherapy (such as psychomotor sculpting) to aid these individuals in gaining greater emotional, cognitive, and behavioral awareness of their addiction. Rummel (1988) suggested the use of hypnoanalysis in the treatment of "manaholic(s)" and others involved in highly dependent interpersonal relationships. Rummel contended that personality changes could be made in relatively short periods of time.

Halpern (1983), Rummel (1988), and others have tended to treat relationship addiction with an intrapersonal focus, not really looking at the system in which the addiction originated or the one in which it is acted out. However, when Peele (Peele & Brodsky, 1975; Miller, 1987) discussed the treatment of relationship addictions, he differentiated it from treatment for addictions to inanimate objects such as food, drugs, or alcohol. He believed that relationship addictions involve a whole new perspective and that their treatment cannot be dealt with solely on an intrapersonal basis. The system within which the addiction is acted out must be considered and dealt with.

Peele (Peele & Brodsky, 1975) suggested that it is necessary, in breaking an addiction, to get out of the "set" of the relationship—that is, to experience life in new ways. This may mean developing a support group of a few significant friends and sharing meaningful parts of one's life with them. Peele suggested that the addicted dyadic system be opened up so that other individuals can enter the system, and people previously caught within the addiction can go outside the relationship for some emotional need fulfillment.

In psychotherapeutic treatment, individuals who are addicted to relationships or love need to perceive therapy as a secure and accepting environment where their false (highly dependent, non-self-reliant) selves can be placed on hold and their true selves can evolve. Treatment should be the antithesis of what these individuals received as children. As with most addictions, those addicted to relationships need to explore their feelings in an environment where all feelings will be understood and open expression of feelings will be encouraged. This is the only way that these people can feel safe enough to confront their false selves.

It is important when working with relationship addictions to conceive of these persons' addictions within the systemic framework in which they are presently acting the addiction out, as well as within the original system in which the tendency to addiction first developed (family of origin). This is a major reason for the introduction of the family into the therapy. As the client gains more access to his or her true self, there is less need for that individual to expend as much psychic energy on internal reality. Therefore, the use of group therapy and family therapy aids in the process of helping the addicted individual risk being involved and emotionally energized with the external world.

The major goal of psychotherapy is not to eliminate the pain that a patient carries around inside, nor to erase an addicted patient's high state of neediness. To do these things would merely provide a substitute partner: a surrogate spouse, lover, or parent with whom the addiction could be further extended. Rather, the purpose of psychotherapy is to provide a way for addicted individuals to develop "transmuting internalization"—the ability to soothe, nurture, and strengthen oneself, often through the open emotional exposure of oneself to significant others (Kohut, 1971). The model that appears most effective in treatment of relationship addictions goes beyond the intrapsychic focus of Halpern and the dyadic, systemic approach of Peele; it includes a focus on the extended family system. This treatment model includes three different but necessary components: individual psychotherapy, group psychotherapy, and family therapy. The therapy is initiated in a sequential manner, with individual therapy being started first, and then family and group psychotherapy being initiated at a later date.

Individual Psychotherapy

Individual therapy is recommended for each member of the addicted couple. If one member refuses, the couple is usually cautioned about throwing the system out of balance and warned that this may result in some change within the system; this can mean separation but many times may lead to divorce. Not coming to therapy means that these individuals are unable to depart from the expectations originally established within the addicted relationship. They are able to maintain hope that there will be another parent figure (rescuer) who will come along and give them the kind of emotional reparation that they desire.

The most important goal in individual psychotherapy is to restructure the self so that an individual is able to venture out of his or her internal world of self-absorption and extend the self into the external world of others. Psychotherapy should "aim at the liberation of the hidden self, and its integration into the central sector of the psyche" (Wood, 1987, p. 71). The goals of treatment are to develop the experience and aliveness of the true self so that an individual may be spontaneous, genuine, and open and not approach the world like a chameleon who *exists* so that he or she can feel secure by performing behaviors that are safe but are not a representation of the genuine self. This process helps the person experience the external world in a more open, less fearful manner. Individuals can then emotionally extend themselves more to others. Part of this shift for addicted individuals is to be able to develop real intimacy and closeness with others. This closeness and intimacy is first developed within the relationship with the therapist.

Wallace (1974, p. 304) described psychological treatment of an addict as the development of "a relatively conflict-free addiction to the analyst (therapist) . . . which catalyzes the working through" of the underlying psychological dynamics. As the emotional connection in individual therapy between patient and therapist becomes more firmly established, the more positive the pull becomes for the patient to invest in an enriching, non-consuming relationship. As the patient-therapist relationship develops greater closeness, it becomes safe for the patient to invest more intensity in the relationship and safe enough to reduce the symbiotic involvement in the addictive relationship.

Group Psychotherapy

Group psychotherapy is an important adjunctive therapy to individual psychotherapy. It significantly aids in the development and practice of reaching out to others, and helping individuals become more open and accessible to others. The timing for placing addicted individuals in group therapy is very important and has very little to do with the length of time they have been in psychotherapy. It has much more to do with how much awareness of their addiction is present, how much awareness of intrapersonal dynamics each individual has, and how much motivation there is to change the addiction. A high degree of trust and intimacy between client and individual therapist must be present prior to the beginning of a group therapy experience. If an addicted individual is prematurely placed in group, he or she will definitely find a way to act out his or her addictive issues, which may well lead to premature termination of psychotherapy. An especially good model for conducting group therapy with this population is the placement of the addicted individual into a very small group (four persons at most). As the group gains cohesion and as individuals are able to handle change while still being able to feel safe and genuine, the group can be enlarged.

Case Study Number 3

William, an individual therapy patient, was placed in group therapy too early. He became overwhelmed with the infusion of emotions regarding the intense emotional presence of others. As a result, he reacted in the same pattern that he had exhibited in his relationship with his addicted partner; he chose a woman in the group with whom he could act out his intense dependency by having an affair with her. Both of these people came from addictive relationships and were not emotionally separate enough from their partners (or originally their parents) to feel confident outside of their closed addictive system. Out of fear and anxiety there was an overwhelming need to fill their unbearable emptiness and attachment hunger. Both acted to rescue each other within the context of the group. When the new relationship was discussed in group therapy, the intensity of carefully examining the symbiotic process, and the resultant fear that he would have to give up his newly found object, to whom he had already transferred his over-dependence, became too great. As a result, William left the group.

When an addicted individual is ready, the group process can produce powerful changes. At it simplest level, it is the extension of that individual into potential relationships outside of the one to which he or she is addicted. Naturally, when an individual is placed in a frightening environment and anxiety is heightened, old addictive behavior patterns, rooted in the family of origin, will once again be replayed.

Group psychotherapy offers further possibility to repair the emotional damage that occurred in early childhood. Through transference, countertransference, and interaction with peers, a person's projection of original family members can be acted out in group therapy and important issues can be worked through. The purpose of therapy is to correct the "repetition of non-functional patterns" (Wood, 1987). Group therapy is an important place to observe the process of projective identification: to understand clearly how others are unconsciously chosen so that individuals can externalize their internal struggles onto them. Through this process in group therapy, people are able to gain insight about internal dynamics and to alter significantly the manner in which they relate to others. This alteration not only affects how they will relate to people in their environment, but also will have major impact on the kinds of relationships they choose in the future.

Family Therapy

Family therapy is also employed as a major component of treatment. This often leads to greater awareness and clarity about communication, adaptation, and cohesion within the family. It also provides the therapist with examples of actual family dynamics. A therapist can quickly observe how the family responds to "outsiders" and whether people can readily enter the family system. Also, the addicted individual's dynamics usually spill out through interactional patterns within the family. This exposure of original interactional dynamics happens much more quickly within the context of family therapy than in group therapy.

In one family, seen in therapy, the dynamics present in the relationship between the patient and his wife were readily observed in the relationship between him and his mother. The dynamic was one in which he and his mother played a pursuer-distancer game. When this man was with his wife, he would play a very dependent, needy individual who pursued his wife much of the time. His wife would continue to distance herself as he pursued. The same was true between him and his mother.

Summary and Conclusions

The treatment of addiction to relationships and love must be based on the intrapsychic dynamics of the individual, the interpersonal dynamics of the addicted dyad, and the systemic dynamics of the nuclear and/or the extended family. To generate significant and long-lasting effects, all three components of treatment are necessary. Although there are some drawbacks to treatment described here, the benefits can far outweigh the deficits. Perhaps the greatest benefit is that other people in the patient's relationship system, including peers in group therapy, extended family members, and nuclear family members, can be affected by positive and significant changes in the addicted patient.

Not only do the intrapsychic and interpersonal dynamics of the patient change; the family system in both generational directions often changes as well. This latter benefit is important for the prevention of future addicted generations in the family. The literature clearly documents that children of parents who are addicted to alcohol (as well as other addictive substances) are more highly predisposed to becoming addicted than are children of nonalcoholic families. Although no such research is reported regarding relationship addiction, it seems likely that the same dynamic is present and that inclusion of the children in the treatment process can have positive benefits into the next generation.

Through treatment, using individual, group, and family therapy, not only can individuals who are in treatment be freed from their addiction to relationships, but their extended family can also be affected. The patients can become more emotionally self-sufficient, self-nurturing, and open to allowing others into their world, and the family can mirror this process and open its system in such a way that communication, cohesion, and adaptation can extend to a social network outside the family.

References

Forward, S. (1986). *Men who hate women and the women who love them.* New York: Bantam.

Fromm, E. (1956). *The art of loving.* New York: Harper & Row.

Greer, G. (1971). *The female eunuch.* New York: McGraw-Hill.

Halpern, H. (1983). *How to break your addiction to a person.* New York: McGraw-Hill.

Kohut, H. (1971). *The analysis of the self.* New York: International Universities Press.

Lionells, M. J. (1986). A reevaluation of hysterical relatedness. *Contemporary Psychoanalysis, 22*(4), 570–597.

McClelland, D. C., Atkinson, J. W., Clark, R. A., & Lowell, E. L. (1953). *The achievement motive.* New York: Appleton-Century-Crofts.

Miller, R. (1987). Some questions for Stanton Peele on addiction to love, stress and alcohol. *Employee Assistance Quarterly, 3*(1), 35–56.

Norwood, R. (1985). *Women who love too much.* New York: Simon & Schuster.

Peele, S. (1985). What I would most like to know: How can addiction occur with other than drug involvements? *British Journal of Addiction, 80*(1), 23–25.

Peele, S., & Brodsky, A. (1975). *Love and addiction.* New York: Taplinger.

Rummel, R. L. (1988). A case study of a manaholic "who loved too much." *Medical Hypoanalysis Journal, 3*(1), 17–38.

Simon J. (1982). Love: Addiction or road to self-realization, a second look. *American Journal of Psychoanalysis, 42*(3), 253–263.

Tennov, D. (1979). *Love and limerence.* Briarcliff, NY: Stein and Day.

Wallace, L. (1974). The psychoanalytic situation and the transference neurosis. *Israel Annals of Psychiatry and Related Disciplines, 12*(4), 304–318.

Wood, B. (1987). *Children of alcoholism: The struggle for self and intimacy in adult life.* New York: New York University Press.

__10__

Eating Disorders: Bulimia and Anorexia

LINDA PAULK
BUCHANAN, M.Ed.

WILLIAM L. BUCHANAN,
Ph.D.

IN THE LAST 15 years, eating disorders have received a great deal of attention. The incidence of bulimia and anorexia appears to be increasing to epidemic proportions. The incidence of eating disorders in young females during the early 1980s was reportedly 5 to 6 percent; however, more recent studies have found 9 to 12 percent of this population had some form of eating disorder (Berg, 1988; Carter & Duncan, 1984).

To describe bulimia and anorexia as two separate eating disorders is somewhat arbitrary. Many of the dynamics, food-related behaviors, and thought processes are similar for both bulimics and anorexics. However, there are differences between these disorders, so each is described separately.

Description and Diagnosis

Bulimia Nervosa

The term "bulimia" literally means "ox-hunger" or voracious appetite, but in recent years has come to mean binge-eating. Typically, bulimics binge on food and then purge by forced vomiting, fasting, or laxative or amphetamine abuse. It is becoming more and more accepted that the binging and purging are the consequences of excessive dieting (Laessle, Tuschl, Waadt & Pirke, 1989), and that factors that influence dieting be-

165

haviors directly increase the incidence of eating disorders (Hsu, 1989). Although there have been more empirical and descriptive studies on anorexia than on bulimia, the latter is addressed first in this chapter because it is far more common.

Historically, there has been controversy and a lack of clarity over the definition and naming of bulimia nervosa. Terms such as "bulimarexia" (Boskind-White & White, 1983), "binge-purge syndrome" (Hawkins, Fremouw & Clement, 1984), and "bulimia nervosa" have been used to identify this disorder that is characterized by overeating and then purging. Because of the confusion as to the name and definition of the disorder, this chapter will apply the *DSM-III-R* (American Psychological Association, 1987) criteria and use the terms "bulimia nervosa" and "bulimia" interchangeably.

Some have supported the idea that a subgroup of women with eating disorders may also have a personality disorder (Sansone, Seuferer, Fine & Bovenzi, 1989). Additionally, some evidence supports the theory that women with eating disorders have a higher incidence of having been sexually abused (Tice, Hall, Beresford, Quinones & Hall, 1989). Thorough assessments must be made in these areas when working with bulimic individuals.

Boskind-White and White (1983) have summarized that bulimics have excessive dependency needs, high need of approval, lack of assertiveness, high level of perfectionism, low self-esteem, a significant degree of depression (often to the point of being suicidal), and difficulties in heterosexual relationships. This cluster of personality factors may be learned in the course of society's traditional female socialization process, which teaches women to be passive, dependent, noncompetitive, and overly concerned with physical appearance, and to become self-sacrificing as mothers. These factors converge in the bulimic to the point that she reacts with undue anxiety or depression to normal life situations.

The Binge-Purge Cycle

Several research efforts have been directed to understanding the specifics of the binge-purge cycle itself. Consumption of large amounts of high-calorie food is common, but patients also commonly label consumption of small amounts of a forbidden food (e.g., one cookie) as a binge (Mizes, 1983). In addition to binge eating, bulimics often alternate between bingeing and periods of very low food consumption or fasting, and may use other forms of purging such as laxatives and excessive exercise.

Binge eating may effectively divert one's attention from upsetting thoughts, as well as induce relaxation (Mizes, 1983). Thus, the binge becomes a way of coping with stress and relieves the pre-binge negative emotional state.

The purge also seems to be a way of reducing guilt after the binge. In essence, a highly reinforcing sequence is enacted, in which the binge relieves the negative emotional state before the binge, and the purge relieves the guilt from the binge. In summary, bulimia nervosa is characterized by pre-binge anxiety, anxiety reduction during the binge, post-binge anxiety for having binged, and anxiety reduction via vomiting (Mizes, 1983).

Anorexia Nervosa

The disorder occurs predominantly in adolescent girls, with 95 percent of all cases being females. It may affect as many as one in every hundred adolescent and college-age girls in the United States. Although hospitalization is often utilized to prevent death by starvation, there is still a 5 to 18 percent mortality rate. Long-term follow-up studies (Hsu, 1980; Swift, 1982) indicate after five years only 35 percent of patients treated for anorexia nervosa are eating normally and free of neurotic fixations on body weight. However, most patients improve weight and menses (75 percent), eventually find full-time employment (75 percent), and function well socially (40 to 75 percent).

Actually, the term "anorexia" is a misnomer, since people suffering from this disorder generally do not report loss of appetite, as the name implies. In fact, they resemble people dying of starvation, in that they are obsessed with eating and food. However, they also have a relentless craving to be thin. Indeed, the German name for this condition, "pubertaets magersucht," means an addiction to thinness (Bruch, 1985).

The Self-Starvation Syndrome

How is it that young females become addicted to thinness? Bruch (1985) suggested that anorexia is more than the culturally prescribed goal of thinness combined with a diet that gets out of control. Anorexics, according to Bruch, use their refusal to eat as a solution to personality difficulties and problems in living. Long before these girls begin to refuse to eat, they feel helpless and ineffective in conducting their lives. They focus on the demands of others, which leads to a lack of ability to identify their own needs and feelings. A concrete number, their weight, becomes their only measure of success and self-esteem. Their rigid discipline, measured by visible weight loss, gives them the experience of being effective and in control. Their defiance to all who notice their excessive weight loss appears to them to be an expression of strength and independence.

Bruch, however, does not view their defiance as a strength; rather, she sees their defiance as a defense against the feeling of not having a core personality of their own. The paradox of this is that their excessive need for control ultimately causes them to lose all control. Conversely, to gain control of their lives, they must give up the one thing that ever gave them a sense of control: their exaggerated discipline in restricting their food intake. The family environment is a key influence on the issues of control, perfectionism, and independence.

The Families of Individuals with Eating Disorders

Minuchin, Rosman, and Baker (1978) describe five characteristics of psychosomatic families that can also be seen in the families of anorexics. These are enmeshment, overprotectiveness, conflict avoidance, rigidity, and parental conflict. Although no single family characteristic seems sufficient, the cluster of these transactional patterns is believed to be characteristic of a family process that encourages somatization.

Enmeshment refers to a smothering closeness in which the interpersonal boundaries between people become blurred. For example, a mother and daughter may form a cross-generational coalition by taking on parallel roles as "girlfriends" so that the boundary between the parental subsystem and the sibling subsystem is unclear. In this framework, loyalty and protection take precedence over autonomy and self-realization. Overprotectiveness, a second characteristic, refers to a family's exaggerated concern for the physical and psychological welfare of its members. Whereas overprotectiveness may be legitimate when a child is very young, it becomes increasingly unwarranted as she becomes older. Because parents are so preoccupied with the children's behavior, the child becomes overly conscious of herself and of other people's expectations.

Extreme denial and avoidance of conflict, a third characteristic, are observed in psychosomatic families. The family presents itself as a unified group devoid of any problems except for the child's "illness." Although members of normal families can disagree among themselves, those in the psychosomatic family cannot. The fourth characteristic is rigidity. Extrafamilial stress, such as a loss or change in occupation, may require adaptations that the family cannot make, which might precipitate illness. As a result, problems in the family are continually left unresolved.

The fifth characteristic of the anorexic family is the use of the child's illness in a parental conflict so that the family detours, avoids or suppresses the conflict. For example, parents unable to deal with each other directly unite in protective concern for their sick child, avoiding conflict by detouring. The effectiveness of the symptom bearer in regulating the internal stability of the family reinforces both the continuation of the symptom and the family organization in which it emerged.

Root, Fallon, and Friedrich (1986) described three patterns that families of bulimics typically manifest. The "perfect" family puts a great deal of emphasis on appearance and the family reputation. The "overprotective" family is very enmeshed, lacks confidence in the bulimic's competence, and lacks rules for age-appropriate behavior in the family. The "chaotic" family is enmeshed, lacks skills in conflict resolution, has inconsistent rules, and is characterized by one or both parents unavailable to the bulimic, a history of victimization of the bulimic, frequent expression of anger, and substance abuse.

When comparing anorexic families with bulimic families, anorexic families were found to have more interpersonal boundary problems and a stable and conflict-avoiding way of interacting that was experienced as nonconflictual and cohesive by the patient and her family (Kog & Vandereycken, 1989). Humphrey (1989) found that parents of anorexics communicated a double message of nurturant affection combined with neglect of their daughters' needs to express themselves and their feelings, and bulimic families expressed more negative emotions and were hostilely enmeshed. These findings suggest that honest communication is more restricted in anorexic families but that both groups of families have patterns that reduce the daughters' ability to develop healthy, separate identities.

Treatment of Eating Disorders

General Treatment Issues

Eating disorders have several components in common with other addictive disorders (Scott, 1983; Zweben, 1987). The obvious component is the compulsive eating behavior, either compulsive restricting of food or compulsive overeating of food. Accompanying the compulsive behavior is a sense of powerlessness and the fear that if the eater takes one bite of forbidden food, she will be unable to stop or control herself. The eating-disordered person is also obsessed with thoughts of food such as when, where, and what to eat, a preoccupation that requires a tremendous amount of mental energy. Another aspect of eating disorders common to addictive behaviors is the learned ability to avoid aversive feelings through the abuse of food and the simultaneous relief. These similarities have led to applying the addiction model for alcoholism and substance abuse to eating disorders. Thus many inpatient units have combined treatment of eating-disordered individuals with that of other addicts. Several aspects of the 12-step programs such as Overeaters Anonymous can be useful for people suffering from an eating disorder: the philosophy of "one day at a time", a focus on having the destructive behaviors cease before other problems are addressed, an emphasis on spirituality that gives many eating-disordered individuals relief from their internal emptiness, a focus on physical recovery and stabilization, and a reframing of the problem as a disease rather than a lack of character.

One dissimilarity between an eating disorder and an addiction must not be overlooked. Unlike the abuse of other substances, food is a substance which cannot be given up. Therefore, treatment must involve management of, not abstinence from, the feared and loved object: food. Vandereyken (1990) warns that rather than abstinence from food, the abstention target should primarily concern all abnormal attempts at weight reduction and should focus on the individual's deficits rather than the "excesses" of overconsumption. No research to date demonstrates that a 12-step approach is an effective intervention for eating-disordered individuals. The addiction model is inadequate in and of itself to treat eating disorders successfully.

Regardless of whether a woman has bulimia or anorexia, several issues are important for effective therapy. A thorough physical examination must be conducted by a physician knowledgeable in the treatment of eating disorders. The therapist may suggest that a session with all members of the treatment team be held early in treatment in the physician's office, and that clear goals be established in terms of medical stabilization. If, for example, an anorexic falls below a predetermined weight decided on by the physician, hospitalization will occur.

A thorough psychological assessment must also be made with each eating-disordered patient. At the minimum, there should be a complete psychosocial history that includes a sexual history and a history of abnormal eating behavior. The latter should include a history of dieting as well as the psychosocial context in which overconcern for weight and eating developed. Finally, a multidimensional approach incorporating aspects from various disciplines, orientations, and treatment modalities is suggested (Garfinkel and Garner, 1982; Anderson, 1987; Stager, 1989), to allow for comprehensive treatment without sacrificing the unique needs of each individual.

Treatment of Bulimia Nervosa

A multidimensional approach is needed for the treatment of eating disorders. Unfortunately, most of what has been written to date has focused either on the cognitive-behavioral treatment, with little attention paid to personality dynamics, or on psychodynamic treatment where the family or past experience take precedence, with little attention paid to symptom management. For people with eating disorders, the cognitive-behavioral phase of treatment must not be overlooked. Eating disorders involve behaviors that are hazardous to the patient's health and may be fatal, and these behaviors must be brought under control. However, for many patients, much work remains to be done when the binging and purging has ended. One patient stated that she had been in seemingly successful treatment several times, but that at some point later, the whole cycle would be manifested again.

A Three-Phase Treatment Model

Suggested in this chapter is a three-phase model conceptualized and developed by Linda Paulk Buchanan. The three distinct phases to the comprehensive treatment for eating disorders are: (1) therapist-patient relationship development and psychoeducation; (2) symptom reduction through cognitive and behavioral interventions; and (3) dynamic-interpersonal psychotherapy.

   This model brings together several modalities, into which any helpful technique may be incorporated. Although in practice the phases overlap, they are conceptualized as distinct because each phase has specific tasks and goals that should be completed.

Phase One: Therapeutic Relationship Development and Psychoeducation
People with bulimia often present themselves as having most other areas of their life under control and desiring only to work on their behavior with food. A useful response is to ask them to talk about what they know about bulimia. Bulimics typically report little accurate knowledge about their disorder. Therefore, the first phase of treatment is to educate the patient by providing accurate information. The bulimic should be informed about the physiological and emotional consequences of starvation (or periods of strict dieting), and the physiological and emotional consequences of purging. The goal of this phase is for the patient to begin to believe that her attempts at self-restraint and perfectionism will eventually backfire.

   Bulimia often starts with a female who is interested in losing a few pounds to feel better about herself. Because she is determined, her diet is often too strict and results in a series of physiological and emotional reactions. Although at this point she is able to ignore her hunger, her body can not. Her body reacts by increasing its metabolic efficiency, which inhibits weight loss (i.e., by needing less food to maintain the same weight) until she begins eating normally again. The longer the diet continues, the more acute the need to conserve energy becomes, and the body's basal metabolic rate (BMR) slows down more and more (Bennett, Williamson & Powers, 1989; Brownell, 1988). Brownell and his colleagues (Brownell, Greenwood, Stellar & Shrager, 1986; Steen, Oppliger & Brownell, 1988) demonstrated that the BMR drops measurably within 24 hours and continues to decline 20 percent within two weeks. Moreover, the lipoprotein lipase (LPL) enzyme which controls how fat is stored in fat cells, becomes more active with reduced caloric intake. More active LPL makes the body become more efficient at fat storage. With physiology and metabolism working against weight loss, the dieter is set up to fail and will eventually gain the weight back.

The cycle above does not stop just with regaining the weight. Dieting and then regaining weight makes later weight loss of the same amount slower and periods of regaining more rapid. This weight cycling or "yo-yo dieting" (Brownell, 1988) also increases the risk of heart disease, increases the proportion of fat to lean tissue in the body, redistributes body fat (shifting fat from the thighs and hips to the abdomen), and increases the desire for fatty foods (setting the dieter up to binge). Thus there is the immediate effect of gaining the weight back and the long-term effect of making future weight loss more difficult. Worse still is the physiological damage done to the body.

Although diets don't work, and actually work against effective weight control, eating-disordered individuals continue to diet and severely restrict food intake. When the bulimic diets, she begins to notice that although she is eating less and less, she is thinking about food constantly. Being a perfectionist, she feels guilty about this obsession with thoughts of food. She needs to hear that the second way the body attempts to adapt to a scarcity of food is by motivating her to find food. Biologically, the body is trying to "save" itself; one could say that the body cannot differentiate between a willful restriction of food and a famine. At this point in the process of dieting, the body's reaction to any food is to demand more so forcefully that the most determined person could not help but yield. Because she probably experiences her obsession and yielding to eating as a moral issue rather than a biological one, the dieter's self-esteem plummets even further.

Eventually the dieter will begin to admit to herself that she cannot help but binge at times and she will learn a way of making up for her "sin" of breaking the diet. Her repentance usually takes the form of forcing herself to vomit. Initially, she feels better in that she has gotten rid of the "sin", but later feels worse as she realizes her helplessness. She swears to herself that she will never do it again and that she will stick to her diet tomorrow.

Often after years of binging and purging, the female's metabolism will have slowed to the point that she really will gain weight even when she eats very little, for the reasons described above. She will also be constantly obsessed with food and have low self-esteem and a myriad of physical problems, depending on which type of purging she has used (Mitchell, Pyle, Eckert, Hastukami & Lentz, 1983; Pomeroy & Mitchell, 1989). Although most people with eating disorders are proud of their attempts at rigid dieting and embarrassed by their overeating, the patient must learn that binging is a consequence of (not the reason for) the rigid, though intermittent, dieting. Her incessant attempts at controlling her weight through restraining her eating are the problem, not a lack of willpower.

As this information is being accepted, concurrent assessment is being conducted. A baseline for the behavior is taken by asking the patient in the first session to change nothing for one week except for keeping a record of her eating. Also included in the record are where she ate, when, with whom, how she felt before and after eating, and if she purged. The patient continues to self-monitor her eating and bingeing throughout treatment until her symptoms stabilize.

Phase Two: Cognitive-Behavioral Therapy for Symptom Stabilization   The phase of psychoeducation and developing a therapeutic relationship usually takes two to three sessions. Following this is a cognitive-behavioral phase that lasts 6 to 15 sessions. If improvement is not apparent within three months from beginning treatment, hospitalization should be considered. The primary goal of the second phase of treatment is for the bingeing and purging to cease and for the patient to begin eating normally. This goal is achieved by helping the bulimic recognize the misbeliefs she holds about herself and eating, by developing a repertoire of alternative behaviors to bingeing and purging, and by increasing a sense of self-esteem. By using a variety of cognitive and behavioral techniques, approximately halfway through the second phase of treatment the bulimic begins controlling her bingeing and purging.

One of the models most associated with effective treatment of eating disorders is the cognitive-behavioral approach, which suggests that cognitive variables play a vital role in maladaptive eating behaviors. Behavioral management without concurrent change in beliefs and attitudes is less effective and/or may lead to rapid relapse (Andersen, 1987; Garner & Bemis, 1982; Bruch, 1974).

Other cognitive theories hold that eating disorders are a problem of cognitive deficits, in that the individual has not developed abstract reasoning or formal operational thinking, has low I.Q., or has characteristics of a thinking disorder. Most research has failed to support these speculations (Strauss & Ryan, 1988). However, lower levels of conceptual organization (Johnson & Holloway, 1988) and lower defense styles (Stager, Goldstein, Mongrain & Van der Feen, 1990) have been found among anorexics when compared to bulimics or controls. Additionally, Strauss and Ryan (1988) found that anorexics made significantly more logical errors than the bulimics or controls but that all groups were indistinguishable on tests for cognitive slippage and conceptual complexity. Taken together, the data suggest that individuals with eating disorders generally have average or better cognitive abilities and therefore should respond to cognitive therapy, which is based on correcting errors in logic, although anorexics may have more difficulty using this approach than bulimics.

In helping the bulimic recognize and change the misbeliefs she holds, the therapist should monitor and challenge automatic, irrational beliefs. For example, the belief that, "I've been a *good* girl all day so I deserve one bite of X", (i.e., the forbidden food) may be written with counterarguments. It is important to note that the bulimic uses words such as "good" and "bad" as perfectionistic labels; the therapist must be careful not to fall into using such labels in similar ways. The emphasis for cognitive therapy in this phase is based on the new beliefs about the consequences of dieting, binging, and purging, with less emphasis on actual personality change (phase three).

The bulimic must become cognizant of some common evasive maneuvers before she will actually be able to maintain change. First, is the concept of irreversibility: the maneuver of repeatedly applying the same responses to old problems. The patient should come to realize that risks must be taken and that anything new is awkward and uncomfortable. Second is the idea that pain is a precursor to change; bulimics have developed a pattern of avoiding pain at all costs. The third evasive maneuver is that of living in the past or future and avoiding the present. The bulimic is usually feeling guilty over the past or wishing magically for the future and is almost unaware of what she is doing during the present binge-purge behavior. Tied in with living in the future is the maneuver of using toxic words such as "never," "can't," and "forever."

For most bulimic patients, there seems to be a constant dialogue between a critical parent-self (often even more critical than her own parents actually were) and a discouraged or rebellious child-self. With a combination of transactional analysis and gestalt techniques, patients become aware of the destructive ways they talk to themselves. Through the "empty chair" technique, their covert internal conversations may be made overt and the feelings generated can be discussed. Bulimics are encouraged to talk back to their critical side with more appropriate talk from the viewpoint of an adult or nurturing parent-self.

As the patient begins to limit her destructive self-talk, she also needs to be developing positive self-talk in its place. A three-part self-esteem exercise can be taught that includes an instruction to the patient to tell herself one thing that she did that day that made her feel good. Second, she is to tell herself one thing she could have done differently and to visualize herself doing it differently next time. Finally, she is instructed to tell herself that since she has a plan to do it differently, she can decide to not let the mistake continue to bother her. She is then to end the exercise by telling herself another thing (or repeating the first thing) she feels good about. The exercise is helpful in that it emphasizes dwelling on the positive. Finally, visualization enables the patient to be ready if the same event should occur in the future.

Behavioral interventions are also initiated in this phase of treatment. Using the self-monitoring of all food intake, which began in the first phase of treatment, patterns and areas of weakness can be identified and targeted for intervention. For example, the patient and the therapist can plan a menu together for one day. The patient is told to choose one day to follow the menu, and that if she can do it just once in the week, the week will be labeled a success. This can be modified to just one meal if the patient is not able to comply for one full day. The changes must be very gradual, with successes labeled as often as possible to create a lasting change.

A behavioral technique we have found to be very helpful includes the use of a kitchen timer. Patients are instructed to set a timer for 15 minutes when they first have the thought that they have overeaten and are going to throw up. They then are asked to sit and explore their feelings during the 15 minutes and to write them down. This task focuses them on the present as well as forcing them to experience the pain of being overly full. They live, at least for 15 minutes, with the consequences of their actions. This is a risk that many patients find very frightening. When the timer rings they may choose to "go about their business" (i.e., do something else and not purge), reset the timer for another 15 minutes, or purge. As the bulimic becomes able to last for 15 minutes without purging, the time period to wait is increased. As this becomes a new habit, the tendency to overeat is decreased, since the patient accepts that she will wait for an uncomfortable period of time before throwing up.

People who are suffering with bulimia have often been observed to omit pleasurable activities from their daily life, based on a subtle belief that they don't deserve to have fun because they are so preoccupied with food. It is helpful to have the patient make a list of things she enjoys doing or has in the past enjoyed doing.

Another helpful strategy for some patients is to pretend they don't have a problem with eating. They are instructed to create in their mind the image of a person who does not have an eating problem and then to act the way they believe that person would act. For the patient to play the part of a created image is often challenging and may result in the patient talking and thinking less about food. As the dieter appears to be less concerned with food, social reinforcement becomes a pleasant side effect. The more comfortable she begins to feel, the more she incorporates the created image into her self-concept.

A strategic technique for teaching the patient to have more control is to have her plan a binge (also known as prescribing the symptom or prescribing a relapse). The planning is very detailed as to when the binge will take place, what will be eaten, etc. With this strategy the patient is instructed to plan to eat some "forbidden food" at distinct times during the week. When the patient is able to eat formerly forbidden foods without later purging, her fear of forbidden foods decreases, and more importantly, her belief in her own power to control her eating is increased.

Several adjuncts to therapy are useful in helping the bulimic give up her symptoms in this second phase. These include couples therapy and family therapy, drug therapy, and group therapy. Each of these will be discussed in separate sections.

Phase Three: Dynamic-Interpersonal Psychotherapy for Treatment Maintenance   The third and final phase of individual therapy for bulimics is the psychodynamic-interpersonal phase. This phase will last from six months to two years, depending on the needs of the patient. For some patients the binge-purge syndrome began as a tragic reaction to a prolonged and rigid diet, and with these patients, therapy may be terminated after the second phase of treatment. This is where traditional cognitive-behavioral therapy usually ends, and unfortunately, where most research into treatment ends as well. For many patients, however, the problem is more complex, involving family of origin dynamics and personality dynamics of perfectionism, guilt, and anger. During this stage, there is less discussion of eating and bulimic symptoms and an increased focus on larger personality factors. In determining which patients need to continue to the third phase of treatment, the therapist should consider several factors.

The therapist may look first at the age of onset of the eating disorder. The earlier the problem developed, the more likely the need for this phase, in that past experiences and early family dynamics probably played a role in the development of the problem. Second, the therapist should consider the number of relapses the patient has suffered following previous treatment. A relapse after successful symptom management clearly suggests that the third phase is indicated. A third factor is the ability of the patient to maintain significant relationships with individuals outside the treatment environment. The patient must have a healthy support system available to maintain the progress of the first two phases of treatment. If she does not, she will need the support offered by a trusted therapist until she develops other supports. Additionally, she will learn through this phase the skills and risks involved in maintaining long-term relationships. Finally, if there is a history of sexual abuse or if a personality disorder is also present, the patient will also need to continue therapy into the third phase.

The goals of the third phase of treatment must be determined individually for each patient and will differ from patient to patient. Generally, an environment should be provided in which the patient feels safe to explore the various experiences that have helped to shape her personality. Also, the therapist must take the risks involved in being in a therapeutic relationship with the patient for a significant amount of time. Because of its intimate nature, this phase of treatment is less conducive to research and may be more conducive to learning through long-term supervision and personal therapy.

In this phase of therapy, the therapist helps the bulimic modify several aspects of her personality that foster the problem and may contribute to a reoccurrence of the problem behaviors. A cluster of personality variables, common among bulimics, are interlocked in a powerful, self-destructive belief system. These broadly include perfectionism, low self-esteem, and high dependency, which tend to lead to unhealthy relationships. The bulimic will often reject the notion that she is a perfectionist, because she believes that she rarely lives up to her own standards. Yet this could almost be a definition of perfectionism. She must learn that it isn't her lack of ability that leads her to feel guilty and unworthy, but rather where she sets her standards.

Therapy for the perfectionist consists partly of helping her begin to understand how she developed these beliefs about herself. Often when exploring the family of origin of a bulimic, one finds a parent who was critical or somehow gave the message to the child that she was not good enough. The other parent was often passive (sometimes alcoholic) and did little or nothing to interrupt the negative messages received by the child. This part of therapy is not aimed at blaming the parents, because it is usually observed that the critical parent, in the patient's mind, is worse than that parent ever was in reality. However, the patient must begin to realize that it is understandable that she developed the perfectionistic tendencies.

At times the parents truly were handicapped in their nurturing abilities, and the bulimic will need to experience the grief and anger associated with this realization. One patient realized that she was still believing "the message that my mother gave me, that I wasn't good enough." Additionally, she perceived her father as passive and wondered why he never protected her or stood up for her. She had been listening to a critical voice tell her that she was only acceptable if she was thin (like mother), and she never questioned or stood up against these messages (like father). Thus she was carrying out in her own behavior both of the negative roles that her parents had played, and had abolished any of the positive roles they may have played. Her task was to begin nurturing and standing up for the inner child in ways that her parents had not been able to do.

The above illustrates the need for the bulimic to deal with the messages that she received in the past and to take an honest look at how she is still obeying these messages. Visualization techniques may be helpful in changing the power of the old messages. The patient is instructed to visualize herself as a child in several settings and then to visualize herself as an adult comforting the child and giving her positive messages in place of the negative ones she originally perceived. The patient must begin to realize that this child is still alive inside her and that she is responsible now for nurturing her. As she begins to develop compassion for the inner child, she is often less able to be as critical or perfectionistic toward herself.

The second major cluster of personality variables attended to in the third phase of therapy involves dependency needs. The bulimic is unlikely to express anger to others, for she is overly concerned with others' evaluation of her and is likely to hold in her own feelings. She is more comfortable giving than receiving in a relationship, and lacks assertiveness. All these variables often lead to a succession of unsuccessful or unsatisfying relationships with others.

A visualization exercise developed by Linda Paulk Buchanan can be used to assess the patient's unique needs. She is asked to imagine herself at a moment when she is feeling a strong urge to binge. Next she is asked to imagine that she had previously activated a "force field" that will last for several hours and allows her to do anything except eat. The feelings that the patient often reports are indications of what she needs or is reacting against. For instance, one patient reported feeling angry and remembered this feeling when her parents were restrictive; another felt relief, which may have indicated a wish for someone to take control.

During this phase of treatment, the therapist needs to monitor consistently the reactions and feelings he or she feels toward the patient. The relationship between the patient and the therapist will be the key in understanding how the patient behaves in interpersonal relationships outside the therapeutic milieu. The therapist will need to be looking for opportunities to ask how the conversation at hand is meaningful to the patient/therapist relationship. For example, one patient was talking in boring detail about how her previous therapist had made her angry. The patient was encouraged to deal directly with her feelings by the therapist asking what the current therapist could do to make her angry. This was followed by an agreement that the patient would speak up if the therapist did anything that made her angry or reminded her of her past experience. Similarly, if a patient is talking about feeling rejected by a friend, the therapist may ask if the patient feels accepted by the therapist. The patient is encouraged to deal directly and honestly in a relationship in which the therapist is also willing to deal with the actual feelings.

The therapist also will need to risk sharing his or her feelings and reactions with the patient. For example, a patient was describing the lack of affection that her mother had shown her. The therapist at this point experienced two reactions that she shared with the patient. The patient was told, "As you were describing that, I wanted to do two things. One was to come over and shake you by the shoulders and ask you how long you were going to let your mother control you, and the other was that I wanted to come over and put my arm around you and tell you that your mother made a terrible mistake." After saying this, the therapist asked the patient to discuss her reactions to both possibilities.

Misconceptions that are addressed may include Riebel's (1989) list of common misconceptions including, "Much of what I think and want is unacceptable, so I must censor outgoing messages," "Other people can read my mind, so if they don't give me what I want, it means they don't want to," "Other people are fragile. They can't stand to hear my opinions," and "Honest communication is devastating. Relationships can't survive the truth."

In this phase of treatment, the therapist helps the patient develop the skills and understanding involved in healthy relationships. The patient is often deeply touched (although anxious) by the therapist's directness. Directness builds trust in a way that the patient has never experienced in a relationship. Using the therapeutic relationship to work through past hurtful relationships enables the patient to begin to believe in her own power as an individual, begin to care for herself in a healthy way, and begin to develop lasting, satisfying relationships with others.

Structural-Strategic Couples Therapy and Family Therapy for Bulimia

Some couples enter therapy because of relationship problems that are in part caused by or contribute to the bulimia in one of the partners. The therapist needs to assess the systemic issues that may be contributing to the problems before deciding whether to see the bulimic individually or the couple conjointly. The goals would be to help the couple establish flexible interactions and comfortable boundaries, and to modify the interpersonal dynamics that may be maintaining the bulimic symptoms.

Structural-strategic family therapy is indicated if an individual with bulimia is under 18 or living at home with her parents. As the disorder often begins as part of a dysfunctional family system, the bulimic will have little chance for success without fundamental changes in the family. Structural family therapy, which was originally applied by Minuchin (Minuchin et al., 1978) to work with anorexic families, can be adapted for use with bulimic families as well. The goals of structural-strategic family therapy for bulimics are to help the patient achieve a greater sense of self-control, become less protective of her family, become genuinely close to people both inside and outside of her family, and let go of the dependent, sickly identity that bulimia symbolizes and maintains. This model will be discussed in more detail in a later section.

Treatment of Anorexia Nervosa

Various treatment approaches have been used to treat anorexia nervosa. Psychodynamic therapy has provided rich theory for understanding the disorder, but has been shown to be ineffective in managing the symptoms. Behavioral treatments have been more successful in initially helping the anorexic gain weight, but follow-up studies of behavioral treatments still indicate a high failure rate. The effectiveness of behavior therapy is often short-lived; although such therapy is effective in helping the anorexic gain weight while in the hospital, long-term effectiveness is questionable. However, the structural family therapy approach has been very effective (Minuchin et al., 1978).

Minuchin's structural family therapy approach focuses primarily on the second phase of treatment advocated in this chapter—symptom reduction through cognitive and behavioral interventions. The other two phases of treatment are also included in their approach, but are given less emphasis. Certainly, a strong relationship develops between the patient and therapist, and psychoeducation occurs as well. What is little acknowledged about this approach is that after the weight and anorexic symptoms are stabilized, intensive individual psychotherapy is necessary with these patients, often for months or years. Recent developments in the structural family therapy model have clearly tried to integrate family and individual therapy for anorexia (Sargent, 1987; Dare, Eisler, Russell & Szmukler, 1990).

Structural Family Therapy for Anorexia

The structural family therapy approach developed by Minuchin (Minuchin et al., 1978), claims an 86 percent success rate in follow-up results from one and a half to five years (Liebman, Sargent & Silver, 1983). By success, the authors mean that the patients demonstrated normal eating patterns, normal weight, and were participating effectively in school, with peers, and with their families at the time of follow-up. To date, this is the most effective treatment reported for anorexia.

This approach begins with a thorough evaluation of the system constituted by the patient, family, and referring physician or agency. This enables the therapist to make an accurate diagnosis of both individual and family dysfunction. Following assessment, a treatment plan is developed to meet the specific needs of the patient and family. In most cases, the pediatrician or family physician is included as an integral member of the treatment team, working in a collaborative fashion with the therapist, patient, and family.

The results of the initial medical evaluation will determine the need for inpatient or outpatient therapy. Originally, about half of the patients in the Minuchin study were hospitalized but, as the structural approach developed more fully, only about 10 to 15 percent of the patients had to be treated on an inpatient basis. The indications for psychiatric hospitalization are the presence of suicidal or severe psychotic symptoms in the patient, prior or current outpatient failures, and/or relapses after previous inpatient treatment. The primary purpose of hospitalization is to stop weight loss and promote weight gain. The family must support the treatment program, which strongly encourages the patient to strive for increased responsibility for weight gain and care for her body. Psychotropic medication is rarely used in this approach. Force feeding, nasogastric intubation, and hyperalimentation are to be avoided if possible, in order to prevent power struggles.

The family therapy lunch session is also used to accelerate weight gain. The lunch session can be used for either inpatient or outpatient therapy. If hospitalization is not needed, the lunch session should be conducted during the first five sessions. The lunch session is usually a two-hour session with the therapist, pediatrician, patient, parents, and siblings. There are three goals of these sessions: (1) change the concept of the identified patient within the family from one of being "sick"; (2) transform the eating problem into an interpersonal problem—the child isn't sick but is disobedient and thus is recognized as having manipulative powers among her symptoms; and (3) disengage the parents from using the child's eating behavior as a conflict-detouring device. The lunch session is divided into two parts.

Initially, the therapist joins the family and develops the therapeutic system: the therapist assumes leadership, develops family trust, and prepares the family for the stress in the following part of the session. One of two treatment strategies emerges. The first strategy is used more frequently with younger and preadolescent patients, in order to highlight issues of control and to enable the parents to become more competent. The goal is to increase parental executive effectiveness. When the patient refuses to eat in front of her parents, the therapist requests that one parent, then the other, make the child eat. Typically, these unilateral efforts fail. By this time, with the support of the therapist, the parents unite, take a firm stand, and work together. Often, they either succeed in feeding the child or she spontaneously begins to eat.

The second strategy is preferred for families with older adolescents, where separation, differentiation, and autonomy are important to establish. The goal is to increase emotional distance between parents and anorexic child. Here again, the therapist instructs the parents, each in turn, to get the child to eat, usually to no avail. The therapist stops these unsuccessful attempts. This sick, helpless little girl has totally defeated the healthy and powerful parents in an explicit and dramatic way. The therapist then disengages the parents from further contact with the patient about food, making this into a private issue between patient and therapist.

In cases where the family structure is more flexible, or where the child is already eating a little, the third strategy is preferred. The goal is to neutralize family interaction with respect to eating. The child may or may not be eating in her parents' presence. No efforts are made to engage parents and child around eating, and all talk about the child's eating is discouraged. The therapist exhibits what appears to be a casual or indifferent attitude toward the child. Instead, the therapist engages the parents in discussions with himself or each other about family background, interpersonal problems, or family problems. When these topics involve the child, she too is drawn into the discussion. Typically, the child spontaneously begins to eat at some point in the session.

In the outpatient phase, the family therapist assumes primary responsibility, with the pediatrician functioning in a supportive-consultative manner. At this point, the top priority is to eliminate the symptom of refusing to eat and to stimulate progressive weight gain. To do this, the therapist attempts to elucidate the dysfunctional family patterns that reinforce and maintain the patient's symptoms and to change the structure and functioning of the family system in order to prevent relapses. Weight gain alone is never considered sufficient; it is only a first step and must be followed by restructuring of the family system.

The goal of family therapy for these families is to change dysfunctional interactional patterns. The therapist intervenes both directly in the session and also by assigning tasks to be carried out at home. For one task the patient is told that she has to gain a minimum of two pounds a week in order to maintain normal weekend activities. If she gains less than two pounds from Friday to Friday, she is not allowed out of the house during the weekend and cannot have friends come to the house. In addition, a member of the family has to stay with her. The parents are told that it is their responsibility as parents to enforce the rules. Setting the above limits produces a great deal of stress in the family system, causing members of the family to join together to ensure that the patient eats.

As weight gain continues, the focus shifts from eating and the behavior paradigm to concern about interpersonal issues. As family issues begin to be solved, emphasis shifts to school and community activities and peer group relationships. Within the family, there is a gradual shift of emphasis to the problems in the marriage. At this point, the parents are seen separately for marital therapy, with periodic family sessions as needed. The patient is also seen individually to discuss age-appropriate developmental issues, such as the complexities of interpersonal relationships, learning to tolerate frustration, and developing problem-solving skills for home, school, and community. At this point Minuchin's approach clearly resembles the third phase of treatment advocated by the authors of this chapter.

Swift (1982), Tseng and McDermott (1979), and Malone (1979) have criticized the Minuchin's structural family therapy model for anorexia treatment on several levels (1) Anorexia nervosa is viewed as a unitary concept and diagnostically ignores the heterogeneity of the disorder. The model is applied to all patients with anorexia nervosa, although mostly teenage anorexics were treated in the study population. (2) Some anorexics were treated individually after the family system stabilized. In fact, some anorexics were treated individually for one to three years after the family therapy was terminated. (3) The follow-up lacked face-to-face interviews with a majority of the patients. (4) The mean duration of follow-up is inadequate (only 2.67 years). (5) No mention was made of menses. (6) No control group was used.

We have found only one controlled study of family therapy for anorexia (Dare et al., 1990). These researchers compared family therapy with individual therapy for 80 individuals with anorexia nervosa. These individuals were divided into four subgroups: (a) early onset, short duration; (b) early onset, duration longer than three years; (c) onset after 18 years of age; and (d) those with bulimia nervosa. Family therapy was found to be significantly better than individual therapy for individuals in the first subgroup only. A trend for the superiority of individual therapy over family therapy was found for individuals in the third subgroup (the older patients).

The family approach utilized in the Dare study was similar to that used by Minuchin and his colleagues, in that therapy focused on concrete specific matters such as weight and diet in the early phases of treatment. With younger patients the focus was on getting the parents to adopt a strategy to make their child eat. With older patients the focus was on having the parents either control their daughter's eating or consistently adopt the attitude that her eating was none of their business. The general focus was on the parents' being consistent. The authors found similar results to those reported by Minuchin but noted that in 51 out of 53 of Minuchin's cases, the patients would have fallen into the first subgroup of the Dare study.

Individual Psychotherapy for Anorexia

As stated above, Minuchin and his associates (Minuchin et al., 1978) treated some anorexics individually after the family therapy stabilized the anorexic symptoms. Individual psychotherapy focused on age-appropriate developmental issues: (a) complexities of interpersonal relationships; (b) learning to tolerate frustration; and (c) developing problem-solving skills for home, school, and community, as well as the emotional issues of depression, anxiety, anger, guilt, perfectionism, and low self-esteem. These emotional, social, and interpersonal issues are very similar to the dynamic issues of the bulimic.

Not all people with anorexia are teenagers, although the majority of them first developed anorexia as children or teenagers. When the patient is older than a teenager, the therapist must decide if the family therapy approach is appropriate for the individual patient. Age alone should not be the determining factor. One goal of structural family therapy is to help the anorexic individuate from her family of origin. Often patients have never successfully individuated from their families, although they are in their thirties or forties. Individuation, however, can also be accomplished through the use of individual psychotherapy and/or group therapy.

The section of this chapter on individual psychotherapy for bulimics is also generally applicable for individual psychotherapy for anorexics. The third phase of treatment is, in our experience, virtually always necessary for anorexics, since anorexia usually has its onset in adolescence and appears to involve an earlier developmental problem. A major difference, of course, is the behavioral issue of weight loss. In working with an anorexic, a range of weight that the patient must maintain must be established. A contract between the therapist and patient must stipulate that if the patient's weight goes below the designated weight limit, she will have to be hospitalized; the therapist must follow through with this natural and logical consequence. Not to do so indicates that the therapist does not mean what he or she says. The second major distinction from bulimics is that anorexics tend to turn inward to cope and have difficulty turning to others, so the therapist-patient relationship is even more vital. If the anorexic can develop trust in the therapist, a major goal has been accomplished. Finally, if the anorexic can stay above a minimum weight limit, therapy can proceed in a manner similar to the three-stage model for bulimia.

Drug Treatment for Bulimia and Anorexia

Recent studies have suggested that various antidepressants may be helpful at least in the short-term treatment of bulimia nervosa. Five placebo-controlled double-blind studies have appeared to date. These studies were reviewed by Pope and Hudson (1988) and Mitchell (1988). Mitchell indicated two difficulties in interpreting the drug studies: multiple treatment modalities were often used, and the mechanism of action is still unclear. Mitchell concluded that the studies suggest that the mechanism of action is not the treatment of an underlying depressive illness.

The antidepressants that have shown the most promise in the treatment of bulimia have been fluoxetine (Pope & Hudson, 1989) imipramine (Pope, Hudson, Jonas & Yurgelun-Todd, 1985), the MAO inhibitor phenelzine (Walsh, Stewart, Wright, Harrison, Roose & Glassman, 1984), and desipramine (Hughes, Wells, Cunningham & Ilstrup, 1986). Pope, Hudson, and Jonas (1983) cautioned that considerable experimentation was often necessary in some subjects to achieve optimum response and that in order to be effective, purging must be minimal. The latter point is often used as information to increase the bulimic's motivation not to purge. If bulimics cannot comply with proper administration of the medication, drug treatment is contraindicated.

The studies of the pharmacological treatment of anorexia nervosa have produced less consistent results than those of bulimia nervosa (Pope & Hudson, 1988). After reviewing the studies to date, Pope and Hudson concluded that pharmacological treatments have yielded unimpressive results. Although fluoxetine (prozac) has been found to be helpful with bulimics (Pope & Hudson, 1989), it has also been shown to inhibit appetite (Clifton, Barnfield & Philcox, 1989). It may therefore be contraindicated for anorexics. Antidepressant agents and lithium may be of value in certain cases. However, none of these agents has been shown to have a clear and substantial effect in anorexia nervosa. Thus, medication is at best an ancillary treatment, to be used in conjunction with an overall program for the treatment of anorexia nervosa.

Eating Disorders Outpatient Psychotherapy Group

The three-phase model for the treatment of eating disorders may be incorporated into a group setting for people with eating disorders. We have found that concurrent individual or family therapy with group therapy is the most effective. Further research is needed to determine the effects of group therapy alone or as an adjunct and to determine the advantages or disadvantages of combining subgroups of eating disorders in the same group.

Summary

This chapter presented a three-phase model for the comprehensive treatment of eating disorders. The three phases are 1) therapist-patient relationship development and psychoeducation, 2) symptom reduction through cognitive and behavioral interventions, and 3) dynamic-interpersonal psychotherapy. These three phases of treatment can be accomplished through individual, family, marital, or group therapy, or a combination of therapies. Many techniques have been borrowed from a variety of schools of therapy, with the goal of describing a unified, integrated approach to the treatment of eating disorders. Interventions and techniques used in the approach described in this chapter include behavioral, cognitive, gestalt, medical, psychodynamic, psychoeducational, psychopharmacological, strategic, systemic, and transactional analysis. No single approach, school of thought, or mental health discipline alone can successfully treat eating disorders. In the case of bulimia and anorexia, integration is not just an intellectual exercise but often a case of life and death.

However, each individual who presents herself for treatment of an eating disorder is unique. Therapists not only must adopt an integrated approach, they must also individualize their approach for each individual patient. Although therapy must be individually tailored to meet each patient's unique needs, it must involve, for all patients, a combination of treatment goals consisting of trust, education, symptom management, and resolution of psychodynamic and family of origin issues.

References

American Psychiatric Association. (1987). *Diagnostic and statistical manual of mental disorders* (3rd ed., revised). Washington, DC: Author.

Andersen, A. (1987). Contrast and comparison of behavioral, cognitive-behavioral, and comprehensive treatment methods for anorexia nervosa and bulimia nervosa. *Behavior Modification, 11,* 522–543.

Bennett, S., Williamson, D., & Powers, S. (1989). Bulimia nervosa and resting metabolic rate. *International Journal of Eating Disorders, 8,* 417–424.

Berg, K. (1988). The prevalence of eating disorders in co-ed versus single-sex residence halls. *Journal of College Student Development, 29,* 125–131.

Boskind-White, M., & White, W. C. (1983). *Bulimarexia: The binge-purge cycle.* New York: Norton.

Brownell, K. D. (1988, March). The yo-yo trap. *American Health,* 78–84.

Brownell, K. D., Greenwood, M. R. C., Stellar, E., & Shrager, E. E. (1986). The effects of repeated cycles of weight loss and regain in rats. *Physiology and Behavior, 38,* 459–464.

Bruch, H. (1974). Perils of behavior modification in the treatment of anorexia nervosa. *Journal of the American Medical Association, 230,* 1419– 1422.

Bruch, H. (1985). Four decades of eating disorders. In D. M. Garner & P. E. Garfinkel (Eds.), *Handbook of psychotherapy for anorexia and bulimia.* New York: Guilford.

Carter, J., & Duncan, P. (1984). Binge-eating and vomiting: A survey of a high school population. *Psychology in the Schools, 21,* 198–203.

Clifton, P., Barnfield, A., & Philcox, L. (1989). A behavioral profile of fluoxetine-induced anorexia. *Psychopharmacology, 97,* 89–95.

Dare, C., Eisler, I., Russell, G. F. M., & Szmukler, G. I. (1990). The clinical and theoretical impact of a controlled trial of family therapy in anorexia nervosa. *Journal of Marital and Family Therapy, 16,* 39–57.

Garfinkel, P. E., & Garner, D. M. (1982). *Anorexia nervosa: A multidimensional perspective.* New York: Brunner/Mazel.

Garner, D. M., & Bemis, K. M. (1982). A cognitive-behavioral approach to anorexia nervosa. *Cognitive Therapy and Research, 6,* 1–27.

Hawkins, R. C., Fremouw, W. J., & Clement, P. F. (Eds.). (1984). *The binge-purge syndrome: Diagnosis, treatment, and research.* New York: Springer.

Hsu, L. K. (1980). Outcome of anorexia nervosa: Review of the literature (1954–1978). *Archives of General Psychiatry, 37,* 1041–1046.

Hsu, L. K. (1989). The gender gap in eating disorders: Why are the eating disorders more common among women? *Clinical Psychology Review, 9,* 393–407.

Hughes, P. L., Wells, L. A., Cunningham, C. J., & Ilstrup, D. M. (1986). Treating bulimia with desipramine: A placebo-controlled double-blind study. *Archives of General Psychiatry, 43,* 182–186.

Humphrey, L. (1989). Observed family interactions among subtypes of eating disorders using structural analysis of social behavior. *Journal of Consulting and Clinical Psychology, 57,* 206–214.

Johnson, N., & Holloway, E. (1988). Conceptual complexity and obsessionality in bulimic college women. *Journal of Counseling Psychology, 35,* 251–257.

Kog, G., & Vandereycken, W. (1989). Family interaction in eating disorder patients and normal controls. *International Journal of Eating Disorders, 8,* 11–23.

Laessle, R., Tuschl, R., Waadt, S., & Pirke, K. (1989). The specific psychopathology of bulimia nervosa: A comparison with restrained and unrestrained (normal) eaters. *Journal of Consulting and Clinical Psychology, 57,* 772–775.

Liebman, R., Sargent, J., & Silver, M. (1983). A family systems orientation to the treatment of anorexia nervosa. *Journal of the American Academy of Child Psychiatry, 22,* 128–133.

Malone, C. A. (1979). Child psychiatry and family therapy. *Journal of the American Academy of Child Psychiatry, 18,* 4–21.

Marlatt, G. A., & Gordon, J. R. (Eds). (1985). *Relapse prevention: Maintenance strategies in the treatment of addictive behaviors.* New York: Guilford.

Minuchin, S., Rosman, B. L., & Baker, L. (1978). *Psychosomatic families: Anorexia nervosa in context.* Cambridge, MA.: Harvard University Press.

Mitchell, J., Pyle, R., Eckert, E., Hastukami, D., & Lentz, R. (1983). Electrolyte and other physiological abnormalities in patients with bulimia. *Psychological Medicine, 13,* 273–278.

Mitchell, P. B. (1988). The pharmacological management of bulimia nervosa: A critical review. *International Journal of Eating Disorders, 7,* 29–41.

Mizes, J. S. (1983, March). *Bulimarexia: Clinical description and suggested treatments.* Paper presented at the annual meeting of the Southeastern Psychological Association, Atlanta, GA.

Pomeroy, C., & Mitchell, J. (1989). Medical complications and management of eating disorders. *Psychiatric Annals, 19,* 488–493.

Pope, H. G., & Hudson, J. I. (1988). Eating disorders. In J. T. Tupin, R. I. Shader & D. S. Harnett (Eds.), *Handbook of clinical psychopharmacology* (2nd ed.). Northvale, NJ: Jason Aronson.

Pope, H. G., & Hudson, J. I. (1989). Pharmacologic treatment of bulimia nervosa: Research findings and practical suggestions. *Psychiatric Annals, 19,* 483–487.

Pope, H. G., Hudson, J. I., & Jonas, J. M., (1983). Antidepressant treatment of bulimia: Preliminary experience and practical recommendations. *Journal of Clinical Psychopharmacology, 3,* 274–281.

Pope, H. G., Hudson, J. I., Jonas, J. M., & Yurgelun-Todd, D. (1985). Antidepressant treatment of bulimia: A two-year follow-up study. *Journal of Clinical Psychopharmacology, 5,* 320–327.

Riebel, L. (1989). Communication skills for eating-disordered clients. *Psychotherapy, 26,* 69–74.

Root, M. P., Fallon, P., & Friedrich, W. N. (1986). *Bulimia: A Systems approach to treatment.* New York: W. W. Norton.

Sansone, R., Seuferer, S., Fine, M., & Bovenzi, J. (1989). The prevalence of borderline personality symptomatology among women with eating disorders. *Journal of Clinical Psychology, 45,* 603–610.

Sargent, J. (1987). Integrating family and individual therapy for anorexia nervosa. In J. E. Harkaway (Ed.), *Eating Disorders.* Rockville, MD: Aspen.

Scott, D. (1983). Alcohol and food abuse: Some comparisons. *British Medical Journal, 3,* 301.

Stager, H. (1989). An integrated psychotherapy for eating-disorder patients. *American Journal of Psychotherapy, 18,* 229–237.

Stager, H., Goldstein, C., Mongrain, M., & Van der Feen, J. (1990). Description of eating-disordered, psychiatric, and normal women along cognitive and psychodynamic dimensions. *International Journal of Eating Disorders, 9,* 129–140.

Steen, S. N., Oppliger, R. A., & Brownell, K. D. (1988). Metabolic effects of repeated weight loss and regain in adolescent wrestlers. *Journal of the American Medical Association, 260,* 47–50.

Strauss, J., & Ryan, R. M. (1988). Cognitive dysfunction in eating disorders. *International Journal of Eating Disorders, 7,* 19–27.

Swift, W. J. (1982). The long-term outcome of early onset anorexia nervosa: A critical review. *Journal of the American Academy of Child Psychiatry, 21,* 38–46.

Tice, L., Hall, R. C. W., Beresford, T. P., Quinones, J., & Hall, A. K. (1989). Sexual abuse in patients with eating disorders. *Psychiatric Medicine, 7,* 257–267.

Tseng, W., & McDermott, J. E. (1979). Triaxial family classification: A proposal. *Journal of the American Academy of Child Psychiatry, 18,* 22–43.

Vandereycken, W. (1990). The addiction model in eating disorders: Some critical remarks. *International Journal of Eating Disorders, 9,* 95–101.

Walsh, B. T., Stewart, J. W., Wright, L., Harrison, W., Roose, S. P., & Glassman, A. H. (1984). Treatment of bulimia with monoamine oxidase inhibitors. *American Journal of Psychiatry, 139,* 1629–1630.

Zweben, J. E. (1987). Eating disorders and substance abuse. *Journal of Psychoactive Drugs, 19,* 181–192.

11

Eating Disorders: Obesity

WILLIAM L. BUCHANAN, Ph.D.

Obesity is defined as a condition in which body weight exceeds ideal weight by 20 percent or more. It is commonly believed that 5 percent to 10 percent of pre-school age children, 10 percent of school age children, and 10 percent to 25 percent of adolescents are obese (Richmond, Blyler & Linscheid, 1983). For adults ages 20 to 75, 26 percent are obese, some 34 million Americans (Van Itallie, 1985). Twenty percent of Americans are obese by 30 percent or more, equalling 2.3 billion pounds (Bray, 1984).

Obesity has been found to contribute to heart disease, hypertension, atherosclerosis, hyperlipidemia, diabetes mellitus, pulmonary and renal problems, carbohydrate intolerance, increased surgical risk, risk with anesthesia, cancer, and complications during pregnancies (Brownell, 1982). A study conducted by the American Cancer Society found the lowest mortality rate was for persons 10 percent to 20 percent below average weight (Lew & Garfinkel, 1979). Mortality rates increased 131 percent for men 20 percent overweight and 185 percent for men 50 percent overweight (Lew, 1985).

In addition to the medical consequences of being overweight, social stigma and discrimination also affect the emotional well-being of the obese person. Obese persons suffer from the stigma of being blamed for their condition and are often labeled with terms that imply personal responsibility such as "lazy" and "weak."

America has become obsessed with thinness, demonstrated in recent surveys that found over 95 percent of American women diet at least part of the time, and that the weight-loss business is currently a $33-billion-a-year industry (Beck, Springen, Beachy, Hager & Buckley, 1990). Despite the billions of dollars spent and the millions of people who have dieted at one point or another, diets have a high failure rate. Only 6 percent of people who diet are able to keep the weight off (Rader, 1981).

Diets not only do not work in helping people lose weight, they actually work against weight loss. Research by Brownell and his colleagues with animals (Brownell, Greenwood, Stellar & Shrager, 1986) and with humans (Steen, Oppliger & Brownell, 1988) indicate that to diet and then regain the weight makes later weight-loss attempts take longer and weight regain more rapid. In other words, the more one diets, the harder it is to lose weight and the easier it is to gain weight. What Brownell calls weight cycling or "yo-yo dieting" (1988) also appears to increase the risk of heart disease, increase the proportion of fat to lean tissue in the body, redistribute body fat (shifting fat from the thighs and hips to the abdomen), and increase the desire for fatty foods. Physiologically, there are two reasons diets do not work (Brownell, 1988). First, whenever there is a significant drop in caloric intake, the body reacts by lowering the basal metabolic rate (BMR). The BMR drops measurably within 24 hours and continues to decline 20 percent within two weeks. Thus, dieting slows metabolism, making it more efficient; as a result, the body requires less food to maintain its weight, the exact opposite of what dieters desire. The second physiological reason diets don't work is that the enzyme lipoprotein lipase (LPL), which controls how fat is stored in fat cells, becomes more active when one reduces caloric intake. More active LPL causes the body to become more efficient at fat storage.

Behaviorally, the reason diets do not work is that diets are only a temporary change in the foods people eat; no permanent change of lifestyle is accomplished. After a diet, people return to the eating habits they had before they went on a diet. Those diets designed to make permanent changes are often so strict that people refuse to adhere to them after a short period of time.

Diets are also designed for people to use willpower in order to lose weight. However, willpower is a faulty concept that usually evokes guilt and does not produce weight loss. What is more important than willpower is "skill power." Learning a skill takes instruction, coaching, practice, and time. In order to lose weight, people must develop the proper skills. The vast majority of people who are overweight are deficient in two basic skills: eating skills and exercise skills.

The Behavioral Treatment of Obesity

Diets have an extremely high failure rate; better results have been found by changing exercise and eating behaviors (Brownell, 1982). The behavioral treatment of obesity has become a major approach not only in the field of weight control but in the field of behavior therapy as well. Currently, more people are receiving behavioral treatment for obesity than are receiving behavioral treatments for all other conditions combined. Obesity has also supplanted snake phobias as the largest single topic of behavioral research and treatment (Stunkard, 1982). The emphasis in the behavioral treatment of obesity is to make changes in the person's life-style so that eating and exercise habits are permanently changed.

To focus on the behavioral aspects of weight control is not to deny the importance of medical and nutritional factors. Every person participating in a weight-control program must first have a thorough physical examination and be cleared medically. Furthermore, the behavioral approach stresses balanced nutrition.

The goal of behavioral weight control is for people to learn to eat "normally." This means eating three meals a day, eliminating between-meal snacks, eating a variety of foods, being able to eat the foods one enjoys, and having balanced nutrition. Stated another way, the goal is to eat to live instead of to live to eat.

Common to all behavioral weight-reduction programs (BWRP) are self-monitoring, control of the stimuli preceding eating, reinforcement of prescribed eating and exercise behaviors, techniques for controlling the act of eating, and cognitive restructuring (Stunkard, 1982). Sandifer and Buchanan (1983) found that eleven specific behaviors accounted for 87.5 percent of the variance in weight loss:

1. Self-monitoring
2. Eating three meals a day and eliminating between-meal snacks
3. Exercise
4. Refraining from other activities when eating (e.g., not watching television while eating)
5. Eating only in a designated area (e.g., eating at the dinner table, not in a car)
6. "Chaining" so that the person is only engaging in one behavior at the time (e.g., the person is not reaching for a drink while chewing)
7. Taking a two-minute break at each meal
8. Limiting the amount of liquid drunk with a meal
9. Eating only one serving of each food
10. Counting calories
11. Using aversive imagery

Effective Treatment Procedures for Obesity

Most BWRPs meet for approximately 90 minutes each week and continue for different lengths of time, usually between 16 and 20 weeks. Behavioral treatment of obesity is significantly improved by lengthening the duration of treatment (Perri, Nezu, Patti & McCann, 1989). Average weight loss during behavioral treatment is 1.4 pounds per week (Brownell & Jeffery, 1987). Weight loss in a BWRP is slow. If a person is 25 pounds overweight, a realistic and reasonable time frame to lose 25 pounds is 5 months.

Self-Monitoring

Starting the first week of a BWRP, participants are to record certain information about their current eating habits. An accurate baseline is important so that later they will know exactly how much change has actually occurred. Weight-loss participants record in a small notebook the following information: date, time, amount and food consumed, where the food was eaten, and their mood while eating. To assure recordings as accurate as possible, clients are asked to carry their notebooks with them and record in them immediately after eating.

Eliminating Between-Meal Snacks

Analyzing Patterns
To analyze eating patterns, participants make frequency counts using the data collected by self-monitoring. From this, certain eating habits and patterns can be identified. Participants often identify places they eat other than the kitchen or dining room table, such as their car, living room sofa or recliner, desk at work, etc. People who skip breakfast and lunch often snack continuously throughout the day. Other people have difficulties with ice cream or popcorn later in the evening. Many people may eat normally throughout the week but have excessive eating on the weekends. Still other people may eat more when they are in a particular mood. Knowing when, where, and in what moods eating occurs identifies the cues that lead to overeating.

Graphing Between-Meal Snacks
A useful task in eliminating between-meal snacks is to graph between-meal snacks on a daily basis by using a histogram. A between-meal snack is defined as any consumption of food greater than one calorie that is not breakfast, lunch, or dinner. Participants use the data already collected in their notebooks to fill in the graph for the first week of the program. The participants then continue to use the graph for the rest of the program by filling in the number of between-meal snacks at the end of each day. The use of the bar graph is a powerful indicator for participants, since they can see the progress they have made over the course of time.

Scheduling Meals
Another method of eliminating between-meal snacks is to have participants schedule the time and place for their meals. Participants are taught to schedule their meals each night for the following day. This procedure typically takes many weeks to master because participants generally

rebel against it at first. Frequently they state that their schedule is too hectic and their life too busy for them to predict accurately when and where they will have time to eat. One rationalization that participants use in order to engage in snacking is, "There is no telling when I'll have time to eat, so I'd better grab something while I can." Participants are encouraged to schedule their meals as best they can, although they may be half an hour to several hours off. Over the course of time, participants become more accurate in predicting the time and the place they eat.

Stimulus Control
The principle of stimulus control is also useful in helping people eliminate between-meal snacks. Schachter (1971) suggested that obese people have more external stimulus control than internal stimulus control, implying that obese people are more likely to eat when they see or smell food (an external stimulus) as opposed to the internal stimulus of hunger. More recent research suggests that obese people are no more susceptible to external stimuli than normal-weight people (Stunkard, 1982). However, the principle is still useful in working with weight-loss participants, for it makes sense to them. The principle of stimulus control predicts that people eat food in response to specific stimuli, even if they are not hungry. Stimulus control can be summarized by the statement, "Out of sight, out of mouth" (Brownell, 1988).

Food Storage   One technique based on stimulus control is to store food only in an appropriate food storage area, which should be out of sight. Often participants have food in their car, bedside table, desk, study, or pocketbook. Thus, people should store food in containers out of sight in the kitchen cabinets or pantry. To go a step further, it is useful to refrigerate leftovers wrapped in aluminum foil instead of clear wrap.

Designated Eating Areas   Another technique based on the principle of stimulus control is to designate a specific eating area and eat only in that eating area. The eating area should be only at the kitchen or dining room table. A particular seat at each table should be designated. The person is not considered to be in a designated eating area unless he or she is seated, with the chair pulled up to the table. Under these guidelines, food should not be consumed in the bedroom, den, or car. Of course when one is not at home, the designated eating area must be determined, e.g., sitting at a table in a restaurant. At a party, a particular spot to consume food should be chosen; the spot chosen should be at least several yards away from where food is displayed.

Aversive Imagery
Using imagery that is repulsive to participants is also useful in helping to eliminate between-meal snacking. A procedure that seems to work extremely effectively in a group is for the instructor to bring ten pounds of

animal fat to the meeting. It is often useful to have participants stick their hands in the fat and squish it with their fingers.

Planned Snacks

When the idea of eliminating between-meals snacks is first introduced, participants are not asked to eliminate all snacks immediately. They are allowed four planned snacks during the first week. Using the techniques described above, over the course of several weeks the number of snacks allowed gradually decreases to zero. Limiting the number of between-meal snacks to a specific number means the participants will either have to plan when to use their allowed between-meal snacks or keep them in reserve and use them spontaneously. The participants are encouraged to plan their use of the between-meal snacks over the next week. For example, if Sunday afternoon is a time when the family goes for an ice cream cone, this could be a good use for a planned snack.

In reducing the number of between-meal snacks to four for the week, the participants are reminded of certain points. For example, foods and drinks of one calorie or less do not count as between-meal snacks. Thus, water, diet soft drinks, and coffee or tea with diet sweetener are encouraged and do not count as between-meal snacks. Nutritionally, this is not sound because of the artificial sweetener, caffeine, and food coloring included in those items. However, the point is to begin shaping the behavior of controlling the times and places that people consume their food. Later in the program, nutrition will be addressed.

Decreasing the Amount of Food Eaten

One Thing at a Time

The concept of stimulus control is also useful in decreasing the amount of food eaten. Participants should not watch television, read the newspaper, or listen to the radio while they are eating. This breaks the association between the stimuli and eating behavior. If participants pay more attention to their food and do not eat merely out of habit, the amount of food eaten can be decreased.

Participants should also enjoy their food and make eating a social time by talking with family or friends. Since they are only eating three times a day, they should enjoy those three times as much as possible. Participants are told to enjoy their food more, not less, and to "eat like a gourmet" (Johnson & Stalonas, 1981). To maximize eating enjoyment, all distractions should be eliminated.

Chaining

The principal of behavioral chaining is the idea that complex behaviors, such as eating, are made up of smaller discrete behaviors. These discrete behaviors are sequentially linked to each other to form a behavior "chain." People collapse the chain, so that instead of performing discrete behaviors sequentially, they are performing three and four behaviors simultaneously. Instead of sitting down, then reaching for a fork, then putting food on the fork, then putting the food in the mouth, many people simultaneously chew food, put more food on the fork with one hand, and reach for a drink with the other. In teaching people to perform only one behavior at a time, a useful rule is that the jaw does not move as long as the hand is moving. To signal that the hand is no longer moving, the hand must touch their knee. This requires putting the fork down between each bite and putting the hands in the lap before starting to chew the food. The major benefit of behavioral chaining is that it forces people to slow down the speed of their eating.

Eating more slowly is another method to help people eat less. Having people slow down their eating will enable them to feel full while eating less. Beyond a certain minimum volume of food for the person to feel satisfied, the single most important factor in feeling full is length of time. People usually feel full approximately 20 minutes after they begin eating, regardless of how much food they have eaten, as long as the minimum amount is consumed. Most people are able to consume this minimum amount of food within a few minutes. People continue to eat between the time they actually have consumed enough food to satisfy them and the end of 20 minutes, by which time they feel bloated from overeating. This is reinforcing because they feel as if they ate until they were full, but in reality they ate far beyond being full. Physiologically, the explanation for this is that it takes approximately 20 minutes for the stomach to signal to the hypothalamus that the stomach is full. Thus, merely by slowing down their eating, people can consume less food and feel satiated. Several additional techniques are useful in helping people slow down their eating.

Two-Minute Pause

Another method to help slow down eating is to take a two-minute pause from eating. During the meal, participants simply stop eating for two minutes. The two-minute pause in eating serves two important functions. First, it allows more time for food to reach the stomach, which in turn uses up 10 percent of the time necessary for the stomach to signal the hypothalamus that it is full. The second important function is that the pause breaks up momentum when eating. Often, people start eating slowly, and as time continues, gain momentum and eat faster. By taking a two-minute time-out approximately six to eight minutes into the meal, the momentum of eating faster is broken up. Sandifer and Buchanan (1983), using multiple regression analysis, found that the best single behavior for successful weight loss was to take a two-minute pause.

Limiting Liquids

Another technique for slowing down eating, thereby decreasing the amount of food eaten, is to limit the amount of liquid drunk during a meal to one glass. The amount of liquid may be gradually decreased over the course of a few weeks. The reason for limiting liquids during the meals is that people often do not thoroughly chew their food and will wash their food down with liquid. Limiting the amount of liquid during a meal prevents them from washing their food down and encourages them to chew longer and swallow more thoroughly. By so doing, participants lengthen the amount of time needed to eat the same volume of food.

One Serving
Participants can also decrease the amount of food they eat by eating only one serving of each food. Before participants begin to eat, all of the food they are going to eat should be on their plate. This helps teach them to become fully aware of how much they are eating so that their "eyes are not bigger than their stomachs".

Throw Away the Last Bite
Participants are also taught to throw away a bite of each food at the end of each meal. Very often, participants are trained as children to clean their plates. The emotional reactions of participants to this particular technique is interesting. In any group, several participants always find this very difficult. This goes back to the issue of whether persons control their eating or their eating controls them. When people are able to use this technique of throwing away bites of food, their sense of self-control is increased.

Exercise

Participants are encouraged to find a specific kind of exercise that they will enjoy and are capable of continuing after the BWRP ends. People will not continue to exercise if it is not practical and enjoyable. Frequently people identify walking as an exercise they enjoy. They are encouraged to increase exercise slowly so that they will not feel sore, not do more than they are capable of doing, and choose a kind of exercise that will fit into their daily routine without disrupting it. The idea of "no pain, no gain" is a myth that should be dispelled in any BWRP; any exercise a participant will do is better than none.

Number of Calories Burned
Exercise can be measured by the amount of calories burned on a daily basis. Participants monitor the amount of time they exercise. The total number of calories burned is determined by multiplying the number of minutes they engaged in exercise by the number of calories burned per minute. Light exercise such as softball, volleyball, bowling, horseback riding, walking, golf, and gardening typically burns four calories per min-

ute. Moderate exercise such as fast dancing, cycling, stationary cycling, tennis, fast walking, and swimming typically burns seven calories per minute. Heavy exercise such as fast calisthenics, racquet ball, jogging, skipping rope, and basketball typically burns ten calories per minute. Johnson and Stalonas (1981) recommend that participants begin by burning 150 calories in planned exercise every day. Planned exercise does not include daily activities such as vacuuming, carrying in groceries, yard work, etc. Often for older individuals, the amount of calories burned through exercise needs to be reduced to 75 to 100 per day.

The number of calories burned per day is not nearly as important as the fact that participants *consistently* exercise. Some people prefer to have formal exercise every other day since they take exercise classes such as aerobic dancing. Nevertheless, participants are encouraged to burn 150 calories per day doing planned exercise. Activities do not have to be the same from day to day; what does have to be consistent is that they plan ahead and engage in activities designed as exercise. As time goes on, participants are encouraged to increase the number of calories burned each day, increasing the daily number by 50 or 100 calories every few weeks.

Participants are also encouraged to increase the intensity of exercise so that eventually they are getting aerobic exercise. As with the graph used for between-meal snacks, participants use a histogram to graph the number of calories burned per day. The maximum the participants are asked to burn is 400 calories per day. Often, participants will burn up to 800 or more calories per day, but this not is required. If participants set their standards too high, they are likely to become discouraged and give up exercising all together. However, if participants set their goal at burning 400 calories a day and burn more, this is allowed as long as the higher number does not become a standard they must attain.

With regard to exercise, the participants should be reminded that the myth that exercise increases appetite is just that; actually, exercise stimulates the hypothalamus so that appetite and hunger feelings are decreased.

Daily and Weekly Feedback Using a Point System

Another useful method of daily feedback is having people record on a tally sheet all the new behaviors to which they adhere. The point system, as designed by Johnson and Stalonas (1981), assigns a certain number of points for each activity on a daily basis. Determining the number of points weight-loss participants earn on a daily basis gives accurate feedback as to how much the participants are adhering to the BWRP. Points are also totaled every seven days to provide weekly feedback. The useful aspect of the point system is not to provide feedback as to how well participants are doing in their weight-loss efforts, but the point system does give an alternative to the weight scale as a measure of progress. Instead of people looking at a number on a weight scale to see how they are doing, participants add up points to measure the degree of lifestyle change. This breaks up the daily ritual of weighing oneself and gives participants a different number to evaluate their progress.

Balanced Nutrition

Another important aspect of changing one's lifestyle is to use balanced nutrition. Although a diet is not recommended, balanced nutrition is. Balanced nutrition is having servings of the four basic food groups each day: four servings of vegetable and fruits, four servings of breads and cereals, two servings of dairy products, and two servings of protein. In general, as long as participants are getting appropriate servings (4-4-2-2) each day, they are getting balanced nutrition. The biggest difficulty Americans usually have is that they eat too much meat and not enough vegetables and fruits. This is the opposite of what cancer experts are recommending in terms of nutrition to reduce the risk of cancer.

In general, Americans need to reduce their level of cholesterol. The primary cause of heart disease is cholesterol, which in 1987 caused 1.5 million heart attacks and 550,000 deaths in the U.S. (Brand, 1988). Cholesterol contributes to the death of more Americans each year than all cancers combined. Over 50 percent of Americans have cholesterol levels that are considered too high; only 8 percent of Americans actually know their cholesterol level. Healthy adults under the age of 65 have a 50 percent chance of suffering a heart attack if they have any two of the following risk factors: high cholesterol level, obesity, smoking, inactivity, or high blood pressure. If a person's cholesterol level is 265 or higher, he or she has 4 times as great a risk of a heart attack as someone who has a cholesterol level of 190 or less.

However, it is not just a matter of reducing cholesterol, as there are two types of cholesterol: high density lipoprotein (HDL) and low density lipoprotein (LDL). An excess of the LDL type of cholesterol and too little HDL poses a danger to health. LDL cholesterol works as a plaque that binds the inner walls of the veins and arteries, thus restricting blood flow (a condition known as atherosclerosis). As the inner diameter of arteries and veins decreases, it takes greater force to pump the blood, thus increasing blood pressure. If a piece of cholesterol breaks off, or if the blood flow is critically reduced, there can be severe damage in the form of a heart attack or stroke.

HDL cholesterol, which is very dense and tightly packed, also attaches to the walls of arteries and veins, but since it is very dense, it does not restrict blood flow. The human body needs HDL to increase elasticity in arteries and veins. HDL may actually play a role in preventing heart disease (Brand, 1988).

Nine out of ten people can substantially reduce their cholesterol level by altering their diet, specifically by reducing the intake of foods containing saturated fats, such as butter, cheese, eggs, liver, and red meat. For every 1 percent reduction in cholesterol, there is a 2 percent reduction in the risk of heart attack. Cholesterol is basically animal fat. Vegetables and fruits have no cholesterol until people add butter or cook them with some other animal fat. Cholesterol can be reduced by eating more fruits and vegetables properly prepared and eating less red meat. Cholesterol can also be reduced by exercise. Aerobic exercise actually increases levels of HDL while decreasing the levels of LDL. Thus, a combination of diet and exercise can significantly alter one's cholesterol level.

Counting Calories

In general, weight-loss participants know how many calories they are burning, because most participants in BWRPs have been through various other programs and have developed great skill at counting calories. The fact that they have skill at it and are still obese strongly suggests that counting calories alone does not result in weight loss. However, there are occasions when counting calories may be useful. If after several weeks the participants still are not losing weight on a weekly basis, they probably are consuming too many calories.

To determine how many calories per day participants are consuming, they should monitor their calories for a period of one to two weeks. The number of calories per day needed to maintain a particular weight is determined by multiplying the current number of pounds by 15 (Johnson & Stalonas, 1981). Since a pound is equivalent to 3500 calories, to lose 1 pound in 1 week, there must be a reduction in caloric intake by approximately 500 calories each day. This is assuming, of course, that the level of exercise remains constant.

Very-Low-Calorie Diets

The above procedures are recommended for all obese people once they are medically cleared. For people who are less than 50 pounds overweight, the behavioral weight-control program appears to be the treatment of choice (Foreyt, 1987). However, for the treatment of moderate to severe obesity, for those individuals who need to lose 50 pounds or more, other and more aggressive approaches are required. One such approach is the use of a very-low-calorie diet (VLCD) combined with behavior therapy (Foreyt, 1987). VLCDs should be considered only one component of a multifaceted behavioral weight loss program and not means to be used by themselves.

The VLCD must be medically supervised and ideally should be a hospital-based program. As outpatients, participants drink a liquid supplement in place of eating meals. Legitimate liquid supplements provide all the minerals, nutrients, proteins, and vitamins that are needed to remain healthy. Typically, the programs are restricted to 300 to 800 calories per day. Average weight loss on VLCDs is between three and four pounds per week. Patients on VLCDs are usually very enthusiastic about them, and after a few days actually report feeling little hunger. However, it is important that after participants lose a significant amount of weight, they slowly return to eating after being thoroughly trained in the behavioral methods described earlier. If they return to previous eating habits without learning the behavioral methods, they are almost guaranteed to regain all of the weight they have lost and more. Thus, *maintenance* of any weight loss achieved through the use of VLCDs becomes critical.

Very low calorie diets have received a great deal of attention in the popular press recently. It has been estimated that in 1990, 20 million Americans will spend one billion dollars on medically supervised liquid diets and over-the-counter liquid diet products (Beck et al., 1990). Indeed, so much attention has been given and so much money has been spent that on May 7, 1990, U.S. Congressional hearings on the weight-loss industry were held before the Subcommittee on Regulation, Business Opportunities, and Energy (Burris, 1990). Unfortunately, there are a great number of unethical and ineffective programs on the market, and many programs imply (although none actually claim) that their VLCD is the "magic bullet" of weight loss.

Wadden, Van Itallie, and Blackburn (1990) provide guidelines for the responsible use of VLCDs. First, VLCDs should only be used by people with moderate to severe obesity. People with mild obesity should lose weight through modifying their lifestyles. Second, patients on VLCDs must have adequate medical supervision. They should have weekly examinations by a physician and have their electrolyte and other laboratory values assessed every other week during the period of rapid weight loss. Third, there should be supervision by a multidisciplinary team of trained professionals—at a minimum including a physician who has specialized training in obesity, a behavioral psychologist, and a dietitian. Fourth, patients should attend weekly group sessions and be instructed to modify their eating, exercise, and other lifestyle habits. The lifestyle modification instruction ideally should continue for at least 6 to 12 months following the medically supervised VLCD.

Long-term effectiveness of VLCDs has been shown to be best when the VLCD is combined with behavior therapy. Follow-up studies of two years (Miura, Arai, Tsukahara, Ohno & Ikeda, 1989) and eight years (Kirschner, Schneider, Ertel & Gorman, 1988) indicate that VLCDs combined with lifestyle modifications provide a reasonable rate of success for achieving and maintaining weight loss for the morbidly obese. However, other follow-up studies at three years (Wadden, Stunkard & Liebschutz, 1988) and five years (Wadden, Sternberg, Letizia, Stunkard & Foster,

1989) found that although people lost weight initially on VLCDs plus life-style modifications, most participants eventually stopped practicing their behavioral weight control methods and regained the weight origi-nally lost. However, people who entered additional treatment seemed to be more successful at not regaining weight. Wadden, Stunkard, and Liebschutz (1988) suggest that dieters may wait too long before seeking additional treatment. If this is the case, it may be best to think of moder-ate to severe obesity as a lifelong problem in which lifelong maintenance and follow-up is necessary. If so, this is similar to the treatment of addic-tions for which alcoholics or drug addicts attend AA or NA meetings on a regular basis for the rest of their lives.

Adjunctive Procedures

The latter stages of treatment are generally considered adjunctive proce-dures to help maintain weight loss. During the early part of treatment, participants alter their lifestyles with regard to their eating and exercise behaviors. During the latter stages of treatment, consistency and routine are focused on, so that these new behaviors become permanent in the participants' repertoire. Such procedures include assertiveness training, cognitive restructuring, stress management, relapse prevention, and fol-low-up booster sessions.

Assertiveness Training
There are two types of assertiveness with regard to eating. The first type is making a request, and the second is in refusing other people's requests. In making requests, participants role-play a situation where they ask that food be prepared a certain way or that certain foods by available at a fam-ily meal. In refusing requests by others, the participants role-play a signif-icant other insisting, "Oh, just have one, you'll love it." A useful tactic in the latter situation is complimenting the host. Often, when people let the host know that they are enjoying themselves and that they have noticed how hard the host has worked, the host will be less insistent that they eat a particular food.

Cognitive Restructuring
Negative self-talk will typically evolve around eating habits, exercise, and generally being overweight. Each of the categories is attacked in session and participants are taught to identify their thought processes and learn to counter automatic critical thoughts. A useful visual tool is a piece of cardboard approximately two feet long with the following letters: "IAMNOWHERE." The instructor flashes the card in front of the partic-ipants for approximately one second, removes it, and asks the weight-control participants what they saw. Some people see "I am nowhere," and

other people see "I am now here." People can look at the same thing and come up with totally opposite conclusions. Most participants, when they have an uncontrolled eating episode, will conclude that they are nowhere. By relabeling a between-meal snack as simply a snack, as opposed to a failure in character, participants are less likely to become discouraged and quit.

Stress Management and Relaxation Training
Participants are taught stress management and relaxation techniques. Many of the procedures already used in the BWRP are also applicable to stress management, since both require a change in lifestyle. Various ways of controlling stress are exercise, cognitive restructuring, assertiveness, and using balanced nutrition. Stress management techniques such as prescribed breathing and progressive muscle relaxation are also taught.

Relapse Prevention
During and following participation in a BWRP, participants will be tempted to stop adhering to some or all of the procedures described above. How this is handled may determine future progress. Lapse, relapse, and collapse have been distinguished as three stages in a process (Brownell, Marlatt, Lichtenstein & Wilson, 1986). A lapse is a single slip or mistake. A relapse is a recurrence of symptoms of the disorder being treated. Thus a lapse is viewed as an event that may or may not lead to an outcome (i.e., relapse). A collapse is a return to the previous state, before treatment. The goal of relapse prevention is to prevent a slip or mistake (lapse) from becoming a relapse, and ultimately, a collapse. A person's reaction to one or more lapses will determine whether there is a relapse or not.

Relapses may be prevented by developing a repertoire of skills aimed at avoiding or overcoming lapses. Cognitive restructuring is important to prevent relapses, since people often have all-or-nothing thinking with regard to eating. For example, eating a bowl of ice cream often leads to thoughts such as, "Well, I've broken my diet now; I might as well eat the whole thing." Predicting or prescribing a relapse can also be applied to weight control. This involves coaching participants to overeat purposefully or gain a small amount of weight, followed by a reinstatement of the weight-loss procedures (Brownell & Jeffery, 1987). Such techniques give participants confidence that they can handle future lapses.

Follow-up Booster Sessions
Maintaining weight loss and a health-oriented lifestyle has been a major problem for BWRPs (Perri, 1987). Booster sessions following treatment can help people continue to lose weight or prevent weight regain. All the above procedures should be periodically reviewed and participants should be monitored for continued adherence to them. Booster sessions are often once a month. The participants have an opportunity to weigh in and see

other participants from their program. Booster sessions that incorporate professional contacts, peer group support, problem-solving skills and relapse-prevention training appear to be more effective in maintaining weight loss (Dubbert, Terre, Holm & Brown, 1987).

Positive Psychological Side Effects

Clinicians using behavioral treatments for weight reduction often report that in addition to their clients losing weight, the clients often have positive psychological changes that were not originally goals for treatment. That is, clients participating in BWRPs often report positive psychological side effects from treatment. This is an important issue to investigate further, because if different treatments produce equivalent weight change but differ in positive side effects, the clinician should favor the strategy that was associated with the most positive side effects (Epstein & Martin, 1977). The side effects most often reported were increased self-esteem, decreased feelings of depression, and improved marital relationships and social functioning (Brownell, 1982; Wing, Epstein, Marcus & Kupfer, 1984). One study found a significant decrease in the level of depression from pre- to post-treatment (Wadden, Stunkard & Smoller, 1986). In reviewing ten studies investigating the relationship between mood and weight loss in BWRPs, Wing et al. (1984) found no negative side effects.

Buchanan, Bennett, Cobb, and Wright (1984) found significant differences in positive psychological side effects for subjects participating in a BWRP when compared to a no-treatment control. The treatment group not only lost significantly more weight, but also had significantly greater self-acceptance and less measured depression. A trend was found, in that the treatment group also had higher self-regard and greater marital satisfaction.

Long-Term Follow-up

Behavioral treatments for obesity appear to have adequate maintenance of weight loss during the following one to two years (Brownell & Wadden, 1986), but beyond two years, regain of 75 to 100 percent of the initial weight loss is common (Wadden et al., 1989). The long-term results of the behavioral approach to weight control need to be improved. A 5-year follow-up of a BWRP (Graham, Taylor, Hovell & Siegel, 1983) indicated that the most successful weight-loss maintainers reported adhering to the behavioral procedures and being more physically active. However, after five years, the participants reported that they had not lost all the weight they wanted to and that they wished to lose an additional 15 to 95 pounds. In another 5-year follow-up (Stalonas, Perri & Kerzner, 1984), most participants gained back a major portion of the weight they lost during treatment.

Participants reported that a number of situational, social, and emotional factors affected their weight control efforts. Families were reported to have a negative role, with spouses reported most often as being counterproductive to the participant's continued weight loss. Depression was also reported as a factor that reduced the participants' long-term adherence to the behavioral principles, thus resulting in their regaining weight. The most striking finding of the latter study was that for the most part, the subjects did not continue the use of the treatment strategies and techniques learned. In other words, the participants did not really change their lifestyle.

Westover and Lanyon (1990) reviewed the literature on the behavioral treatment of obesity and found three factors that related to the long-term maintenance of weight loss: (1) adherence to treatment and use of the behavioral skills, (2) post-treatment vigilance regarding both weight fluctuation and the skills learned in therapy, and (3) intraindividual physical and emotional factors. In terms of adherence to treatment, Westover and Lanyon concluded that subjects who continued to use behavioral skills after therapy terminated were more successful in maintaining weight loss. With regard to post-treatment vigilance, regain of weight served as a cue to reinstitute or increase the use of the behavioral skills learned in therapy. Factors related to vigilance included: attending therapy with a spouse who is coached to aid the subject; attending further programs after the termination of treatment; having contact (in person, by phone or by mail) with the therapist; and daily monitoring and recording of calorie intake, weight, and physical activity. Intraindividual factors included gender, personal and environmental stresses, percentage of body fat before treatment, age of onset, weight loss early in treatment, and confidence in the ability to lose weight. Westover and Lanyon concluded that weight-loss maintenance could be improved by relabeling weight control as a continuing, lifelong process and by directing subjects to be constantly vigilant of both their weight fluctuations and their use of behavioral skills.

In general, it appears that exercise is the single most important variable in long-term weight loss (Graham et al., 1983). People who continue to exercise are the most likely to lose weight and keep the weight off over the course of the years. Stalonas and Kirschenbaum (1985) maintain that social and psychological factors also contribute to long-term weight loss. Stunkard (1980) declared that social factors are among the most important factors, if not *the* most important factor, in the prevalence of obesity today, and that the social context of obesity needs to be better controlled if long-term maintenance is to be improved. The family is the most obvious social context.

The Family and Obesity

Stuart and Davis (1972) found that husbands of women who lose weight often feel that they lose overeating as a shared activity, lose bargaining power in arguments, worry about the unfaithfulness of their wives, and worry about the possibility of losing their wives through divorce. They concluded that husbands may actually be exerting a negative influence on their wives, and that this negative influence serves to sabotage the wives' weight-loss efforts.

Obesity and the Couple System

From the behavioral literature, Stuart and Davis (1972) reported several findings about obesity that relate to marital interactions. The husband is more likely to discuss food, offer food, and accept offered food than is his wife. Husbands also criticized their wives' eating behavior 12 times more frequently than they were criticized by their wives. Stuart and Davis suggest that the treatment of obesity should include the marital partner, because without the partner's participation, the intervention may be seen as a disruption of a shared lifestyle. They report that although 91 percent of husbands want their wives to lose weight, only 61 percent were willing to assist them in weight loss.

Sandifer and Buchanan (1983) asked the spouse of the participant to make unobtrusive observations of the participant's eating behavior in their natural environment. Family members' ratings were significantly related to both the self-report of the participants and to weight loss. A serendipitous finding (not reported in this study) was that participants whose spouses were involved indicated that spousal sabotaging was diminished.

Several studies examined whether involving a family member, most often the spouse, affected weight loss for the participant. The first study to vary social support systematically in a weight-loss program was conducted by Wilson and Brownell (1978). All subjects received the standard behavioral therapy program. Half of the participants attended all the sessions with a family member; the other half attended alone. The family members were taught behavioral principles and how to help the participant change the conditions and consequences of eating. The family intervention made no difference in outcome at the end of treatment or at the 6-month follow-up. The authors concluded that it is difficult to interpret this finding without having any measure of the degree to which family members cooperated with the program. Perhaps the family members need more structure if they are to improve outcome.

Brownell and his colleagues conducted another study, this time controlling the variables mentioned above (Brownell, Heckerman, Westlake,

Hayes & Monti, 1978). Three groups were examined, two of which had "cooperative" spouses, in that spouses agreed to participate by helping their mates, and a third group in which the spouse refused to cooperate (thus called "uncooperative"). In the first cooperative-spouse group, the spouse was made an active participant instead of a passive observer, with the spouse and the participant each having assignments to do between sessions. In the second cooperative-spouse group, the spouse was not involved in the program, although spouses had indicated they were willing to be involved. Participants in this second group attended the group alone. The third group consisted of the participants who had spouses who had refused to participate. Brownell et al. found that patients treated with their spouses lost more weight than the other two groups who were treated alone. They also found that those with a cooperative spouse, even though the spouse did not attend the sessions, lost more weight than those with an uncooperative spouse. The weight loss increased at the end of a 6-month follow-up for both cooperative-spouse groups. Not only did the participants with cooperative spouses lose more weight than the participants with uncooperative spouses, the weight loss was nearly triple what is commonly reported in other behavioral weight-loss programs for the same amount of time, with one-third of the weight loss occurring during the follow-up period, after the end of treatment.

The positive findings of the Brownell study have been replicated in several other studies (Fremouw & Zitter, 1980; Israel & Saccone, 1979; Pearce, Lebow & Orchard, 1981; Rosenthal, Allen & Winter, 1980; Saccone & Israel, 1978). However, five other studies failed to replicate Brownell's findings of greater weight loss resulting from involvement of the spouse (Brownell & Stunkard, 1981; Dubbert & Wilson, 1984; O'Neil, Currey, Hirsch, Riddle, Taylor, Malcolm & Sexaur, 1979; Weisz & Bucher, 1980; Zitter & Fremouw, 1978). An interesting point is that many of the same researchers who found data replicating Brownell's findings in one study found contradictory data from another study.

Buchanan (1987) investigated changes in the levels of depression, marital satisfaction, and intimacy for participants in a BWRP by involving the spouse in treatment; 63 obese subjects participated in a BWRP in which 48 of the participants were married. Of the married participants, 37 had cooperative spouses and 11 had uncooperative spouses (Brownell et al., 1978). The cooperative spouses were divided into three conditions: attending the program as a participant with their mates; attending a meeting for the spouses, designed to prevent spousal sabotage (Pearce, Lebow & Orchard, 1981); and no spousal involvement. All weight-loss participants lost a significant amount of weight by the end of the program, with no significant differences between groups. The married participants had a significant decrease in depression and a significant increase in marital satisfaction and emotional intimacy. By the end of the weight-loss program, participants with cooperative spouses were more satisfied in their marriage than participants with uncooperative spouses. There were no significant differences between the three cooperative-spouse conditions for any dependent variable with the exception of depression. Participants whose spouses attended the program with them had the lowest level of depression at both pretest and posttest.

The future of couples training is now uncertain (Stunkard, 1982) but appears promising and deserves more attention. It is apparent that the family can play a useful role in the treatment of obesity, and that family involvement has worked well on occasion. What is unknown is *when* family involvement will work. The variance found between studies concerning whether or not spouse involvement affected weight loss may be due to the different ways various groups involved the spouse. Brownell and Stunkard (1981) speculate that the active participation of the spouse seems to be the key to enhancing effectiveness, but this has not been demonstrated empirically. Spousal support appears to be promising for enhancing weight-loss maintenance, but so far how to best involve the spouse is unclear. Decisions to involve the spouse are best made on a case-by-case basis (Dubbert et al., 1987).

Summary

Obesity is a serious health risk for people in this country. Recent surveys suggest that up to 26 percent of Americans are clinically obese. In addition to a greater incidence of physical disorders and earlier death for obese people, a number of psychological factors are affected by obesity. Obese people suffer a great deal of social stigma and discrimination and generally feel negative about their body image. Helping people lose weight helps lower their level of depression and enhances self-esteem.

Although diets have not been effective in the long run, the behavioral treatment of obesity appears to be promising. For mildly obese people, changing lifestyle through the use of behavioral techniques appears to be the treatment of choice. For moderate to severe obesity, more aggressive treatments are necessary, including very low calorie diets used with behavioral treatments. Current trends in behavioral weight-loss programs are to increase the length of treatment and to focus on maintaining weight losses. The most significant treatments for helping maintain weight loss include relapse-prevention training, exercise, and social support. Follow-ups from three to five years are beginning to appear in the literature and the long-term follow-up appears to be most important. It appears that the best treatment over the long run will be a continued collaboration among psychologists, physiologists, physicians, biochemists, dieticians, and practitioners from related disciplines to better treat this complex, refractory disorder (Foreyt, 1987).

References

Beck, M., Springen, K., Beachy, L., Hager, M., & Buckley, L. (1990, April 30). The losing formula. *Newsweek*, pp. 52–58.

Brand, D. (1988). Searching for life's elixir. *Time, 132*(24), pp. 62–66.

Bray, G. A. (1984, July). Obesity: Benefits and risks of treatment. *Drug Therapy,* 60–73.

Brownell, K. D. (1982). Obesity: Understanding and treating a serious, prevalent and refractory disorder. *Journal of Consulting and Clinical Psychology, 50,* 820–840.

Brownell, K. D. (1988, March). The yo-yo trap. *American Health,* 78–84.

Brownell, K. D., Greenwood, M. R. C., Stellar, E., & Shrager, E. E. (1986). The effects of repeated cycles of weight loss and regain in rats. *Physiology and Behavior, 38,* 459–464.

Brownell, K. D., Heckerman, C. L., Westlake, R. J., Hayes, S. L., & Monti, P. M. (1978). The effect of couple training and partner cooperativeness in the behavioral treatment of obesity. *Behavior Research and Therapy, 16,* 323–333.

Brownell, K. D., & Jeffery, R. W. (1987). Improving long-term weight loss: Pushing the limits of treatment. *Behavior Therapy, 18,* 353–374.

Brownell, K. D., Marlatt, G. A., Lichtenstein, E., & Wilson, G. T. (1986). Understanding and preventing relapse. *American Psychologist, 41,* 765–782.

Brownell, K. D., & Stunkard, A. J. (1981). Couples training, pharmacotherapy and behavior therapy in the treatment of obesity. *Archives of General Psychiatry, 38,* 1224–1229.

Brownell, K. D., & Wadden, T. A. (1986). Behavior therapy for obesity: Modern approaches and better results. In K. D. Brownell & J. P. Foreyt (Eds.), *Handbook of eating disorders.* New York: Basic Books.

Buchanan, W. L. (1987). Effects on weight loss and marital interaction by involving the spouse in a behavioral weight reduction program. Unpublished doctoral dissertation, Georgia State University, Atlanta, GA.

Buchanan, W. L., Bennett, K., Cobb, S., & Wright, K. (1984, March). Positive psychological side effects resulting from participation in a behavioral weight reduction program: A pilot study. Poster session presented at the annual meeting of the Southeastern Psychological Association, New Orleans, LA.

Burris, B. (1990, May 9). Congressional hearings. *New Direction Media Alert.* Unpublished memo.

Dubbert, P. M., Terre, L., Holm, J. E., & Brown, M. (1987). Maintenance in behavioral weight reduction programs. *The Behavior Therapist, 10,* 225–230.

Dubbert, P. M., & Wilson, G. T. (1984). Goal-setting and spouse involvement in the treatment of obesity. *Behavioral Research and Therapy, 22,* 227–242.

Epstein, L. H., & Martin, J. E. (1977). Compliance and side effects of weight regulation groups. *Behavior Modification, 1,* 551–558.

Foreyt, J. P. (1987). Issues in the assessment and treatment of obesity. *Journal of Consulting and Clinical Psychology, 55,* 677–684.

Fremouw, W. J., & Zitter, R. E. (1980). Individual and couple behavioral contracting for weight reduction and maintenance. *The Behavior Therapist, 3,* 15–16.

Graham, L. E., Taylor, C. B., Hovell, M. F., & Siegel, W. (1983). Five-year follow-up to a behavioral weight-loss program. *Journal of Consulting and Clinical Psychology, 51,* 322–323.

Israel, A. C., & Saccone, A. J. (1979). Follow-up effects of choice of mediator and target of reinforcement on weight loss. *Behavior Therapy, 10,* 260–265.

Johnson, W. G., & Stalonas, P. M. (1981). *Weight no longer.* Gretna, LA: Pelican.

Kirschner, M. A., Schneider, G., Ertel, N. H., & Gorman, J. (1988). An eight-year experience with very-low-calorie formula diet for control of major obesity. *International Journal of Obesity, 12,* 69–80.

Lew, E. A. (1985). Mortality and weight: Insured lives and the American Cancer Society studies. *Annals of Internal Medicine, 103,* 1024–1029.

Lew, E. A., & Garfinkel, L. (1979). Variations in mortality by weight among 750,000 men and women. *Journal of Chronic Diseases, 32,* 563–576.

Miura, K., Arai, K., Tsukahara, S., Ohno, M., & Ikeda, Y. (1989). The long term effectiveness of combined therapy by behavior modification and very low calorie diet: 2 years follow-up. *International Journal of Obesity, 13* (suppl. 2), 73–77.

O'Neil, P. M., Currey, H. S., Hirsch, A. A., Riddle, F. E., Taylor, C. I., Malcolm, R. J., & Sexaur, J. D. (1979). Effects of sex of subject and spouse involvement on weight loss in a behavioral treatment program: A retrospective investigation. *Addictive Behaviors, 4,* 167–178.

Pearce, J. W., Lebow, M. D., & Orchard, J. (1981). Role of spouse involvement in the behavioral treatment of overweight women. *Journal of Consulting and Clinical Psychology, 49,* 236–244.

Perri, M. G. (1987). Maintenance strategies for the management of obesity. In W. G. Johnson (Ed.), *Advances in Eating Disorders.* Greenwich, CT: JAI Press.

Perri, M. G., Nezu, A. M., Patti, E. T., & McCann, K. L. (1989). Effect of length of treatment on weight loss. *Journal of Consulting and Clinical Psychology, 57,* 450–452.

Rader, W. (1981). *Dr. Rader's no-diet program for permanent weight loss.* New York: Warner.

Richmond, D. A., Blyler, E. M., & Linscheid, T. R. (1983). The obese child. *American Family Physician, 28,* 129–134.

Rosenthal, B., Allen, B. J., & Winter, C. (1980). Husband involvement in behavioral treatment of overweight women: Initial effects and long-term follow-up. *International Journal of Obesity, 4,* 165–173.

Saccone, A. J., & Israel, A. C. (1978). Effects of experimenter versus significant other controlled reinforcement and choice of target behavior on weight loss. *Behavior Therapy, 9,* 271–278.

Sandifer, B. A., & Buchanan, W. L. (1983). Relationship between adherence and weight loss in a behavioral weight reduction program. *Behavior Therapy, 14,* 682–688.

Schachter, S. (1971). *Emotion, Obesity, and Crime.* New York: Academic Press.

Stalonas, P. M., & Kirschenbaum, D. S. (1985). Behavioral treatments for obesity: Eating habits revisited. *Behavior Therapy, 16,* 1–14.

Stalonas, P. M., Perri, M. G., & Kerzner, A. B. (1984). Do behavioral treatments of obesity last? A five-year follow-up investigation. *Addictive Behaviors, 9,* 175–183.

Steen, S. N., Oppliger, R. A., & Brownell, K. D. (1988). Metabolic effects of repeated weight loss and regain in adolescent wrestlers. *Journal of the American Medical Association, 260,* 47–50.

Stuart, R. B., & Davis, B. (1976). *Slim chance in a fat world: Behavioral control of obesity.* Champaign IL: Research Press.

Stunkard, A. J. (1980). The social environment and the control of obesity. In A. J. Stunkard (Ed.), *Obesity.* Philadelphia: W. B. Saunders.

Stunkard, A. J. (1982). Obesity. In A. S. Bellack, M. Hersen, & A. E. Kazdin (Eds.), *International Handbook of Behavior Modification and Therapy.* New York: Plenum.

Van Itallie, T. B. (1985). Health implications of overweight and obesity in the United States. *Annals of Internal Medicine, 103,* 983–988.

Wadden, T. A., Sternberg, J. A., Letizia, K. A., Stunkard, A. J., & Foster, G. D. (1989). Treatment of obesity by very low calorie diet, behavior therapy, and their combination: A five-year perspective. *International Journal of Obesity, 13*(suppl. 2), 39–46.

Wadden, T. A., Stunkard, A. J., & Liebschutz, J. (1988). Three-year follow-up of the treatment of obesity by very low calorie diet, behavior therapy, and their combination. *Journal of Consulting and Clinical Psychology, 56,* 925–928.

Wadden, T. A., Stunkard, A. J., & Smoller, J. W. (1986). Dieting and depression: A methodological study. *Journal of Consulting and Clinical Psychology, 54,* 869–871.

Wadden, T. A., Van Itallie, T. B., & Blackburn, G. L. (1990). Responsible and irresponsible use of very-low-calorie diets in the treatment of obesity. *Journal of the American Medical Association, 263,* 83–85.

Weisz, G., & Bucher, B. (1980). Involving husbands in treatment of obesity: Effects on weight loss, depression and marital satisfaction. *Behavior Therapy, 11,* 643–650.

Westover, S. A., & Lanyon, R. I. (1990). The maintenance of weight loss after behavioral treatment: A review. *Behavior Modification, 14,* 123–137.

Wilson, G. T., & Brownell, K. (1978). Behavior therapy for obesity: Including family members in the treatment process. *Behavior Therapy, 9,* 943–945.

Wing, R. R., Epstein, L. H., Marcus, M. D., & Kupfer, D. J. (1984). Mood changes in behavioral weight loss programs. *Journal of Psychosomatic Research, 28,* 189–196.

Zitter, R. E., & Fremouw, R. E. (1978). Individual versus partner consecration for weight loss. *Behavior Therapy, 9,* 808–813.

12

Gambling

ROBERT W. WILDMAN II, Ph.D.*

Of all the socially acceptable addictions, gambling may seem to be the most innocuous. It does not seem to produce any physiologically dangerous condition as do alcohol and substance abuse. We even build casinos and entire cities devoted to catering to individuals who like to gamble. Here, probably more than in other addictions, the differentiation between usage, abuse, and addiction seems the most apt. Many of us gamble occasionally. Some of us gamble regularly, provided the stakes remain within certain well-defined limits. A few cannot limit themselves to either occasional or mild usage. To these people gambling becomes a way of life. It reaches extremes that indicate an out-of-control abuse at the expense of other activities and at the expense of other family members. Like most addictions, it may have to reach destructive, pathological extremes to be recognized as needing treatment. The gambler, like most addicts, will go to untold damaging extremes before recognizing the need for treatment. Even then, there remains the unspoken attitude of, "I know better! What applies to other addicts does not apply to me." This omnipotent attitude becomes a component part of playing for the "big score," the magical nirvana that will cure all of the individual's ills (in this case debt), and will make everything all right. This drivenness parallels the loss of contact with reality experienced by most addicts. Negative consequences, immediate or delayed, are denied. There is a better reality: the one of the gambler's own making!

The purpose of this chapter is to summarize the literature on the treatment of pathological gambling.

*Appreciation is expressed to Julian Ingersoll Taber, Ph.D., who generously shared his file of unpublished materials on gambling and gambling-related problems.
An expanded version of this chapter is available from the author.

A Review of Treatments for Pathological Gamblers

The treatment literature relating to pathological gambling has been reviewed by Lester (1980), Wolkowitz, Roy, and Doran (1985), and Allcock (1986). The review and recommendations of Harris (1989) are particularly enlightening.

Gamblers Anonymous

Because of the nonprofessional and anonymous nature of Gamblers Anonymous (GA), scientifically acceptable treatment outcome studies have been difficult. It seems evident, however, that numerous individuals who have had severe gambling problems convincingly attribute their long-term abstinence to involvement in this inspirational fellowship. The brightness of this picture is clouded by the fact that Gamblers Anonymous retains for extended periods only about 30 percent of those who attend a first meeting (Brown, 1984). Brown and Stewart (1988) estimated that only 8 percent of all first-comers to GA maintain total abstinence from gambling for a year, and 7 percent achieve this goal for 2 years. They estimate that approximately 20 percent of those who join GA will experience some degree of substantial improvement.

Brown (1986) surveyed continuers and dropouts from GA. Surprisingly, there were few differences between those who appeared to benefit from this group and those who did not. Individuals who later dropped out seemed to have higher, unrealistic expectations of GA. There was probably a greater amount of initial debt among those who continued in Gamblers Anonymous. Dropouts appeared to feel superior to other GA members (Brown, 1987a), and they expressed more dissatisfaction with the format and procedures of GA (Brown, 1987b, 1987c, 1987d).

Theoretically, GA can be conceptualized as focusing on the stimulus conditions that control gambling. It gives the individual a nongambling environment (GA meetings) to frequent and a new set of enthusiastically nongambling companions. This process is well discussed by Cromer (1978) who attended Gamblers Anonymous meetings in Israel.

Institutionally Based Programs

At last report, sixteen programs in this country were specializing in the treatment of pathological gambling (Franklin & Ciarrocchi, 1987). The first inpatient treatment program for problem gamblers was initiated at a Veteran's Administration Hospital in Cleveland, Ohio, in 1972 by Robert L. Custer (Taber & McCormick, 1987). At various times, Alida Glen, Julian Ingersoll Taber, and Durand F. Jacobs worked with Custer, and all three subsequently went on to extend work in this area in new directions.

The description of this 28-day inpatient program seems to indicate that a matter-of-fact, even confrontive, approach was taken with the pathological gamblers. The staff accepts the fact that problem gamblers tend to be charming and polished manipulators, and efforts are made to prevent this superficial approach to life from being successful.

A component of the Cleveland VA program is the daily group therapy session. Taber (1981) describes the goals and strategies of these sessions in great detail. The specific techniques involved included "the ideographic experimental approach, learning theory, behavior analysis, the recovery philosophy of AA and GA, stress management, Zen philosophy, Gestalt methods, Rational-Emotive Therapy, and values clarification." Also stressed in these meetings was the gambler's need to take responsibility for his own behavior; issues related to impulse control were major topics. In order to expedite the progress of each patient within the group, each member is required to prepare and present verbally an autobiography (Adkins, Taber & Russo, 1985). More information on this use of group psychotherapy is contained in the report of Taber and Chaplin (1988).

Fortunately, the Cleveland program described by Taber and McCormick (1987) appears to have been highly successful. At a 6-month follow-up, over half of their graduates reported having been abstinent from gambling (Taber, McCormick, Russo, Adkins & Ramirez, 1987). Adkins (1988) discussed discharge-planning issues; she notes a high incidence of physical disease in this population.

Greenberg and Rankin (1982) described an in-hospital treatment program for gamblers. The specific techniques employed included urging the patient to avoid stimuli associated with gambling, surrender money to the wife or girlfriend, and punish the urge to gamble by using images or by snapping the wrist with a rubber band. These procedures were successful in only 5 of the 26 cases reported when using the standard that the patients "gained and maintained control over their gambling." The authors speculated that treatment outcomes could be improved by addressing more directly the patients' marital problems.

Lesieur and Blume (1987) noted the existence of an inpatient program for pathological gamblers at the South Oaks Foundation in Amityville, New York. Taber and McCormick (1987) cited Politzer, Morrow, and Leavey (1981) as having developed a program at Johns Hopkins Hospital in Maryland. Politzer, Morrow, and Leavey (1985) provide a description of the Johns Hopkins program. It is an abstinence-oriented program that involves the use of a team composed of both peer counselors and professionals. Specific techniques described included goal-setting, education, family therapy, financial counseling, and post-release referrals to a therapist in the community and/or to GA. The authors report a 6-month post-treatment abstinence rate of 80 percent for their inpatient program and a

90 percent abstinence rate for their concurrently operated outpatient program.

In an outpatient program funded by the New York State Office of Mental Health, which included many of the features of the one described by Politzer, Morrow, and Leavey (1985), Blackman, Simone, and Thomas (1986) reported a decrease in percentage of patients who rated their gambling as severe from 67 percent to 28 percent. Another program apparently based on the same general model, particularly the use of a team composed of both professionals and peers, is the one at Taylor Manor Hospital in Maryland (Franklin & Ciarrocchi, 1987).

Individual Behavioral Treatments

The use of behavioral techniques with gambling dates back to the 1960s with the report of Barker and Miller (1968). The authors delivered electrical shocks as their patients gambled or were exposed to gambling-related stimuli. One of the cases thus treated appeared to have been an immediate success. Another individual suffered a minor relapse, and the third experienced an increased post-treatment problem with gambling. Happily, both of the latter two cases returned to abstinence from gambling after a series of "booster sessions" for at least a 6-month interval.

Seager (1970) followed up on this work be using electrical aversion therapy with 14 compulsive gamblers. Substantial improvement was reported by half of the cases. However, there were reasons for questioning the validity of the reports by one of the patients, and another "had occasional small bets on horses, well within his means." Koller (1972) reported on the effects of electrical aversion therapy with 12 "poker machine addicts." Six ceased gambling, as reported in reviews from six months to two years. Some substantial degree of improvement was noted in another two cases, bringing the overall success rate to two-thirds. Koller noted that the subjects who benefited most from treatment were those who had established the best relationship with the behavior therapist.

The most completely described case of the use of aversion therapy in the treatment of compulsive gambling was contributed by Goorney (1968). This case involved a 37-year-old horse race gambler. His gambling problem appeared after his marriage, which, from his report, had never been satisfactory. He described his wife as "cold, undemonstrative, highly strung, and wearing the pants." He admitted that his gambling, "might be an attempt to hurt her—can't stand up to her in any other way." The treatment procedure involved delivering shocks at five points during the patient's gambling activities. Not only did this man cease gambling, but at a 12-month follow-up he reported no desire to gamble. The patient also noted a significant improvement in his relationship with his wife.

McConaghy, Armstrong, Blaszczynski, and Allcock (1983) interpreted some of their earlier work with aversion therapy in treating homosexuality as indicating that this procedure merely suppressed the behavior without affecting the underlying sexual orientation. Applying this conclusion to the gambling problem leads to the concern that such aversion therapy would artificially dampen the probability of gambling but leave the underlying desire intact, to emerge at a later time. In an attempt to test this hypothesis, these researchers worked with 20 compulsive gamblers. Half were assigned to an aversion relief condition, and the other ten received imaginal desensitization. The aversion relief procedure involved 12 phrases associated with gambling by the subject and three alternative nongambling phrases, all written on cards. The subjects were instructed to turn over the cards in a randomly presented order and read the phrases. Unpleasant shocks followed the gambling descriptions but not the nongambling phrases. The imaginal desensitization condition involved pairing deep muscle relaxation with scenes in which the subject successfully resisted the urge or opportunity to gamble. At a 1-year follow-up, the members of the imaginal desensitization group reported significantly greater improvement than those in the aversion relief group, both in terms of actual gambling and feeling an urge to gamble. The authors interpreted their results as being consistent with their theory that "compulsive gambling is driven by aversive tension."

Certainly, these results would appear to put to rest the simplistic theory that *all* gambling is motivated by a desire for "action," in the sense of bringing about an increase in level of stimulation. Additionally, these results are promising from the standpoint of the behavioral handling of such cases. Aversion relief training is an unpleasant procedure, and it is gratifying to discover that a gentler treatment is at least as effective. Interestingly, four of the subjects, one in the aversion relief group and three in the imaginal desensitization group, reported "controlled gambling" at one year after treatment (McConaghy et al., 1983).

Cotler (1971) described a multifaceted and individualized behavioral intervention with a single case of compulsive gambling. He cited as the inspiration for this approach a theoretical paper presented by Montgomery and Kreitzer (1968).

The treatment began with a careful history and by explaining to the patient, a 32-year-old card player, the effects of such psychological phenomena as intermittent reinforcement. Next, he was asked to substitute for his gambling behavior an activity that he felt would be rewarding. Visits with his wife were made contingent upon his not gambling. He was also instructed to keep records on his gambling, including amount of money lost and his associations with gambling. Next, the patient was "instructed to take a set amount of money into the casino . . . and to bet the maximum amount allowed each time he put money into the pot." The instructions were to leave the gaming environment as soon as all of his money had been lost, which meant a rather short time spent gambling, since he had been told to make the maximum bet at all opportunities. Nights when the patient did not gamble were reinforced by his engaging in alternate pleasurable activities. By using this DRO schedule (Differential Reinforcement of Other Behaviors), the man was encouraged to reduce his gambling activities to two nights per week. When he happened to win, he self-administered a shock to the hand. At the end of two weeks, a seemingly paradoxical procedure was employed:

> . . . he was instructed to gamble consecutively for the next 7 days under the following conditions: He was to take a fixed amount of money to the casino, he was to bet the maximum on every wager regardless if the hand was good or bad, he was to use the hand shocker before reaching for winning chips and on the draw of every third hand, and he was to leave immediately after the money was gone and stay isolated in his apartment for the rest of the evening.

His estranged wife allowed him to "earn his way back into the family," and the couple was seen in marital therapy. Not only was Cotler's treatment regime successful in reducing the frequency of gambling to zero, but the patient reported that he did not even have the urge to gamble.

Certainly from a clinical point of view, Cotler's (1971) treatment was successful, at least at 3-month follow-up, and impressive in terms of the variety of interventions and the author's ingenuity in implementing and combining them. Scientifically, however, the range of procedures makes it difficult to determine exactly what the effective components were. The patient's subjective report, which appeared to be consistent with the behavioral records, was that " . . . massing the opportunities to lose coupled with shock in the actual environmental situation" were the most effective elements. There was a subsequent relapse, and this was dealt with by a series of booster sessions consisting of "covert sensitization, hand shocks, and family contingency contracting."

A follow-up to Cotler's work was the case study contributed by Bannister (1977). He was successful by combining covert sensitization (for example, the male pathological gambler imagined himself being thrown into an outdoor toilet following the visualization of gambling scenes) with Rational Emotive Therapy. RET was used to shift the locus of control to the patient so that he could bring the excessive gambling under his own control.

Individual Psychotherapy

Taber and McCormick (1987) painted a bleak picture of the state of the art and the results of traditional individual psychotherapy with pathological gamblers. They cite some of the same analytic writers who were quoted in the earlier theoretical section of this chapter as illustrating this low level of scientific development, and they strongly question Bergler's (1958) report of a 75 percent success rate. The most dramatic conclusion to be reached from this review is that in the great majority of cases the pathological gambler in psychotherapy is being treated by a professional who is almost totally naive about pathological gambling! It should be noted, however, that after using standard analytic techniques, Harris (1964) reported some success in treating the problem gambling of an adolescent male.

Miller (1986) is pioneering in the development of specific "dynamic" strategies with this population. This author appears to accept much of the behavioral and physiological theorizing that links problem gambling to a need to obtain a comfortable level of stimulation and to escape the problems and worries of life. He goes on to describe a deep attachment to this activity that has provided temporary relief and comfort, and he notes that what to the behaviorist is simply a reduction or termination of a behavioral excess would represent to the pathological gambler the potential loss of a significant "love" object. Miller goes on to describe the grief process involved in this loss, and he argues that this grief must be worked through therapeutically for the treatment of the pathological gambler to be truly successful from comprehensive and long-range points of view.

A particular issue to which Miller (1986) is sensitive is that of low self-esteem in the problem gambler. The experience of being a "high roller" artificially boosts self-esteem, and having to give up this "crutch" while at the same time admitting that one has lost control over one's gambling can have a devastating effect on the patient. Holtgraves (1988) supported this position through showing that gambling allows one to present one's self in a romantic light.

Like all other treatments for pathological gambling presented in this review, Miller's (1986) does not hold all the answers. It does, however, advance and illustrate a refreshing alternative to the stern confrontational approach taken by many previously reviewed workers. As Miller warned, "A manipulative and/or adversarial relationship is not apt to prove effective and may cause premature termination of therapy. Therapeutic engagement is important. The therapist should be authentic and involved. Anxiety must also be managed well" (p. 103).

Aubry (1975) made suggestions for the treatment of the pathological gambler from Freudian, transactional analysis, and Adlerian standpoints.

Paradoxical Intention

Victor and Krug (1967) treated a 36-year-old male who had been gambling most of his life. After a modestly successful course of group therapy, the patient was seen in individual psychotherapy. The use of paradoxical intention began in the third session. He was told to gamble every day during three hours that the therapist selected. He was then to go to his office and "write, in detail, about his feelings when gambling." At the next session, the patient described himself as "confused," stating that he had to force himself to gamble as he had not really wished to engage in this activity! He explained, "I cannot stand being controlled, and now you are trying to control me." When the therapist informed the patient that the prescription for further gambling was being renewed for the coming week, he told the therapist, "You are going to ruin me, Doctor." He did follow the directives, although reluctantly and intermittently. For a period of time the patient was unable to follow the paradoxical instructions because he had lost so much that he was absolutely out of cash. The doctor suggested that he sell some valuables in order to resume gambling, a suggestion to which the patient responded with horror. The patient's subsequent attempts at gambling were described as "feeble." He rejected a suggestion that he establish a pattern of "controlled gambling," citing his commitment to his work. He made a $700 bet with another gambler that he would never be seen in a gambling joint again, and he stopped gambling entirely. At this juncture, he directed his need for excitement into the sexual area and had intense arguments with his wife.

An Emerging Theoretical and Treatment Issue: Abstinence Versus Controlled Gambling

Rankin (1982) reviewed the similarity with which professionals and laypersons alike conceptualize pathological gambling and alcoholism. Just as workers in the area of alcoholism were considering adopting a goal of treatment involving controlled drinking (Sobell & Sobell, 1973), Rankin argued the possibility that controlled gambling might be a desirable and feasible outcome for the post-treatment pathological gambler.

The first attempt to try controlled gambling was a case study contributed by Dickerson and Weeks (1979). Their patient was a 40-year-old married man whose gambling had been out of control for the preceding three years. He was spending approximately one-sixth of his income on gambling, in this case, horse races. He displayed a pattern of "chasing" (Lesieur, 1976, 1979, 1984), in that he would increase the size of his next bet following a series of losses.

A contract was negotiated in which the gambler agreed to participate in a certain number of social outings with his wife. If he fulfilled his part of the contract he was allowed to place a 50-pence bet on Saturday. He was required to give his salary to his wife without opening the packet. She supervised his weekly bet, which was actually placed by a third person because the gambler had been instructed to avoid betting shops. A 20-week course of this treatment resulted in the patient completely restricting his betting to the Saturday 50-pence wager. Additionally, he began calling frequent gamblers "mugs," and improvement in the marriage was noted. These gains were maintained at a 15-month follow-up. The authors offered the opinion that the goal of therapy (controlled gambling) was an incentive to the gambler.

In Rankin's own report (1982), work with a 44-year-old man who had been gambling for 20 years was described. His gambling had been escalating to the point where it was affecting adversely his career and his marriage, and he also displayed the pattern of "chasing" bets. The patient strongly indicated to the therapist that he simply couldn't imagine a life completely without gambling. A 5-pound (approximately $10) per week limit on gambling was agreed upon. His wife handled the remainder of the couple's funds. The patient was seen monthly for the first six months, then every three months, and finally every six months. The patient stuck to the limits with only three exceptions during a 2-year follow-up. Ironically, he scored a big win on one of these occasions, and his transgressions netted him a profit of 365 pounds. Significantly, he did not gamble away all of his winnings, having apparently overcome the compulsion to "chase" losses. The patient came to the point where he did not gamble every week, and he claimed to be able to take or leave gambling. He was then able to hold an important position involving the handling of money, and some improvements in the marital situation were reported.

Wellins and Steinitz (1977) described a gambling game for winners. The rationale for this game, which involves the placing of "fantasy bets," was taken from transactional analysis. The authors reports that this game helped the two gamblers with whom they worked to stop gambling entirely.

Marital/Family Interventions

While marital/familial problems and implications of problem gambling have emerged spontaneously and dramatically in the previously reviewed treatment reports, professional workers have been surprisingly slow to utilize a couples/family approach to this disorder. It should be noted, however, that GA has Gamanon for the spouses of members and Gamateen for their children. These meetings are separate and do not involve joint sessions with the gamblers.

Boyd and Bolen (1970) noted the "chaotic, turbulent marital relationships and the frequent, severe characterological problems of both the gambler and his spouse." They went on to state, "It became apparent that having both marital partners involved was indicated, and hence, marital couple group therapy was selected because of the chronic and severe marital difficulties, the relationship of specific marital stress to the onset of problem gambling, and the anticipated poor prognosis in individual therapy'' (p. 78). The report involved nine male pathological gamblers and their wives, who were seen within the context of two marital therapy groups. Boyd and Bolen (1970) characterized these marriages as being similar to the "character object relationship" type described by Giovacchini (1965). This type of marriage is maintained by the bond of complementary psychopathology.

The initial phase of Boyd and Bolen's therapy groups involved a discussion of gambling itself, with the husbands recounting their "war stories." The wives responded by telling of the deprivations to which they had been subjected and by denying any involvement in the husbands' problems with gambling. The couples then fell into a pattern of rehashing old disagreements that were not necessarily relevant to the problem of gambling. The therapists moved in to point out how "mind-reading" had brought about numerous misunderstandings and arguments. An atmosphere was fostered in which each spouse made active efforts to understand the thoughts and feelings of the partner. At this point the wives became quite depressed when they "became increasingly aware that their husband's gambling was a mutual problem symptomatic of marital discord. They recognized the loss of their 'martyr' role and became aware of their previous scapegoating of the husband, gambler, and bad object who functioned as the primary localization of their projected personal conflicts" (pp. 81–82).

The spouses alternated in playing the "sick" role during the course of therapy. The authors describe a turbulent course of therapy that frequently required crisis intervention. A directive approach was required with their immature clients. Fortunately, the members did improve in their ability to interpret and analyze past problems, particularly those of a neurotic nature, and in the expression of empathy. It was discovered that, while attempting to do the opposite, they had chosen mates startlingly similar to their own parents. The focus of therapy turned at this point from gambling to working through the previously achieved insights. The many disruptions in therapy were interpreted by Boyd and Bolen as relating to the "negative therapeutic reaction" described by Fairbairn (1952), and it would seem that this paradoxical effect of correct therapeutic interventions is one for which other workers in this area should be on the lookout.

For the eight couples who remained in treatment, Boyd and Bolen's group marital therapy proved quite successful from the standpoint of improvements in both the gambling and the marriages. Three of the husbands stopped gambling altogether, and the other five achieved a state of "near cessation."

Tepperman (1985) reported on the effectiveness of short-term conjoint group marital therapy with pathological gamblers and their wives. All couples in the study were drawn from Gamblers Anonymous/ Gamanon. Ten of the couples were involved in the therapy and the other ten couples, for various reasons, were unable to do so. Tepperman followed Boyd and Bolen (1970) in assuming that pathological gambling has the effect of distracting a couple from the underlying problems in their relationship, and that purely symptomatic treatment of the gambling addiction, if successful, would leave the couple at the mercy of the underlying psychopathology. A major goal of therapy is to undo the defense of denial in the spouse, thereby releasing underlying emotions such as insecurity and anger. Therapy was guided by the FIRO (Fundamental Interpersonal Relationship Orientation) therapy put forward by Schutz (1958). The therapy was conducted by a clergyman who had been trained in client-centered therapy and was also familiar with the GA recovery program. As a matter of fact, each session focused on one of the twelve AA-like steps. Half of the couples dropped out of treatment/GA prior to the conclusion of the study. Six of the experimental couples and four of the control couples remained in therapy and/or GA until the conclusion of the study. The treated couples showed improvements on various psychometric measures of marital functioning, particularly relating to interpersonal sensitivity. A decrease in level of depression was also noted. Obviously, the group therapy was considered a valuable addition to the ongoing work with GA, in that all but one of the couples wished the group to continue. It was found that continuing in the group contributed to retention in the GA program.

A marital intervention using a form of paradoxical intention was reported by Walker (1985). In this case only the wife appeared for treatment, as the problem gambler himself refused even to acknowledge that he had a problem. The wife returned from the therapy sessions acting thoughtful and sad. When the husband pressed her for the reason for her depressed mood, she replied that she had been told in therapy that compulsive gambling was an incurable disorder and that she would have to resign herself to a life of debt and other associated problems. The man became so enraged at Walker and the way that these pronouncements had wounded his wife that he immediately turned over the family finances to her and suspended all further gambling.

Heineman (1987) noted differences between the treatment issues involved in working with the wives of pathological gamblers and those dealt with in treating the wives of alcoholics. One of the most significant of these was the need to deal with the financial problems created by the gambling.

Chemotherapy

The proposal that psychotropic agents might have a role to play in the general treatment of pathological gambling was put forward in a panel discussion in which a number of physicians, including R. L. Custer, participated (Cohen et al., 1984). The basic ideas to emerge were to use drugs that counteract the euphoria induced by opiates, such as naltrexone, to combat the thrill of the "action" associated with gambling. It was suggested that perhaps propranolol or clonidine might be useful in managing the withdrawal symptoms from gambling. About the components of gambling withdrawal, Custer stated, "The most common one is restlessness, but they may get cold sweats, clamminess, headaches, abdominal pain, nausea, vomiting—mostly autonomic symptoms with poor sleep, similar to mild alcohol withdrawal" (p. 39).

A more specific use of medications was suggested by the report of McCormick, Russo, Ramirez, and Taber (1984). Using the Schedule for Affective Disorders, they found that two-thirds of hospitalized pathological gamblers qualified for a diagnosis of major depression; 38 percent were hypomanic. Linden, Pope, and Jonas (1986) subsequently found that 18 (72 percent) of their 25 pathological gamblers had had at least one episode of major depression. Recurrent affective disorder was found for 13 of the subjects, of which 2 were of the manic type. Taber and Boston (unpublished) have explicated what they consider to be the role of dysphoria in all addictive behaviors, and Taber and Harris (unpublished) note that some cases of dysphoria-induced addictions may have an etiology based in thyroid disease.

The only case of the direct chemotherapeutic treatment of problem gambling uncovered in this review is that of Moskowitz (1980). Noting the similarity between the "high" of gambling and mania, he tried a course of lithium carbonate with three problem gamblers. The gambling of all three of these patients appeared to be associated with a dramatic elevation in their mood, which occurred on a cyclical basis. A decrease in the gambling behavior of all three patients was noted, as well as a decrease in general life problems. One patient went so far as to say, with respect to gambling, "The thrill is gone."

Suggestions for the Treatment of the Pathological Gambler

The Importance of Evaluation

The present formulation of problem gambling stresses the importance of individual differences. Consequently, the first step in treatment should be an analysis or diagnosis of the disturbance in the psychological substrate. Obviously a variety of techniques are available to assist in accomplishing this goal, but the instrument that is most directed and best validated would appear to be the MMPI. This device should inform the clinician as to the nature of the source of psychological distress. Common examples would be depression, anxiety, hypomania, and the thought disorders. Obviously, a major focus of treatment should be in remediating the syndrome that emerges from a complete clinical analysis of the case, which, at minimum, should include an interview and review of available records, in addition to the MMPI. The clinician often will find other evaluation techniques to be relevant or even essential. A social/family history immediately comes to mind in this category.

A Treatment Menu

This section on the specifics of treatment assumes that the reader/therapist is working with clients on an outpatient basis and that problem gamblers will periodically find their way into his or her practice. The clinician contemplating working with pathological gamblers in a hospital setting should carefully review the literature on inpatient treatment that was summarized earlier in this chapter, particularly Taber's writings.

The first issue addressed in treatment should be, according to Jacob's (1986) formulation, whether the patient is chronically under-or over-aroused. For the over-aroused, the anxious, and harried, the following treatment procedures would appear to be indicated:

1. Relaxation training/systematic desensitization (Wolpe, 1958). Particularly important is the use of this procedure as a self-control device in the manner put forward by Goldfried (1971). This variant involves teaching the client Jacobsonian progressive muscle relaxation in such a way that he or she may use this technique to combat symptoms of nervousness and related discomforts.

2. Various forms of meditation and Eastern-inspired techniques for achieving relaxing, mind-altering states.

3. The regular use of exercise. Particularly helpful in this regard would appear to be walking, jogging, and swimming.

4. The short-term use of tranquilizing medications to help the client through a particularly stressful period, such as dealing with the legal/financial consequences of past excessive gambling. It is recommended that great care be exercised in the use of drugs in that, quite obviously, dependency might occur.

5. The use of the old and standard advice to take a vacation should not be dismissed out of hand. Time away can allow the client to escape temporarily from impending stressors and to short-circuit a buildup of stress to an unbearable level. Closer to home, activities like soaking in a warm tub of water, listening to soothing music, a walk through the woods, a heart-to-heart talk with an intimate, and going out for supper can be prescribed as appropriate.

The management of cases involving hypo- or underarousal would appear to be more problematic. In general, the strategy is one of helping the client to find some source of stimulation and challenge that does not involve gambling. Some possibilities to consider are:

1. Hobbies or sports that might give the gambler the needed amount of excitement. Gamblers, like alcoholics, tend to be deficient in recreational skills, and the therapist may find referral to a university physical education department or a YMCA helpful.

2. A challenging activity like taking a course or undertaking a project such as building a boat.

3. Vocational assessment and guidance, in an effort to help the pathological gambler find a job in which more of his or her needs are met. It would appear to be a theoretical possibility for an assembly line worker to find gambling no longer necessary after switching to work as a private investigator.

The second level of issues to be dealt with relates to the presence of some form of mental problem or disorder that places the person in a state of psychological distress (Jacobs, 1987). Some of the primary problems in this area for which the clinician should be on the lookout are: anxiety, depression, mania, sociopathy, marital/family dysfunction, feelings of rejection and "hurt," inferiority complexes, and unresolved psychological issues and conflicts.

The treatment of all of these dysfunctions obviously goes beyond the scope of a chapter on pathological gambling. Clinicians are trained in the treatment of all of these disorders. Since the position taken here is that these psychological problems need to be addressed *prior* to the beginning of a heavy focus on the gambling itself, it is obvious that the great bulk of treatment in this area will need to be conducted by comprehensively trained clinicians. One general suggestion involves the need for the use of some variant of client-centered therapy throughout treatment of the pathological gambler, particularly in addressing the last three problems of the eight listed above. This procedure and other related talk therapy techniques give the patient an opportunity to work through his or her underlying psychological problems. This opportunity would not be provided by a lay self-help organization.

After underlying, general issues have been dealt with, the therapeutic process can focus on the gambling itself. At this point, the following techniques are recommended:

1. Cognitive restructuring. An abundance of data shows how poorly people understand odds and the concept of randomness (Corney & Cummings, 1985). The bulk of the verbalizations of roulette players are irrational; they assume some illusory control over the outcome or suggest departure from established laws of probability (Ladouceur & Gaboury, 1988). Lamentably, problem gamblers are even more afflicted with such misconceptions than the general population (Malkin & Syme, 1985). Anecdotally, it can be reported that numerous statements were made at GA meetings that reflected gross misunderstandings of the laws of chance. For example, one "pit boss" (casino floor supervisor) made the statement that the wise gambler will, in effect, sample the gambling atmosphere to "see if you're hot" (the odds are with you) or not!

On the bright side, some evidence indicates that training in statistics can improve an individual's ability to make probabilistic judgments (Shoemaker, 1979). The therapist should stress that almost all gambling activities involve random and independent events. There are no "runs," and hence it is not possible to devise a system for breaking the bank, as was attempted in the pitiful case study reported by Israeli (1935). Demonstrations with coin tosses or mock gambling games might prove useful in convincing the gambler of the immutability of the laws of chance.

2. Relaxation training. The gambler whose excesses appear to be triggered by neurotic types of problems should be taught to use deep muscle relaxation instead of resorting to gambling.

3. Covert sensitization (Cautela, 1968). Through this procedure the gambler can be taught to associate such unpleasant states as anxiety and nausea with gambling-related stimuli.

The author uses this technique with one patient with some success. The problem gambler was told to imagine himself entering a casino. As he approached the slot machines he became anxious and nauseated. He saw himself vomit as he touched the lever. He was instructed to experience his physiological status as returning to normal as he retreated from the gambling devices and to feel a surge of health and joy as he cleared the casino door.

4. Alternate activities. The pathological gambler may be instructed to respond to the urge to gamble by engaging in an alternate, incompatible activity, such as the hobbies mentioned in the section on general treatment. Obviously, the alternate activity should be matched as closely as possible to the mood-altering qualities of the preferred gambling outlet. For example, a craps player will theoretically require a more stimulating hobby, like hang-gliding or stock-car racing, than will the slot machine addict, who might achieve the desired amount of relaxation by reading the Audubon Nature Encyclopedia and listening to classical music.

5. Gamblers Anonymous. While this author has doubts about GA's model of this disorder, an attempt to integrate attendance at GA meetings into treatment should be made in most cases. While GA is not right for everyone, a potential resource at this level of development should not be overlooked entirely. Suggest to the patient that he or she attend a few meetings with the therapist to inspire permission to take only that which is useful to the individual and to discard the rest. It should be made clear to the client that going to GA meetings is entirely optional, and that he or she may continue attending for as long or short a time as is helpful.

      6. Relapse prevention. The client needs to be warned that mere thoughts about gambling are not as harmless as they might seem. In fact, they represent a threat to continued recovery. Parenthetically, the therapist might be alerted to an acute danger of relapse when the client suddenly displays a striking sense of serenity and contentment, which might well mean that the heretofore recovering addict has decided to treat her- or himself to a gambling binge. Thought stopping (Rimm, 1973) can be useful well in advance of this precarious juncture, to help stop the cognitive chain of events that might spill over into the behavioral.

The recovering addict needs to be carefully warned about the abstinence violation effect (Donnell, 1984). This effect is the mistaken assumption that one slip into gambling, however small, means that a full-blown relapse has occurred. Assure your patient that it's never too late to leave the table.

To summarize the treatment strategy advocated here, the problem gambler should first be carefully and professionally assessed clinically. The beginning of treatment should focus on remediating the underlying mental disorders or imbalances. Only then should therapy move toward attacking the symptom of pathological gambling.

Conclusion

The present review reveals that the motivations for pathological gambling are complex and vary from individual to individual. It is argued that the treatment procedures reviewed should be selected and utilized only after the client/patient is assessed comprehensively. The theoretical formulation advanced by Jacobs (1986, 1987) is recommended as the basis for making these selections.

References

Adkins, B. J. (1988). Discharge planning with pathological gamblers: An ongoing process. *Journal of Gambling Behavior, 4,* 208–218.

Adkins, B. J., Taber, J. I., & Russo, A. M. (1985). The spoken autobiography: A powerful tool in group psychotherapy. *Social Work, 30,* 435–439.

Allcock, C. C. (1986). Pathological gambling. *Australian and New Zealand Journal of Psychiatry, 20,* 259–265.

Aubry, W. E. (1975). Altering the gambler's maladaptive life goals. *The International Journal of the Addictions, 10,* 29–33.

Bannister, G. (1977). Cognitive and behavior therapy in a case of compulsive gambling. *Cognitive Therapy and Research, 1,* 223–227.

Barker, J. C., & Miller, M. (1968). Aversion therapy for compulsive gambling. *The Journal of Nervous and Mental Disease, 146,* 285–302.

Bergler, E. (1958). *The psychology of gambling.* New York: International University Press.

Blackman, S., Simone, R. V., & Thomas, D. R. (1986). Treatment of gamblers. *Hospital and Community Psychiatry, 37,* 404.

Boyd, W. H., & Bolen, D. W. (1970). The compulsive gambler and spouse in group psychotherapy. *International Journal of Group Psychotherapy, 20,* 77–90.

Brown, R. I. F. (1984). The effectiveness of Gamblers Anonymous. Paper presented at the sixth National Conference on Gambling, Atlantic City, NJ.

Brown, R. I. F. (1986). Dropouts and continuers in Gamblers Anonymous: Life context and other factors. *Journal of Gambling Behavior, 2,* 130–140.

Brown, R. I. F. (1987a). Dropouts and continuers in Gamblers Anonymous: Part 2: Analysis of free-style accounts of experiences with GA. *Journal of Gambling Behavior, 3,* 68–79.

Brown, R. I. F. (1987b). Dropouts and continuers in Gamblers Anonymous: Part 3: Some possible specific reasons for dropout. *Journal of Gambling Behavior, 3,* 137–151.

Brown, R. I. F. (1987c). Dropouts and continuers in Gamblers Anonymous: Part 4: Evaluation and summary. *Journal of Gambling Behavior, 3,* 202–210.

Brown, R. I. F. (1987d). Pathological gambling and associated patterns of crime: Comparisons with alcohol and other drug addictions. *Journal of Gambling Behavior, 3,* 98–114.

Brown, R. I. F., & Stewart, R. M. (1988). An outcome study of Gamblers Anonymous. *British Journal of Psychiatry, 152,* 284–288.

Cautela, J. I. (1968). Behavior therapy and the need for behavioral assessment. *Psychotherapy: Theory, Research, and Practice, 5,* 175–179.

Cohen, S., Custer, R. L., Goodwin, D., Henningfeld, J. E., Kleber, H.D., O'Brien, C. P., Jasinski, D., Taylor, I. J., & Taylor, B. T. (1984). Panel discussion. *Journal of Clinical Psychiatry, 45,*(12,2) 39–44.

Corney, W. J., & Cummings, W. T. (1985). Gambling behavior and information processing bias. *Journal of Gambling Behavior, 1,* 111–118.

Cotler, S. B. (1971). The use of different behavioral techniques in treating a case of compulsive gambling. *Behavior Therapy, 2,* 579–584.

Cromer, G. (1978). Gamblers Anonymous in Israel: A participant-observation study of a self-help group. *The International Journal of Addictions, 13,* 1069–1077.

Dickerson, M. G., & Weeks, D. (1979). Controlled gambling as a therapeutic technique for compulsive gamblers. *Journal of Behavior Therapy and Experimental Psychiatry, 10,* 139–141.

Donnell, P. J. (1984). The abstinence violation effect and circumstances surrounding relapse as predictors of outcome status in male alcoholic patients. *Journal of Psychology, 117,* 257–262.

Fairbairn, W. R. D. (1952). *An object relations theory of personality.* New York: Basic Books.

Franklin, J., & Ciarrocchi, J. (1987). The team approach: Developing an experiential knowledge base for the treatment of the pathological gambler. *Journal of Gambling Behavior, 3,* 60–67.

Giovacchini, P. L. (1965). Treatment of marital disharmonies: The classical approach. In B. L. Green (Ed.), *The psychotherapies of marital disharmony.* New York: Free Press.

Goldfried, M. R. (1971). Systematic desensitization as training in self-control. *Journal of Consulting and Clinical Psychology, 37,* 228–234.

Goorney, A. B. (1968). Treatment of a compulsive horse race gambler by aversion therapy. *British Journal of Psychiatry, 114,* 329–333.

Greenberg, D., & Rankin, H. (1982). Compulsive gamblers in treatment. *British Journal of Psychiatry, 140,* 364–366.

Harris, H. J. (1964). Gambling addiction in an adolescent male. *Psychoanalytic Quarterly, 33,* 513.

Harris, J. L. (1989). A model for treating compulsive gamblers through cognitive-behavioral approaches. *The Psychotherapy Patient, 4,* 211–226.

Heineman, M. (1987). A comparison: The treatment of wives of alcoholics with the treatment of wives of pathological gamblers. *Journal of Gambling Behavior, 3,* 27–40.

Holtgraves, T. M. (1988). Gambling as self-presentation. *Journal of Gambling Behavior, 4,* 78–91.

Israeli, N. (1935). Outlook of a depressed patient, interested in planned suicide, before and after his attempt at suicide. *The American Journal of Orthopsychiatry, 5,* 57–63.

Jacobs, D. F. (1986). A general theory of addictions: A new theoretical model. *Journal of Gambling Behavior, 2,* 15–31.

Jacobs, D. F. (1987). A general theory of addictions: Application to treatment and rehabilitation planning for pathological gamblers. In T. Galski (Ed.), *The handbook of pathological gambling.* Springfield, IL: Thomas.

Koller, K. M. (1972). Treatment of poker machine addicts by electrical aversion therapy. *Medical Journal of Australia, 1,* 742–745.

Ladouceur, R., & Gaboury, A. (1988). Effects of limited and unlimited stakes on gambling behavior. *Journal of Gambling Behavior, 4,* 119–126.

Lesieur, H. R. (1976). *Compulsive gambling: The spirals of options and involvement.* Ph.D. Dissertation, University of Massachusetts.

Lesieur, H. R. (1979). The compulsive gambler's spiral of options and involvement. *Psychiatry, 42,* 79–87.

Lesieur, H. R. (1984). *The chase: Career of the compulsive gambler.* Cambridge, MA: Schenkman.

Lesieur, H. R., & Blume, S. B. (1987). The South Oaks Gambling Screen (SOGS): A new instrument for the identification of pathological gamblers. *American Journal of Psychiatry, 144,* 1184–1188.

Lester, D. (1980). The treatment of compulsive gambling. *The International Journal of the Addictions, 15,* 201–206.

Linden, R. D., Pope, H. G., & Jonas, J. M. (1986). Pathological gambling and major affective disorder: Preliminary findings. *Journal of Clinical Psychiatry, 47,* 201–203.

Malkin, N. D., & Syme, G. F. (1985). Wagering preferences of adolescent gamblers, *Journal of Abnormal Psychology, 94,* 86–91.

McConaghy, N., Armstrong, M. S., Blaszczynski, A., & Allcock, C. (1983). Controlled comparison of aversive therapy and imaginal desensitization in compulsive gambling. *British Journal of Psychiatry, 142,* 366–372.

McCormick, R. A., Russo, A. M., Ramirez, L. F., & Taber, J. I. (1984). Affective disorders among pathological gamblers. *American Journal of Psychiatry, 141,* 215–218.

Miller, W. (1986). Individual outpatient treatment of pathological gambling. *Journal of Gambling Behavior, 2,* 95–107.

Montgomery, H. R., & Kreitzer, S. (1968). *Compulsive gambling and behavior therapy.* Paper presented at the meeting of the California State Psychological Association, Santa Barbara, CA.

Moskowitz, J. A. (1980). Lithium and lady luck. *New York State Journal of Medicine*, 785–788.

Politzer, R. M., Morrow, J. S., & Leavey, S. B. (1981). Report on the societal cost of pathological gambling and the cost-benefit/effectiveness of treatment. In W. R. Eadington (Ed.), *The gambling papers: Proceedings of the 1981 Conference on Gambling*. Reno: University of Nevada.

Politzer, R. M., Morrow, J. S. & Leavey, S. B. (1985). Report on the cost-benefit/effectiveness of treatment at the Johns Hopkins Center for Pathological Gambling. *Journal of Gambling Behavior, 1*, 131–142.

Rankin, H. (1982). Control rather than abstinence as a goal in the treatment of excessive gambling. *Behavior Research and Therapy, 20*, 185–187.

Rimm, D. C. (1973). Thought stopping and covert assertion in the treatment of phobias. *Journal of Consulting and Clinical Psychology; 41*, 466–467.

Schutz, W. (1958). *FIRO: A three dimensional theory of interpersonal behavior.* New York: Holt, Rinehart, and Winston.

Seager, C. P. (1970). Treatment of compulsive gamblers by electrical aversion. *British Journal of Psychiatry, 117*, 545–553.

Shoemaker, P. J. H. (1979). The role of statistical knowledge in gambling decisions: Moment vs. risk-dimension approaches. *Organizational Behavior and Human Performance, 24*, 1–17.

Sobell, M. B., & Sobell, L. C. (1973). Individualized behavior therapy for alcoholics. *Behavior Therapy, 4*, 49–72.

Taber, J. I. (1981). *Group psychotherapy with pathological gamblers.* Paper presented at the Fourth Annual Conference on Gambling. Lake Tahoe, NV.

Taber, J. I., & Boston, M. D. Developmental vulnerability and dysphoria in the etiology of addictive behavior. Unpublished manuscript. Veteran's Administration Medical Center, Reno, NV.

Taber, J. I., & Chaplin, M. P. (1988). Group psychotherapy with pathological gamblers. *Journal of Gambling Behavior, 4*, 183–194.

Taber, J. I., & Harris, R. L. Thyroid disease, dysphoria, and personal vulnerability in pathological gambling. Unpublished manuscript. Veterans' Administration Medical Center, Reno, NV.

Taber, J. I., & McCormick, R. A. (1987). The pathological gambler in treatment. In T. Galski (Ed.), *The handbook of pathological gambling.* Springfield, IL: Thomas.

Taber, J. I., McCormick, R. A., Russo, A. M., Adkins, B. J., & Ramirez, L. F. (1987). Follow-up of pathological gamblers after treatment. *American Journal of Psychiatry, 144*, 757–761.

Tepperman, J. H. (1985). The effectiveness of short-term group therapy upon the pathological gambler and wife. *Journal of Gambling Behavior, 1*, 119–130.

Victor, R. G., & Krug, C. M. (1967). "Paradoxical intention" in the treatment of compulsive gambling. *American Journal of Psychotherapy, 21*, 808–814.

Walker, G. (1985). The brief therapy of a compulsive gambler. *Journal of Family Therapy, 7*, 1–8.

Wellins, L., & Steinitz, A. (1977). And they're off: A gambling game for winners. *Transactional Analysis Journal, 7*, 323.

Wolkowitz, O. M., Roy, A., & Doran, A. R. (1985). Pathologic gambling and other risk-taking pursuits. *Psychiatric Clinics of North America, 8*, 311–322.

Wolpe, J. (1958) *Psychotherapy by reciprocal inhibition* Stanford, CA: Stanford University Press.

13

Workaholism

JACK E. FARRAR, Ph.D.

WITHIN THE LAST few years, counselors, psychotherapists and the public in general have become more aware of the dysfunctional consequences of many addictive disorders. It is now becoming clear that addictions can take many forms. Some aspects of addiction are not always overtly dysfunctional. In many cases, the addiction can even have socially acceptable and admirable consequences. Such is the case with an addiction to work, or workaholism.

In many ways addictions that are socially acceptable place the addicted individual in a much more precarious position than the addict whom society openly pushes toward treatment. The workaholic, like those suffering from some other socially accepted addictions, is reinforced for his or her compulsive behaviors. Society in various ways reinforces the addictive behaviors. It is no accident that the workaholic becomes addicted to work. One of the underlying dynamics of workaholism is that the individual is driven by a need for external confirmation through status, position, and materialism, due to lack of internal self-worth and unconditional self-acceptance. This dynamic, in which the focus is external rather than internal, has been repeated throughout the life of those addicted to work.

One of the major problems experienced by such an individual in childhood was that he or she was not reinforced for being his or her real self; instead, through subtle maternal and paternal modeling and reinforcement, the child developed a false self or chameleon-like personality that the parental subsystem needed to maintain a homeostatic environment. The false self formed by impostor behaviors (Clance, 1985) placed such children in good stead with their parents and reduced their fear of parental displeasure or possible parental rejection.

In this chapter, I will acquaint the reader with a general background on work addiction by looking at who is affected and how these individuals choose this particular addiction. Also, discussed will be approaches to treatment of individuals who are addicted to work.

Nature of Workaholism

Addiction to work falls under several headings: compulsion to work, workaholism, Type A personality, and obsessive-compulsive personality disorders. Given the varied ways that work-related disorders are expressed, how then is workaholism defined?

According to Oates (1971), the workaholic is someone who spends most of his or her time and energy on work, to the exclusion of other important elements in life. The workaholic, depending on how addicted he or she is, will exclude many of the traditionally meaningful life activities (i.e. personal relationships, hobbies, etc.) in favor of work. The workaholic tends to be terrified of intimacy or any closeness that will bring him or her face to face with emotional intensity and possible rejection. As an adult, this person is destined to repeat in adult relationships similar behavioral patterns to those first developed in childhood, as a way to redo and correct what failed in the past and also to flee the intensity of relationships and potential rejection. This is the dilemma of the workaholic: how to establish real relationships with significant others and at the same time deal with emotional intensity and potential rejection without retreating into what Winnicott and Guntrip (1983) have called the false self.

Development of the false self is one of many adaptations that a person might use to escape closeness. Fogarty (1988) described closeness as movement toward another, with an attempt to get as close as possible without fusing. There must be enough space between individuals so it is clear where each self begins and ends. Fogarty emphasized that closeness requires clarity regarding both self-identity and self-differentiation.

Characteristics of Workaholism

Pietropinto's (1986) research has focused on the general characteristics of workaholism. He found that the workaholic was most often motivated to devote inordinate amounts of time and effort to work due to inferiority feelings and a fear of failure. Also, he found that work served as a compulsive defense against strong anxiety. Other less important reasons cited for working long hours and putting excessive effort into work were need for approval and fear of personal intimacy. These results demonstrated that the workaholic is not primarily driven by need for material profit or external material reinforcers, but by inferiority feelings, anxieties, and need for approval.

The workaholic tends to have tremendous difficulty with free time. A sense of extreme emptiness surfaces when the workaholic is confronted with unstructured time. This intense emptiness is so overwhelming that the workaholic prefers to remain highly structured and working rather then face the psychic pain that the confrontation of not working would bring. Miller (1981) aptly described this feeling.

> *Understand these patients complain of a sense of emptiness, futility, or hopelessness, for the emptiness is real. A process of emptying, impoverishment, and the partial killing of his potential actually took place when all that was alive and spontaneous in him was cut off. In childhood these children have often had dreams in which they experienced themselves as partly dead. (pp. 12–13)*

Fogarty proposed (1988) a basic model of the sequence that results in a response choice of work addiction for many. The model is: stimulus —→ emptiness ——→ hurt ——→ emotional upset (frequently in the form of anger or its equivalent)——→ response (p. 6). The response is work and more work to compensate for the uncomfortable emotions stimulated by no work. Work addiction is one of many adaptations to the emptiness that is felt by the workaholic.

Free time is a dilemma for the workaholic. Rather then face the tremendous sense of emptiness during these times, the workaholic distracts him- or herself with detailed planning and over-structuring of free time. Thus, free time often becomes as demanding as the work schedule.

When confronted with conflict, the workaholic tends to behave in a predictable manner. Pietropinto (1986) found that this individual avoids confrontation much of the time. At other times the approach to confrontation is through passive-aggressive maneuvers, such as sulking and silence.

The System of the Workaholic

The system within which the workaholic functions is both complicated and somewhat predictable. For instance, given the little time available for intimacy, it would be expected that the workaholic would be likely to have affairs and superficial relationships with others, but this does not appear to be the case. Pietropinto (1986) ascertained that workaholics were 48 percent less likely to have affairs than non-workaholics. However, he found that 74 percent of workaholic spouses are likely to have affairs.

The apparent reason that the workaholic is reported to have fewer affairs than the spouse is lack of time. However, the actual reasons appear more complicated: the workaholic wishes to avoid the increased demands that an affair would place on him or her.

The workaholic has difficulty with emotional demands from others, especially demands for intimacy. This is further complicated by the heightened dependency needs present between workaholic and spouse, which result in the formation of an over-attachment with the spouse; an intense loyalty appears to develop between workaholic and spouse. This over-attachment frightens the workaholic and work is used to defend against the feelings that accompany this over-attachment. Issues such as these prevent intimacy needs of the workaholic from being acted out through an affair. Instead, intimacy is acted out within the structured environment of work. Relationships with people in a work environment are much easier for the workaholic to handle.

Since the workaholic is minimally intimate with the spouse, it is understandable that spouses of workaholics would go outside the relationship to find intimacy. When the workaholic spouse actually has an affair, this would act to bring homeostasis to the marriage. As a result of this balanced situation the relationship could continue for long periods of time. However, the relationship is not alive, spontaneous, or intimate.

Ways in Which the Workaholic Handles Stress

The workaholic deals with stress in a variety of ways. One way is with alcohol; a majority of workaholics abuse alcohol to escape stress (Pietropinto, 1986). Why is the workaholic inclined toward alcohol abuse? The workaholic appears to use alcohol and caffeine primarily for utilitarian reasons. Both alcohol and caffeine are used to structure the workaholic's day; The caffeine lifts the workaholic into the day, because the work schedule and hours required are viewed as highly demanding. Alcohol acts as a decompression chamber for the workaholic; it is a way to "come down" and to switch gears from the working mode.

Characteristics of Workaholics

To gain a clear picture of the workaholic, Oates (1971), Farrar (1988), and others have suggested several characteristics that generally describe the parameters of the workaholic syndrome. These general characteristics are listed below.

1. There is an over-involvement in the area of preoccupation (work).
2. Like the drug addict and alcoholic, the workaholic is viewed as powerless to kick the habit.
3. The workaholic has the illusion that he or she is indispensable.
4. The workaholic tends to be noted in the family of origin as the self-sufficient, highly responsible and highly resourceful individual;

these characteristics receive a great deal of reinforcement throughout childhood.

5. The workaholic starts the day immediately from the moment the alarm clock sounds; he or she does not waste time getting into the day. This individual tends to hit the floor running.

6. The workaholic plans time so that every minute is controlled and scheduled. Emergencies and sudden changes in the schedule are very disruptive and not easily handled.

7. The workaholic has tremendous difficulty with unfinished business or tasks. If it is necessary to leave work without completing something or at least having it under control, the workaholic carries the unfinished work home and frets about it until he or she can get back to the task. This often means that sleep and social activity are disrupted.

8. The workaholic arrives at work earlier than most people and stays later than most.

9. The workaholic often eats lunch in a very short time or, more commonly, does not take time for lunch at all. If lunch is eaten, it is usually functional and structured around business.

10. The workaholic constantly weighs the effectiveness of daily activities. Often a productivity scorecard is kept.

11. The workaholic is constantly on the move. He or she is restless and feels as if time is being wasted if he or she does not hurry when going from place to place. Also, the workaholic is quite (often secretly) judgmental of others who do not fit this mold.

12. The workaholic takes pride in doing at least two things at the same time; if possible, three or more tasks at the same time are attempted. Time and efficiency are most important.

13. The workaholic has great difficulty taking vacations, including planning, preparation, and actually going on them. Often vacation times are cut short. On vacation, the workaholic may call the office daily; for many workaholics at least two calls per day are necessary.

14. Often planned vacations are postponed; vacations more frequently are taken at the spur of the moment. Long-range planning for a vacation becomes too frightening, so the workaholic delays decisions about the vacation as long as possible.

15. The workaholic has little time in his or her schedule for socializing. In fact, socializing, if not work-related, is viewed as a waste of time, especially if it is with anyone who does not value the use of time as much as the workaholic does.

16. The workaholic is much more at ease with other hard workers or workaholics than with non-work-oriented individuals.

17. The workaholic wants to work only with people who have the same level of motivation. His or her motto is, "I don't mind you making mistakes, but I can't stand a person not trying as hard as possible."

18. The workaholic thinks that almost anything can be accomplished if he or she is efficient and well enough organized. Greater organization is something for which the workaholic constantly strives.

19. Control and structure are two characteristics that the workaholic requires to feel safe and comfortable.

20. The workaholic feels safest when he or she is socially isolated and working at a task.

21. The workaholic tends to experience negative feelings in an extreme way. For instance, when he or she experiences disappointment, the effect often becomes exaggerated, leaving the workaholic feeling devastated and overwhelmed. The intensity of this kind of emotion for the workaholic is as extreme as the drive toward work.

Treatment Guidelines

Let us first look at the kinds of emotional conflicts that bring the workaholic to treatment or psychotherapy. This individual will probably never come to treatment on his or her own initiative without some kind of major challenge to his or her perception of life, if life is not following the carefully designed path that was established. This challenge can come in many forms. Ackerman (1980) stated that there were four essential ways in which families or people generally present themselves for therapy: (1) a school referral for one of the children; (2) emotional problems within the sibling subsystem; (3) marital problems; and (4) emotional difficulty with one of the parents, related to problems with the extended family. Whichever significant event leads to therapy tends to act as a major break in the strong defense system (primarily denial) that the workaholic has constructed. The workaholic tends to be so well defended that it is difficult to perceive the depth of emotional reaction following a traumatic problem or loss. The workaholic is a master at hiding and protecting true feelings.

Although stress reduction techniques including reduced workloads, social support, relaxation therapy, and more frequent contact with professional peers may be helpful, it is difficult to rectify the workaholic's deeply entrenched human problems with recommendations for behavioral change (Penzer, 1984). A more self-enhancing philosophy of life and work can be implemented for accomplishment of significant change. This is usually accomplished through individual therapy.

Individual Psychotherapy

Once the workaholic enters treatment, what direction does the therapist take? There are two key components to treating a workaholic. One is to let the individual do the work; remember that the workaholic is a very motivated and driven individual. The second and most important factor in treating a person afflicted with an addiction to work is to learn to speak that person's language: efficiency. Words are employed as tools to say something in as short and forthright a manner as possible.

The therapist must be aware that trust will be the paramount theme throughout this person's therapy. Because the workaholic is accustomed to presenting what he or she imagines others want to hear, the false self or chameleon self will initially be presented. The therapist must not become a cheerleader, which would only result in the reinforcement of the workaholic's false self (Masterson, 1986). Then the workaholic would view the therapist as being like everyone else, so that for the workaholic to be recognized and validated, chameleon-like characteristics should be shown.

The therapist must be cautious regarding what the workaholic brings to therapy, and must be aware that a great deal of skepticism (not necessarily obvious) will be present, almost as if the workaholic is able to remove him- or herself from the dyadic interaction with the therapist and become a third-party observer. While the therapist and patient are interacting, the patient is also observing very carefully the dynamics that are perceived to be happening. At times it seems that the workaholic is rather paranoid and frightened of what the therapist might do or say, so the patient must be constantly vigilant.

When the therapist gets to know the patient better it becomes clear that two connected processes are going on within the patient. One relates directly to the patient's ability to do two things at one time (participate in the treatment process with the therapist and at the same time be a constant observer), and the other relates to a repetition compulsion going on within the therapeutic process. Through the repetition compulsion process, the workaholic is creating an environment reflective of what went on in the early childhood years with the parent; that is, that he or she had to be on constant guard against rejection and emotional indifference and thus learned to portray only a false self to the world. This false self allowed the workaholic to appear natural and close with others. Although therapy provides the workaholic with the opportunity to have access to the true self, pre-therapy expectations dictate that suspicion and constant vigilance must be present. Once a consistent and trusting environment is established and it becomes clear that a "good performance" is not what is expected, the workaholic can slowly reduce defenses and open up to the actual and genuine feelings of the true self.

Because all of these dynamics come out in the initial meetings in the therapy process, it is important that the therapist attempt to make the therapy as safe as possible. In terms of therapist experiential reactions to this patient, this often means being as straight and direct as possible. Since direct expression of most feelings is withheld by the patient, passive-aggressive behavior becomes fairly routine. Thus direct responses to the workaholic act as a model for further work in therapy and over time the passive-aggressive behavior decreases.

Case Study Number 1

A patient who was angry and scared in the initial sessions of therapy often expressed his feelings by arriving 30 to 40 minutes late for the therapy session. This went on for several sessions, with a different "legitimate" reason being presented each time. When held to his allotted 50 minutes, he became enraged and made accusations that the therapist lacked caring and understanding. As might be expected, the rage had little to do with the situation at hand. This manner of expression was the only way that the anger and rage could be justified, accepted, and expressed by the workaholic. Over time, through therapist modelling of directness and establishment of clear (although gently implemented) limits, this patient gave up this form of defensive behavior.

Behavioral therapy and strategic techniques such as paradoxical interventions should not be employed with workaholics. These kinds of therapies and techniques might seem successful, because there will be the appearance of change at the behavioral level. However, it will soon become evident that what has appeared is the compliant and chameleon-like behavior of the false self. The best form of treatment appears to be an experimental psychodynamic approach that both focuses on the individual's early emotional development and stresses the formation of a real relationship. This relationship should be oriented toward corrective work in which the workaholic can be encouraged to develop his or her real self. As the real self begins to evolve and continues to emerge, the therapist can both recognize the true self and validate the patient's experience and feelings.

One way of starting therapy with the workaholic is to give homework assignments at the end of the first four or five sessions. It is important that the homework assignments be open-ended, with the goal being for the workaholic to learn more about him- or herself, and secondarily for that information to be shared with the therapist. Often at the end of the first few sessions, the workaholic will be asked to write an outline of family history dynamics that is viewed as important in the development of work as a central theme in life. The homework assignments emphasize a feeling component. The focus on feelings in assignments is primarily due to the workaholic's history of having had tremendous difficulty with experiencing genuine feelings. Feelings usually have been very difficult, painful, and not validated within the family, and thus have been buried. This kind of homework assignment also provides the opportunity to look at the actual role the parents played in this process.

Unfinished business with the parents is important to elicit, so that the therapist can gather information about how the patient's dynamics are going to be acted out. Many workaholics act out their projections in the work place. Bosses, supervisors, and others in positions of authority receive projections related to unfinished business associated with the family of origin.

Case Study Number 2

One patient who was seen in therapy over a 5-year period went from job to job making massive projections upon female supervisors whom he saw as too powerful and overwhelming. It was not surprising that the boundaries between this man and his mother were very fused. This man would manage either to find women with similar boundary issues or attempt to push other women supervisors into a role similar to his mother's. This man worked extremely hard and was highly productive and successful. Initially, he refused to address the fused boundary issue, and constantly demanded that these women recognize him as special due to the positive results of his work. Problems consistently arose when these women would set external limits that the man was unable to set for himself. Once the limits were clearly set, the patient would become furious and act out his feelings in non-direct, passive-aggressive ways. Often, without discussion with the supervisor, he would find another job (usually a higher-level position) and abruptly leave the position he was in. It would not be long before the same dynamics were again replayed.

It continues to be amazing how readily the workaholic is hired for new positions, although he or she often seems to leave positions prematurely. The workaholic usually does not get fired but is considered to be a hard worker and a high producer in the workplace. It is difficult to say if the workaholic would actually be fired if he or she were to remain on the job for very long after eruption of the intense interpersonal struggle with the supervisor. Many workaholics choose these intense periods as justification for leaving their jobs. It appears that the workaholic views the interpersonal struggle and resultant premature leaving as a punishment to the parent-figure substitute. In an indirect manner, this is one way the workaholic expresses the intense anger, and sometimes rage, toward the original parent.

It is important to the therapy process that the therapist allow the patient to be in charge of changing this repeated pattern of behavior. The task of the therapist is to help the patient understand whom these people (objects of projection) represent in the patient's life.

Once trust has begun to be established within the context of individual psychotherapy, it is time to add a second component to the therapy process. Group psychotherapy, perhaps the most important part of the therapy process for workaholics, is necessary for workaholics to practice some of the emotional and interpersonal skills that they have acquired in their individual therapy.

Group Psychotherapy

The model that seems most effective is concurrent individual and group psychotherapy, with group therapy starting after the relationship with the individual therapist has been established. The importance of group psychotherapy will be realized shortly after the workaholic is placed in the group setting. The workaholic often begins by unconsciously choosing various members of the group on whom to project underlying issues. When this happens, it will be important that the group be experiential and relationship-oriented. Minimal structure is also important, since the workaholic tends to use structure to shield himself or herself from closeness with others. Minimal structure will allow this individual the opportunity to explore feelings with others without the crutch of structure.

Also important in the treatment of the workaholic is the use of an individual therapist who will also be one of the group therapists. This provides a double benefit. Group, the arena for development of interpersonal relating, will then be less frightening for the workaholic and he or she will be less likely to show the false self, which will increase the likelihood of showing and working on the real self. Additionally, with the workaholic's individual therapist as one of the group co-therapists, the workaholic's need for repetition compulsion (or the need to replay the historical dynamics through projections onto group members) can more readily be observed and challenged.

Group psychotherapy with workaholics tends to operate best when there are two therapists of opposite gender. This allows group members to project onto mother and father figures, as well as other representative members of their families.

Several of the primary issues that the workaholic deals with will crop up during the group process. The major issue needing attention will involve the issue of limit setting and the ability to say no. The workaholic will get the opportunity to decide whether he or she really wishes to do things that other members of the group might ask. At first the workaholic will say yes all of the time. When this issue is addressed in group, it is often discovered that the workaholic had not wished to say yes, but could not say no. The therapists should then suggest to the workaholic that he or she experiment with saying no to others in group, and then ask for feedback from other group members. The workaholic is usually surprised to discover that he or she is not disliked for setting limits, and more often is respected for it.

The above issue reflects the original early childhood conditioning that was established: that saying "no" and setting limits with the parent caused an intense reaction. Early parental responses, quashing limits set by the child, supported the child's assumption that he or she was the cause of this negative parental reaction. This resulted in extreme fear of limit-setting. Overbeck (1976) suggested that setting limits for the workaholic was helping the patient to establish workable psychic space between what he or she ought to do, wants to do, can do, and will do. In therapy, the workaholic is able to learn that other adults are not necessarily like the parent and, in fact, are often resentful of others trying to take responsibility for them by preventing a natural interpersonal exchange. The workaholic also learns that a person can be liked and even loved for being truly him- or herself, and not someone whom he or she really is not.

Family Therapy

Laing (1971) stated that emotional difficulty was the result of an individual not only being isolated from a sense of self but also from his or her roots. Laing viewed the social network of the family as a necessity for emotional healing to occur. Lockwood (1986) viewed the family as the underlying foundation in the development of addictions. She also believed that family systems therapy along with other social system support groups (AA, NA, OA, etc.) were a necessary component in the treatment of addictions.

The family of the workaholic is certainly an important component of the emotional and behavioral change process. An effective model appears to be one in which the family is initially brought into therapy on a routine basis. Once the family becomes cooperative and a reduction in family defenses is clear, the frequency of family sessions can be decreased. However, until the family actively and cooperatively participates in therapy with the workaholic, routine sessions are a must. Only after the family becomes open, non-defensive, and cooperative has the therapist won the power struggle, breaking the fused boundaries of the closed system. It is often helpful to give the parents of the family system homework assignments that are both focused on opening the highly dependent and closed system, and on encouraging development of interpersonal relationships with couples outside the family system.

Summary and Conclusions

In summary, when doing therapy with the workaholic, the primary goal is not to get the workaholic to transform the working habits into a more leisurely framework. Rather, the fundamental goal for the therapy is to help the workaholic relate to others in a real manner, which results in the workaholic feeling significant, recognized, and genuine. What transpires in the work arena will vary from workaholic to workaholic. Work to the workaholic is the process by which significant meaning in life is realized. The therapist's role is not to take away that source of meaning, but to focus on helping the workaholic develop an interpersonal world in which the workaholic can experience his or her real self.

An additional goal of therapy is to assist the workaholic in giving up the addiction to work, and replacing the addiction with the pleasure and significance that work can provide. For the workaholic who has successfully been involved in therapy, work often becomes an arena where spontaneous and creative feelings can be experienced.

In conclusion, therapy for the workaholic does not remove work as the source of security in life. Instead, therapy tries to bring meaningful, significant, and genuine relationships into the world of the workaholic. Thus, the value of work to the workaholic is altered; it no longer is the structuring life force, but rather becomes one of many avenues for an individual to enjoy and find meaning in life.

References

Ackerman, N. J. (1980). The family with adolescents. In E. A. Carter & M. McGoldrick (Eds.), *The family life cycle: A framework for family therapy* (pp. 147–169). New York: Gardner.

Clance, P. (1985). *The imposter phenomenon.* Atlanta: Peachtree Publishers.

Farrar, J. (1988). Case study information regarding characteristics of the workaholic. Unpublished case study data.

Fogarty, T. F. (1988). *Why a workaholic?* (Newsletter). Rye Brook, NY: Center for Family Learning.

Laing, R. D. (1971). *The politics of the family and other essays.* New York: Random House.

Lockwood, D. (1986). Three generations of addiction: Who is colluding? *Journal of Strategic and Systemic Therapies, 5*(3), 4–12.

Masterson, J. F. (1986). *The disorder of the real self: Borderline and narcissistic personality disorders* (Cassette Recording No. 2-1). New York: The Masterson Group.

Miller, A. (1981). *Prisoners of childhood.* New York: Basic Books.

Oates, W. (1971). *Confessions of a workaholic.* New York: World.

Overbeck, T. J. (1976). The workaholic. *University of Santa Clara Jesuit Community Psychology, 13*(3), 36–42.

Penzer, W. N. (1984). The psychopathology of the psychotherapist. *Psychotherapy in Private Practice, 2*(2), 51–59.

Pietropinto, A. (1986). The workaholic spouse: Survey analysis. *Medical Aspects of Human Sexuality, 5,* 89–96.

Winnicott, D. W., & Guntrip, H. (1983). Ego distortion in terms of true and false self. In J. R. Greenberg & S. A. Mitchell (Eds.), *Object relations in psychoanalytic theory.* Cambridge, MA: Harvard University Press.

_14

Excessive Exercise

JACK E. FARRAR, Ph.D.

A SOCIALLY ACCEPTED ADDICTION seems to be a contradiction in terms. How can an addiction be viewed as socially accepted or socially supported? Glasser's term (1976) "positive addiction" addressed this issue. Glasser referred to positive addiction as the energy, heightened enthusiasm, and internal meditative process (sometimes called a runner's high) observed in persons who run and jog.

Webster (1965) defines addiction as the process of devoting or surrendering oneself to something habitually or obsessively. Peele and Brodsky (1975) described addiction as "not a chemical reaction. Addiction is an experience—one that grows out of an individual's routinized subjective response to something that has special meaning for him—something, anything, that he finds so safe and reassuring that he cannot be without it" (p. 18).

Attitudes appear to play a major role in developing an adherence to exercise routines and possible addiction. According to the subjective expected utility theory (Kendzierski & Lamastro, 1988), a weightlifter's attitude and underlying belief system are more important in the development of strong, routinized exercise behavior than is adherence to a workout schedule. This research emphasizes the importance of belief system and emotional subjectivity in the development of behaviors that can later become addictive.

Exercise addiction is often so extensive that daily exercisers (especially runners) have reported withdrawal symptoms when deprived of exercising. Peele (1978) presented several issues that are central to the discussion of addiction. He emphasized that addiction should be viewed as a process rather than a condition, and not as an all-or-none state of being, either totally present or totally absent. Addiction was described as an extension of ordinary behavior, a pathological habit, dependence, or compulsion. It refers not merely to the inherent characteristics of drugs or activities per se, but to the involvement a person develops with these substances or behaviors. When involvement eliminates basic choices in all other areas of life, an addiction has been formed.

The peak period for research into exercise addiction was during the late 1970s and early 1980s. Relatively little research has been conducted in this area since the early 1980s. Much of the earlier research focused on addiction to running rather than addiction to exercise in general.

Definition of Exercise Addiction

Running (exercise) addiction has been defined as the psychological and physiological habituation to a regular, ongoing routine of physical activity, characterized by withdrawal symptoms (Glasser, 1976). Glasser stated that withdrawal symptoms occurred within 24 to 36 hours without the activity. Withdrawal symptoms referred to were anxiety, restlessness, guilt, irritability, tension, frustration, hostility, bloatedness, muscle twitching, discomfort, apathy, sluggishness, weight loss resulting from lack of appetite, sleeplessness, headaches, and stomachaches (Glasser, 1976; Morgan, 1979).

Sachs and Pargman (1984) further clarified what specifically is meant by an addiction to running. They stated that an addiction can occur even if an individual runs (exercises) a minimum number of times a week (as few as one or two times). The conditions for addiction were that individuals had to have a planned regimen of running (exercising), and if they missed their running (exercising) days, they would experience withdrawal symptoms within 24 to 36 hours. Withdrawal symptoms occurred only on those days when the individual had expected to run (exercise).

Glasser (1976) stated that positive addictions to such activities as running and meditation promoted psychological strength, and increased life satisfaction. Sachs (1984) indicated that this definition was in sharp contrast to those of negative addictions such as alcohol or heroin, which were described as often undermining psychological and physiological integrity.

Runner's High

Glasser (1976) additionally proposed that runners became addicted to exercise largely because of beneficial psychological effects. He described positive running addiction as an "altered state of consciousness" during which the runner experiences a euphoric "runner's high."

The phenomenon of runner's high commonly occurs after a runner has run for 25 or 30 minutes. Csikszentmihalyi (cited in Harris, 1978) described the runner's high as an altered state of consciousness that often accompanied intense exertion. The intense exercise was often accompanied by a loss of self-consciousness and an immersion into one's physical activity that resulted in euphoria, heightened sense of aliveness, increased energy, and good feeling. During this period of time the mind was reported to be able to focus without interruption. This explained one of the major reinforcing qualities in the process of running. Although the runner's high is well documented and reported by many, it is not actually known what causes this phenomenon to happen. Perhaps, as Wagemaker and Goldstein suggested (1980), it may be the result of the reversal of right-left brain confusion, or it may involve changes in norepinephrine levels. Research has been conflicting and highly subjective in this area. Although runner's high or its equivalent has not been definitively demonstrated, it is clear that some powerful form of physiological and psychological motivation is present in exercising.

Physiological Effects of Exercise

Some researchers have suggested that running produces endorphins and as a result causes a heightened possibility of physiological addiction. Moore (1982) indicated that there was no real evidence that runners actually achieve an opiate-intensity high from their exercise. However, it was determined that a physiologically based general feeling of well-being resulted from running. Farrell (1981) suggested that exercise might simply be a general stress on the body, resulting in secretion of hormones and other substances from the pituitary, such as adrenocorticotropic hormone and endorphins. No one as yet has determined the exact function of the pituitary secretions. The physiological nature and basis of exercise addiction is also still unresolved.

Psychosocial Factors in Exercise Addiction

Robbins and Joseph (1981) looked at the interrelationship of running, family, and work. Their initial thesis was that addictive running would lead to neglect of the family and scaling down of vocational aspirations. The findings indicated that there was direct conflict between the runner and the spouse or partner on such issues as neglect, loss of shared interests and friends, fatigue, and neglect of work. These issues were found to be directly related to commitment to running (synonymous with addiction). Perhaps the most significant finding of Robbins and Joseph's work was that 42 percent of full-time runners reported having to reappraise a primary relationship because of their commitment to running.

Summers, Machin, and Sargent (1983) found that running showed a consistent pattern of sex differences, concluding that females became more highly addicted to running than males. Even given the many research problems, the underlying addictive characteristics of running have been well studied. Research has found that training for a marathon required the commitment of a major part of one's life. Summers, Machin, and Sargent (1983) suggested that it was among the most strongly committed runners that the characteristics of negative addiction tended to apply. Using Carmack and Marten's (1979) "commitment to running scale", runners finishing a marathon in three hours or less appeared to be more addicted to running than those who required more then three hours to complete a marathon.

Although research did not demonstrate that neglect of work was a function of negative running addiction (Morgan, 1979), questions did arise regarding the relationship between quality of work and job satisfaction and negative addiction to exercise. Most of the subjects considered to be addicted to running tended to run outside of work hours, and work quality was generally not affected.

Treatment Considerations

The treatment of an addiction to exercise is very difficult. Not only is there confusion about what level of exercise is unhealthy, but more important is the difficulty of actually getting individuals involved in a negative addiction to enter treatment.

Presence of Positive or Negative Addiction

When treatment for addiction to exercise is considered, a distinction must be made between whether the individual is positively addicted or is experiencing a negative addiction to exercise. Evaluation of negative addiction should include the individual's recognition of exercise as an interference with the functioning of his or her daily life, a desire to change the behavior, and the support of the person's extended functional systems (such as family or work environment) in the change process.

There are many reasons for running. Some individuals exercise to escape the "anxiety of terminal helplessness." Some runners seem to be using running to ward off the debilitating effects of aging (Graham, 1979). Others tend to use exercise to ward off the pressures of life. Still others use running and exercise to maintain their desired body shape and weight. Sachs and Pargman (1979) described how a positive addiction to running can shift to become a negative addiction to running. The shift appeared to occur when exercise (running) became a controlling activity in an individual's life, eliminating all other choices.

Glasser (1976) addressed the value of remaining in the positive end of the dedication-addiction continuum. In positive addiction, running represented a positive addition to a person's life style, a tool or technique that better enabled a person to manage the normal stress, anxiety, and depression of life.

For a small percentage of others, running began to control their lives, eliminating other choices. Morgan (1979) cited a number of case studies of runners who were consumed by their need to run. These runners dramatically altered their daily schedules, continued to run even when seriously injured, and neglected the responsibilities of work, home, and family. Morgan suggested that the behavior of hard-core exercise addicts resembled that found in other major addictions.

Consequently, it appeared that runners must be alert to the possibility of a positive addiction evolving into a negative one. Hailey and Bailey (1982) found a linear relationship between time spent in running and level of addiction. As a runner's running experience increased, his or her progression toward negative addiction also increased.

Social Network and Family System

Many runners do not have the necessary emotional introspection to perceive the negative addictive qualities of their exercise. In addition, as when working with any addicted population, there is a high level of denial. Thus, it is important to interview the other members of the addicted person's family and work systems before a full and accurate assessment of the exercise addiction can be established. Often it is the family's dissatisfaction that leads to the addict's referral to treatment.

When Is Treatment Necessary for Exercise Addiction?

Harper (1984) stated that it is important to differentiate between state-specific personality characteristics and trait-personality characteristics. Trait-personality characteristics were considered to be deeply entrenched, chronic problems similar to those underlying negative addiction. Exercise or running as treatment was not recommended for such chronic problems. State-specific personality characteristics were considered to be situational and acute. These characteristics included: anxiety/tension, loneliness, alcoholism, depression, and weight control. Harper (1984) and others have used programs of prescribed running to combat such state-specific personality characteristics. For all of these problem areas, exercise treatment was paired with some form of non-running therapeutic group. Gary and Gutherie suggested that use of jogging treatment or jogotherapy (Harper, 1984) be followed by attendance at an Alcoholics Anonymous meeting for alcoholic clients. For alcoholics, jogging paired with AA provided them with something substantive to replace their alcoholism. Recovery from alcoholism was reported to be shortened by a program of jogging. Also, jogging was reported to improve an alcoholic's self-concept and attitude toward physical health. Kostrubala (1984) reported using running as a therapeutic tool in treatment of patients with both state-specific and trait-personality characteristics. Some of the problems treated were: schizophrenia, depression, organic brain syndrome, alcoholism, anxiety states, and acute depression following severe interpersonal loss.

Shipman (1984) developed and researched running programs with emotionally disordered children. One remarkable outcome of his work was that all of the emotionally disordered children in the study were maintained on a much-decreased dose of medication when placed on a consistent, regularly prescribed running program.

At the present time researchers and clinicians using running as therapy perceive its use as an adjunct to psychotherapy and not as the sole treatment. Running is merely another tool in which clinicians can become trained, and can apply in those cases that most dictate its use. This is no different from psychotherapists employing different adjunctive techniques such as gestalt, psychomotor, or behavioral therapy in their psychotherapeutic treatment.

Kostrabula (1976) and other therapists with expertise in the use of running as a therapy have been certifying clinical professionals in the use of this kind of therapy. One of the criteria for the certification process was that those certified were required to run in at least two marathons per year.

Treatment of Negative Addiction

When Glasser (1976) wrote about development of a positive addiction, he was ruling out the development of negative addiction. The key quality described by Glasser was that the activity must be able to be performed without engendering any self-criticism; establishment of a negative addiction certainly involves self-identity problems including self-criticism.

A therapist's work with clients to help them develop a positive addiction to exercise often can be a very good form of treatment, especially as an adjunct to a patient's ongoing therapeutic process. A great deal of caution must be demonstrated when working with a client in this regard; ethical concerns should be addressed. As specified in research reported in this chapter, not everyone is a good candidate for the approach Glasser suggested.

A person might either be immersed in another addiction or actually could be an addictive personality. For a number of reasons, a good pretreatment assessment is recommended. Minimally, the assessment should include some form of personality testing, like the Minnesota Multiphasic Personality Inventory; some more physical measure of a client's state of drive or compulsivity, like a Type A/B personality assessment (Roskies et al., 1986); and a measure of compulsivity of running or exercise, like the Commitment to Running Scale.

Persons caught in a negative addiction may use exercise to avoid or escape themselves and others, as well as any criticism they may perceive. To encourage these individuals to sharpen their addictive potential would not serve them well. Cavalier attitudes regarding diagnosis of exercise addiction or using prescribed running as a blanket treatment may underestimate the power of the addictive quality in the personalities of some people.

A major issue in treatment is the manner in which a therapist helps a negatively addicted client become less dependent on the addiction. For this process to be successful two factors need to be considered. First, as with any addiction, those highly addicted to exercise are not going to back away from their addiction easily. The addictions serve a real function, which tends to be based on an individual's personality dynamics, and is unique for each person. Therefore, a good assessment and a psychosocial and family history are important prior to the initiation of treatment.

A second factor important in treating negative addiction to running is that a resocialization process must be introduced and successfully established. People who have a negative addiction to running and exercise tend to be socially isolated and emotionally disengaged from their families and friends. A fundamental part of the resocialization process is the evaluation of the social system of the addict. Treatment must be based on an accurate assessment of the nuclear and extended family. Questions such as functionality of the closeness-distancing dynamics must be understood. The purpose of the addicted individual's withdrawal from his or her social system should be found. The extended family can provide the therapist with a sense of repetition dynamics across generations. Understanding the function of closeness and distance in the extended family makes it easier to understand how the addicted individual went about setting up similar dynamics in the present family.

Some of the factors most requiring evaluation are:

1. Emotional triangulation. Addicted individuals have triangled their exercise addiction into their lives. In this regard, exercise for an individual with a negative addiction can be seen as similar to an affair within a marriage. There is something that these individuals cannot get from their partner or family, and they substitute exercise.

2. Separation/enmeshment issues. How emotionally separate is the addict from his or her partner? Has that individual achieved a clear sense of self in the process of separation from the family of origin? Is the distance from family a function of lack of availability of the partner, because the partner is overinvolved with other members of the family sys-

tem, and thus overinvolvement with exercise becomes a compensation for the lack of availability? Which person in the couple backed away from the other partner first, and for what perceived reason?

3. Family hierarchy. Is there an appropriate hierarchy in the family system? Are the parents actually in charge of the family? Are the children limited to child roles or is too much power given them? Do the grandparents act as friends to the nuclear family, or do they overcontrol when visiting?

4. Family subsystems. Are the subsystems clearly delineated within the nuclear family? Are there clear formations of the parental, spousal (marital), sibling, and individual subsystems? Does each possess its own sense of appropriate power and control?

5. Intimacy avoidance. How does the addict use the exercise addiction to avoid intimacy within the family system, as a parent, family member, and as a spouse?

All of the above information is necessary for an appropriate assessment. Once the function, purpose, and manner of perpetuation of the addiction are understood, then a treatment approach can be established. Since the negative addiction is usually acted out in more isolated ways, establishment and social support of relationships should be primary concerns in treatment. Thus, treatment should be concerned with the formation of a social network. Two components to this resocialization treatment model should be a psychoeducational aspect, and an experiential component.

The psychoeducational part of the model involves teaching addicted individuals about a range of family dynamics and peer-relating skills. The genogram can prove a useful tool to define graphically the dynamics within the family (McGoldrick & Gerson, 1985). The genogram depicts important emotional dynamics that are not clear from merely interviewing these individuals. In addition to providing more information about the family, the genogram teaches families about the ways in which they relate to one another. The design of the genogram often is the therapist's first powerful input into the family, and it can be a potent change agent. The following dynamics are of greatest concern when conducting a genogram with people who appear to be addicted to exercise:

1. Emotional triangles that reflect the role and position the addict plays in the family system. Often the exercise addict is the "outsider" or distancer, especially regarding closeness/distance to another.

2. Alliances are often found between the other members of the triangles. The closeness in these alliances tends to exclude the addict and to include others.

3. Subsystems should be delineated through the use of the genogram.

In a nonaddictive family the four subsystems should be functioning in positive and supportive ways. There should be clear individual, spousal, parental, and sibling subsystems.

4. Overinvolvement and distance between family members should be noted. This will reflect where and with whom the family's psychic energy is concentrated.

5. Hierarchy issues should also be noted. Often the addicted individual has been relegated, or has relegated himself or herself, to a childlike, nonparental role, which provides further reinforcement for the sense of isolation that these individuals feel.

The experiential component involves initiation of individual therapy first and group therapy at a later date. The focus is the development of a genuine caring and understanding personal relationship with the addict. This therapy approach is an attempt to reverse the addict's tendency toward social isolation and is an attempt to encourage investment in interpersonal exchange and relationship rather than continuing absorption in the addict's intrapersonal world. Individual therapy is started after the family system is understood and the exercise addict has made some movement toward less isolation and more family involvement. Some evidence of change in the alliances within the family is also necessary. The marital bond should show a degree of positive change and begin to look stronger. Also, the addict should be pushed toward greater responsibility in the parenting, not working in isolation but becoming part of a more functional parenting team.

As these changes come about, the exercise addict should begin a relationship-oriented group psychotherapy process. The goal is to generalize the greater closeness established within the family and with the therapist to peers in a supportive network. Group therapy continues as individual therapy is tapered off, until it is clear that individuals are comfortable with being themselves with others and are able to form significant and meaningful relationships—ones in which a range of both positive and negative feelings are expressed. Group therapy should be an essential change agent for individuals negatively addicted to exercise. Group therapy can be the primary source of change, providing addicted individuals with an opportunity to get in touch with their real selves and to be emotionally present in an accepting, open, and trusting environment, yet one that provides ongoing, honest feedback (Flores, 1988).

Conclusions

Treatment of exercise addiction requires knowledge, awareness, and at least minimum capability in the area of exercise. In other words, the therapist, in addition to being knowledgeable about exercise addiction, also must value the usefulness of exercise. If the therapist has no awareness of, or does not value the importance of exercise, the client is unlikely to give the trust necessary for the relationship to develop. The relationship established with the therapist is the foundation and model for the addict to establish trust with members of the therapy group and the family system. Also, the investment in significant relationships is the key factor in turning around negative addictions of this kind. Genuine relationships are built on the model of trust established between the addict and the therapist.

The overall transition process for the exercise addict is movement from a position of negative addiction to exercise to a position of positive addiction to exercise, and then to the gradual development of a genuine relationship with the spouse and family members. Then, over time a significant relationship with a few members of a social network outside the family system should be established. Since exercise addicts are so sensitive to criticism, initially there should be close monitoring of potential critical remarks from the newly acquired social network, including the new relationship with the therapist and group members, and the renewed and different relationship with the addict's family.

References

Anxious or depressed. (1985). *The Health Letter, 25*(10), 1–2.

Carmack, M. A., & Martens, R. (1979). Measuring commitment to running: A survey of runners' attitudes and mental states. *Journal of Sport Psychology, 1*(1), 25–42.

Farrell, P. A. (1981). Plasma beta-endorphin/beta-lipotropin immunoreactivity increases after treadmill exercise in man. *Medical Science Sports Exercise, 13*(2), 134.

Flores, P. (1988). *Group psychotherapy with addicted populations.* New York: Haworth Press.

Glasser, W. (1976). *Positive addiction.* New York: Harper & Row.

Graham, W. F. (1979). The anxiety of runner: terminal helplessness. *The Christian Century*, pp. 821–823.

Hailey, B. J., & Bailey, L. A. (1982). Negative addiction in runners: A quantitative approach. *Journal of Sport Behavior, 5,* 150–154.

Harper, F. D. (1984). Jogotherapy: Jogging as psychotherapy. In M. L. Sachs & G. W. Buffone (Eds.), *Running as therapy* (pp. 83–93). Lincoln: University of Nebraska Press.

Harris, D. V. (1978). The happy addict. *Women's Sports, 5*(1), p. 53.

Kendzierski, D., & Lamastro, V. D. (1988). Reconsidering the role of attitudes in exercise behavior: A decision theoretic approach. *Journal of Applied Social Psychology, 18*(9), 737–759.

Kostrubala, T. (1976). *The joy of running.* Philadelphia: Lippincott.

Kostrubala, T. (1984). Running and therapy. In M. L. Sachs and G. W. Buffone (Eds.), *Running as therapy* (pp. 112–125). Lincoln: University of Nebraska Press.

McGoldrick, M., & Gerson, R. (1985). *Genograms in family assessment.* New York: W. W. Norton.

Moore, M. (1982). Endorphins and exercise: A puzzling relationship. *The Physician and Sportsmedicine, 10*(2), 111–114.

Morgan, W. P. (1979). Negative addiction in runners. *The Physician and Sportsmedicine, 7,* pp. 56–63, 67–70.

Peele, S. (1978). Addiction: The analgesic experience. *Human Nature, 1*(9), 61–67.

Peele, S., & Brodsky, A. (1975). *Love and addiction.* New York: Taplinger.

Positive interval addiction to speed. (1978). *Runner's World, 13*(6), 70–79.

Robbins, J. M., & Joseph, P. (1981). Commitment to running: Implications for the family and work. *Sociological Symposium, 30,* 87–108.

Roskies, E., Sevaganian, P., Oseasohn, R., & Hanley, J. (1986). The Montreal Type A intervention project: Major findings. *Health Psychology, 5*(1), 45–69.

Runners similar to anorexics? (1983). *Health Letter, 21*(8), 1.

Sachs, M. L., (1984). The runner's high. In M. L. Sachs & G. W. Buffone, (Eds.), *Running as therapy* (pp. 273–288). Lincoln: University of Nebraska Press.

Sachs, M. L., & Pargman, D. (1979). Running addiction: An indepth interview examination. *Journal of Sports Behavior, 2,* 143–155.

Sachs, M. L. & Pargman, D. (1984). Running addiction. In M. L. Sachs & G. W. Buffone (Eds.), *Running as therapy* (pp. 231–253). Lincoln: University of Nebraska Press.

Sacks, M. H., & Sachs, M. L. (Eds.). (1981). *Psychology of running.* Champaign, IL: Human Kinetics Publishers.

Sheehan, G. (1978). *Running and being.* Indianapolis, IN: Warner Books.

Sheehan, G. (1980). *This running life.* New York: Simon & Schuster.

Shipman, W. M. (1984). Emotional and behavioral effects of long-distance running on children. In M. L. Sachs & G. W. Buffone (Eds.), *Running as therapy* (pp. 125–138). Lincoln: University of Nebraska Press.

Summers, J. J., Machin, V. J., & Sargent, G. I. (1983). Psychosocial factors related to marathon running. *Journal of Sport Psychology, 5*(3), 314–331.

Wagemaker, H., & Goldstein, L. (1980). The runner's high. *Journal of Sports Medicine, 20*(2), 227–229.

Waters, B. (1981). Defining the runner's personality: For years, theories have been expounded on what type of person runs. But can running change personalities? *Runner's World, 16*(6), 48–51.

Webster's Dictionary. (1965). Chicago: Rand McNally & Company.

15

Excessive Spending

LUCIANO L'ABATE, Ph.D.

HISTORY REPORTS THE excessive and repetitive (i.e., compulsive) spending habits of President Lincoln's wife. Born into a moneyed Kentucky family, Mary Todd Lincoln lived long before the invention of instant credit via credit cards—not that she needed it; as the president's wife, she received open credit anywhere she cared to shop. Merchants were happy to oblige in indulging her whims. She enjoyed shopping sprees that, of course, pale in comparison to the recent ones of Imelda Marcos, whose accumulations of goods and clothes have surpassed anything that Mrs. Lincoln may have purchased. Mrs. Lincoln shopped freely and, some would say, frivolously. In fact, she overspent her husband's salary by so much that she asked special friends in Congress for an advance on her husband's four years stipend, *before* he started his term of office! Her free-spending habits came to a halt with the assassination of her husband in 1865. After her death as a destitute in 1882, more than 60 pairs of lace curtains were found in her room. What could she possibly have intended to do with them?

The purpose of this chapter is to review what factors (cultural, familial, and individual) lead people toward such excessive spending that either bankruptcy or criminal prosecution may result as the ultimate price that has to be paid for this form of addiction. An understanding of these factors should be helpful in treating people who are afflicted with this pattern of abuse.

The Dynamics of Excessive Spending

Patterns of overuse of credit, as shown by credit card usage, indicate that some individual characteristics can be identified (Garcia, 1980; Hirschman, 1981). Married individuals with a high income who maintain a number of bank accounts are more likely to use credit cards. Usage is made to seem easy by advertising and TV; banks and credit corporations make money in the long run by just issuing a credit card (Martell & Fitts, 1981). Also, personal characteristics in one partner may interact with the characteristics of the other partner, especially but not exclusively in the area of money management (Ater & Deacon, 1972; Lee, 1979).

The idea of personal characteristics interacting with demographic and socioeconomic variables seems to be supported by a great deal of evidence, both normative and deviational. Bergler (1984) probed what he termed "money neurosis," whose unconscious roots can be found in every culture, in every group of every society, and in any period of history. Money neurosis is by no means solely the result of political, social, or economic disorders or injustices, but these factors may certainly aggravate the condition. From his clinical practice and experience, Bergler considered the psychological problem of money as related to various personality profiles. His clinical impressions elaborated on variations on the theme of money addiction, such as the success hunter, the gambler, the golddigger and the playboy, as well as the other side of the coin: the miser, the impostor, the embezzler, the dependee, the con-person, the bargain hunter, and the sucker for easy money. Krueger (1988) extended the same kind of thinking to distinguish compulsive shopping from other symptomatic uses of money and other impulsive acts: "The distinction between compulsive shopping and the occasional shopping 'spree' is that compulsive shopping represents an attempt at affect regulation, especially to remedy depression and emptiness and is a chronic pattern. The compulsive shopper often experiences an inner tension that is released only when something is bought" (p. 574). Krueger also considered what he called "revenge spending," directed against a spouse, as a retaliatory, revengeful act, based on fear of success that derives from "various unconscious and conscious motivations" (p. 574). "In instances where the parents had been involved . . . it emerged that they, too, viewed possessions and money as means of expressing love" (p. 575). Krueger added, "In my experience, compulsive shopping occurs in individuals who are very conscious of how they look and appear to others, who attempt to be pleasing to others, and whose fragile esteem and sense of self depend on the responses of others" (p. 575).

Other explanations for excessive spending have focused on the concept of "greed," which is then linked to such concepts as "need," "temptation," and "opportunity" (Caudill, 1988; Poppe & Utens, 1986; Rappoport, 1987; Yamagishi & Sato, 1986). In fact, on the basis of these studies, one would conclude that greed has started to achieve a modicum of legitimacy in social psychology, although its contruct validity, its developmental roots, and its nomological network of personality correlates have not yet been investigated. Indeed, one could add that greed is a relatively new concept in the psychological literature, in the sense that it has not been operationalized sufficiently to deserve attention. How is greed different from need? How is greed related to desire for immediate gratification? What are its antecedents? We know full well what the consequences of greed are, yet we know very little about what makes some people greedier than others. Other explanations for excessive spending are based on psychoanalytic theory, as in the work of Boris (1986) and McWilliams (1984), using such vaguely defined and questionable concepts as "unconscious guilt" and "identification with the victim."

Feinberg (1986) conducted four experiments to test the hypothesis that stimuli associated with spending can elicit spending responses. He used 135 restaurant customers and 154 undergraduates. In all four experiments, credit card stimuli were either present or absent in situations in which subjects were given the opportunity to spend. Overall findings indicated that credit card stimuli enhanced the magnitude, probability, and decision time involved in spending, suggesting that the presence of credit card stimuli may elicit spending responses. Feinberg proposed that, by ownership of a credit card, a form of conditioning may occur. Credit card stimuli become associated with spending, which, in turn, is conceptualized as an instrumental response run by the positive affect/feeling generated by the acquisition of goods, and possibly by the affect generated by the spending itself.

Paulsen, Rimm, Woodburn, and Rimm (1977) conducted another study based on the same behavioral view as Feinberg. These authors located 16 undergraduate volunteers who had experienced problems with impulsive overspending. They were randomly assigned to either a self-control experimental treatment condition or to a placebo condition. The self-control condition stressed self-reinforcement for non-spending, keeping a budget, and avoiding carrying checkbooks or credit cards. The placebo condition involved discussing financial problems in terms of psychoanalytic constructs, such as the pleasure versus reality principles. Both groups received a 1-hour session for 4 weeks. The results showed that, in terms of self-recorded spending, subjects in the self-control condition evidenced a significantly greater change (55 percent reduction in spending) than subjects in the placebo group, who showed only a limited increase. These differences between groups were maintained at a 3-month follow-up.

Financial problems due to excessive spending are traceable to at least three different patterns that take place in three different constellations of individual and family factors. The first constellation is traceable to *family crises,* such as divorce or illness; personal difficulties that lead individuals to spend lavishly to bolster low self-esteem and alleviate depression; attempts to resolve personal deficits such as inadequate maturity, poor education, or limited experience in dealing with money matters; and family life-cycle considerations, such as marriage and increasing family needs of spouses and children.

The second constellation is represented by the sudden and one-time-only *spending spree* of two or more adolescents, who on the spur of the moment, and probably under the influence of alcohol or drugs, decide to rob a car and squander stolen money in a frantic orgy of unplanned spending. Many of these youngsters cannot explain why this sudden explosion took place, but their denials and inadequate awareness of rational bases for their behavior should not exonerate them of responsibility. On the contrary, the relationship of the spree to possible family and contextual (peer) antecedents should be explored fully with their families. Such behavior does not take place out of the blue, without any connection to other situational factors that may not be directly causal, but may, in some way, be related to their suddenly irresponsible behavior.

The third constellation, on the other hand, takes place with a clearly *criminal* and callous intent to defraud and cheat others for one's own gain. Under these conditions, one would not find anxiety, guilt, or remorse, as one would find in the first constellation. One would find instead an unthinking and unfeeling opportunistic viewpoint that the end justifies the means, with a callous disregard for the rights of others, and a deliberate plan to take away from others what is seen as superflous or unnecessary for them but not for the addict. The first two patterns may result in bankruptcy; the third has a greater likelihood of resulting in criminal behaviors and punishment. Both outcomes will be considered briefly before the remainder of this chapter deals with therapeutic guidelines.

Bankruptcy

Bankruptcy may be the outcome of excessive or irresponsible spending, which may be based on individual, marital, and family characteristics or on legitimate factors outside the control of the individuals involved. In other words, bankruptcy can be an outcome resulting from a variety of reasons, legitimate and illegitimate. Some authors (Robbins, 1983) even advocate "the advantages of a timely bankruptcy." As far as individual personality factors in bankruptcy are concerned, Ginsburg and Ginsburg (1983) reported a psychoanalytic study of a bankruptcy lawyer to illustrate the stages of ego disintegration under state-imposed constraints, where each bankruptcy was seen as representing death. Two additional case examples are of a middle-aged man and a woman in her thirties, where grandiose narcissism was used as a defense against the terror associated with the financial disintegration of the self.

Criminality

Spending behavior is a corollary to excessive acquisitive behavior that may or may not result in excessive spending. The need to acquire sudden or excessive wealth, no matter what the means of acquisition, may be a form of addiction that results in criminal behavior, although its roots and processes may be different from those relevant to excessive spending. Both may be based on greed or an overreliance on money and possessions to bolster one's sense of self-importance. Thus, these processes raise questions about criminality in general as addictive behavior, a viewpoint that is worthy of consideration among the many others about this behavior. Excessive spending and bankruptcy may not be criminal behaviors, but often excessive spending may be the result of the same desire for acquisition of money and possessions through illegal means.

The Issue of Gender Differences in Criminality

There is a widespread belief that white-collar crime is mostly a female undertaking (Heidensohn, 1985). In terms of different socialization patterns for males and females and the possibility of gender differences, it may be important to devote some space to this issue, which is especially relevant to the issue of differential treatment for men and women. For instance, Hoffman-Bustamante (1973) maintained that the issue of whether criminal women are uniquely different from criminal men "remains largely unanswered" (p. 136). She argued that when crimes are committed by women, they seem to be the outcome of five factors: (1) different role expectations for men and women; (2) sex differences in socialization patterns and application of differential social controls; (3) structurally determined differences in opportunities to commit particular offenses; (4) differential access or pressures toward criminally oriented subcultures; and (5) careers and sex differences built into the crime categories themselves. From national and regional crime statistics, Hoffman-Bustamante found that in 1970 women averaged 14.4 percent of all arrests. With the exception of prostitution, the only other categories in which women constituted more than 15 percent of all arrests were murder/manslaughter, larceny, forgery and counterfeiting, fraud, embezzlement, larceny, narcotic usage, vagrancy, curfew violations, and runaways.

Simon (1975, 1976) argued that female criminality has received less attention from the criminal justice system and from the mental health enterprise than male criminality. Two positions have been maintained about this issue. One position views women offenders as "poor benighted victims of male oppression and of society's indifference" (1975, p. 105). The second position views these women "as being more cunning and more crafty than men, as having learned how to commit crimes that are more difficult to apprehend, and as believing that they can count on the chivalry of male law enforcement officers to avoid arrest, conviction, and imprisonment" (1975, p. 105). The first position does not take into consideration that in proportion to men, women may well be underrepresented in crime statistics; proponents of the second position argue that statistics "distort rather than describe the real picture of the amount of crime that women commit" (1975, p. 105). A third position, in between the two presented above, is taken by the women's liberation movement, which argues against a double standard that favors men and that belittles women. An equal-rights position would argue for similar punishments for similar crimes, regardless of sex. Simon's review of statistics relevant to these points revealed an increase in women's involvement in four types of crime: "theft, forgery, fraud, and embezzlement, but not in crimes of violence or in the traditional female crimes, prostitution and child abuse" (1975, p. 107). The gender ratios were 6.5 arrests for men for 1 female arrest; 1 woman convicted in comparison to 9 men; and 1 prison sentence per woman for every 30 men sentenced.

Simon also interviewed 30 criminal trial court judges and state attorneys in 4 large Midwest cities, finding that indeed these judges, mostly men, dealt (or at least reported dealing) with women less harshly than with men. "Most often the women are accomplices that get involved because of their commitment to a boyfriend or a husband. In drugs, they tend to be the users, rarely the pushers, and not at all the organizers. Women are not connected with organized crime" (1975, p. 109). In other words, women are supposedly followers rather than leaders in crime. Simon predicted that as women gain wider access to the business and economic spheres, and also obtain greater personal independence, the trend of increased white-collar crime by women will continue. On the international scene (Simon, 1976), comparisons among 25 different countries showed that American women ranked first and second for financial and property crimes and sixth and seventh for crimes involving violence and drugs.

Austin (1982) argued that previous studies had not determined a satisfactory starting point for female emancipation in order to examine the question of whether this variable caused an increase in female criminality. This author set the years 1967 to 1968 as the time when female emancipation, as measured by female labor force participation and divorce rates, should be followed by noticeable effects on crime rates. The same procedures to measure female emancipation were applied to show take-off points for the increasing percentage of female contribution to various criminal offenses subsequent to changes in female emancipation and the 1976 founding of the National Organization for Women. Increases in female involvement for serious offenses of auto theft and robbery, which may be attributed to women's increased liberation, were found to be greater than increases in larceny/theft and fraud/embezzlement, increases that may be attributed to the same cause.

Kramer and Steffensmeier (1977) assessed conceptions of appropriate punishment for males and females among prison inmates, to judge the extent to which prison inmates recognize the authority of law. A questionnaire asking survey participants to rate various offenses was completed by 100 criminology students and 75 male prison inmates. Significant differences were found on appropriate punishment for shoplifting, embezzlement, resisting arrest, and seduction of a minor, but not for public drunkenness, murder, homosexual acts, or child beating. Inmates and students differed most strongly on homosexual acts, about which inmates were more punitive, and on embezzlement and shoplifting, about which students were more punitive. Inmate answers were also affected by demographic, institutional, and arrest history variables.

Steffensmeier (1978) used data from the Uniform Crime Reports to examine female property crime trends since 1960. The effects of the women's movement on female property crime were also examined. Results indicated that female levels of property crime were rising at a faster rate than male levels only for offenses of larceny (theft and fraud/embezzlement). Absolute differences between the two genders in crime frequencies still exist and, in fact, have generally increased. Female property crime levels have continued to lag far behind those of males. The patterns of data also suggested that the upward trend in female property crime was not due to the women's movement. Women, according to Steffensmeier, are still typically nonviolent, petty property offenders, and the concept of the "new female criminal" remains more of a social invention than an empirical reality.

Zeitz (1981) examined case records and interviewed 100 women offenders in a prison, who represented about 25 percent of the population convicted of property offenses. She suggested a tentative classification for two major types of crime: forgery or embezzlement versus fraud and theft. Among the first group of "honest" women who embezzled or defrauded, thus violating financial trust, Zeitz described four subgroups: (a) obsessive protectors, who "sacrificed" themselves to meet marital and parental responsibilities; (b) romantic dreamers who "sought to preserve what they considered their most important possessions (a husband's love), or to enhance a relationship with a lover or a relative" (p. 148); (c) greedy opportunists, who "began their illegal activities to meet financial needs involving the welfare of significant persons or their relationships with such persons" (p. 148); and (d) victims of persuasion or pressure exerted by another person. Among the second group of women sentenced for stealing, Zeitz found three different subgroups: (a) vindictive self-servers, who believed they were "entitled" to goods or money to "provide an emotional outlet for pent-up feelings of loneliness, envy, frustration, disillusionment, or self-pity" (p. 149); (b) asocial entrepreneurs, who wanted creature comforts no matter how they were achieved, and contrary to other subgroups, operated in association with other criminals; and (c) reluctant offenders, who denied responsibility for their crimes, accusing their husbands or lovers as being mainly responsible for the crimes. A third category involved women who had previously and repeatedly committed drug-related offenses, many of them before 16 years of age. While the obsessive protectors and the romantic dreamers seem to gravitate toward the self-sacrificing selfless extreme, the vindictive self-servers and asocial entrepreneurs seem to gravitate towards the selfish extreme.

Ohberg, Haring, and Marsh (1982) described the case of a woman with multiple personality who embezzled funds from a bank and was subsequently successfully treated by a psychiatrist, a psychologist, and an attorney. She presented herself as being depressed, reporting severe headaches, with frequent memory lapses on her job. Under hypnosis, she began to describe an alter personality with a separate identity, with activities inconsistent with those of the presenting personality, with a different voice, and even with differences in visual acuity. Treatment was accomplished by a progressive application of the test of criminal responsibility. The recognition and acceptance of the hypnotic method as a tool in forming an opinion as to a defendant's competency needs to be stressed within the context of understanding and compassion on the part of the court and the prosecuting authorities.

Pogrebin, Poolem, and Regoli (1986) studied records of 23 males and 39 females found guilty of embezzlement, in an effort to construct a profile of the contemporary bank embezzler. Data were extracted from records by probation officers. The typical embezzler was a 26-year-old Caucasian woman with a high school education, who had been married nearly 5 years and had 1 or 2 children. Income of these women averaged under $10,000 annually. Most of them worked in low, entry-level positions. They indicated that family and personal debts were the reason for the thefts. Most were without accomplices and had been at the job for less than one year. Motivations for a first-time embezzler may not be identical to those of an individual who has embezzled for several years.

Welch (1988) discussed the practical implications of previous studies that have revealed identifiable differences between the value systems of prison inmates and of the general population. These findings suggest a link between an individual's value system and a criminal lifestyle. These value systems are capable of being changed if confronted situationally, through value clarification.

How is one to explain sex ratios in crime, white collar or otherwise? Since women tend to have been socialized for selflessness more often than men, and men have been socialized for selfishness more often then women, one would expect and predict this kind of outcome. Women would tend to be followers rather than leaders, being more indirect than direct, and in some ways, more passive than active. Men, on the other hand, would tend to gravitate towards the other end of this dimension, behaving actively, directly, and certainly more aggressively, for their own gains rather then the benefit of others.

Treatment Guidelines

The following guidelines are concerned with helping families in trouble for excessive spending and do not apply to the treatment of individuals guilty of criminal behavior, to whom an altogether different set of treatment guidelines would apply. Family financial counseling has received very little recognition from the psychotherapeutic community, but deserves to be appreciated as a professional discipline in its own right. Often this form of counseling is offered by well-meaning therapists, who, because they think they know how to manage their own finances, believe that they can help families in need of this specialized form of help (Bagarozzi & Bagarozzi, 1980). Whether training in financial management should be part of the training of most family therapists remains to be seen, but it certainly would not hurt them. Family financial counseling is a discipline in its own right that has a great deal to contribute to the betterment of families in general and especially those in financial trouble (Davis, 1970; Deacon & Firebaugh, 1981; Feldman, 1976; Fetterman, 1976; Jaffe & Senft, 1966; Nichols, Mumaw, Paynter, Plonk & Price, 1971; Shuptrine & Samuelson, 1976).

Beattie (1962) collected and validated a survey of opinions concerning personal finances. This and other questionnaires concerning money management may be worthwhile to evaluate values and attitudes toward finances. This evaluation could serve as a baseline to compare any changes in individuals and families who need financial counseling. Furthermore, by using the same items one could make up questions that could be put together to develop a paratherapeutic workbook. Rolfe (1974) developed a Financial Priorities Inventory designed to assist individuals and couples to become more aware of their relative priorities and expectations in money management. In consists of ten parts, the first part lists 36 budget items, which are ranked by each respondent according to perceived importance. The other nine parts deal with estimations of net income needed for comfortable living and with expectations about expenses and debt accumulation. An instrument of this kind should serve as one way of establishing a financial baseline for individuals and families in trouble with excessive spending.

Part of the treatment with many bankrupt individuals, as with former offenders released from prison, involves helping them find a suitable job. In the process, a therapist needs to know employers' attitudes toward work-release programs and the hiring of former offenders. Atkinson, Fenster, and Blumberg (1976) designed a questionnaire for group administration to assess these attitudes from potential employers involved in retail sales, trade, banking, and service industries. Most of these employers were middle-aged college graduates, making over $10,000 a year in 1975. Their answers revealed that a clear majority of this group were sympathetic, although with some reservations. Crime victims showed a significantly lesser willingness to hire criminal offenders than did those who were not crime victims. Employers who had previously employed ex-offenders were somewhat less willing to hire other ex-offenders than were those with no such experience. Murderers, rapists, and muggers were listed as the three least desirable types of potential employee; the best chances for employment went to car thieves, burglars, drug addicts, and embezzlers. The majority of the respondents felt that they should have access to a work-release employee's records. Overall results suggest that effective planning, administration, research, and especially public relations would be vital for the expansion, survival, and eventual success of work-release programs; this would also apply to programs encouraging employers to hire bankrupt individuals.

After one evaluates not only the specific dimensions of financial trouble and possibly personal and contextual reasons for this trouble, one may also need to evaluate how this trouble is related to personality and relationship variables before beginning counseling. There are three different types of financial counseling programs: (1) credit union programs that provide remedial counseling to overcome immediate problems or learn long-range financial management, preventive advice on how to avoid possible pitfalls in the future, and productive services to individuals who want better investments for their money; (2) consumer credit service programs that concern themselves mostly with the establishment of a sound program of debt repayment; and (3) corporate financial counseling programs for employees who want advice on investments, estate planning, and utilization of tax shelters (Bagarozzi & Bagarozzi, 1980).

According to Bagarozzi and Bagarozzi (1980), the goals of family financial planning are: teaching responsible financial practices through management, decision-making, and planning; setting up and achieving realistic financial goals on the basis of the family's own value system; generation and exploration of various alternatives and strategies that will allow concrete implementation of stated goals; selection of appropriate management strategies consistent with the family's life-style and value system; and utilization of available information to improve problem-solving and to assure the achievement of stated goals (p. 398).

Financial management and planning, however, cannot take place until an initial stage of crisis has been resolved or at least reduced. One needs to deal with the feelings of guilt, inadequacy, and shame that many of these families carry with them after a financial failure. Once the tensions and anxieties in the family have been lowered, one can start asking specific questions about the nature, duration, intensity, extent, and outcome of the particular financial problems. One needs to separate facts from fantasies, reality from wishful thinking, and ascertain how much personal responsibility is assumed by family members for the present situation. Are all their financial troubles externalized onto other causes such as being laid off, having a nasty boss, etc.? How does the family feel about being a victim of external or internal circumstances? What are their expectations about the future? Do they want an immediate handout or do they want to work for their own betterment? In other words, as in any initial interview, the therapist needs to ascertain: (1) the antecendents that led to where the family is now, (2) what they have attempted to do to correct the situation, and (3) what they are willing to do for the future. How willing are they to assume responsibility for their own financial failure(s)?

Hence a thorough assessment and evaluation of the family's perceptions of the situation and their motivations in asking for help should take place from the outset. In this regard, Lopez (1983) discussed a counseling approach with individuals who lose their jobs due to corporate bankruptcy, to clarify marketable skills, review vocational test results, and focus on developing short-range plans to help clients reorient themselves to changed financial circumstances. DiGiulio and Janosik (1982) presented a rationale for a counseling program that provided both family and credit counseling, where the causes of financial problems as well as treatment and goals were dealt with in such a program, as part of a family service agency.

In sum, interventions with bankrupt families or families at risk for financial failure should focus on promoting money-management skills, as well as on alleviating the personal and interpersonal problems that lead to excessive spending, and on managing client hostility or passivity.

Money Management

Money management skills can be learned like any other skill, if there is sufficient motivation to learn. Guadagno (1981) performed a factor analysis of items defining the bill-paying domain of financial management. This analysis yielded five factors: planning an action sequence or schedule to pay bills, dividing bills into routine and non-routine ones, and scheduling specific times of payment for bills; implementing and checking by date the receipt of payment, recording amount of payment in a designated place, and keeping records of cash payments; deciding which bills need to be paid on time and which can be delayed; facilitating payment by paying through the bank or payroll deductions, and setting blocks of time to pay bills routinely; and feedback—that is, informing the spouse whether one has overspent and how much, and calling creditors to check on possible disagreements, discrepancies, or errors.

Working on a Budget It is also important to help the family learn to make up a budget sheet, with all the expected, actual income and possible ways of improving this income (predicted income) on the left side of the sheet. Expenses are listed on the right side and include all *fixed* expenses (rent or mortgage payments, car payments, insurance, etc.); all *variable* expenses (food, clothing, transportation, etc.); and all *discretionary* expenses (entertainment, vacations, travel, gifts, etc.). Expenses should be calculated on the basis of the actual income rather than on the basis of expected or predicted income. It is important to impress on the family the difference between *needs* and *wants*. Previous purchases were probably made on the basis of wants; to live within a stated budget, purchases will need to be limited to those that satisfy needs.

Lowering Expectations   Clearly the family needs to adjust to lowered expenditures, even if this means moving to cheaper housing, selling the family home, avoiding vacations or travel, and not giving gifts to anyone. Here it is important to discuss the discrepancy between the present and their past presentation facade—the impression they wanted to convey to others, to impress them through material goods and to keep up a front of affluence. In other words, the family has to face, adjust to, and contemplate an unpleasant reality, to give up fantasies of acquiring importance through external and material means. Can they learn to feel important even when they have little or no money? What kind of values were they accustomed to in the past? Who taught them these values, and why did they accept them uncritically and unquestioningly? What kind of values will they need to substitute and implement to lead them into moral and financial reliability and ultimate personal satisfaction?

Setting Realistic Goals   Goals should be differentiated into short- and long-term, concrete and intangible, realistic and unrealistic, responsible and irresponsible ones. Is fiscal responsibility and reliability more important than the superficial impression the family wants to make on others? What can the family aspire to within a year? Within two years? Within five years? What are the long-range goals of the family? Ultimately, as trite as it may seem, each family member has to ask about the meaning of life. How do they want to live their lives? As winners or as losers? Why? What are the consequences of winning? What are the consequences of losing? If they spend more than they earn, who is going to suffer the consequences?

Implementing Workable Strategies   What are the possible ways of increasing the income of the whole family? Should the unemployed mate get a job? Should the already-employed mate get a second part-time job or make sure that the full-time position already acquired is stable and secure? Should adolescents in the family learn to work and thus alleviate family expenditures by earning pocket money? How about baby-sitting or employment in fast-food shops? How about learning to become a trusted and respected employee, to earn credit for future recommendations and new jobs? By the same token, on the expenditure side of the ledger, what kind of sacrifices will have to be made to limit expenses? Is an extra car necessary or can public transportation suffice for the needs of family members? Which expenses can legitimately be cut and which cannot? Everybody needs to participate in the decision-making process because every member of the family counts, and all of their input is needed.

Decreasing Tensions

Before training to help a family learn new skills begins, their level of stress should be lowered considerably. It would be quite inappropriate and futile to try to teach a family new skills while that family is in the midst of a crisis, facing possible bankruptcy or, worse, inprisonment of one of its members!

Crisis Intervention   The goal of the first session is not only to gather information relevant to plan tailor-made treatment, but also to establish rapport and trust and to decrease as much as possible the feelings of guilt, shame, remorse, embarrassment, and hurt. In addition to helping express these and other feelings, the therapist should lower the emotional temperature of the family by assigning homework tasks related to lowering tensions and allowing the non-destructive and non-judgemental expression of feelings. "Why don't you meet tomorrow at 8 P.M. to allow each of you to express how you feel for 5 minutes by the clock. Make sure you use only the personal pronoun 'I'; start a sentence with 'I feel,' followed by whatever feelings you have about the subject. Dad, you preside at this meeting, and I will hold you responsible for it. Who will be the secretary and take notes? I want to see what you all say at this meeting."

Another way of lowering tensions in the family right from the beginning is to have each family member complete on paper sentences like: "What I appreciate about me is ———. What I do not appreciate about me is ———. What I appreciate about you (husband, wife, child, etc.) is ———. What I do not appreciate about you is ———." In this fashion, the family is taught to express both hurtful and helpful emotions in a non-destructive fashion. In addition, this exercise allows the therapist to evaluate how the family functions or fails to function on the basis of what they feel and say about one another.

An additional exercise to access feelings is to ask everybody in turn to complete ten sentences using the stem "I feel ——— because ———." Once this sequence is finished and practiced to the point of everyday usage, the next exercise consists of completing as many sentences as possible using the stem "I hurt when ———," or "It hurts me if ———." If people cannot complete this exercise, it may help to have them complete it on a "pretend" basis.

Lowering Anger, Frustration, and Anxiety   By the same token, the therapist can start to explore how hurtful feelings are kept in and unexpressed, or expressed directly or indirectly, verbally or nonverbally. "Who cries in this family? What happens when ——— cries? Who gets angry? Who leaves the room? Who stays and comforts her or him? How is anger expressed in this family? Explosively? Hurt collecting and then exploding? Is anger expressed at all?" Here is where patterns of approach-avoidance (distance regulation), and discharge-delay (control) need to be assessed in their impact between family members—how each family member acts and reacts in relation to other family members' behavior.

Dealing with Depression   Under the distraction of many addictions, and excessive spending is no exception, lurks the influence of avoided and denied depression—sad, hurt feelings from past traumas, abuses, neglects, and frustrations that have been repressed, suppressed, and short-circuited (L'Abate, 1987). Since this is the most pervasive, frequent, and influencial condition in everyday life, it is important to have a definite plan for dealing with it, rather than dealing with it reactively. Consequently, each therapist should develop such a plan and use it either in the office therapy or in written homework assignments (L'Abate, 1986). Such a program is available in workbook format and is being evaluated in comparison to two other workbooks developed from Beck's cognitive therapy approach to depression and the Depression Content Scale on the MMPI-2 (L'Abate, 1992). An example of how this approach was coupled with ongoing marital therapy was presented by Johnston, Levis, and L'Abate (1986).

Planning for the Future to Avoid Relapse

The temporal perspective of many addicts is limited to the moment and to the immediacy of personal or interpersonal gratification, no matter what the long-term consequences may be. A long-range temporal perspective on financial responsibility should be introduced in terms of outcomes and costs. Emphasis should be on how every minute, day, and week count now and how they will affect the future of the family. Historical and situational reasons for past failures should be discussed in terms of how they have affected the family's bankruptcy. The establishment of more realistic and consistent goals and strategies for the future must be reinforced concretely, by implementing step-by-step sequences of actions. In some cases the inevitability of specific steps in establishing a different life style must be stressed: "I know it is hard. If you can come up with something better, please do so. This is all I can think of at this time."

Working for the Long Haul   Often these families want better working conditions or will want to move somewhere else to avoid dealing with what they perceive as shameful stigmas and impaired reputations. Fantasies of moving to more inviting towns or states may be abundant. Sometimes such fantasies may be based on knowledge and reality, but more often these fantasies of a nirvana elsewhere are based on wishful thinking and avoidance of a painful reality. The nature of these fantasies should be pointed out: "You need to make decisions on the basis of what *is*, no matter how painful, rather than on what *could be*, no matter how pleasant it may seem. What would happen if, after the move, you find yourselves in the same condition you are now?" It is not unusual for some of these families to have moved frequently in search of the fantasized perfect job, perfect working conditions, perfect neighborhood, etc. These experiences should be clarified as examples of the family being controlled by unrealistic perceptions of what life is, and as indications of futile attempts to avoid unpleasantness whenever it occurs in their lives.

Learning to Negotiate Win-Win Conditions   Negotiation skills can be learned through regular family conferences or through a programmed negotiation workbook, consisting of eight lessons dealing with such topics as setting family goals; learning the norm of reciprocity; becoming conductive after becoming aware of one's apathy and reactivity; clarifying personal, marital, and familial priorities; and going through the various steps of negotiating (L'Abate, 1986). The process of learning how to negotiate may take place through the medium of money and possessions. Given that all budgets have limits, how can various goals be reached with a minimum of emotional turmoil and cost to everyone involved?

Increasing Intimacy   Ultimately, to survive emotionally as well as economically and materially, the family needs to learn to express and share their hurts, to stress the importance of being present and available to each other, rather than valuing material success and achievement as the (substitute) way of achieving personal satisfaction. Money and goods are important, but they are not substitutes for being close with each other. The therapist should stress the importance of expressing and sharing painful, sad, and unpleasant feelings with each other: "If you cannot share your hurts, how can you share your joys together?"

Conclusion

Excessive spending, no matter what its roots, can lead to bankruptcy or, worse, to imprisonment. Like other addictions, such spending is another illegitimate way to bolster an inadequate sense of self-importance. The therapist needs to help these individuals, couples, and families to establish a more adequate sense of self-worth through constructive means, such as teaching better ways of managing money and of relating to each other, and giving them a more future-oriented perspective without fantasized nirvanas. Many bankrupt families are so ashamed of their failure that they will avoid asking for help until forced to do so by a judge or a welfare agency. Responsibility will be externalized on everybody else, so bankrupt families are no easier to help than families with seemingly more serious addictions. Excessive spending is just as serious as any substance abuse or violence.

References

Ater, C., & Deacon, R. E. (1972). Intersection of family relationship qualities and managerial components. *Journal of Marriage and the Family, 51,* 257–262.

Atkinson, D., Fenster, C., & Blumberg, A. S. (1976). Employer attitudes toward work-release programs and the hiring of offenders. *Criminal Justice and Behavior, 3,* 335–344.

Austin, R. L., (1982). Women's liberation and increases in minor, major, and occupational offenses. *Criminology, 20,* 407–430.

Bagarozzi, J. I., & Bagarozzi, D. A. (1980). Financial counseling: A self-control model for the family. *Family Relations, 29,* 396–403.

Beattie, A. D. (1962). *Relationships between high school pupils' information and attitudes toward personal finance.* Unpublished doctoral dissertation, University of Minnesota, Minneapolis.

Bergler, E. (1984). *Money and emotional conflicts.* Edison, NJ: Inernational Universities Press.

Boris, H. N. (1986). The "other" breast: Greed, envy, spite and revenge. *Contemporary Psychoanalysis, 22,* 45–59.

Caudill, D. W. (1988). How to recognize and deter employee theft. *Personnel Administrator, 33,* 86–90.

Davis, H. L. (1970). Dimensions of marital roles in consumer decision making. *Journal of Marketing Research, 7,* 168–177.

Deacon, R. E., & Firebaugh, F. M. (1981). *Family resource management.* Boston: Allyn and Bacon.

DiGiulio, J. F., & Janosik, G. J. (1982). Successful partners: Credit counseling and family services. *Social Casework, 63,* 482–488.

Feinberg, R. A. (1986). Credit cards as spending facilitating stimuli: A conditioning interpretation. *Journal of Consumer Research, 13,* 348–356.

Feldman, F. L. (1976). *The family in today's money world.* New York: Family Service Association of America.

Fetterman, E. (1976). *Money management: Choices and decisions.* Boston: Houghton Mifflin.

Fowler, R. L., & Hunt, C. A. (1977). Awarding of credit cards: Reactive and nonreactive results compared. *Psychological Reports, 41,* 735–745.

Garcia, G. (1980). Credit cards: An interdisciplinary survey. *Journal of Consumer Research, 6,* 327–337.

Ginsburg, L. M., & Ginsburg, S. A. (1983). Some clinical and psychobiographical aspects of personal bankruptcy: A psychoanalytic inquest. *Journal of Psychiatry and the Law, 11,* 19–28.

Guadagno, M. A. N. (1981, October). *A systems approach to family financial management implications for family research.* Paper presented at the annual meeting of the National Council for Family Relations, Milwaukee, WI.

Gurin, G., & Gurin, P. (1976). Personal efficacy and the ideology of individual responsibility. In B. Strumpel (Ed.), *Economic means for human needs.* Ann Arbor, MI: Institute for Social Research.

Heidensohn, F. M. (1985). *Women and crime: The life of the female offender.* New York: New York University Press.

Hirschman, E. C. (1981). Comments on credit cards: An interdisciplinary survey. *Journal of Consumer Research, 7,* 420–424.

Hoffman-Bustamante, D. (1973). The nature of female criminality. *Issues in Criminology, 8,* 117–136.

Jaffe, L. J., & Senft, H. (1966). The roles of husbands and wives in purchasing decisions. In L. Adler & I. Crespt (Eds.)., *Attitude research at sea.* Chicago: American Marketing Association.

Johnston, T. B., Levis, M., & L'Abate, L. (1986). Treatment of depression in a couple with systematic homework assignments. *Journal of Psychotherapy and the Family, 2,* 117–128.

Kramer, J. H., & Steffensmeier, D. J. (1977). Reactions of male inmates to male and female offenders: Sex bias in prison? *International Journal of Contemporary Sociology, 14,* 169–184.

Krueger, D. W. (1988). On compulsive shopping and spending: A psychodynamic inquiry. *American Journal of Psychotherapy, 42,* 574–584.

L'Abate, L. (1986). *Systematic family therapy.* New York: Brunner/Mazel.

L'Abate, L. (1987). The denial of depression and its consequences. In L. L'Abate, *Family psychology II: Theory, therapy, enrichment, and training* (pp. 153–165). Washington, DC: University Press of America.

L'Abate, L. (1992). *Programmed writing: A self-administered approach for interventions with individuals, couples, and families.* Pacific Grove, CA: Brooks/Cole.

Lee, G. (1979). Marital structure and economic systems. *Journal of Marriage and the Family, 41,* 701–714.

Lopez, F. G. (1983). The victims of corporate failure: Some preliminary observations. *Personnel & Guidance Journal, 61,* 631–632.

Martell, T. F., & Fitts, R. L. (1981). A quadratic discriminant analysis of bank credit card user characteristics. *Journal of Economics and Business, 33,* 153–159.

McWilliams, N. (1984). The psychology of the altruist. *Psychoanalytic Psychology, 1,* 193–213.

Nichols, A., Mumaw, C. R., Paynter, M., Plonk, M. A., & Price, D. Z. (1971). Family management. *Journal of Marriage and the Family: A Decade of Family Research and Action—1960-1969* (pp. 91–97). Minneapolis, MI: National Council for Family Relations.

Ohberg, H. G., Haring, G. F., & Marsh, R. F. (1982). Embezzlement and multiple personality. *Medical Hypnoanalysis, 3,* 153–163.

Paulsen, K., Rimm, D. C., Woodburn, L. T., & Rimm, S. A. (1977). A self-control approach to inefficient spending. *Journal of Consulting and Clinical Psychology, 45,* 433–435.

Pogrebin, M. R., Poolem, E. D., & Regoli, R. M. (1986). Stealing money: An assessment of bank embezzlers. *Behavioral Sciences and the Law, 4,* 481–490.

Poppe, M., & Utens, L. (1986). Effects of greed and fear of being gypped in a social dilemma situation with changing pool size. *Journal of Economic Psychology, 7,* 61–73.

Rappoport, A. (1987). Research paradigms and expected utility models for the provision of step-level public goods. *Psychological Review, 94,* 74–83.

Robbins, M. A. (1983). The advantages of a timely bankruptcy. *Family Advocate, 5,* 15.

Rolfe, P. J. (1974). The financial priorities inventory. *The Family Coordinator, 23,* 139–144.

Shuptrine, F. K., & Samuelson, G. (1976). Dimensions of marital roles in consumer decision-making revisited. *Journal of Marketing Research, 13,* 87–91.

Simon, R. J. (1975). *Women and crime.* Lexington, MA: Lexington Books.

Simon, R. J. (1976). American women and crime. *Annals of the American Academy of Political and Social Science, 423,* 31–46.

Steffensmeier, D. J. (1978). Crime and the contemporary woman: An analysis of changing levels of female property crime, 1960–1975. *Social Forces, 57,* 566–584.

Welch, M. (1988, August). *Integrating value systems research, value clarification and sociological practice in prisons.* Paper presented at the annual meeting of the American Sociological Association, Atlanta, GA.

Yamagishi, T., & Sato, K. (1986). Motivational bases of the public goods problem. *Journal of Personality and Social Psychology, 50,* 67–73.

Zeitz, D. (1981). *Women who embezzle or defraud: A study of convicted felons.* New York: Praeger.

16

Religious Fanaticism

LUCIANO L'ABATE,
Ph.D.
GREGORY T. SAMPLES,
L.C.S.W.

DORIS W. HEWITT,
Ph.D.

RELIGIOUS FANATICISM IS DEFINED as any abuse or overuse, in word or deed, of the deity and of religious ideals or values that control or are controlled by an individual's rigid and unbending behavior, and make that individual want to control others by imposing these values on them and/or requiring others who depend on him or her to exhibit absolute conformity to his or her beliefs. Religion becomes an addiction when it is used to control and manipulate self and others at the expense of other people and/or at the expense of appropriate behaviors, such as taking care of oneself and one's responsibilities, both emotional and practical, toward members of one's family. Religious fanaticism should be distinguished from other forms of fanaticism concentrated on political or non-religious bases (Haynal, Molnar, & de Puymege, 1983; Rudin, 1969). There may be considerable overlap among fanatics, regardless of ideological content, so religious fanaticism could be considered as one subspecies of fanaticism in general.

Rudin (1969) suggested that fanaticism, regardless of its nature, is a problem of intensity that could range from a positive extreme, as a spontaneous expression of one's vitality, to a negative extreme, as compensation for denied inadequacies, with an obsessive drive towards absolutism. In fact, Rudin described the self-concept of the fanatic as being based on compensatory mechanisms made up of "escape-values"—that is, substitute or artificial values—as seen in the avoidance of personal realities that are too painful and unacceptable to consider or confront. He suggested a classification of the fanatic personality as being: psychopathic, hysteric, schizoid, or obsessive-compulsive. Thus far, the major explanations for the development of fanaticism in general have been based on psychoanalytic thinking (Haynal et al., 1983; Rudin, 1969), reducing the phenomenon to unconscious factors that the addict has repressed and denied.

Incidence and Implications of Religious Fanaticism

Where can one draw the line between religious fanaticism and legitimate spiritual yearning? In America, religion has been so much a part of the historical and cultural heritage ever since the Pilgrims' landing, that one would find it impossible to draw a clear line. For an interesting historical review of religious fanaticism in America, the reader is referred to Smith (1976). General sources are Clemen (1931) and Spiegelberg (1956). Any estimate of incidence for this addiction is bound to be off the mark. In spite of possible difficulties, it is important to attempt to differentiate between fanaticism and healthy religion.

Characteristics of religion-dominated individuals are: (a) restricted awareness and relative insensitivity to feelings; (b) codependency of the wife on the husband, which indicates the importance of considering addictions within a context of mutual attraction (i.e., the selfish attracting the selfless) and the inability to draw firm lines and boundaries to protect the self (as discussed in greater detail in Chapter 17); (c) the husband's passivity and sexual acting out whenever he cannot live up to expectations, although he demands to have authority without carrying out marital and parental responsibilities, a role in which he feels supported by the pastor; (d) rigid, dichotomous, either/or thinking that makes the religious fanatic come close to the stereotype of the fascist personality, characterized by prejudice and discrimination against anyone who does not have the same beliefs. The explicit or implicit demand for blind acceptance and conformity to one's beliefs makes the overly religious individual fit within the continuum of selfishness-selflessness. Many charismatic religious leaders and TV evangelists would fit at one extreme of this continuum, and their followers would fall into the other extreme.

Support for some of the foregoing conclusions can be found in the literature. For instance, Allport's (1966) description of religion as extrinsic, and therefore an end in and by itself, was studied by Watson, Hood, and Morris (1984) in 225 undergraduates. These authors found a positive relationship between religion as an end in itself and the emotional and cognitive aspects of empathy.

Moon and Fantuzzo (1983) emphasized how indicators of positive mental health have a great many similarities (and some differences) with Christian maturity and wholeness. These differences were investigated by Elzerman and Boivin's study (1987) with 120 undergraduates. They found few if any relationships between two measures of religiosity and of Christian maturity, suggesting that religion, at least at the present time is independent of personality and psychopathology; or, to put it another way, there are as many personalities and psychopathologies in believers as there are in non-believers.

Wilson (1989) concluded that persons with certain personality types or pathology may be less able than others to benefit from evangelical religion, for unknown reasons. She compared 67 adult children of alcoholics and 62 adult children of non-alcoholics who were affiliated with a variety of evangelical churches. The adult children of alcoholics appeared to be significantly more depressed, self-blaming, distrustful, and guilt-prone, and they reported more difficulty trusting God's will, experiencing divine love and forgiveness, believing God's promises, and forgiving others than did the adult children of non-alcoholics. The Christians who were adult children of alcoholics continued striving to experience God's love and care, and yet appeared to suffer emotionally just as much as adult children of alcoholics in the general population. This process raised a question as to why the faith of these individuals from alcoholic families failed to make more of a practical difference in their lives. Wilson suggested that this phenomenon may relate to a primary defense mechanism in which people from dysfunctional backgrounds may tend to either ignore or blindly accept discrepancies between what is postulated and what they experience in their own relationship with God.

More recently, Bergin, Stinchfield, Gaski, and Masters (1988) in an extensive and intensive study of lifestyles of religious undergraduates, found that students with continuous religious development and mild religious experiences appeared healthier psychologically than those students with discontinuous development and intense religious experiences. The intense religious experiences, however, tended to enhance adjustment. These investigators found no evidence for an overall negative or positive correlation between religiosity and mental health. However, some modes of religious involvement appeared to be related to disturbance, and other modes seemed related to enhanced stability and resilience, supporting the conclusions reached above. There is no question that the issue of religiosity and adjustment will continue to generate spirited debates.

The sole exception to the above conclusion of no relationship between religiosity and adjustment may be found in cases of extreme and excessive religiosity, i.e. fanaticism, where religion is used to mask personal inadequacies. Washburn (1982), in his study relating spiritual attachment to Ainsworth's differentiation of secure versus anxious types of attachment (Ainsworth, Blehar, Waters & Wall, 1978), found that the same types of distinction can be applied to religious attachments as well: secure versus insecure attachments. This conclusion is supported by McAdams' (1988) findings concerning the relationship between ego development, as defined by Loevinger (1976), Kohlberg's stages of moral development (1969), and religiosity. Starting from two basically intrapsychic dimensions of power and intimacy, derived from Bakan's (1966) notions of agency and communion, McAdams found that individuals high on intimacy motivation, as measured from Thematic Apperception Test stories, would describe a "meaningful religious experience" in terms of giving and sharing feelings with people. This sharing included tender touching as part of this experience, and also participation in religious rituals with a sense of community or togetherness, with God as an intimate companion (pp. 225–226). Students high on power motivation, on the other hand, described meaningful religious experiences primarily in terms of heroism, inspiration, and power from above. Subjects' religious views seemed related also to their level of ego development; that is, the higher the ego development, the more complex and well articulated were their religious beliefs.

Ego development, as measured by Loevinger's (1976) sentence completion test, may be a helpful tool to evaluate the level of ego development in addictions. Most but not all addicts, especially individuals on the selfish extreme, would score at what Loevinger called the impulsive stage, one of the lowest levels of ego development.

Although it may be difficult to judge the extent of religious fanaticism in the American population, there seems to be a pattern sufficiently pervasive to have a possible negative impact on many lives. For instance, popular TV evangelists have apparently influenced the lives of many, especially the old and invalids (mostly women) who send much of their Social Security money to the evangelists (mostly men) for the aggrandizement and glory of the evangelists themselves (the selfish leading the selfless!). Thus, these naive citizens lose financial resources and in some instances are ultimately disillusioned upon learning the true motives of these leaders.

In spite of our inability to estimate adequately the extent of religious addiction, it is pervasive enough to warrant some extrapolations from existing evidence. For instance, the 1985 Gallup Poll on religion found that 91 percent of Americans reported a religious preference, with 56 percent of that group stating that religion was very important for them. In fact, 61 percent of this sample believed that religion can answer all or most of today's problems! In a more recent Gallup Poll of 539 college students, nearly 80 percent said religion was important in their lives and 55 percent reported that they had attended at least one worship service during the month preceding the survey. A conservative assumption, that 1 percent of the total American population follows extreme religious attitudes and practices, would show a minimum of 2.5 million fanatics. An increase of another percentage point would double that figure. Even the lowest estimate would warrant professional interest in this form of addiction.

How are religious fanatics different from cult followers? Cults, of course, are allegedly religious or quasi-religious organizations that function outside the mainstream of the predominant organized religions

(Beckford, 1985; Evans, 1973; Pavlos, 1982). Most cult followers share many of the characteristics of religious fanatics, although religious fanatics may not necessarily be cult followers. Enroth (1977) listed some of the characteristics of cultic commitment that may also be present in fanatics: (a) willingness to strive for goals that seem impossible to achieve, such as converting the whole world; (b) unswerving loyalty and extreme commitment to the cause and the attainment of its goals; (c) demands that one give away material possessions; (d) isolation and rejection of worldly values, habits, and associations, including family and friends.

The last two points may be especially useful to distinguish cult followers from those with extreme religious attitudes. Many religious people may share some commonality with the first two points above, but may fail to follow the last points of the list. They would hold on to their possessions, although they might give part of their income to their church and contribute to special religious causes and/or to TV evangelists. They would also support old, established, and familiar patterns of religious belief and practice. Fanatics might do these same things but with a great deal of isolation from non-believers. Once a distinction between religious people and those who are religiously fanatical is achieved, one must still address the following question: How are religious fanatics different from other addicts?

In the first place, religious fanaticism is socially acceptable due to the puritanical background on which this nation was founded, and it is generally within the laws of the land. What harm could one do with religion? Perhaps very little. However, one must ask how many lives and families have been destroyed by cults' requests that, in order to prove their faith, neophytes must leave their homes and families, or even give all of their belongings and earnings to the cult? How many people have been driven crazy or to suicide by rigid demands for blind conformity, especially those made by parents, who blame and make abusive and punitive judgements under the guise of religious attitudes? How many character disorders, with oppositionality and rebellion among others as their major characteristics, are the result of a reactive pattern to one's parents' religious beliefs that were used as a big stick to obtain unquestioning obedience, docile passivity, and continuing acquiescence? Except for cults that are so outlandish in their customs and obnoxious in their practices that they are widely rejected, many cults and sects flourish freely, usually under the leadership of a charismatic figure (Beckford, 1985; Evans, 1973; Pavlos, 1982). After the leader dies or leaves, these cult groups are usually terminated or disbanded.

In the second place, by specifying the characteristics of religious fanaticism, we should be able to distinguish it from other addictions. This distinction can be made clearer once we examine the functions religion serves in people's lives. As discussed earlier, religion serves many legitimate purposes, like enhancing spirituality, giving existential meaning, uplifting and upgrading values and expectations, giving encouragement and a greater sense of self-worth, etc. By the same token, religion can also perform many illegitimate, abusive functions, those very functions that define religious fanaticism.

The Functions of Religious Fanaticism

Religious fanaticism in America is much more socially acceptable and per-haps more pronounced and extreme than in many other countries, because of the relative freedom with which we can worship. Consequently, religion can perform negative functions that may change from individual to individual, but that are nevertheless important. Religion can function as an escape or avoidance of reality, as shown by denial and other defenses against what is perceived as dysphoric, sad, and unpleasant, i.e., depressive affect.

Religious addictions, like most others, have the function of filling up a weak, chaotic, inconsistent, and incomplete internal self-structure (i.e., self-definition and identification) with an externally given structure. This incompleteness in self-structure is one of the characteristics of the obsessive, driven personality (Salzman, 1968, 1980) that leads to excesses, such as perfectionism. Gibson (1983) found the same characteristics in extreme cases of evangelism. "Seeking God" and "seeking God's will" may be manipulative words to control others or to free oneself from personal responsibility for decisions, externalizing one's behavior into "God's hand." In extreme cases, for instance, daily devotions may become repetitive, compulsive rituals, like buying favors from God: "If I behave and am good, I will be rewarded."

Under these conditions, the individual fills up the incompleteness of the self with an external object that does not belong there. A study of the God images of seven women with multiple personalities (Bowman, Coons, Jones & Olstrom, 1987), for instance, found that many of these images derived from severe parental abuse, both physical and sexual. A model of self-definition, presented and expanded in greater detail elsewhere (L'Abate, 1992b) posits a dimension defined by extremes in selfishness versus extremes in selflessness. This dimension suggests that in the extreme of selflessness, experienced mainly by women, there would be a borrowed identification, like victim or martyr, where the deity, the mate, or both becomes the saviour and rescuer of the woman's helplessness. Some men, on the other hand, abuse religion as a way of satisfying their selfishness by attracting and using selfless women as wives and as followers. Some men have become skilled at quoting scriptures out of context in an effort to justify their selfish behavior, such as quoting Paul's admonition to the Ephesians, "Wives, submit yourselves unto your husband," but ignoring Paul's instructions several verses later exhorting *both* husbands and wives to submit themselves to each other. The selfish individual's identification is one of rescuer and saviour, images that are strongly supported by McAdams' work (1988).

Since many religious fanatics come from abusive and apathetic family backgrounds with irrational and contradictory rules and practices, religion under these circumstances may furnish a source of control over what is perceived as evil (i.e., a chaotic and incomprehensible reality) both within and outside the self. Natural human feelings, emotions, urges, and drives, especially anger, are perceived as overwhelming, because there are no words to express them appropriately. Hence, all of these undifferentiated internal urgings and tensions are viewed with further fear and anxiety. What is one to do with them, especially if previous models (parents) expressed them inconsistently and contradictorily, varying from being mainly violent and abusive to being apathetic? The tendency is for these people to do the opposite of what they were doing before. If they were uncontrolled, they make sure the feelings become controlled. If they were dominated by "irrational" emotions, if strong emotions were acted out rather than talked out, then they avoid, deny, suppress and repress them, sometimes to the point of dissociation.

From L'Abate's (1992b) model, we could surmise that religion is one way of achieving self-importance. The less important the individual feels, the greater the tendency to rely on religion and its rituals to replace incomplete feelings of self-importance. The reparation function of religion is commensurate to the degree of self-importance and self-reliance. The less self-important individual will rely on external structures to make up for inadequate internal self-structures.

Treatment Guidelines

One of the many issues in the treatment of extreme religious attitudes is identification of the limits where legitimate and enhancing religiosity ends and illegitimate and destructive fanaticism begins. In this regard, Smith's (1986) Christian life assessment scales may go a long way toward the beginning of this identification. Subjective criteria for identification may include finding out how reactive the family is to itself and to the external reality—i.e., is religion exploited, abusively and/or apathetically, to avoid taking personal responsibility for one's actions? Another aspect might be to examine the extent of polarization in the marriage; that is, whether selflessness and codependent passivity in one partner corresponds to selfishness in the other. Religious fanaticism is also characterized by singularity and rigidity of purpose, to the extent that religion colors and controls all aspects of life, not only within the individual but also within his or her personal relationships, so that beliefs and practices are imposed on others or are used to denigrate others. In other words, no respect is shown for others' individuality, differentness, beliefs, lifestyle, and practices.

Religious fanaticism is one of the most difficult addictions to treat because the fanatic feels so righteous and correct in his or her position that to consider the condition as a sickness would be abhorrent. Religious fanaticism poses a contradiction in terms, for to those who are fanatical, to be "saved" (or its equivalent to those who use other terminology) means automatically to be healthy. How can one be a "true" or "real" Christian and still be depressed, or anxious, or worried? For many who believe this way, treatment would be equated to losing one's identity and one's reason for living.

In fact, religiously fundamental people tend to be quite reluctant to seek professional mental health services (Wicker & Johnson, 1988). Extreme beliefs have become so central to the addict's identity that to consider these beliefs as invalid would be tantamount to abandoning God, being abandoned by God, and/or being bereft of any defenses that would justify existence. In addition, if the patient is a member of a cult or congregation with similar beliefs that serves as a support group or as surrogate parents and counselors, it is practically impossible to change that person's views unless something drastic happens. Many extremely fanatic cults and sects maintain a completely adversarial position with the mental health and psychotherapy establishments, seeing them as the product of the devil at worst, or representatives of a sinful, worldly, and decadent society at best.

Quackenbos, Privette, and Klentz (1986), in discussing the relationship between religion and counseling, suggested that the four possible positions with regard to this relationship (orthodox, atheistic, agnostic or neutral, and moderate) contain the seeds for an understanding. Professional therapists need to be aware of and prepared to address religious issues regardless of intensity and pervasiveness. In fact, these authors suggest that the time has come "to seriously consider specialized education and certification in religious counseling for secular psychotherapists" (p. 82).

What could happen that would encourage someone with a fanatic religious orientation to seek professional help? Often these individuals are unable to see the inconsistencies and illogical contradictions, not only within their belief system, but also between that belief system and reality. Apart from outright kidnapping and debriefing, as done by the parents of some youthful converts, one has to wait for a crisis within the individual and/or within the individual's family or religious group. In the face of such a crisis, beliefs may no longer make sense, and the individual is left without an internal support system, either in self-definition or in the defensive self-structure. For instance, a person may be so driven by devotion to a given cult that he or she gives it everything in terms of money, time, and energy until a financial or health crisis or loss of employment occurs. One or more such crises may help the individual face reality and see the need to abandon the cult. Also, a cult or other religious group may have rules and regulations that a person eventually finds unacceptable for a wide variety of reasons, thus leading to abandonment of religious extremes.

The reason for referral to therapy may seem completely independent of the belief system, as in cases of depression, attempted suicide, psychotic break, etc. The treatment and the rapport to be established should be based on the referring symptom and not on religious beliefs. However, the initial reason for referral may become the basis by which the fanatic may start to share with the therapist his or her fears, worries, and anxieties. From these concerns, the therapist can start, very carefully, to draw out historical background information, past traumas, experiences, and events that may have, in part, produced a need to rely on a rigid religious system to survive. In other words, the fanatic may see the religious system as the rescuer from a fate worse than death: depression, nonexistence, and the fear of hell and damnation.

Therefore, religious fanaticism will often come to the fore of the therapeutic relationship after the referral symptom has been treated more or less successfully, or when extreme religious attitudes interfere with treatment. Switching the focus of treatment from one symptom to another (religious belief) is a crucial step. Often the therapist cannot straightforwardly inform the client that his or her religious attitudes are related to the existence or maintenance of the original symptom. Such a confrontation could be perceived as a challenge and a criticism that the individual is frequently not ready to accept. At this point, he or she may abandon treatment. Therefore, the therapist should be very careful about the timing and phrasing of any direct or indirect confrontation related to the belief system. Here anecdotes, metaphors, and even appropriate quotations or stories from the Bible may be useful. Whatever confrontation is eventually made must take place within a context of positive affirmation, unconditional support, care, and compassion.

In dealing with religious fanatics, the following points should be considered for at least the first interview, in order to decide whether and how help can best be given (outpatient, inpatient, individually, maritally, familially, or in a group).

1. The initial acceptance of the belief system and of the defensive structure must be coupled with unconditional regard, warmth, and acceptance of the individual. Positive reframings of the reason for referral are crucial at the beginning stage of treatment: "Only strong (responsible, caring) people ask for help. You must be pretty strong to ask for help now," or "You must be here because you care about yourself. Is that right?"

From the outset the therapist must assess the sense of self-importance that the individual attributes to himself or herself. Probably this sense will be either defective ("I am not important") or missing, so that the individual cannot even conceive of being important. ("What is that? I never thought of it.") With the spouse or other family members one can readily assess how disparagement of the patient may take place verbally, non-verbally, directly, or indirectly, by omission and commission. This disparagement may be expressed according to religious absolutes, with acceptance and love being conditional on "being saved" or on attending church and performing good deeds.

2. Above all, do not challenge any statements that indicate the validity of a rigid, extreme religious belief system. In fact, avoid getting involved with beliefs and concentrate on the reason for the referral. If the client asks whether the therapist shares the same kind of belief system ("Are you a Christian?"), the therapist at this point may answer according to whatever he or she feels is in keeping with his or her standards of personal and professional integrity. One therapist may feel that people deserve a brief, honest answer that would lessen the chance of religion becoming a premature and inappropriate focus at this time in the relationship. Another therapist may ask why this information is important to the client and accept whatever explanation is given. Here the therapist may indicate that his or her primary commitment is to the welfare and well-being of the client, that religion is important, but this topic should be deferred to a later date, perhaps after the referral symptom has been treated. However, if the therapist prefers to answer the question directly, this is certainly acceptable, provided it is done briefly and with an accompanying comment that the therapist hopes the client is able to use his or her inner spiritual reserves in dealing with the current difficulty.

3. The therapist should concentrate on a thorough investigation of historical background, with emphasis on losses, abuses, rejections, and traumas that may have weakened the individual's internal identification and may have led him or her to substitute deity or religious leaders for self. Often the family background may suggest the presence of apathetic or abusive parental practices, deprivation, abandonment, and/or neglect. The family background may be a reactive one, in which the family is not able to negotiate crucial issues and to be intimate and close, especially at times of crisis and stress when being close matters the most. ("How were feelings expressed in your family?") The expression of anger is especially taboo in these families, thus reducing the entire gamut of emotional experiences and expressions.

4. The therapist should focus on the symptomatic behavior (tension, stress, anxiety, depression, etc.), if necessary reframing it as being a positive manifestation of God's plan: "Depression is God's way to make us stop and reflect." Particularly when the name of God or scripture is used and abused to defeat the self and others, they can also be used by the therapist to enhance. If an extreme religious belief is stated as a challenge to the therapist and a reply seems appropriate and expected by the client,

a simple reflection of feelings may often suffice: "You really feel strongly about this issue."

Here is where the therapist must be alert to keeping his or her boundaries firm, to avoid becoming enmeshed in a power struggle with the client. Sometimes the name of the deity is used as a club to control and manipulate the therapist (or anybody else) through challenges to his or her value system. These are probes that indicate the need to affiliate and to come close, since closeness is felt to be in conforming: "If you behave as I do, you are okay, and I will accept you." By the same token, any indication of differentness is perceived as oppositeness: "You are either saved or you are not. If you are not, you need to be saved so I can come close to you." Again, religious beliefs determine the degree of distance from other people, regardless of personal likes or dislikes. The therapist must somehow gain a degree of closeness and acceptance before he or she can be listened to or respected enough to help the client recognize such patterns and the need to change them.

5. The therapist should encourage the active involvement of family members as much as possible, to evaluate how the belief system is supported, reinforced, and encouraged by them, or whether the religious fanatic is rejected as being an exception to the family's norms. At the outset positive reframings should concentrate on the nature and function of the symptom in keeping the family together and unchanged. Often the therapist's opinion will be challenged as being invalid and incorrect. When this negation takes place, the therapist should qualify his statements with humility: "Maybe you are right, and I am wrong about this issue." Since the individual and the family place a great deal of emphasis on being "right," the therapist should not be afraid to be "wrong," should avoid becoming defensive, and should appear to accept the family's viewpoint as given, without questioning it, since such questioning may be perceived as an attack on the family.

6. Only in time, after a trusting and caring relationship is established, can the therapist begin to raise questions about inconsistencies in the individual's and family's belief system and in their relationship with the external world. Helping to develop a more critical, questioning, and flexible attitude about self versus others and deity should be done through questioning rather than through direct statements or authoritative pronouncements.

7. Ideally, the therapist may go as far as helping the patient and his or her family to grasp the possibility that this addiction is defeating the individual and the family, and, ultimately, God's purpose. Such a possibility, however, should be raised as a question and never as a statement: "I wonder how much your need to be 'right' prevents all of you from being close."

8. Initially, if a therapeutic contract is agreed upon, the therapist may indicate that the patient and family should set aside some individual,

marital, or family time, perhaps one hour a week, to learn to negotiate issues with loved ones. Materials for written systematic homework assignments on depression, negotiation, and intimacy can be found in L'Abate (1986, 1992a).

9. Ultimately, the therapist might be able to help the family develop an ability to love unconditionally rather than conditionally, as fanaticism requires: "I will love you if you believe as I do!" This unconditional love is based on seeing the good in oneself and others and responding to that good with physical, practical, and economic caring, forgiveness, and intimacy (L'Abate, 1986). If the therapist is not aware of these elements of love, it will be impossible for the clients to grasp the nature of unconditional love and intimacy: the sharing of hurts and of fears of being hurt.

10. At times it may be helpful to ask the client to invest in his or her belief system in a new way: "Are your current spiritual investments working? If not, it may be that God wants you to learn and grow in a different way, such as spending more time with your spouse and children or spending time with yourself to reflect about your past, present, or future. If you plan to devote more time to yourself, you may find it helpful to make appointments to be by yourself at a specific time and place, to write down whatever comes into your head at the time" (L'Abate, 1986, 1987).

It may be helpful to change the structure of the marital relationship by asking the client to give more control of the spouse to God and to allow God to keep control: "What would happen if you gave up your control?" Often control is a basic issue with fanatics; the therapist should explore why so much control is needed and how such a need developed.

If the therapist is able to establish a flexible and helpful rapport with the client(s) over a period of time, she or he may eventually be able to provoke the beginning of independent and constructive thinking with surprising statements and questions: "Do you suppose it is possible that your mate will ever be able to achieve as direct a line to God as you have?" or "You have taken on a tremendous responsibility. Don't you ever get tired of filling in for God in the family?"

11. Measured and timely self-disclosure by the therapist is always helpful, provided it is not used to indicate how much better or better off the therapist is in comparison to the client: "I too wanted to force others to do what seemed right to me, but I finally realized that God himself doesn't force them, so what right do I have to do so?" or "I used to assume a lot of responsibility, as you seem to, by trying to play God and make things happen, but then I tried giving up that responsibility, and I was surprised to see that the sun still rose at the same time every morning!" "On the issue of control, it took me a lot of time, years, and effort to understand that I cannot control anybody. It's a full-time job just to control myself! I cannot control others unless I want to coerce and manipulate them!" On the issue of forgiveness, where religious fanatics are especially vulnerable, the therapist can admit to fallibility: "I am so surprised by how stupid I am, and after I forgive myself for all of my immense stupidity, I can forgive almost everybody, except perhaps Hitler!"

12. Another effective form of intervention may be introduced by encouraging the religious fanatic to talk about his or her religious concepts and how they have evolved since childhood. Many addicts are surprised to discover that they are unable to articulate such concepts, having never examined them closely or critically. This exploration may take place through the written word as a homework assignment to be done at specified, pre-arranged times: "Write what 'faith' means to you," or "Write down why being right seems more important to you than being close to the ones you love." Once this homework is brought back to the therapist, it can be used for a discussion of personal and interpersonal implications, carefully avoiding judgments or criticism.

Conclusion

Treatment of religious fanatics requires a thorough knowledge of Biblical or religious issues by the therapist. If the therapist is scornful, critical, or disdainful of such issues, he or she should perhaps avoid treating religious fanatics. This addiction is as challenging and difficult to deal with as any life-threatening addiction, especially if the deity is used and abused as a big club or stick in the sky to keep people (and the therapist) under control.

Although some addictions require a great deal of directness and firmness, religious fanaticism may require a great deal of indirectness by the therapist. Any direct confrontation or challenge to the belief system will be perceived immediately as criticism and rejection of the individual, since religious beliefs are so basic that they are often perceived as actually *being* the individual.

References

Ainsworth, M. D. S., Blehar, M., Waters, E., & Wall, S. (1978). *Patterns of attachment.* Hillsdale, NJ: Erlbaum.

Allport, G. W. (1966). Religious context of prejudice. *Journal for the Scientific Study of Religion, 5,* 447–457.

Bakan, D. (1966). *The duality of human experience: Isolation and communion in human experience.* Boston: Beacon Press.

Beckford, J. A. (1985). *Cult controversies: The social response to new religious movements.* London: Tavistock.

Bergin, A. E., Stinchfield, R. D., Gaskin, T. A., & Masters, K. S. (1988). Religious life-styles and mental health: An exploratory study. *Journal of Counseling Psychology, 35,* 91–98.

Bowman, E. S., Coons, P. M., Jones, R. S., & Oldstrom, M. (1987). Religious psychodynamics in multiple personalities: Suggestions for treatment. *American Journal of Psychotherapy, 41,* 542–554.

Clemen, C. (1931). *Religions of the world: Their nature and their history.* New York: Harcourt, Brace.

Cornwall, M. (1989). The determinants of religious behavior: A theoretical model and empirical test. *Social Forces, 68,* 2–18.

Donahue, M. J. (1985). Intrinsic and extrinsic religiousness: Review and meta-analysis. *Journal of Personality and Social Psychology, 48,* 400–419.

Elzerman, J. H., & Boivin, M. J. (1987). The assessment of Christian maturity, personality, and psychopathology among college students. *Journal of Psychology and Christianity, 6,* 50–64.

Enroth, R. (1977). *Youth, brainwashing, and the extremist cults.* Grand Rapids, MI: Zondervan.

Evans, C. (1973). *Cults of unreason.* New York: Farrar, Straus & Giroux.

Gibson, D. L. (1983). The obsessive personality and the evangelical. *Journal of Psychology and Christianity, 2,* 30–35.

Haynal, A., Molnar, M., & de Puymege, R. (1983). *Fanaticism: A historical and psychoanalytic study.* New York: Schocken.

Kohlberg, L. (1969). Stage and sequence: The cognitive-developmental approach to socialization. In D. A. Golin (Ed.), *Handbook of socialization theory and research* (pp. 347–480). Skokie, IL: Rand McNally.

L'Abate, L. (1986). *Systematic family therapy.* New York: Brunner/Mazel.

L'Abate, L. (1987). Therapeutic writing through homework assignments. In L. L'Abate, *Family Psychology II: Theory, therapy, enrichment, and training* (pp. 123–136). Lanham, MD: University Press of America.

L'Abate, L. (1992a). *Programmed writing: A self-administered approach for interventions with individuals, couples, and families.* Pacific Grove, CA: Brooks/Cole.

L'Abate, L. (1992b). *A theory of personality development.* New York: Brunner/Mazel.

L'Abate, L., & Samples, G. T. (1983). Intimacy letters—invariable prescription for closeness avoidant couples. *Family Therapy, 10,* 37–45.

Loevinger, J. (1976). *Ego development: Conceptions and theories.* San Francisco: Jossey-Bass.

McAdams, D. P. (1988). *Power, intimacy, and the life story: Personological inquiries into identity.* New York: Guilford.

McFarland, S. (1988, August). *Religious orientation and the targets of discrimination.* Paper presented at the annual meeting of the American Psychological Association, Atlanta, GA.

Moon, G. W., & Fantuzzo, J. (1983). An integration: Christian maturity and positive mental health. *Journal of Psychology and Christianity, 2,* 27–47.

Moy, S., & Malony, H. N. (1987). An empirical study of ministers' children and families. *Journal of Psychology and Christianity, 6,* 52–64.

Pavlos, A. J. (1982). *The cult experience.* Westport, CT: Greenwood.

Quackenbos, S., Privette, G., & Klentz, B. (1986). Psychotherapy and religion: Rapprochement or antithesis? *Journal of Counseling and Development, 65,* 82–85.

Rudin, J. (1969). *Fanaticism: A psychological analysis.* Notre Dame, IN: University of Notre Dame Press.

Salzman, L. (1968). *The obsessive personality.* New York: Science House.

Salzman, L. (1980). *Treatment of the obsessive personality.* New York: Aronson.

Smith, D. E. (1986). The Christian life assessment scales: Christian self-perception. *Journal of Psychology and Christianity, 5,* 46–61.

Smith, H. W. (1976). *Religious fanaticism.* New York: AMS Press.

Spiegelberg, F. (1956). *Living religions of the world.* Englewood Cliffs, NJ: Prentice-Hall.

Washburn, D. A. (1982). Dimensions of spiritual attachment. *Journal of Psychology and Christianity, 1,* 2–11.

Watson, P. J., Hood, R. W., Jr., & Morris, R. J. (1984). Dimensions of religiosity and empathy. *Journal of Psychology and Christianity. 4,* 73–85.

Wicker, D. A., & Johnson, R. W. (1988, August). Effects of counselor's Christian values on the client's perception of the counselor. Paper presented at the annual meeting of the American Psychological Association, Atlanta, GA.

Wilson, S. D. (1989). Evangelical Christian adult children of alcoholics. *Journal of Psychology and Theology, 17(9),* 269–279.

_17

Treating Codependency

LUCIANO L'ABATE,
Ph.D.

MARY G. HARRISON,
M.S.

CODEPENDENCY IS THE NEW buzz word in the counseling and psychotherapy of addictions (Treadway, 1990). Both professional and popular literature have focused on the plight of the spouse or partner of the addict, relating gender differences to the existence of destructive attractions between codependents and addicts (Beattie, 1987; Cermak, 1986; Friel & Friel, 1988; Forward & Torres, 1987; Langley & Levy, 1977; Leman, 1987; Norwood, 1985, 1988; Mellody, 1989; Mendenhall, 1989; Potter-Efron & Potter-Efron, 1989; Schaef, 1986; Whitfield, 1987, 1989). These and other sources too numerous to cite have highlighted dangerous polarizations between genders in adult children of dysfunctional families who marry each other. Most sources have focused in one way or another on the relative masochism of women and the relative sadism and narcissism of men in our society.

Definitions of Codependency

There are as many definitions of codependency as there are books on the topic. At last count there were 128 books written since 1978. Our review of the definitions is illustrative rather than exhaustive. Most definitions of codependency tend to stress the addictive, driven quality of this pattern, in the sense that, in keeping with the definition given in Chapter 1, codependency controls the individual's life at the expense of other spheres of activity. Beattie (1987), for instance, defines the codependent as a person who allows another person's behavior to affect him or her and who is obsessed (and therefore controlled) with controlling that person's behavior. Schaef (1986) sees codependency as an emotional, psychological, and behavioral condition that develops as a result of an individual's prolonged exposure to and practice of a set of oppressive rules that prevent the open expression of feelings and the direct discussion of personal and interpersonal problems. This characteristic is especially relevent to the treatment of codependents. The codependent seeks a partner who "should" live by a set of rules that are similar to his or her own. Subby and Friel (1984) expanded on the rules that control codependency as a dysfunctional pattern of living and problem solving that is reinforced by a set of rules within the family system. These rules prevent open expression of feelings as well as direct confrontation and discussion of personal and interpersonal problems (Schaef, 1986, p. 15). Additional rules are: (a) it is not acceptable to talk about problems; (b) feelings should not be expressed openly; (c) communication is best if indirect, with one person acting as messenger between two others (triangulation); (d) be strong, good, right, and perfect; (e) make us proud of your performance (at the expense of presence); (e) don't be selfish; (f) do as I say, not as I do; (g) it's not acceptable to play or be playful, laugh and enjoy life; and (h) maintain the status quo and do not rock the boat.

Schaef (1986) saw codependents as "anyone who has been affected by the person who has been afflicted by the disease of chemical dependency . . . in close association over a prolonged period of time with anyone with a neurotic personality" (pp. 17–18). One aspect of this personality consists of "self-defeating, learned behaviors or character defects that result in a diminished capacity to initiate or participate in loving relationships" (Larsen, 1987, p. 17). Cermak (1986, 1988) defines codependency diagnostically as a recognizable personality pattern of traits that is predictably found in most members of chemically dependent families. This pattern is capable of creating sufficient personal dysfunctionality to warrant a diagnosis of Mixed Personality Disorder, according to the DSM-III.

What is an acceptable working definition of codependence? We tend to agree with Schaef (1986), who sees it as just one more form of the addictive process—an underlying, generic, primary behavioral pattern that is promoted by the addictive society in which we live. Furthermore, we need to understand codependency as another form of addiction that lends itself to treatment. This treatment, however, must go beyond the verbal modality.

Treatment Considerations

For purposes of treatment we must understand that as a result of past and present training, the codependent is unable to assert his or her importance, as shown in Table 17–1. This table summarizes the process

TABLE 17–1   Discriminating Signs Between Addicted (i.e., Selfish) and Codependent (i.e., Selfless) Individuals

Selfishness	*Selflessness*
1. Not taking precautions during intercourse before marriage	Allowing it to happen
2. Not taking responsibility if and when girl gets pregnant	Allowing it to happen
3. Not holding a steady job and expecting to be taken care of by others including wife or woman friend	Allowing it to happen
4. Using job or job pressures to avoid taking responsibilities in the home	Allowing it to happen
5. Not sharing in household chores	Allowing it to happen
6. Watching TV or drinking or whatever while spouse is still working	Allowing it to happen
7. Not taking initiative in house care and child care	Allowing it to happen
8. Having to be reminded of duties and responsibilities relevant to the role of husband/wife and partner	Allowing it to happen
9. Spending leisure time away from home, with friends, or in away-from-home pursuits related to fame and glory	Allowing it to happen
10. Being or becoming addicted to work, TV, alcohol, gambling, or worse	Allowing it to happen
11. Verbally and physically abusing spouse and/or children	Allowing it to happen
12. Running around with other men or women ("friends")	Allowing it to happen
13. Spending more on clothes than the rest of the family does, to look good at work.	Allowing it to happen

whereby a (usually selfless) codependent is unable to set limits with the addict (usually selfish) from the very beginning of the relationship, because of the attribution of importance to the partner rather than to the self. The first line of defense ("the condom line") relates to how one is going to protect his or her body during courtship.

The polarization of selfishness-selflessness is at the basis of most conflicts found in addict-codependent couples, no matter what the nature of the abuse may be. From this basic polarization arise a variety of polarizations, as illustrated in Table 17–2.

Consequently, a therapist initially needs to consider some general objectives with the codependent partner.

1. Do Something New That We Have Never Done Before   Doing something *new* means doing something new *for ourselves.* Something new means changing a behavior that was the least and the last in the past, such as shopping for ourselves *before* shopping for others, or insisting on watching a favorite TV program rather than allowing everybody else in the family to watch their favorites. In other words, to do something new means to affirm, to assert, and to insist that we are important and that no one will be allowed to put us down. If they do, as they inevitably will, they are going to do it at their peril! We need to introduce the idea that choos-

TABLE 17–2 Polarizations between Two Reactive Stances in Codependent Relationships

Addicted (Selfishness)	*Codependent (Selflessness)*
Denial of personal errors	Acceptance or admission of personal errors
More able to receive than to give love	More able to give than to receive love
Spoiled (picky)	Neglected
Self-absorbed & enhancing	Self-effacing or self-debasing
Self-indulgent	Self-sacrificing or self-neglectful
More critical of others than self	More critical of self than others
Blaming others rather than self	Blaming self rather than others
Committed to self more than others	Committed to others more than self
Decisive	Indecisive
Dominant-authoritarian	Submissive-permissive
Rigid	Flexible (pliable)
Neither trusting nor trustworthy	Naively trusting, gullible
Unconventional	Conventional
Uses anger to manipulate others	Uses fear, anxiety, worry and sadness to manipulate self
Driven	Pushed
Unreflective and/or impulsive about consequences	Anxious, worried about consequences
Dominant	Submissive

ing things to buy or a TV program to watch are all negotiable processes. What is not negotiable is a sense of importance, and our love for those who love us. We are willing and able to negotiate *provided* there is *equality of importance and equality and balance of reciprocity* in what we give or give up, and in what we receive. In fact, intimacy between partners and among family members is impossible unless there is equality of importance and reciprocity in giving and getting.

2. Do Something New That Is Also Positive   We now have a way of finding out what is *positive* in a relationship. Something is positive when it does not put anybody else down or is not done at anybody's expense, including our own. We cannot get something at someone else's expense. If there is no loss to anyone and one partner wins without defeats to others, this behavior is positive. We need to ask, "Will anybody suffer for or from this behavior? Will somebody become frightened if I assert my importance?" If we are convinced that whatever we do: (a) enhances the self, (b) would make us feel proud and pleased, (c) would bring a new perspective to the self and to the relationship, and (d) does not hurt anyone else, then that behavior is positive and can be implemented.

The addicted partner will object to almost anything new and positive that the codependent partner does. Consequently, his or her permission or that of anybody else is not needed to do something new and positive. If the addicted partner gets mad, the codependent is probably on the right track, because addicted individuals are usually afraid of anything that may threaten the status quo, especially any behavior that may show that the codependent partner wants to behave like a grown-up person in his or her own right.

It is inevitable that the addicted partner will react negatively to new and positive behavior on the codependent's part. When this negative reaction takes place, the addicted partner should be asked to come up with at least three reasons why this new behavior should not take place. Here the rule of three should be practiced; that is, the codependent should have three relevant and positive reasons for doing what he or she wants to do, provided no one else is hurt by this behavior. The codependent can easily find at least three reasons for advocating new behavior: "I like it," "It makes me feel good," and "It does not hurt anybody."

3.   *Do Something New, Positive, and Strong*   "Strong" means doing whatever we need to do to express our inherent importance and determined commitment to change. The action has to be intense and powerful enough to make a difference in the codependent's life and in the relationship with the addicted partner.

To fulfill these three objectives, the codependent must go through the following successive sieves or hurdles: drawing lines; dealing with attacks; writing an individualized bill of rights; going on strike; forming or joining a support or study group on the topic of codependency; and dealing with the resistance to therapy. Each of these suggestions is more difficult to implement than the preceeding one. The codependent should expect that the more he or she changes or wants change, the greater the resistance from the addicted partner will be.

Drawing Lines

How and when do we draw lines orally, nonverbally, and in writing? First of all, drawing lines or setting limits orally with an addicted partner is often useless. Words, most of the time, lead to escalations, explosive arguments, and fights. Before speaking and trying to talk sense with the addicted partner, we should avoid engaging in another round of useless and destructive arguments unless we have thought an issue through and the rule of three has been used successfully. If we cannot come up with at least three good (appropriate, relevant, positive, helpful) reasons, it means that not enough thought has been given to the issue at hand. Instructions for drawing lines are found in Table 17–3; use a blank, unlined piece of paper. The codependent should draw lines without speaking, using a yellow or red colored pen or pencil for lines 1, 2, and 3, and a black pencil or pen for lines 4 and 5. After what is requested on table 17–3 has been completed, attach to each line various behaviors that can be identified for each

TABLE 17–3   Helping Codependents to Draw Lines

1. Draw two straight, parallel, uninterrupted yellow or red lines.
2. Draw two straight, parallel yellow or red lines with one (just one!) break.
3. Draw one straight, uninterrrupted yellow or red line.
4. Draw one straight, uninterrupted black line.
5. Draw one straight, interrupted (dotted) black line.

of these lines, where *in the past the codependent failed to draw a line* for his or her partner.

The codependent should write down what is completely non-negotiable with him- or herself, that which would never be stood for, tolerated, or accepted in self or partner. For instance:

Line No. 1   What would we consider nonnegotiable in an intimate relationship? Infidelity? Violence? Rape? Incest? What would the partner have to do for the codependent to draw a line? Commit murder? Is anything and everything he or she does acceptable or non-acceptable? Is the codependent trying to make excuses for his or her behavior, to allow him or her to get away with murder?

Line No. 2   What behavior would we put up with just once, not to be repeated *ever again?* Running around with other people? Rape? Incest? Violence? Abuse? Getting drunk or hitting the codependent more than once? Just because we failed to draw a firm line the first time, it does not mean that we cannot draw a firm line now. The codependent needs to write down exactly what he or she would do if the addicted partner were to do something to him or her that legally, morally, emotionally, and personally would be hurtful to himself or herself or to loved ones. The codependent should make it very clear that the first time he or she was hurt, it was the responsibility of the addict. However, if the offense occurs again, responsibility belongs to the codependent to protect himself or herself.

Line No. 3   What would be negotiable over an extended period of time? Everyday decisions? Who is going to take care of the house? What chores should be taken on by whom? Who is going to clean what? Who is responsible for doing what? Who will draw up a budget? Who will follow it? How are disagreements going to be settled? By fighting? By sitting down at a table at a pre-arranged time with an agenda? How are purchases to be made? Separately? Jointly? How should vacations be negotiated with relatives, away from relatives? How is money to be spent, etc.? Ideally, negotiation implies *both* partners working, talking, discussing, and solving problems without blaming and without using negative or abusive behaviors, such as "you" statements, bringing up the past, mind reading, making threats and ultimatums, using emotional blackmail or bribery, etc.

Line No. 4   What is still unclear in the relationship that would require further negotiation? In the previous line, it would have been helpful if we made a list of all the issues that are affecting the relationship. Some of these issues may have been dealt with under line 3. Other issues are still unresolved and are still affecting the relationship. Here we may find issues that should be upgraded to line 3, kept in line 4, or downgraded to line 5.

Line No. 5   What issues are taken for granted by both partners, are accepted or already implemented, and do not require negotiation? In other words, here we may list issues that have been resolved, do not need more negotiation, and do not present a problem to anyone in the family.

Once the first draft of this line-drawing assignment is completed, the codependent should put the draft aside and sleep on it for one or more nights. Then he or she should go back to see whether it needs any improvement and change whatever needs to be changed. Then, the final draft should be photocopied with at least three copies: one for the therapist, one for the codependent, and one for the addicted partner.

An appointment with the partner should be made at least 24 hours in advance, *because important things need to be discussed by appointment.* In asking for an appointment, the codependent should try to avoid the semblance of an ambush or a confrontation and *should not, under any conditions,* give in to the addict's inevitable request for immediate explanations. The codependent should present a copy of the draft to the partner because he or she needs the partner's feedback. However, no immediate reaction is desired or needed. Allow time to read it in comfort (at least 24 hours) and decide at what time both partners can get together to talk about it. Then, the codependent should listen to the partner's reactions, if they are positive, and write down whatever helpful suggestions he or she may make to improve or clarify the lines. If the partner's reaction is one of put-down, criticism, and negativity, the codependent should indicate the destructive aspects of this behavior and express his or her feelings about it. If the addict is not willing to sit down and talk at an agreed-upon time, he or she is failing to behave like a partner. The addict should not be allowed to control the relationship any more than the codependent should. The codependent should keep cool and avoid reacting and escalating.

Codependents need to learn about setting boundaries. This learning means behaving as much as possible at their very best, *regardless of their partner's worst behavior.* Just because one's partner robs banks, this behavior would not excuse the codependent for robbing banks also! Setting boundaries means not getting hooked by the partner's provocations and set-ups. The addicted partner is involved in getting the codependent to behave like a "bitch" or a "bastard," to provide self-justification that he or she is reasonable in behaving the way he or she does (i.e., like a bitch or a bastard). In other words, he or she is willing to make a monster out of the codependent partner to prove himself or herself right! The addicted partner will push the codependent to the limit. Once the codependent explodes, the addicted partner will receive the greatest gift of all: control of the relationship! Will the codependent allow himself or herself to be controlled, to be pushed to the point of explosion? If the codependent loses control, the addicted partner has won! Probably that is the way the addicted partner learned to behave with his or her parents. Why shouldn't it work with the partner?

If the codependent starts to set boundaries and draw lines, the addicted partner will probably escalate immediately. At best, apathetic-lethargic individuals will reach repetitively reactive and manipulative levels of intimate interaction. The addict will not tolerate any self-assertion and initiative from the codependent. Change for the better in the codependent will be extremely threatening for the addict. Consequently, the therapist must be very careful about this process. The addicted partner will become very upset whenever the codependent does something that is new, positive, and strong. The best-case scenario would be that the addicted partner would not escalate in offensive behavior. However, if and when he or she does, and the method of drawing lines does not work, the codependent may need to try the next, more difficult hurdle.

Dealing with Attacks

Throughout this process, it is important for the codependent to learn how to cope *non-reactively but not passively* with the inevitable ambushes and attacks from the partner. He or she should be helped to develop a written plan of how to behave under such circumstances. An example of such a plan is found in Table 17–4. In spite of having such a plan, many codependents fail to maintain a non-reactive stance in the face of an onslaught of abusive and manipulative behavior from their partners. Reaching a non-reactive level is especially important in trying to implement the next step in treatment. Reading, remembering, and applying the suggestions made in Table 17–4 may be helpful. These suggestions are given to help the codependent get "unhooked" from the partner whenever the addict is trying to draw the codependent out, to get her or him to lose control.

The therapist should expect the codependent to make mistakes, fall for the partner's provocations and lose her or his cool. The process must be experienced little by little. There will not be any giant steps, only small ones.

TABLE 17-4   Possible Strategies for Codependents to Avoid Becoming Involved with or "Hooked" to Provocation by Addicted Partner

1. Avoid using the seven deadly, suicidal patterns: blaming ("You always. . . . You never. . . .); bringing up the past; mind-reading; ultimatums; threats; blackmail or bribery; and distracting.
2. Instead use all of the opposite patterns consistently, that is: use "I" or "we" only; stay in the present; deal with what is said or done in front of your eyes; suggest possible consequences of destructive behavior; use natural consequences of what *will* happen and not what *could* happen; be mindful that even unconditional love has limits on behavior (i.e., we can love a person but not like what he or she is doing); stay on the topic of discussion and make sure it is important and relevant to the relationship.
3. Respond to feelings rather than to behavior. For instance, reflect on the feelings of hurt, helplessness, and frustration that the addict may experience even if he or she denies them.
4. Rather than react in kind, muse on what would happen if you were to indulge in the same behavior. For instance: "If I were to bring up the past, we would be both unable to deal with the present, even if the present is worse than the past."
5. Consider alternatives in how to respond by asking for more information and suggesting possible solutions, even if the solutions are rejected. In that case, comment to the effect that "I guess that the only solution possible is for me to lose and you to win. I wonder whether we can ever win together. I guess that's too much to ask."
6. When he or she asks "hooking" questions, designed to upset you and make you lose control, if you do know not how to answer, say, "I will have to think about it before I give you an answer," or "I am not ready to give you an answer right now, so let me sleep on it," or "I doubt I can come up with a helpful answer when I am upset. Let me calm down and I'll get back to you."
7. When he or she accuses or criticizes you, try to avoid defending yourself; instead say, "You may be right about that," or "I am not perfect and I am entitled to make mistakes."
8. When the attack goes on, suggest the following, "Since we are both upset, wouldn't it be better if we stop this discussion and postpone it until we have both calmed down?" or "I do not think well when I am under attack, please give me a break," or "I really need some time to think about what you said. If you'll excuse me, I'll go for a walk."
9. When an ambush is sudden and unexpected, excuse yourself to go to the bathroom. While there, review possible strategies to use, without reacting or overreacting as he or she wants you to do. Your overreaction would give him or her more ammunition to avoid confrontation, and therefore more power.
10. If all of the previous strategies fail and you are at the point of "losing it," get to the phone and call your doctor (therapist, minister, friends, relatives) for support and suggestions.
11. Make it clear that you will not stand for any verbal or physical abuse: "That is completely unacceptable."
12. If there is a threat or danger to you in the form of physical abuse, leave the house immediately. Do not come back until you are sure that you are perfectly safe and that no harm will come to you. If promises are made to make you come back, make sure that these promises are made in writing *and* in front of a witness.

Writing a Bill of Rights for Codependents

Writing a bill of rights is a process rather than a task to be accomplished in a few easy lessons. It will take some time to complete this process, which must be broken down into three separate steps: learning to write a bill of rights; introducing it to the addicted partner; and learning to deal with the consequences of attempting to change an entrenched and rigid relationship.

Learning How
A bill of rights is based on a single principle—the same principle of *boundaries* discussed under the previous task of drawing lines. It involves drawing boundaries as to what one will or will not tolerate. This is how a self is manifested and expressed. If a person does not decide what will be acceptable or unacceptable, how can any lines be drawn? How do we learn to set boundaries? Metaphorically at least, setting lines or boundaries starts with the condom line. If a woman does not know how to set a boundary to protect herself and her body at the very outset of a relationship, she has lost. By the same token, a man should use a condom to protect both himself and his partner. Lines should be set before sexual intercourse in either a casual or a committed relationship, to avoid either unwanted pregnancy or any diseases. If a person cannot set boundaries at this point, he or she probably will not be able to set firm boundaries about any other issues in the relationship. The selfish partner usually could not care less, and wants to get whatever possible whenever possible; how he or she gets it is not a concern. Immediate needs of the addict are more important than those of the partner. If the codependent does not think about being important, why should the addict care?

Step No. 1   Have the codependent write down various areas of concern, where he or she has not been able to set boundaries *in the past.* After identification of these areas, which may take some time for the codependent to do, he or she should write down plans for intended behavior. Whatever the chosen behavior, it should follow the rule of three presented earlier in this chapter: think of three positive, relevant, and realistic reasons for the new behavior. An example of a bill of rights written by a codependent individual, the wife of an alcoholic, is shown in Table 17–5.

    Of course, the codependent does not have to follow this example exactly. A bill of rights should apply specifically to the person writing it. However, the example can be used as a model to be improved. The therapist should go over several drafts, paying special attention to the use of language. For instance, the bill of rights should avoid accusations, putdowns, and name-calling. The codependent needs to use the "I" position, referring to her or his thoughts and feelings, and not attempting to read the partner's mind or make negative comments. Complaints should refer

TABLE 17–5 A Bill of Rights for Codependent Relationships

I WILL NOT ALLOW MYSELF TO:

1. ARGUE when my partner has been drinking or is angry, upset, strung out, etc., BECAUSE:
   a. when I argue, it causes me to become defensive and to justify myself.
   b. arguments when we are upset accomplish absolutely nothing.
   c. arguments cause me to become sad and/or mad.
   d. during arguments we say things we regret later.
2. BE PUT DOWN and be abused verbally, BECAUSE:
   a. I am human and I am entitled to make mistakes.
   b. Put-downs cause me to become defensive. I do not need to defend myself. I am a responsible, caring, and loving individual.
   c. I cannot use put-downs. They do not give me any helpful information about myself or anything else. However, I can use support and guidance if this is a reciprocal process and my support and guidance are listened to.
   d. Put-downs cause me to become sad, mad, and lose control of myself, and I do not like myself when I lose control, even when my partner provokes it.
3. ACCEPT more than my share of RESPONSIBILITIES, BECAUSE:
   a. Eventually, I would become resentful and angry.
   b. I would then feel used and abused.
   c. It would increase the stress I am feeling.
   d. I already have more responsibilites than I can handle. The more responsibilities I have taken on in the past, the greater the chances of my having been criticized, put down, and abused. Therefore, I will only assume responsibilities that enhance me and that will not debase my partner and my relationship with him or her.
   e. If I accept more than my share of responsibilities, I would not have energy and time left for myself first and others second.
4. HOLD IN my emotions, BECAUSE:
   a. I could become physically sick.
   b. I am entitled to express my feelings, provided I do not put anybody else down.
   c. If I hold in my feelings, I could build them up to the point of a blow-up.
   d. Expressing my feelings lets other people know that my feelings are important, because they are *my* feelings and I am important.
   e. Feelings are to be shared with those I love and who love me. If people do not care about my feelings, maybe they do not care about me.
   f. Sharing my feelings with those I love will give them a chance to share their feelings with me.
   g. Sharing my feelings will help people I love learn to know me better and appreciate me for what I am: an important person.
5. LET ANYBODY KEEP ME FROM DOING THE THINGS I ENJOY DOING, BECAUSE:
   a. I deserve some enjoyment out of life.
   b. My family is part of my life. I enjoy being with them and I should be able to spend time with them without feeling guilty.
   c. It makes me happy and content to do things I enjoy, including doing absolutely nothing! I am important even when I am doing nothing.

strictly to the behavior and not to the person. This should be a bill of rights about how the codependent is going to behave, not about the partner's behavior. The codependent cannot control the partner's behavior, only his or her own. Help the codependent give up fantasies or hopes that he or she is going to change the addicted partner, to concentrate instead on how his or her own behavior is going to change.

Another important step needs to be undertaken here; the points made in Table 17–5 are all written in a negative form: what the codependent will allow herself or himself *not to do.* The therapist should stress the reverse of this negativity and emphasize support and permission to think about *what to do positively.* Thus, for each negative point on the table, the codependent should be helped to think of some positive behavior he or she wants to start, then write down at least three reasons why he or she wants and needs to do it. "Think of the rule of three: are you doing what you *want* to do, are you doing what you *need* to do, and are you doing what you *wish or like* to do?" After the therapist thinks a reasonable document has been completed, three copies should be made: one for the therapist, one for the codependent, and one for the addicted partner. This step cannot be taken lightly.

Step No. 2   Presenting the bill of rights to the partner is not as easy as it may seem at first glance. The codependent will become anxious, wondering fearfully about the partner's reactions and perhaps thinking that this bill should not be shown at all. This option is still open to the codependent, who does not have to show this document, but can keep it to himself or herself and act accordingly. However, the codependent must have at least three reasons for choosing this course of *no action.*

If the codependent chooses to show the partner the product of his or her work, he or she should be prepared for an angry, if not explosive, reaction. Thus, it may help to put a preamble or introduction at the top of the paper, such as "I know that this paper is going to upset you a great deal. However, it is important for me to learn to control myself, regardless of how you behave. Go ahead and respond the way you usually do (get mad, stamp your feet, holler, have a temper tantrum, etc.). After you have finished, I would like to set a time, at least 24 hours from now, to discuss this paper with you, if you are interested in our welfare."

What is the purpose of presenting this bill of rights to the partner? There are at least three reasons for doing it: (1) to make a strong statement about being an independent human being; (2) to show the partner that the codependent no longer wants to behave like a doormat, that the codependent has a will of his or her own, and is interested in making things better for himself or herself; and (3) to point out that neither can win at the other's expense. Both partners must win. If one wins, they both win; if one loses, both lose. Presenting the bill of rights is the first step in the process of learning how to win, preferably for *both* partners.

Another and most important reason for presenting the bill of rights is to start a dialogue between the two partners that will lead to a helpful outcome. What would this helpful outcome be? The outcome cannot be predicted at this point in therapy. One successful outcome, for instance, would be for both partners to agree on a conjugal contract that would direct both of them to work as real partners and not as enemies. This contract *must* be in writing, to avoid distortions and deletions through forgetting, misunderstanding, etc. Thus, the major reason for presenting a bill of rights is to have both partners start talking as friends and not as adversaries.

The therapist should warn and prepare the codependent that if he or she lets the partner start an argument when the document is presented, this step is lost. The codependent must be very clear about wanting the partner to read this document first and then think about it before discussing it: "I want you to have time to think it through." The codependent should be coached in not allowing the partner to bully or bulldoze him or her into a replay of past fights: "I am not ready to discuss it now. We should talk about it when we are both calm." If the partner persists or becomes angry, the codependent may need to leave the room or if necessary leave the house. At worst, if the partner becomes violent or abusive, the codependent should call the police.

The issue here is one of control: *Who controls whom?* If the codependent loses her or his cool because of the partner's inevitable provocations (put-downs, blame, accusations, criticism, etc.), the codependent is giving up control of the situation. That is what the partner wants the most: to have the codependent at his or her beck and call, to dominate, manipulate, and bully him or her at will. If the codependent gives up on the stated appointment and responds immediately to provocation when a copy of the bill of rights is given, control is lost on both sides. Both partners must negotiate when and where they will have the proposed meeting. Time and place may be negotiable, but the need for a meeting is not negotiable. The codependent must beware, because after the meeting has been set, the partner will try distracting and distancing tactics to get the codependent to lose her or his cool.

This is a crucial time that may make or break everything the codependent is trying to do. The partner cannot bear for the codependent to become more detached, more in control of situations, and more reasonable, instead of being what the codependent is often accused of being: volatile, capricious, and irrational. The codependent is no longer reacting to the partner as the addict wants him or her to. Change is very frightening for both. The partner may try anything, including threats of suicide or murder, to induce the codependent to go back to being the way he or she was. Under these circumstances, the codependent is to set clear, firm, and non-negotiable limits: "I am sorry, but I am not ready to talk about it now. I am too upset to think rationally. Let's set a time for us to talk about it calmly." The codependent may need to refer to behaviors suggested in Table 17–4.

Step No. 3   If and when the partners meet, the codependent should be prepared. The first step to maintaining control is to write down what is going on. Even better would be a tape-recorder: "My memory plays tricks on me, and I want to be sure I record everything we say." Why record what is going on at this meeting? For three reasons: (1) to help the codependent keep cool and in control; (2) to aid memory, which during critical situations can play tricks on us, so that we forget, distort, and delete some of what was said; and (3) to start a *record* that must be kept for reference at future meetings, if there are going to be others. This record will allow both partners to go back and see whether any change or improvement has taken place over time.

In addition, a time limit for the meeting must be set, preferably no longer than one hour. The kitchen timer should be set to one hour and this limit should be kept, in spite of the addicted partner also pushing these time limits, as with everything else. If the time limits are not kept, control is lost. Instead of running over the limit set for this meeting, an appointment for another meeting should be set for at least 24 hours later. Why should this limit be set beforehand? Time limits are a form of control. We are controlled by time and space and we achieve control by setting clear space and time boundaries. If we go beyond the allotted time, we start losing control and boundaries, and this meeting might deteriorate into a shouting match, not an outcome favorable to the codependent. Not much can be settled in one hour. Both partners should set up a weekly "relationship hour" on a predictable basis. The written or recorded record will allow the therapist to determine what areas of the relationship need improvement.

Before starting the meeting, the codependent must set some rules for how he or she is going to behave. It would be marvelous if the partner were to follow the same rules, but that much cannot be expected. The codependent may inform the partner that he or she will try to keep control by following these instructions to the letter. The codependent must avoid the seven deadly, suicidal ways of fighting, which are so deadly that they will be called the seven deadly sins. The codependent may need to memorize them, or to keep them in front of him or her during this meeting, making sure to do *exactly the opposite.* To avoid:

Deadly Sin No. 1. Use "I" instead of "you." If you find yourself saying "you," you are getting hooked. Use "we" when it is appropriate, but avoid using "you" altogether. If you do use it, you are starting to lose the most important part of yourself: your identity as a person, as a human being, and as a partner. This identity is expressed by the use of the pronoun "I."

Deadly Sin No. 2. Avoid making generalizations containing "never" and "always;" if you find yourself saying: "You never ———," or "You always ———," you have already lost the struggle.

Deadly Sin No. 3. Do not bring up the past; when the addicted partner does so, say: "I cannot change the past mistakes I have made. However, I can change what I am doing now and what I plan to do in the future."

Deadly Sin No. 4. Avoid reading the partner's mind and telling him or her what he or she should or shouldn't do, think, or feel. How do you like it when he or she does these things to you? When he or she does so, answer: "I am responsible for what I do, say, think, and feel. You are responsible for what you do, say, think, and feel." If he or she pushes, remind him or her that you will not stand for any mind-reading.

Deadly Sin No. 5. Do not use emotional blackmail or bribery such as, "If you do not do as I want, I will ———." Part of this blackmail involves giving ultimatums and using dates, etc., as part of the blackmail.

Deadly Sin No. 6. Do not make up or use excuses to justify your behavior. If you goofed, you goofed; what else is new? Can you forgive yourself and accept that mistakes prove that we are human? If you wanted to be as perfect as your partner, an individual who admits to no mistakes, you would have married someone else! When he or she starts making excuses for his or her behavior, say, "We cannot change the mistakes we have made in the past. However, we can learn from them and try to avoid making them again."

Deadly Sin No. 7. These are patterns that must be discovered and extrapolated from the written or recorded interactions. The most frequent and destructive patterns are *distraction,* or use of irrelevant behavior, and *intellectualization,* using computer-like reactions that are devoid of feelings.

The goals of this first meeting are to see whether the partner can understand and accept the codependent's position, to work out an agenda including issues that are important to both of them, and to start working on solving those issues *for the long haul* by negotiating and problem-solving together. It would be helpful if at this meeting, the partners were to start listing the problems facing both of them, such as what rules of conduct should be followed with each other, like avoiding the seven deadly sins, and how the partners are going to work out these problems—by shouting at each other, by command, by instant decisions without prior discussion—or are they going to start working together by *making regular appointments with each other?*

How does the rest of the world get things done? By appointment and by the written record. Why shouldn't we follow the same practices used by everybody else in the world? What makes us think that intimate relationships should follow different practices than those common in the rest of the world? Thus, through weekly meetings at times that are mutually agreeable and through written records, partners may start to work. After they have a list of issues, whatever those may be, both should rank the issues in order of importance. For instance, how do they talk with each other about money, sex, children, in-laws, friends, work, etc. Divide these issues in terms of special interests. For instance, if one partner takes the issues of money, in-laws, and friends, the other partner takes the remainder. During the next week and before the next meeting, the partners should write down a proposal on how to resolve each particular issue. If possible each partner should give three reasons for suggested solutions. At the next meeting, if there is one, partners should avoid talking as much as possible. Instead, they should exchange their written proposals, add whatever new issues each may have thought of during the week, and end the meeting, even if it lasts only a few minutes. Talking should be kept to a minimum. They have done enough talking in the past, and did it help?

Issues are not going to be solved by arguing. If one partner loses control, a meeting should end immediately, but a time for a future appointment should be agreed upon ("We are not ready to solve problems when we are upset. We can negotiate only when we are calm and have thought through how to solve problems."). During the next week, each partner should look over the other partner's suggested solutions. Each should write down whatever pros and cons are seen in each proposal. On the basis of these criticisms without put-downs, a counter-proposal should be written. These counter-proposals should be presented at the next meeting and exchanged. Each partner should look these proposals over and decide whether they are now ready to write down a final solution that would be acceptable to both of them. For instance, let's take a single issue.

Problem   How should we treat each other and solve issues together?

Goals   (1) To treat each other with the utmost respect and care; (2) to assert each other's importance; (3) to enhance each other and our relationship; (4) to work as partners and not as enemies.

Proposed Solutions   (1) To meet regularly at pre-arranged, clearly stated times; (2) to keep most of our discussions in written form, so as to avoid distortions and deletions and our getting upset, as we have done in the past; (3) to avoid using the seven deadly sins listed above and rely instead on their opposites; (4) to end our meetings when we become upset, and (5) to set another meeting at the earliest convenient time, at least 24 hours later.

Follow the same process for each point, that is: (1) definition of the problem area; (2) goal(s) to achieve in that area; and (3) proposed solutions. The resulting document is the final contract. Allow the partners three months to see how well this contract is working or not working and what changes are needed to improve it. The therapist needs to be convinced that partners must *do everything through the written word.* If they rely mainly or only on spoken words, they will lose control of themselves and of the relationship. If this suggestion does not work, however, work can begin toward the ultimate step in the process of possible change.

Going on Strike

Helping codependents go on strike may be the most difficult thing therapists have ever done in their professional lives. It requires that codependents give up being the over-responsible, overnurturing, overcompetent, and overcaring persons they want to be. After all, their sense of importance is derived from what they do—cooking, cleaning, washing, driving, buying, and working for the benefit of everybody (especially their partners) except themselves! Now they are asked to stop doing anything. Probably they will not be able to do it right away. Codependents are as addicted to those chores (performance and production over personal presence) as their addicted partners are to anything else. Before the strike, both therapist and codependent need to consider the repercussions if the codependent agrees to do it. The codependent should write down at least three reasons why he or she would be better off doing it (to bring change) than keeping things as they are. Going on strike is new, positive, and powerfully change-producing. By going on strike the codependent is announcing that he or she is important, wants change, and intends to work for it. Going on strike may not be the best frame for some codependents. For instance, one codependent chose to use the term "having a nervous breakdown" instead of "going on strike," as a way of telling her partner and the rest of her family about her inability to take care of all of them as she had done in the past.

Sometimes going on strike has been called the Gandhi technique. What are the goals of going on strike? As usual, one must have at least three reasons for doing it: (1) to bring attention to a problem such as lack of change in the relationship, being taken for granted, being demeaned as not important, assuming too much responsibility, etc.; (2) to make the partner or the rest of the family understand that without negotiation and without cooperation in efforts to change, the relationship is doomed; (3) to bring the partner to the negotiating table and start putting some order in the relationship. Without negotiation, there is no hope that things will change for the better.

Before going on strike, codependents must write down their reasons for doing what they want to do. They have to decide whether they want to be taken for granted and keep their role as chief bottle-washer, maid, servant, chauffeur, chambermaid, etc. They need to think through *why* and *how* they are going to change, writing everything down step by step. They must expect a strong, negative reaction from everybody in the family, especially the addicted partner. For once, a family member is acting instead of just talking! Once the partner or the family is assembled, after an appropriate 24 hours notice has been given, the codependent will announce the decision to continue not doing anything for anybody else, since doing for everybody thus far has not brought about any change.

At this point, however, one should keep in mind that recognition is the watchword. Codependents should be reminded that they would not be in the fix they are now in if they had not allowed the situation to grow over the years. They must admit that they are mainly but not solely responsible for this fix. However, since they are 50 percent responsible for the situation, they are now at least 50 percent responsible for getting out of it. Partners and the rest of the family members will not like the strike. Everybody will have to think about what they are going to eat, get things washed, take care of the house, shop and buy whatever is needed in the home, etc. The striker should give the partner or family options such as, "Would you like me to go to bed or would you like me to go to a motel?" or "Would you like me to have a nervous breakdown at home or should I wait until things are so bad that I will have to go to the hospital?"

If codependents choose to stay home, it should be made clear that they will not play the role of consultants who tell partners and family members what they have to do and how to do it. They should act as if they were sick and let the rest of the family find out how to deal with all these issues by themselves. Once the announcement about what is going to happen is made, the codependent should follow this path and write down the partner's reactions, so they can be read afterwards to see whether anything has been learned. Codependents should avoid getting into any arguments with family members. If they are drawn into arguments, they are again going to lose control. During this process the therapist should be continuously available by phone for support and direction.

If going on strike works, the codependent can go back to the bill of rights step. If that does not work, the codependent may need to see a lawyer. If seeing an attorney works (and it may not), the codependent should keep in mind that marriage is slavery when the possibility of divorce does not exist. Before seeking divorce, however, codependents need to ask themselves if they have changed enough and are feeling proud and pleased with themselves enough to warrant taking this final step. If going on strike works, in addition to learning to negotiate, codependents can go on to the next suggestion and do both negotiating and studying together.

Forming or Joining a Study or Support Group

The United States is blessed with many courses and study groups about a myriad of subjects such as parenting, marital encounter, relationship enhancement, etc. Some of these courses are formal and some are informal. Especially in large metropolitan areas, courses and workshops about marital and parental relationships are available. Usually these courses include some practical hands-on or experiential training, between partners or with their children. Most universities and colleges have faculty members who are qualified to give these courses. The codependent should be helped to search and to ask. Doing nothing will not change anything. The partner should be asked if he or she is interested in involvement and active participation in such a course.

Some study groups focus on learning self-help negotiation skills, and others work as support groups without skills training. There is less teaching and more support in the latter groups, as in Alcoholics Anonymous and similar groups. Whether the partner becomes involved or not is a measure of his or her motivation to change for the better. If he or she refuses, the codependent may want to proceed to the next step—starting a support group by asking around and checking how many codependents there are in the neighborhood, church, community, etc. This process implies getting on the phone and calling potential study group members by passing the word around through friends and acquaintances. If codependents start a group, they should make sure they are committed to come at a regular time and for a definite number of sessions. Before starting they should write down a tentative outline of topics that might be of interest and use to this group. Better yet, the first session of the group should be to set specific times and durations for weekly, biweekly, or monthly meetings, to make sure that the group decides about the number of meetings they are going to have. Then they should also work out what specific agenda of topics the group needs to follow. The codependent, even as a founder, should not take responsibility for the whole process. Each member of the study group should be responsible for leading at least one session of the series, deciding on topics to be discussed beforehand, and distributing phone numbers so that each member of the group can get in touch with everybody else.

Another approach is to ask the church's director of education or the members of one's church, temple, or synagogue about organizing such a study group. Codependents may also be able to start such a study group with co-workers with a supervisor's approval and/or assistance.

Dealing with Denial and Resistance to Treatment

If the codependent is unable to get the partner to cooperate on any of the previous suggestions, asking for professional help as a couple may be an issue. This issue, of course, may come up at any time during the process of the codependent's therapy. The addicted partner typically will continue his or her denial and avoidance of change and confrontation, refuse to see anybody, and use all sorts of excuses and rationalizations to support this avoidance. For instance:

"I am not crazy, and I don't need a crazy doctor." (Being in trouble does not mean being crazy, it means being human.)

"Those guys need to be crazy to work in that field." (It takes one to cure one!)

"I knew someone who did go and wasn't helped a bit." (How about the flip side, those who have been helped?)

"All they are interested in is money." (So the therapist should work for charity?)

"I do not need any help from anybody." (That's the syndrome of the macho-man or wonder woman.)

"What could those guys tell me that I don't know already?" (Of course, he or she knows better! Who is going to tell him or her anything?)

"I knew somebody who went to see one of those doctors and they put him in the hospital for life." (He or she forgets to say that that somebody was a certified psychotic!)

"I can quit (name of addiction or habit) anytime I want if I really put my mind to it." (When was the last time he or she quit?)

"You need to go, because if it wasn't for you I would be all right." (It's all your fault.)

"I wouldn't get anything out of it." (How does he or she know?)

"It's too expensive." (He or she just bought a new car!)

If the codependent wants to discuss these self-destructive excuses, he or she should remember that all of the above excuses indicate only one thing: tremendous fear of the unknown and of breaking down, possibly going crazy, and losing control. Seeing professional help in a negative light is part of the process of denial that controls the lives of all driven, selfish, and addicted individuals.

Conclusion

This chapter has attempted to give some suggestions on how therapists can help codependent partners reach a higher level of self-realization. We must warn them, however, that obtaining this higher level may destroy the codependent relationship. The addicted partner may not be able to tolerate change for the better. How can he or she cope without an always-available partner, a caring friend, a sex object, a cook, a purchasing agent, etc.? Thus, although any changes for the betterment of the relationship may motivate the addicted partner to do better, such changes may also produce a deterioration in the addicted partner and in the relationship. Improving oneself may incur the risk of losing one's partner. Is change worth that kind of price? Some codependents are so afraid of losing their partners that they prefer to stay the same and avoid changing, just to please their addicted partner, to avoid conflict, or for the children's sake. Other codependents feel that the financial security they enjoy is too valuable to jeopordize it in any way. If that is the price they want to pay, to be stepped on and demeaned every day, they can continue doing what they have been doing all along. They only need to avoid changing for the better and implementing any of the suggestions made by the therapist.

References

Beattie, M. (1987) *Codependent no more.* New York: Harper & Row.

Carruth, B., & Mendenhall, W. (Eds.). (1989). Codependency: Issues in treatment and recovery (special issue). *Alcoholism Treatment Quarterly, 6.*

Cermak, T. L. (1986). *Diagnosing and treating co-dependence: A guide for professionals who work with chemical dependents, their spouses and children.* Minneapolis, MN: Johnson Institute Books.

Cermak, T. L. (1988). *A time to heal: The road to recovery for adult children of alcoholics.* Los Angeles: Jeremy P. Tarcher.

Forward, S., & Torres, J. (1987). *Men who hate women . . . and the women who love them.* Toronto: Bantam.

Friel, J., & Friel, L. (1988). *Adult children: The secrets of dysfunctional families.* Deerfield Beach, FL: Health Communications.

Kasl, C. (1989). *Women, sex, and addiction: A search for love and power.* New York: Ticknor & Fields.

L'Abate, L. (1990a). A theory of competencies × settings interactions. *Marriage and Family Review, 15,* 253–269.

L'Abate, L. (1990b). *Building family competence: Primary and secondary prevention strategies.* Newbury Park, CA: Sage.

Langley, R. & Levy, R. C. (1977). *Wife beating: The silent crisis.* New York: Dutton.

Larsen, E. (1987). *Stage II relationships: Love beyond addiction.* San Francisco: Harper & Row.

Leman, K. (1987). *The pleasers. Women who can't say no—and the men who control them.* Old Tappan, NJ: Fleming H. Revell.

Mellody, P. (1989). *Facing codependence.* San Francisco: Harper & Row.

Mendenhall, W. (1989) Co-dependency treatment. *Alcoholism Treatment Quarterly, 6,* 75–86.

Norwood, R. (1985). *Women who love too much.* New York: St. Martin's Press.

Norwood, R. (1988). *Letters from women who love too much.* New York: Pocket Books.

Potter-Efron, R. T., & Potter-Efron, P. S. (1989). Assessment of co-dependency with individuals from alcoholic and chemically dependent families. *Alcoholism Treatment Quarterly, 6,* 37–57.

Schaef, L. T. (1986). *Co-dependence: Misunderstood and mistreated.* Minneapolis, MN: Harper/Winston.

Subby, R., & Friel, J. (1984). Co-dependency: A paradoxical dependency. In *Codependency: An emerging issue.* Pompano Beach, FL: Health Communications.

Treadway, D. (1990). Codependency: Disease, metaphor, or fad? *The Family Therapy Networker, 10,* 38–43.

Whitfield, C. L. (1987). *Healing the child within: Discovery and recovery for adult children of dysfunctional families.* Pompano Beach, FL: Health Communications.

Whitfield, C. L. (1989). Co-dependence: Our most common addiction—Some physical, mental, emotional, and spiritual perspectives. *Alcoholism Treatment Quarterly, 6,* 19–36.

Woititz, J. G. (1987). *Home away from home.* Pompano Beach, FL: Health Communications.

18

The Prevention
of Addictive Behaviors

JACK E. FARRAR, Ph.D.
DANIEL SERRITELLA, Ph.D.

LUCIANO L'ABATE,
Ph.D.

THE LAST DECADE has seen an upsurge of many types of preventive approaches for addictions, based on psychoeducational training models. In fact, there are those who would make prevention a national priority (Milgram & Nathan, 1986). It is too early to say whether these approaches are indeed preventive. It takes years, even generations, to prove that an effective psychoeducational approach has preventive results (L'Abate, 1986). Nonetheless, the technology of psychoeducational training programs, focused on teaching psychosocial, interpersonal, communication, and problem-solving skills to children, adolescents, adults, couples, groups, and families, is abundant and readily available (Bond & Wagner, 1988; Gelfand, Ficula, & Zarbatany, 1986; L'Abate & Milan, 1985; Levant, 1986; Nietzel & Himelein, 1986; Price, Cowen, Lorion & Ramos-McKay, 1988; Weissberg & Allen, 1986). Even though many of these programs have been designed with the promise of being preventive, it remains to be seen which among the many are effective from the viewpoint of evaluating results years after implementation. Some treatment approaches for addictions do include preventive components (Haugaard & Reppucci, 1988; Lawson & Lawson, 1989; Lawson, Peterson & Lawson, 1983). Many psychoeducational programs that focus on marital and parental skills have been reviewed by L'Abate (1987) and Levant (1986). These programs can be used in conjunction with and in addition to ongoing therapeutic approaches. For prevention to be successful, professionals will have to learn to let go of many of their clients after the crisis period has been successfully overcome. The clients in these cases should be encouraged to attend various psychoeducational training and support groups. In fact, professionals should learn to deal with and encourage both psychoeducational training and support groups (Ryan, Ryan, Rosen & Virsida, 1986).

Prevention programs are available for numerous problem areas, including those in the addiction field. A comprehensive discussion of addictions and their treatments must also include a discussion on the promotion of health and prevention of psychopathology. As shown in Chapter 3, prevention can be looked at on three levels: primary, secondary, and tertiary. Primary prevention includes the promotion of mental health, prevention of addictive disorders, and prevention of psychosocial disorders through enrichment and related programs. Secondary prevention involves the early identification of addictive/mental health problems. Tertiary prevention is described as crisis-oriented rehabilitation or returning the patient to optimal functioning as soon as possible by concentrating on his or her assets. For addictive behaviors, the goal of prevention is to stop the misuse of all destructive substances or activities and to help the individual find alternative, more constructive methods of expressing anxiety and frustrations. Some researchers and clinicians think that addictions will never disappear, as they hold "great attraction for the hopeless, the depressed, and the anxious as temporary cures" (Cohen, 1984, pp. xxi–xxii). Often, the long-term negative effects of addictions are not immediately noticeable or perceived by the addict. Rather, the short-term effects of stress or anxiety reduction are extremely reinforcing. The short-term positive reinforcement far outweighs the less immediate and more remote detrimental long-term effects. By the time the negative long-term effects are realized, the addict has become powerless to alter the addictive pattern of behavior.

A number of studies have recognized the impact of stress, anxiety, frustration, and depression on the addictive cycle (Ashenberg, 1983). For those recovering from an addictive disorder, a relapse-prevention program needs to concentrate on five components to help the individual: (1) recognize high-risk situations; (2) learn and rehearse coping strategies; (3) avoid the abstinence violation effect; (4) balance the lifestyle to include diet and exercise; and (5) develop a system of self-rewards (Brown & Lichtenstein, 1980; Marlatt & Gordon 1980, 1985). Primary prevention for addictions and mental health has become associated more and more with health promotion. Many U.S. companies that employ more than one hundred people offer prevention programs for their employees. Some programs stress smoking cessation; others emphasize physical fitness, hypertension control, nutrition, weight loss, stress management, or substance abuse control (Mann, 1985). Primary prevention occurs in schools, churches, civic groups, and community centers across the country for most of the addictions discussed in this book. Additionally, the concept of social support, an important consideration in prevention, is also increasing through community professionals such as psychologists, clergy, physicians, attorneys, and legislators. A good example is in the field of domestic violence, which until the last decade was one of our most hidden social problems. Today there are a number of primary prevention programs geared to high school students, to attempt to alter their attitudes and behavior around the issues of domestic violence (Walther, 1986).

Primary prevention programs typically revolve around skill building. Skills deficit is fairly common across the addictions. Addicted individuals frequently have not developed the abilities needed to handle emotional turmoil, conflict, or anxiety. Model skill-building programs include lectures, workbooks, readings, and an active learning component through role-play and rehearsal. A model prevention program also takes into account the developmental needs and abilities of the audience it intends to reach (Krazier, 1988). However, some evidence suggests that prevention programs and concepts are being taught to children who are too young to understand these concepts (Landers, 1988).

Secondary prevention, or early identification, is a method for attacking the roots of addiction through identifying those who are at the greatest risk of becoming addicted: identifying those in greatest need. There is some evidence that through their teachers, parents, and peers, individuals who are at risk of becoming addicted can be identified by a process termed "multiple gating" (Loeber & Dishion, 1983). Parents, teachers, and peers can be used as "successive sieves" to direct those most at risk into treatment (see Chapter 3). Addictive potential is best dealt with early, preferably before the active addictive behavior (such as drug taking) begins and before antisocial peer groups are formed. A second level of prevention must be oriented toward establishment of positive peer groups within the school systems. These groups would act as counter-groups, providing youngsters with positive alternatives to the values associated with antisocial peer groups (Wurmser, 1978).

Prevention should ideally coordinate and revolve around the formation of community-based self-help groups. The purpose of these self-help groups, according to Wurmser (1978), would be social reform and the raising of consciousness of social issues related to addiction.

Today it seems that our society has a superabundance of programs for all types of addictive disorders. The most successful, it appears, are those that utilize established community-based support groups. These support groups are both prevention- and treatment-oriented. Individuals who are combating addiction receive from these groups a number of principles for guiding their lives. The more effective programs go one step further and integrate these principles with tools and skills needed for individuals to improve their relationships and the skills necessary to communicate effectively.

Support Groups

In their review of social and community interventions, Gesten and Jason (1987) distinguished between two types of preventive approaches that fit into an original differentiation between two basic abilities: the ability to love and the ability to negotiate. The authors distinguished between two types of groups. Mutual help and social support groups are directed toward *empowerment* of individuals, couples, and families by giving them a feeling and sense of importance. Competence-building, problem-solving, and negotiation training groups are oriented toward *enablement*—providing skills that are complementary to what is received from support groups. We will follow the same distinction in reviewing various support programs directed toward the primary and secondary prevention of addictive behaviors. For references concerning skill building, the reader may wish to consult Gesten and Jason (1987) or L'Abate and Milan (1985).

Approaches to treatment of addiction have historically included some form of group experience. Alcoholics Anonymous is the prototypical model of group support. Until recent years the focus has primarily been on treatment of the problem, with little emphasis on prevention of addictions. However, group experiences such as the AA model and many other support groups can have a major impact on deterring the development of addictive patterns in people.

For support groups to be successful as tools of prevention, there must be a commitment to working with an entire family system that may be targeted as at high risk for addiction. Individuals with family histories of some form of addiction would be at highest risk. The AA model and Al-Anon provide not only treatment for the family member afflicted by the addiction, but also offer a parallel support group for other members of the family system. The model for such support groups is similar to Al-Anon and Alateen programs. These groups not only provide a supportive community for members of a family system less directly involved in the addiction, but also serve as tools for prevention by heightening awareness of the dynamics of both addiction and codependency.

Alcoholics Anonymous (AA)

The AA model is based on alcoholics working together to keep each other sober (Alibrandi, 1982). Gellman (1964) evaluated the functions of the therapeutic process of AA groups and concluded that the functions of these groups were permissiveness, support, stimulation, verbalization, and reality testing. Essentially, AA gives alcoholics a place to be accepted and emotionally supported. The environment allows for reality testing of ideas and behaviors (Robertson, 1988). Additionally, AA is a place to share personal recovery with others. AA literature relates that "The therapists in AA already have their doctorates in the four fields where the alcoholic reigns supreme: phoniness, self-deception, evasion, and self-pity" (Alibrandi, 1982, p. 983). Sponsorship is an essential component of the recovery process. The emotional connections established through newcomer-sponsorship appear to provide alcoholics with both a source of modeling and an accepting, honest, and confronting support person to aid in the recovery process. Sponsors are responsible for emotionally introducing newcomers into AA and coaching them through their early crises (Ablon, 1982).

One of the reasons that AA seems to be so successful is that it is a leadership-less organization made up of members who have experienced many of the same behaviors, feelings, and thoughts. The environment fosters trust through telling of similar experiences. Self-report of personal success stories, within the context of "one day at a time," provides newcomers with a source of modeling and gentle expectation of success. Programs for individuals abusing substances other than alcohol have been based on the A.A. model; the two most recognized are Narcotics Anonymous and Cocaine Anonymous.

Al-Anon and Alateen (Nar-Anon and Narateen)

At present there are more than 15,000 Al-Anon groups (including over 2,300 Alateen groups) in 80 countries throughout the world (Ablon, 1982). Al-Anon groups were first formed in the late 1940s for spouses and relatives of members of AA to come together to discuss the dynamics of living with an alcoholic. Although Al-Anon is not formally affiliated with AA, the philosophy is similar in the two organizations, with belief in the 12-step process. The AA 12-step model is presented in Table 18–1.

Alateen groups are for children of alcoholics. These groups were formed by members of Al-Anon and are considered to be a component of the Al-Anon program. Alateen groups appear to be an attempt by Al-Anon to include a prevention model in the Alcoholics Anonymous approach. Alateen was started in 1957 by teenagers whose parents were members of Al-Anon and AA. Members attempt to focus their lives back onto themselves, striving to take responsibility for themselves and at the same time attempting to separate emotionally from the alcoholic parents and their related problems. Information on where to find help through AA is presented in Table 18–2.

Adult Children of Alcoholics (ACOA)

Undoubtedly our society pays the price of having to deal not only with the immediate but also the long-term effects of addictive behaviors. Nowhere is the need greater than with the children of alcoholics, at all ages and

TABLE 18–1   Alcoholics Anonymous 12 Steps

Step 1. We admitted that we were powerless over alcohol—that our lives had become unmanageable.

Step 2. Came to believe that a Power greater than ourselves could restore us to sanity.

Step 3. Made a decision to turn our will and our lives over to the care of God as we understood Him.

Step 4. Made a searching and fearless moral inventory of ourselves.

Step 5. Admitted to God, to ourselves, and to another human being the exact nature of our wrongs.

Step 6. Were entirely ready to have God remove all these defects of character.

Step 7. Humbly ask Him to remove our shortcomings.

Step 8. Made a list of all persons we have harmed and became willing to make amends to them.

Step 9. Made direct amends to such people whenever possible, except when to do so would injure them or others.

Step 10. Continued to take personal inventory and when we were wrong, promptly admitted it.

Step 11. Sought through prayer and meditation to improve our conscious contact with God as we understood Him, praying only for knowledge of His will for us and the power to carry that out.

Step 12. Having had a spiritual awakening as the result of these steps, we tried to carry this message to alcoholics, and to practice these principles in all our affairs.

Alcoholics Anonymous. (1953). *Twelve Steps and Twelve Traditions.* New York: Alcoholics Anonymous Publishing.

stages of the life cycle, from infancy to old age (Lawson & Lawson, 1989; Lawson, Peterson & Lawson, 1983; Martin, 1988). Consider the melancholy fact that there may be at least 28 million of these children. They may account for just a fraction of all children who have been either directly abused or have experienced seeing adults abusing. Many of these

TABLE 18–2   Alcoholics Anonymous Information

Alcoholics Anonymous: With 76,184 local groups worldwide, AA publishes a set of four meeting directories: eastern United States, western United States, Canada, and International. The cost is 75 cents each, and they are available from Alcoholics Anonymous, Box 459, Grand Central Station, New York, New York 10163; (212) 686–1100.

As with AA, information regarding Al-Anon and Alateen meetings can be obtained by calling the phone number listed in the area phone book or writing to the Al-Anon/Alateen headquarters as follows: Al-Anon Family Group Headquarters, Inc., P.O. Box 182, Madison Square Station, New York, NY 10010.

Cocaine Anonymous: The organization maintains a directory of meeting places and times. By calling the central office, you can find the location of the group nearest you. Information: Cocaine Anonymous Worldwide Services Office, P.O. Box 1367, Culver City, CA 90239; (213) 559–5833.

Sober Vacations International schedules vacations for those who are recovering. For information about trips offered, contact: Sober Vacations International, 2365 Westwood Boulevard, Suite 21, Los Angeles, CA 90064; (213) 470-0606.

children have now reached adulthood with a variety of dysfunctional developments; they represent the major argument for making prevention of addictive behaviors a primary national goal. Bennett, Wolin, and Reiss (1988), for instance, found that these children perform more poorly than children of non-alcoholic parents on 9 of 17 different measures of emotional, cognitive, and behavioral functioning. Ultimately, these children, like most children of abusive relationships, will grow up to become either dysfunctional and/or addictive personalities (Goglia, 1985; Thaxton, 1988). Children growing up in addictive families have often been found to assume roles that were functional for them for survival as children, but dysfunctional for them as adults. Table 18-3 outlines identified roles that children play in addicted families.

What can be done for these children that we have not already discussed? Certainly, they can join support groups of their own, often without their families. Fortunately, the family social support movement is growing to add to various support groups necessary to help many of these children learn to cope (Fehr & Perlman, 1985; Kagan, Powell, Weissbourd & Zigler, 1987). Thaxton (1988) has collected a variety of exercises that in three group sessions are designed to help ACOAs learn to articulate and express feelings and emotions that have been bottled up during many years. Some useful hints and guidelines for self-help are contained in Watson and Tharp (1988). These suggestions assume that many children of abusive parents are strong and functional enough to be able to implement

TABLE 18-3   Roles People Play in a Substance-Abusing Family

Different roles may be assumed by different children in addicted families, depending on their circumstances at any given time in their lives. Four identified roles are:

1. The Family Hero is the overachiever who always does what is right. He or she will probably grow up to be a workaholic, need to control and manipulate, marry a dependent person, and never be able to say "no." The Family Hero has low self-esteem, feels hurt and confused, and can never do enough.
2. The Problem Child is the irresponsible one, always defiant, in trouble, withdrawn, and sullen. He or she will probably be the one who becomes dependent on alcohol and/or drugs. He or she feels angry, rejected, hurt, abandoned, and inadequate and has low self-worth.
3. The Lost Child is the loner or daydreamer. He or she is ignored during a crisis, withdrawn, shy, and lonely, and may not be missed for days. These children feel unimportant, fearful, defeated, and apathetic and can grow up to be indecisive, have no zest or fun in life, be lonely or promiscuous, and tend to die early.
4. The Family Mascot or Clown will do anything for a laugh or attention. He or she is supercute, immature, fragile, hyperactive, or has a short attention span. These children are usually anxious and may be learning-disabled. They feel unimportant, lonely, fearful, and have low self-esteem. They will probably grow up to be compulsive, unable to handle stress, dependent, and always on the verge of hysterics.

Adapted from Wegshneider-Cruse (1981).

self-directed instructions. However, we doubt the all-encompassing generalizability of this conclusion, in the absence of supporting evidence. As indicated in Chapter 3, we need to distinguish among three different groups: individuals *at risk* for future abuse; individuals *in need* of help; and individuals *in crisis*. Unless this conceptual differentiation is adopted, it is doubtful whether preventive efforts will become individualized to the point of offering multiple treatments for addictive behaviors. To aid in making this differentiation, a list of questions concerning ACOA issues is contained in Table 18–4.

Gamblers Anonymous (GA)

There are 10 to 14 million alcoholics nationwide and approximately 5,000 inpatient programs for them, thousands of alcohol counselors, and volumes of educational material available (Fulcher, 1988). The same is true for drug abusers. However, for the more than 8 million compulsive gamblers in the nation today, fewer than 20 inpatient facilities, fewer than 50 counselors, and virtually no meaningful literature are available (Fulcher, 1988). The growth of Gamblers Anonymous (GA) during the past decade has been phenomenal, which speaks to the growing number of individuals who are compulsive gamblers. As of this date GA is the only self-help group available for them.

Gamblers may have more in common with other addicts than we know. There is evidence to suggest dual addictions to gambling and substance abuse. Many are addicted to both, and others replace their substance abuse with compulsive gambling behavior (Lesieur, 1988). Additionally, as high as 12 percent of compulsive gamblers are physically abusive to their wives and children (Fulcher, 1988). Table 18–5 contains information on where individuals can find help for their gambling problems.

Sexually Addicted

A number of alcoholics and drug-addicted individuals have also been found to suffer from sexual addiction (Scott, 1988). For years, many researchers and clinicians thought that the actual substance use was the cause for inappropriate sexual behavior. In fact, substance abuse is often a concurrent illness. Twelve-step programs, modeled after AA have been developed for individuals suffering from a sexual addiction. Sex Addicts Anonymous (SAA) encourages members in treatment to set and adhere to their own boundaries for sexual behavior. Sexaholics Anonymous (SA), by contrast, has a strict doctrine of sexual sobriety (Scott, 1988). A few chapters of SAA also provide groups for family members through

TABLE 18-4   ACOA Survey

Directions: Answer each question with either a yes or no. Fill in the answer that best describes your feelings, behavior, and experiences related to a parents' alcohol use. Take your time and be as accurate as possible. Answer all 30 questions.

1. Have you ever thought that one of your parents had a drinking problem?
2. Have you ever lost sleep because of a parent's drinking?
3. Did you ever encourage one of your parents to quit drinking?
4. Did you ever feel alone, scared, nervous, angry, or frustrated because a parent was not able to stop drinking?
5. Did you ever argue or fight with a parent when he or she was drinking?
6. Did you ever threaten to run away from home because of a parent's drinking?
7. Has a parent ever yelled at or hit you or other family members when drinking?
8. Have you ever heard your parents fight when one of them was drunk?
9. Did you ever protect another family member from a parent who was drinking?
10. Did you ever feel like hiding or emptying a parent's bottle of liquor?
11. Do many of your thoughts revolve around a problem-drinking parent or difficulties that arise because of his or her drinking?
12. Did you ever wish that a parent would stop drinking?
13. Do you ever feel responsible for and guilty about a parent's drinking?
14. Did you ever fear that your parents would get divorced due to alcohol misuse?
15. Have you ever withdrawn from and avoided outside activities and friends because of embarrassment and shame over a parent's drinking problem?
16. Did you ever feel caught in the middle of an argument or fight between a problem-drinking parent and your other parent?
17. Did you ever feel that you made a parent drink alcohol?
18. Have you ever felt that a problem-drinking parent did not really love you?
19. Did you ever resent a parent's drinking?
20. Have you ever worried about a parent's health because of his or her alcohol use?
21. Have you ever been blamed for a parent's drinking?
22. Did you ever think your father was an alcoholic?
23. Did you ever wish your home could be more like the homes of your friends who do not have a parent with a drinking problem?
24. Did a parent ever make promises to you that he or she did not keep because of drinking?
25. Did you ever think your mother was an alcoholic?
26. Did you ever wish that you could talk to someone who could understand and help the alcohol-related problems in your family?
27. Did you ever fight with your brothers and sisters about a parent's drinking?
28. Did you ever stay away from home to avoid the drinking parent or your other parent's reaction to the drinking?
29. Have you ever felt sick, cried, or had a knot in your stomach after worrying about a parent's drinking?
30. Did you ever take over chores and duties at home that were usually done by a parent before he or she developed a drinking problem?

Any positive response to the above questions may be indicative of the potential for an ACOA related problem to develop.

TABLE 18–5   Help for Gambling Addiction

Gamblers Anonymous: This organization has about 600 chapters in 450 United States communities, as well as chapters in England, Scotland, Ireland, West Germany, Australia, and New Zealand. A directory is available by sending $2 to cover postage to Gamblers Anonymous, P.O. Box 17173, Los Angeles, CA 90017; (213) 386-8789. In most major cities the number for a local GA chapter can be obtained from the local phone book.

Codependents of Sex Addicts (Co-SA). Table 18–6 contains information on where help is available.

Domestic Violence Groups

During the past two decades the plight of the battered woman has gradually come to the forefront of the nation's consciousness. It was not until 1975 that individuals began to focus their attention on batterers and abused children (Sonkin, Martin & Walker, 1985). Many commonalities exist between those growing up in violent homes and those growing up in homes where there is substance abuse (Wood, 1987).

Today there are a number of programs on the local, county, state, and federal levels to help alleviate the devastation of domestic violence/abuse. The diversity of programs precludes them from being listed here. Most states today have mandatory reporting laws for children who are abused. Child abuse has perhaps seen the best coordination of treatment and prevention approaches, with a cadre of professionals and agencies working together on behalf of the child. Educational awareness has been an important component in prevention/protection efforts. Awareness training is available for school personnel, psychologists, medical personnel, and other professionals to identify possibly abused children. Additionally, training is available for parents, to help them break their abusive cycle by learning alternative parenting methods (Pagelow, 1984). Table 18–7 contains information regarding child abuse.

The battered women's movement has been instrumental in estab-

TABLE 18–6   Help for Sexual Addictions

Numbers for most of these programs can be obtained in your local phone book or you can write to:

Sex Addicts Anonymous (S.A.A.), P.O. Box 3038, Minneapolis, MN 55403
Sexaholics Anonymous (S.A.), P.O. Box 300, Simi Valley, CA 93062
Sex and Love Addicts Anonymous (S.L.A.A.), P.O. Box 529, Newton, MA 02258
Codependents of Sex Addicts (CO-SA), P.O. Box 14537, Minneapolis, MN 55414

TABLE 18–7   Child Abuse Facts

1. The average victim of child abuse is between 8 and 11 years of age.
2. Some experts estimate that 5 or 6 children in a typical classroom of 30 have been affected by sexual abuse, regardless of geographic area, race, or socioeconomic class.
3. Ninety percent of abusers are men, at least in cases presently reported.
4. Offenders usually are not strangers to the children. Approximately 85 percent of offenders are known to the children.
5. The offender who rapes and is incarcerated has had an average of 65 victims in his lifetime.
6. The average pedophile will have approximately 244 victims in his lifetime.
7. Forty-one percent of pedophiles begin their sexual-abusing behaviors before the age of 14.
8. Fifty percent of child victims are molested in their own homes or in the offender's home.
9. Heterosexual males present greater risk to boys and girls than do homosexual males.
10. Incest (sexual contact) between parent and child is the most harmful form of sexual abuse.
11. Incestuous parents love their children but put their sexual-intimacy needs before those of the children. Sometimes this due to a crisis period in their lives or because boundaries in the family get confused or unclear.
12. The average length of an incestuous relationship is three years; it is rarely a one-time occurrence.
13. The victim may cope in many ways: by being withdrawn or delinquent or by becoming an overachiever in school. Victims of sexual abuse are typically not as involved with their peers as other children.
14. Emotional scars not dealt with may result in future problems with self-concept and possibly violent or self-destructive tendencies.
15. In the treatment of incestuous families, the prognosis is best when treatment continues long enough, when the entire family is involved, and when a self-help group is utilized.

Adapted from *Good touch, bad touch: Child sexual abuse prevention curriculum.* For information contact the Houston Drug Action Council, P.O. Box 1004, Warner Robins, GA 31099; (912) 922-4144.

lishing shelters that enable women and their children to have a safe haven to escape the violence. Services that shelters provide include parenting training, employment counseling, psychological counseling, legal counseling, and assistance in obtaining housing and public services (Pagelow, 1984). Many feel that women that use shelters "are just one subset of battered women, often those who are most severely beaten and have the fewest resources" (Schecter, 1982, p. 235). Middle-class women are often underrepresented in most statistics at shelters but these women benefit indirectly from the shelter movement. Many women engaged in a violent relationship may be suffering from a codependency syndrome. Table 18–8 presents characteristics of individuals suffering from a codependency syndrome; see also the checklists in Chapter 1.

Groups for men who batter and/or have trouble with their violent behavior are slowly beginning to develop in most major cities. Most programs help men learn how to communicate and deal with their feelings.

TABLE 18-8 Characteristics of Codependency Syndrome

1. Inability to know what is normal behavior
2. Difficulty in following a project through
3. Difficulty in knowing how to have fun
4. Judging the self without mercy and having low self-esteem
5. Difficulty in developing or sustaining meaningful relationships
6. Overreacting to change
7. Constantly seeking approval and affirmation, yet having no sense of self-identity
8. Feelings of being different
9. Confusion and sense of inadequacy
10. Being either super-responsible or super-irresponsible
11. Lack of self-confidence in making decisions; no sense of power in making choices
12. Feelings of fear, insecurity, inadequacy, guilt, hurt, and shame are denied
13. Inability to see alternatives to situations; responding very impulsively
14. Isolation and fear of people, especially authority figures
15. Fear of anger and criticism
16. Being addicted to excitement
17. Dependency upon others and fear of abandonment
18. Confusion between love and pity
19. Tendency to look for "victims" to help
20. Rigidity and need to control
21. Lying when it would be just as easy to tell the truth

Adapted from Seymour & Smith (1987).

Other goals include: decreasing isolation and developing an interpersonal support system; increasing feelings of control, power, and self-esteem; increasing responsibility for behavior; developing stress-reduction skills; developing control over alcohol and drug use; and participating in ongoing therapy (Sonkin, Martin & Walker, 1985). Services for battered men are usually, although not always, coordinated with or through a shelter. A few progressive organizations offer services for both men and women.

Food Addictions

Over 46 percent of all Americans think they are overweight. The weight-loss industry in the United States is a multibillion dollar industry, with specialized programs seeming to spring up daily. Perhaps weight control is one of the most recognized problems in the country but the least understood. Prevention efforts have seemingly failed. For years most people have been exposed to elementary nutrition through the schools and private physicians. Clearly, the dissemination of information alone is not enough.

A number of programs are available nationwide, including Overeaters Anonymous (OA). The OA program was formed in the 1970s and is like that of Alcoholics Anonymous (Overeaters Anonymous, 1980). The program utilizes AA's 12 steps, substituting the word "food" for "alcohol" and "compulsive overeater" for "alcoholic." Table 18–9 presents a self-help test to determine if one may need to seek help for his or her compulsive overeating.

Compulsive overeating contributes to illness on three levels: emotional, spiritual, and physical. OA does not subscribe to a particular diet or method of weight loss, but advocates abstinence through staying away from all eating between planned meals and from all individual food binges (OA, 1980, pp. 2–3). This is based on the idea that once the individual becomes abstinent, the preoccupation with food diminishes. Also postulated is the idea that the individual needs to find new ways of living in order to deal with his or her inner turmoil.

Another popular and successful program is Weight Watchers. Both programs are available in most communities. Table 18–10 presents information about where help is available.

Bulimia and anorexia nervosa are well-documented among adults, teens, and children. Common symptoms of anorexics and bulimics are presented in Table 18–11.

TABLE 18–9   Are You a Compulsive Eater?

1. Do you eat when you are not hungry?
2. Do you go on eating binges for no apparent reason?
3. Do you have feelings of guilt and remorse after overeating?
4. Do you give too much time and thought to food?
5. Do you look forward with pleasure and anticipation to the moment when you can eat by yourself?
6. Do you plan these secret binges ahead of time?
7. Do you eat sensibly in the presence of others and make up for it when you are alone?
8. Is your weight affecting the way you live?
9. Have you tried a diet for a week (or longer) and given up before you reached your goal?
10. Do you resent it when people tell you to "use a little willpower" and lose some weight?
11. Despite evidence to the contrary, have you continued to insist that you can diet on your own whenever you wish?
12. Do you crave food at a definite time of day or night other than mealtime?
13. Do you eat to escape from worries or disappointment, and reward yourself with something forbidden, to cheer yourself up?
14. Has your physician ever treated you for being overweight?
15. Does your obsession with food make you or others unhappy?

If you answered yes to three or more of these questions, you have a potential problem with compulsive overeating. If you answered yes to seven or more of these questions, you have a serious eating problem.

Overeaters Anonymous, 4025 Spencer Street, No. 203, Torrance, CA 90503.

TABLE 18–10   Help for Compulsive Overeating

Weight Watchers: About 25,000 weekly meetings are scheduled in 24 countries; about 17,000 of them are in the United States. Weight Watchers groups are in Puerto Rico, Canada, most West European countries, Australia, and New Zealand. An initial registration fee of $25 is charged and the fee for attending a weekly meeting ranges from $7 to $10, depending on the locale. A participant can go to a meeting daily for one weekly payment. Weight Watchers advises travelers to look in the telephone book for the number of the nearest group. For other information write: Weight Watchers International, Department 924, Jericho, New York 11753

Overeaters Anonymous: OA chapters are available in most communities, and most can be found by looking in the local phone book. For further information, write: Overeaters Anonymous. World Service Office, 2190 190th Street, Torrance, CA 90504.

Smoking Addiction

Smoking as an addiction affects millions of Americans annually. It enjoys widespread preventative efforts from a number of private and public sources. The American Cancer Society provides thousands of pamphlets, posters, and cessation programs each year. Their prevention programs are primarily carried out through the schools by utilizing a number of programmed units designed to teach elementary students the need to take care of their own bodies

The American Lung Association is also a strong supporter of a comprehensive school education program as a vehicle for teaching children the need to adopt a healthy lifestyle that does not include smoking. The

TABLE 18–11   Common Symptoms of Anorexics and Bulimics

1. Abnormal or severe weight loss
2. Refusal to eat, except for very small portions
3. Binge eating
4. Preoccupation with food
5. Vomiting
6. Denial of hunger
7. Excessive exercising
8. Distorted image of one's body
9. Absence of or irregular menstruation (in girls who have menstruated regularly)
10. Abuse of laxatives, diuretics, emetics, or diet pills
11. Low sense of self-worth
12. Dental problems or periodontal disease (due to nutritional deficiencies)

Not all symptoms need be displayed for a problem to be present. If one or more of these signs is noticed, contact your physician. For more information write or call: ANAD National Association of Anorexia Nervosa and Associated Disorders, P.O. Box 7, Highland Park, IL 60035; (312) 831-3438. For the names and numbers of other self-help organizations call the National Self-Help Clearing House in New York at (212) 642-2944.

Table 18-12   Help for Smoking Addiction

American Cancer Society, 90 Park Avenue, New York, NY 10016; (212) 599-8200
American Lung Association, 1740 Broadway, New York, NY 10019; (212) 315-8700
American Heart Association, National Center, 7320 Greenville Avenue, Dallas, TX 75231; (214) 750-5300
U.S. Department of Health and Human Services, National Audio-Visual Center, 8700 Edgewood Drive, Capitol Heights, MD 20743; (301) 763-1896

American Heart Association offers a multiple-risk-factor prevention program that is designed for implementation in the workplace; its prevention efforts focus on smoking, hypertension, nutrition, and exercise as preventative efforts.

Finally, the U.S. Department of Health and Human Services (HHS) offers a broad range of prevention efforts through its public information efforts and the school programs they offer.

Table 18–12 lists the addresses of the major organizations that work in the field of smoking prevention. Each organization usually has a state chapter whose address and phone number can be obtained from your local phone book.

Skill-Training Programs

There are at least four sets of skills that many addicts, regardless of specialization, need to develop, acquire and practice: assertiveness, communication, cognitive skills, and life skills. Most programs rely on role-playing and role-rehearsal with actual practice, rather than on just information acquisition, although some introductory lecturing seems to be necessary at the outset of the program. Not all of the skill-training programs with addicts or with people at risk for addiction can be reviewed here, but the ones presented are representative of what can be done in the area of skill training with addicts.

Assertiveness

One example of a program for children is that developed by Rotheram-Borus (1988), who divided skills necessary for assertive behavior into verbal-nonverbal and passive-assertive-aggressive. From this scheme she developed a model of social interaction process, with associated prerequisite cognitive, behavioral, and emotional responses for effective interpersonal style. This model is so well-developed and validated that it should be expanded for adolescents and adults.

Communication

These skills usually consist of active listening, reflective responding, and I-messages, among others. One application of these skills can be found in the program developed by the Metropolitan Atlanta Council on Alcohol and Drugs (Kramer, undated). Most of these skills have been incorporated in Guerney's (1988) relationship enhancement program, which could be applied to the families of most addicts (Levant, 1986).

Cognition

The most researched and applied of the programs in this area was developed by Shure and Spivack (1988) to aid interpersonal cognitive problem solving. Originally it was applied to teach acting-out adolescents (Spivack & Cianci, 1987), but it could be applied to most adult addicts and children of most addicts, to teach alternative solutions to disruptive and dominating behavior (Shure, 1988).

Life Skills

The best work in this area has been done by Botvin and his colleagues (Botvin & Tortu, 1988). Their program consists of 18 sessions focusing on myths and realities of substance abuse, decision making and independent thinking, self-directed behavior change, coping with anxiety, and social skills in communication and assertiveness.

Discussion

Society at present is becoming more aware and accepting of the tremendous presence of addictions and the problems they bring. This chapter and this book have attempted to examine the characteristics, development and differential treatment of a multitude of addictions. The authors have attempted to present an overall perspective of the many addictions facing society, as well as suggestions by which the commonalities of these addictions can be understood. Additionally, a prevention model for dealing with addictions and psychopathology has been proposed in Chapter 3. Those addicts most at risk might benefit from a primary prevention approach; people not at risk but in high emotional need might require a secondary prevention approach; and those actively in the crisis stage of addiction would receive tertiary prevention (crisis intervention). Although it is most important that those in crisis and the most evident need tertiary prevention, it is paramount that this society also move toward primary prevention. The overall state of addictions in this country is so great that a bandaid, quick-fix, reactive prevention approach is no longer adequate to turn around the long-term, multigenerational effect of addictions. As a society, we must have a conscious movement toward primary prevention approaches. We must go one step further and gradually replace reactive responses with pro-active, para-active, and para-therapeutic measures.

By the time tertiary prevention approaches are necessary, it is often too late for the addict and the surrounding family system. Primary prevention can aid and potentially prevent the detrimental effects of an addiction on a family system. Family systems, through primary prevention, are encouraged to correct emotional system problems before the problems have an irreversible negative impact on the family system.

We need to refocus on health rather than on correction of illness. This may mean figuring out how the wellness movement in this country can be financed through the public and private health system. It may mean that insurance companies will need to include incentives for participation in primary prevention programs, and de-emphasize reinforcement of the present tertiary prevention approaches.

Realizing that school-based, educationally oriented prevention programs as a sole intervention are not sufficient (Botvin, 1986), other means of prevention must be developed. The best primary prevention approaches seem to have two major components: skill development and some form of support-group experience. For primary prevention to be effective, it must use both educational and experiential intervention processes. This double-barreled approach not only provides knowledge, but also gives the emotional awareness that others have similar shared experiences and concerns. To develop adequate prevention programs in areas of addiction, such as those in this chapter, programmed workbooks are now being developed. The purpose of these workbooks is to provide individuals potentially at risk for developing addictive behaviors with both additional knowledge and a format to experience alternative behaviors. Experiences are developed as a result of written and experientially based assignments. These written assignments encourage development of greater knowledge and an interpersonal arena to practice the assignments with partners and family members. The interpersonal emotional interaction and support leads to significant changes, especially on an emotional awareness level.

To deal with the sheer number of addicts and emotionally disturbed individuals, couples, and families, the psychotherapeutic community will need to rely more and more on the written rather than on the spoken word. The latter medium may be necessary for establishment of rapport with some individuals, but we would argue that with many addicts and with many character disorders, the spoken word as a means of therapeutic exchange may be too expensive, too ineffective, and even therapeutically counterproductive. Externalizing addicts and impulse-ridden individuals need to learn to think in more constructive ways than just talking. Therapeutic dialogue based on the oral medium is too inefficient. Addicts use the spoken word to distract, manipulate, con, and control. They are not accustomed to using the spoken word to think in a more constructive, self-enhancing fashion. Consequently, we would argue that with many addicts the written, programmed word of workbooks can be used as a cost-effective medium of teaching better (i.e., more self-enhancing) ways of thinking and behaving.

Conclusion

The field of psychotherapy is made up of at best 500,000 trained professionals who give direct service. They are a drop in the bucket compared to the amount of addiction and psychopathology in our country. There will never be a sufficient number of psychotherapists to deal with the growing number of addicts and children of addicts. We need to develop better models of intervention and a wider range of pre-, para-, and therapeutic personnel with specific primary and secondary prevention skills to work together with full-fledged professionals involved in tertiary prevention. In accordance with the model presented in Chapter 3, we should develop hierarchical teams that will provide crisis intervention therapy *together with* secondary and eventually primary prevention approaches. Verbal therapy should be limited to group therapy and family approaches, bolstered by individually administered programmed materials and workbooks in secondary prevention. Both approaches can be bolstered by skill-training and enrichment programs at the primary prevention level. With addictions and psychopathology, we can no longer try to build skyscrapers with our bare hands as we have done heretofore.

We must develop a differentiated hierarchy of specializations, with all the various preventive psychoeducational technologies that are by now as abundant as therapeutic approaches. We do have technologies available to start building skyscrapers in the fields of mental health, addictions, and criminalities. We need to develop a new group of dedicated personnel who will be trained to use these preventive technologies with the same rewards, status, security, and salaries awarded up to now to therapists. The word "preventer" should be used with as much pride as the word "therapist." Until the new prevention-oriented training and personnel are in place, it is doubtful whether we will be able to build even cabins, let alone skyscrapers.

References

Ablon, J. (1982). Support system dynamics of Al-Anon and Alateen. In E. M. Pattison & E. Kaufman (Eds.), *Encyclopedic handbook of alcoholism* (pp. 987–999). New York: Gardner.

Alibrandi, L. A. (1982). The fellowship of alcoholics anonymous. In E. M. Pattison

& E. Kaufman (Eds.), *Encyclopedic handbook of alcoholism* (pp. 979–987). New York: Gardner.

Ashenberg, Z. S. (1983). *Smoking recidivism: The role of stress and coping.* Unpublished doctoral dissertation, Washington University, St. Louis, MO.

Bennett, L. A., Wolin, S. J., & Reiss, D. (1988). Cognitive, behavioral, and emotional problems among school age children of alcoholic parents. *American Journal of Psychiatry, 145,* 185–190.

Bond, L. A., & Wagner, B. M. (Eds.). (1988). *Families in transition: Primary prevention programs that work.* Newbury Park, CA: Sage.

Botvin, G. J. (1986). Substance abuse prevention research: Recent developments and future directions. *Journal of School Health, 56* (9), 369–374.

Botvin, G. J., & Tortu, S. (1988). Preventing adolescent substance abuse through life skills training. In R. H. Price, E. L. Cowen, R. P. Lorion & J. Ramos-McKay (Eds.), *Fourteen ounces of prevention: A casebook for practitioners* (pp. 98–110). Washington, DC: American Psychological Association.

Brown, R. A., & Lichtenstein, E. (1980). *Effects of a cognitive behavioral relapse prevention program for smokers.* Paper presented at the 88th Annual Convention of the American Psychological Association, Montreal.

Cohen, S. (1984). A glance at the future. In R. O'Brien & S. Cohen (Eds.), *The encyclopedia of drug abuse.* New York: Facts on File.

Fehr, B., & Perlman, D. (1985). The family as a social network and support system. In L. L'Abate (Ed.), *Handbook of family psychology and therapy* (pp. 323–356). Chicago: Dorsey.

Fulcher, G. T. (1988). Resources lacking for compulsive gamblers. *Alcoholism and Addiction, 8,* 24.

Gelfand, D. M., Ficula, T., & Zarbatany, L. (1986). Prevention of childhood behavior disorders. In B. A. Edelstein & L. Michelson (Eds.), *Handbook of prevention* (pp. 133–152). New York: Plenum.

Gellman, I. P. (1964). *The sober alcoholic: An organizational analysis of Alcoholics Anonymous.* New Haven, CT: College and University Press.

Gesten, E. L., & Jason L. A. (1987). Social and community interventions. *Annual Review of Psychology, 38,* 427–460.

Goglia, L. (1985). *Personality characteristics of adult children of alcoholics.* Unpublished doctoral dissertation, Georgia State University, Atlanta, GA.

Guerney, B. G., Jr. (1988). Family relationship enhancement: A skill training approach. In L. A. Bond & B. M. Wagner (Eds.), *Families in transition: Primary prevention programs that work* (pp. 99–134). Newbury Park, CA: Sage.

Haugaard, J. J., & Reppucci, N. D. (1988). *The sexual abuse of children: A comprehensive guide to current knowledge and intervention strategies.* San Francisco: Jossey-Bass.

House, J. S. (1981). *Work, stress, and social support.* Reading, MA: Addison-Wesley.

Kagan, S. L., Powell, D. R., Weissbourd, B., & Zigler, E. F. (Eds.). (1987). *America's family support programs.* New Haven, CT: Yale University Press.

Kramer, E. (Ed.). (undated). Substance use: Prevention and education resource. Available from Metropolitan Atlanta Council on Alcohol and Drugs, 2045 Peachtree Rd., Atlanta, GA 30309.

Krazier, S. K. (1988). Rethinking prevention. *Child Abuse and Neglect, 10,* 259–261.

Kurtz, E. (1979). *Not God: A history of Alcoholics Anonymous.* Garden City, MN: Hazelden Educational Services.

L'Abate, L. (1986). Prevention of marital and family problems. In B. E. Edelstein & L. Michelson (Eds.), *Handbook of prevention* (pp. 177–193). New York: Plenum.

L'Abate, L. (1987). Recent developments in psychoeducation skills programs for families: A review of reviews. In L. L'Abate (Ed.), *Family psychology II: Theory, therapy, enrichment, and training* (pp. 195–203). Washington, DC: University Press of America.

L'Abate, L., & Milan, M. (Eds.). (1985). *Handbook of social skills training and research.* New York: Wiley.

Landers, S. (1988). Abuse education efforts abstract to preschoolers. *APA Monitor, 19,* 35.

Lawson, G. W., & Lawson, L. A. W. (1989). *Alcoholism and substance abuse in special populations.* Rockville, MD: Aspen.

Lawson, G., Peterson, J. S., & Lawson, A. (1983). *Alcoholism and the family: A guide to treatment and prevention.* Rockville, MD: Aspen.

Lesieur, H. R. (1988). Treating gamblers in an alcoholism setting. *Alcoholism and Addiction, 8,* 22–23.

Levant, R. D. (Ed.). (1986). *Psychoeducational approaches to family therapy and counseling.* New York: Springer.

Loeber, R. & Dishion, T. (1983). Early predictors of male delinquency: A review. *Psychological Bulletin, 94,* 68–99.

Mann, P. (1985). *Marijuana alert.* New York: McGraw-Hill.

Marlatt, A., & Gordon, J. R. (1980). Determinants of relapse: implications for the maintenance of behavior change. In P. O. Davidson & S. M. Davidson (Eds.). *Behavioral medicine: Changing health lifestyles.* New York: Brunner/Mazel.

Marlatt, A., & Gordon, J. R. (Eds.). (1985). *Relapse prevention: maintenance strategies in the treatment of addictive behaviors.* New York: Guilford.

Martin, S. H. (1988). *Healing for adult children of alcoholics.* Nashville, TN: Broadman Press.

Milgram, G. A., & Nathan P. E. (1986). Efforts to prevent alcohol abuse. In B. A. Edelstein & L. Michelson (Eds.), *Handbook of prevention* (pp. 243–262). New York: Plenum.

Nietzel, M. T., & Himelein, J. J. (1986). Prevention of crime and delinquency. In B. A. Edelstein & L. Michelson (Eds.), *Handbook of prevention* (pp. 195–221). New York: Plenum.

Orford, J., & Velleman, R. (1982). Alcoholism halfway houses. In E. M. Pattison & E. Kaufman (Eds.), *Encyclopedic handbook of alcoholism* (pp. 907–923). New York: Gardner.

Otto, S. & Oxford, J. (1978). *Not quite like home: Small hostels for alcoholics and others.* Chichester, UK: Wiley.

Overeaters Anonymous. (1980). *Overeaters Anonymous.* Torrance, CA: Overeaters Anonymous.

Pagelow, Mildred D. (1984). *Family violence.* New York: Praeger.

Price R. H., Cowen, E. L. L., Lorion, R. P., & Ramos-McKay, J. (Eds.). (1988). *Fourteen ounces of prevention: A casebook for practitioners.* Washington, DC: American Psychological Association.

Robertson, N. (1988). *Getting better: Inside Alcoholics Anonymous.* New York: William Morrow.

Rotheram-Borus, M. J. (1988). Assertiveness training with children. In R. H. Price, E. L. Cowen, R. P. Lorion & J. Ramos-McKay (Eds.), *Fourteen ounces of prevention: A casebook for practitioners* (pp. 83–97). Washington, DC: American Psychological Association.

Ryan, W. G., Ryan, N. J., Rosen, A., & Virsida, A. R. (1986). Collaborating with self-help groups for substance abusers. In P. A. Keller & L. G. Ritt (Eds.), *Innovations in clinical practice: A source book* (pp. 83–90). Sarasota, FL: Professional Resource Exchange.

Schechter, S. (1982). *Woman and male violence: The visions and the struggles of the battered women's movement.* Boston: South End Press.

Scott, N. (1988). Help and hope for the sexually addicted. *Alcoholism and Addiction, 8,* 46.

Seymour, R. B., & Smith, D. E. (1987). *Drugfree: A unique, positive approach to staying off drugs and alcohol.* New York: Facts on File.

Shure, M. B. (1988). How to think, not what to think: A cognitive approach to prevention. In L. A. Bond & B. M. Wagner (Eds.), *Families in transition: Primary prevention programs that work* (pp. 170–199). Newbury Park, CA: Sage.

Shure, M. B., & Spivack, G. (1988). Interpersonal cognitive problem solving. In R. H. Price, E. L. Cowen, R. P. Lorion & J. Ramos-McKay (Eds.), *Fourteen ounces of prevention: A casebook for practitioners* (pp. 69–82). Washington, DC: American Psychological Association.

Sonkin, D. J., Martin, D., & Walker, L. E. (1985). *The male batterer: A treatment approach.* New York: Springer.

Spivak, G., & Cianci, N. (1987). High-risk early behavior patterns and later delinquency. In J. D. Burchard & S. N. Burchard (Eds.), *Prevention of delinquent behavior* (pp. 44–74). Newbury Park, CA: Sage.

Thaxton, L. (1988). *Issues of control among adult children of alcoholics.* Unpublished doctoral dissertation, Georgia State University, Atlanta, GA.

Walther, D. J. (1986). Wife abuse prevention: Effects of information on attitudes of high school boys. *Journal of Primary Prevention, 7*(2), 84–90.

Watson, D. L., & Tharp, R. G. (1988). *Self-directed behavior: Self-modification for personal adjustment.* Monterey, CA: Brooks/Cole.

Wegshneider-Cruse, S. (1981). *Another chance: Hope and health for the alcoholic family.* Palo Alto, CA: Science and Behavior Books.

Weissberg R. P., & Allen, J. P. (1986). Promoting children's social skills and adaptive interpersonal behavior. In B. A. Edelstein & L Michelson (Eds.), *Handbook of prevention* (pp. 153–175). New York: Plenum.

Wood, B. L. (1987). *Children of alcoholism: The struggle for self and intimacy in adult life.* New York: New York University Press.

Wurmser, L. (1978). *The hidden dimension: Psychodynamics in compulsive drug use.* New York: Jason Aronson.

AUTHOR INDEX

SUBJECT INDEX